Young People and the Future of News

Young People and the Future of News traces the practices that are evolving as young people come to see news increasingly as something shared via social networks and social media rather than produced and circulated solely by professional news organizations. The book introduces the concept of connective journalism, clarifying the role of creating and sharing stories online as a key precursor to collective and connective political action. At the center of the story are high school students from low-income minority and immigrant communities who often feel underserved or misrepresented by mainstream media but express a strong interest in politics and their communities. Drawing on in-depth field work in four major urban areas over the course of ten years, *Young People and the Future of News* sheds light on how young people share news that they think others should know about, express solidarity, and bring into being new publics and counterpublics.

Lynn Schofield Clark is Professor and Chair of the Department of Media, Film, and Journalism Studies and Director of the Estlow International Center for Journalism and New Media at the University of Denver. She is author of *The Parent App: Understanding Families in a Digital Age* (2013) and *From Angels to Aliens: Teenagers, the Media and the Supernatural* (2005), and is coauthor of *Media, Home and Family* (2004).

Regina Marchi is Associate Professor of Journalism and Media Studies at Rutgers University. Before entering academia, she worked as a journalist, community organizer, and teacher. Her first book, *Day of the Dead in the USA: The Migration and Transformation of a Cultural Phenomenon* (2009), won the 2010 national James W. Carey Award for Media Research and an International Latino Book Award in the category of "Best History/Political Book."

Other Books in the Series

(*continued after the Index*)

Young People and the Future of News

Social Media and the Rise of Connective Journalism

LYNN SCHOFIELD CLARK
University of Denver

REGINA MARCHI
Rutgers University

CAMBRIDGE
UNIVERSITY PRESS

CAMBRIDGE
UNIVERSITY PRESS

University Printing House, Cambridge CB2 8BS, United Kingdom

One Liberty Plaza, 20th Floor, New York, NY 10006, USA

477 Williamstown Road, Port Melbourne, VIC 3207, Australia

314–321, 3rd Floor, Plot 3, Splendor Forum, Jasola District Centre, New Delhi – 110025, India

79 Anson Road, #06-04/06, Singapore 079906

Cambridge University Press is part of the University of Cambridge.

It furthers the University's mission by disseminating knowledge in the pursuit of education, learning, and research at the highest international levels of excellence.

www.cambridge.org
Information on this title: www.cambridge.org/9781107190603
DOI: 10.1017/9781108116015

© Lynn Schofield Clark and Regina Marchi 2017

First published 2017

Reprinted 2017

Printed in the United Kingdom by Clays, St Ives plc

A catalogue record for this publication is available from the British Library.

ISBN 978-1-107-19060-3 Hardback
ISBN 978-1-316-64072-2 Paperback

Contents

Acknowledgments

This book has benefitted from the insights of many colleagues and friends. We were fortunate to have opportunities to interact with many people who listened, read, and commented on our research at differing stages, and we are grateful to our families and to colleagues at our home universities of the University of Denver and Rutgers University for their support.

Special thanks are due especially to Adrienne Russell for reading and commenting throughout and for being such a great inspiration and friend; to Margie Thompson for her inspiration and collaborations as a scholar activist; and to University of Denver alumna Rachel Monserrate for her early and important work interviewing high school journalists. We also want to thank Lance Bennett, Director of the Center for Communication and Civic Engagement, for his helpful feedback on the manuscript, as well as the anonymous reviewers and staff at Cambridge University Press.

Lynn wishes to thank University of Denver colleagues Erika Polson, Yoli Anyon, and Heather Kennedy, and Critical Participatory Action research collaborators Hava Gordon, Nicole Nicotera, and Kate Willink, as well as colleagues Nancy Wadsworth, Mary Stansbury, Derigan Silver, Nadia Kaneva, Renee Botta, Sheila Schroeder, Christof Demont-Heinrich, Rod Buxton, Diane Waldman, Elizabeth Henry, Tony Gault, Bob Handley, Steven Barnard, Rachel Liberman, and Taylor Nygaard. She also thanks University of Denver research assistants and associates Grace Chiou, Mike Mwirigi, Ben Peters, Badiah Haffejee, Maggie Lautzenheizer-Page, Courtney Dunson, Lilly Kautz, Andrea Ring, Diana Aqra, Maria Lewis, Elle Mohs, Mario Fierro, and Jen O'Connor for such wonderful support and valuable insights. She also thanks friends and colleagues at the University of Colorado who provided encouragement and wisdom,

including Stewart Hoover, Nabil Echchaibi, Benjamin Thevenin (now at
Brigham Young University), and Deborah Whitehead, and friends who
read and commented on earlier versions via Academia.edu, including
Andrea Stanton, Maria Jose Brites, David Feltmate, and Timothy Beal.

A key opportunity to formulate research and writing for this book
occurred during Lynn's time in 2014 as a visiting fellow at RMIT University
in Melbourne. Special thanks are due to Heather Horst at RMIT for her
wonderful friendship and her generous offerings of listening and providing feedback on the earliest formations of this book's main thesis. Thanks
to other colleagues at RMIT who are members of the wonderfully col-
legial Digital Ethnography Research Center, including John Postill, Sarah
Pink, Larissa Hjorth, and Jo Tacchi, Antonio Castillo, Peter Horsfield,
and Elisende Ardevol (from the University of Barcelona) for hospitality
and timely conversations; Zala Volcic, Mark Andrejevic, Graeme Turner,
Pradip Thomas, and Nick Carah at the University of Queensland; Gerard
Goggin and Fiona Martin at the University of Sydney; and Anita Harris
and Amy Dobson at Monash University.

Colleagues at the University of Copenhagen, where Lynn serves as
an Affiliate Professor, have provided invaluable feedback and sugges-
tions, as well. Thanks to Stig Hjarvard, Christa Lykka Christensen, Nete
Christensen, Mette Mortensen, and the mediatization project at the
University of Copenhagen for providing generous funding that enabled
Lynn to have time to write and think in a wonderfully rich intellectual
setting. Lynn also thanks colleagues Klaus Bruhn Jensen, Kjetl Sandvik,
and Rasmus Helles in Copenhagen and Gitte Stald at IT; Annette
Markham, Stine Liv Johanssen, Kirsten Frandsen, Maja Sonne Damkjaer,
and Helle Strandgaard Jensen at Aarhus University; Line Nybro Petersen,
Kim Schroder and Kirsten Drotner at Southern Denmark University, and
offers a special thanks in memoriam for Kevin Barnhurst, who offered
early inspiration for this project when both Lynn and Kevin served as
visiting professors in Denmark back in 2007. During a sabbatical at the
University of Copenhagen in 2014, Lynn also had an opportunity to visit
Stockholm and learn from Jenny Sunden, Alexandra Segerberg, and long-
time friend Mia Lovheim.

This project was also developed through interactions at conferences such as the meetings of the Association of Internet Researchers,
International Communication Association, the International Conference
on Media, Religion, and Culture, and the Social Media and the
Transformation of Public Spaces conference, as well as a thinking session
with Microsoft scholars Nancy Baym, Dan Green, Tarleton Gillespie,

Andre Brock, and Sara Hamid. Thanks to Zizi Papacharissi, Diane Winston, Mara Einstein, Knut Lundby, Gordon Lynch, Jolyon Mitchell, Nick Couldry, Thomas Poell, Jose Van Dijck, Irene Costera Meijer, Dan Mercea, Maria Bakardjieva, Lina Dencik, Nick John, Goran Bolin, Stina Bengtsson, Mark Deuze, Peter Dahlgren, Sonia Livingstone, Peter Lunt, Terri Senft, Holly Kruse, Jenny Korn, Kishonna Gray, Sun Sun Lim, Ian Gordon, Michele Rosenthal, Mirca Madianou, Danny Miller, Jean Burgess, Karine Nahon, Eszter Hargittai, Karin Wahl-Jorgensen, Jen and Michael Olin-Hitt, Laurie Menzies, Julie Janson, Geoff Baym, Jeffrey Jones, Cornel Sandvoss, Jonathan Gray, Rodney Benson, Paul Mihailidis, Lou Rutigliano, Marie Gillespie, and Clemencia Rodriguez. Thanks also to media activists, educators, and advocates Adan Medrano, Tony Shawcross, Gia Irlando, Nina Horton, Carlo Kriekels, Kris Rollerson, Daniel Weinshenker, Peggy Holman, Steven Silha, Marla Crockett, Linda Miller, Larry Greene, Adrian Barboa, Andrea Quijada, Raphael Nevins, Lorna Samraj, Josh Stearns, Diane Alters, Mario Montano, and Alan Michel.

Thanks to the many collaborators in Denver, including David Brennan, Rich Cole, Ruthann Kallenberg, Haines Eason, Rob Duren, Kristin Waters, Karen Duell, and Jen Hanson, as well as Denise, Abel, Ezana, Yonas, Karim, Jennifer, Prinsela, Samira, Rosemund, Richard, Helena, Christmas, Nabaa, Kunita, Azeb, Gio, Rebekah, Marvon, Barwaga, Joon, Jeneba, Tram, Milad, Sabrina, Seraphina, Fuwei, Jo, Wilfred, Sordum, Barikwa, Amran, John, Tugi, Ace, and Cesar.

Regina wishes to thank the youth at Zumix and Z-Radio in Boston, as well as Zumix staff and parents who shared their insights in interviews with her, and especially Zumix Director, Madeleine Steczynski, who was extremely supportive of this research. She also wants to thank Debra Cave, Director of Boston's City Roots Alternative Education Program and the City Roots high school students who participated in the interviews. In addition, she is grateful to her former student research assistants at Rutgers, Christine Schneider, who coordinated the interviews with young documentary filmmakers at WHYY in Philadelphia, and Carina Sitkus and Cristabel Cruz, who helped interview high school journalism students in New Jersey. She thanks her Rutgers colleagues in the Department of Journalism and Media Studies and in the Social Media and Society Cluster of the School of Communication and Information for helpful conversations and feedback over the years. In addition, a special thanks is due to her family and friends for their encouragement and, particularly, to Roberto Verthelyi for his ongoing moral support during the long research and writing process. Regina also wishes to thank Lynn for inviting her to collaborate on this book. It has been wonderful working together! Early research for this project was funded by a generous grant from the Lilly Endowment, and additional funding came from the University of Denver's Center for Community Engagement and Service Learning and from research funds provided by the Rutgers School of Communication and Information, for which we are very grateful. While we are extremely thankful for the support of so many, we recognize that any errors in this manuscript are our own.

We would like to dedicate this book to our families. To Jon, Jonathan, and Allison and the Schofield and Clark families, and to Roberto and the Marchi and Cave-Madaro families along with Mary Ellen Welch and Kevin Farrell. Thank you for sustaining us and inspiring us throughout this very long project.

Introduction

Young People and the Future of News

It was the dawn of a chilly November morning, and a small group of adults had gathered on the sidewalk across the street from a diverse urban high school in Denver. They carried signs reading, "Fags doom nation" and "God hates fags" – visible reminders that these adults were members of the infamous anti-gay Westboro Baptist Church, recognized for its well-publicized and hateful attempts to garner attention. The word had been leaked that the group might stage something at the high school so that, in the colorful words of one of the protesters, they might "warn this wicked generation that their sins will take them straight to hell."[1] The possibility of a protest hadn't been covered in the mainstream media, but teachers, students, and parents had heard the rumors, and on Facebook and other social network sites in the days before the event, many had been involved in conversations about how to respond.

On the morning of the protest, the first students on the scene began texting photos to friends, who in turn texted the news to others and then rushed to the school with handmade signs. Within ten minutes after the protest had begun, three hundred people had reportedly shown up for a silent counterprotest, holding signs that read, "We were born this way," "Spread love, not hate," and "Why is love wrong?"

The camaraderie was palpable. Students who did not usually discuss their own sexual orientation stood alongside those who openly identified as gay or lesbian, straight allies, bisexual, transgender, or questioning. In the crowd were students from a variety of friendship circles and from differing racial/ethnic and economic backgrounds. They stood together in proud opposition, their phones held high to document their participation in the event for themselves and for one another.

We first learned of this event almost two years after it had occurred, when we happened to be interviewing a group of students from that school about news and social media. We'd asked the students to talk about a moment when their interactions on a social network site had helped them to become informed about events that were of importance to them. We didn't know at the time that this event would come to be one of many, as US society was then in the early days of a marked upsurge in high school and college student protest movements. A perceived increase in the suppression of youth voice and experience was building, leading to numerous protests, rallies, and acts of civil disobedience. We might date the dramatic increase in protests to the 2014–15 academic year. That was when tens of thousands of high school students and their parents participated in various forms of civil disobedience. Among other things, students opted out of mandated standardized school testing, demonstrated against related cuts to educational and community programs, protested rising university tuitions and soaring student debt, and advocated for the Development, Relief, and Education for Alien Minors (DREAM) Act and other immigrant rights. And perhaps most prominently, students and their family members involved themselves in a variety of activities loosely related to the #BlackLivesMatter movement emerging in the aftermath of teenager Michael Brown's death at the hands of Ferguson Missouri police officers, protesting the overly harsh disciplining of youth by members of law enforcement and calling for more respect for young Black men and women.[2] Student protest movements continued in the 2015–16 and 2016–17 academic years in high schools from Oregon to Texas and on college campuses from the University of Missouri to the University of Washington, Clemson University and Rutgers, first in relation to disparate resources, relations between students of color and police, and poor on-campus racial climates, and later in response to hate crimes and anti-immigrant rhetoric that took place in response to the election of Donald Trump as US president, stimulating student activism across the country for "sanctuary campuses."[3] Students from around the country marked their identification and solidarity with student activism through the circulation of messages with hashtags such as #StandUpFG, #ReclaimOSU, #jeffco4kids, #DismantleDukePlantation, and Rutgers' #LikeAMinority. The years 2014–2016 also saw the growth of a national movement to end sexual violence on university campuses, with hundreds of victims speaking out, pressing charges against their universities, and organizing protest events.[4]

The eruption of outrage on social media over the light sentence given to convicted rapist and former Stanford University swimmer Brock Turner in 2016 was an event that some saw as a turning point in the discussions of campus sexual assault, as the victim's grisly and stirring statement was widely disseminated via social media.[5] Millions of young people gathered around the world in solidarity after learning through social media about vigils following the June 2016 mass shooting in Orlando that left more than a hundred lesbian, gay, bisexual, and transgender (LGBT) young people of color dead or wounded.[6] And thousands traveled to Standing Rock, North Dakota, to join Native Americans there in solidarity against the building of the Dakota Access Pipeline that would transport crude oil across sacred tribal lands and pose a threat to safe drinking water.[7]

Not surprisingly, when high school and college students today are asked about how social media play a role in informing them about the events that matter to them, they talk about Facebook event pages, twitter hashtags, snaps, and text messages that keep them up-to-date on where varied events like these are occurring and how they or their peers might be participating in them. One study found that 88 percent of young people in the United States got news from Facebook or another social media site, whereas another found that worldwide, 28 percent of those aged 18–24 said that social media was their main source for news.[8] Young people may or may not be familiar with the particulars of related news stories unfolding in neighboring cities, as many do not follow news sources regularly at all.[9] But mention a local protest, demonstration, or counterprotest involving students, and young people will immediately regale one another and any interested adults with breathless stories of where they were and from whom they learned about it, who was involved, how it unfolded, and how they or others they knew had participated in the event in person or through social media.

As students discussed the protest that opened this chapter, we wondered: had we found an example of a vibrant civic impulse among young people, evidence of a spark that could be fanned into a flame of outrage and political action? Or, more cynically, was this evidence for the argument that youth are so disconnected from broader communities and their news that only events at the hyperlocal level can come to matter to them?

Within the traditions of political communication and journalism, the Westboro event's impact would be considered miniscule. The protest/ counterprotest was over within forty-five minutes, as students needed to depart for the beginning of the school day. A blogger for an alternative weekly was the only reporter who documented the event for a wider audience. And even he published the photos and words of a student's mother while including none of the students' own voices.[10] There was no indication that the event made an immediate difference in the activities of the school, the organization that had staged the protest, or in any of the state-level policy or legislative debates taking place at the time. Because most of the students were not of voting age and others did not have US citizenship due to their undocumented immigration status, the question of whether or not such an event would translate into political action at the ballot box seems beside the point.

And yet in this event are clues about changes that have long been taking place at the intersection of politics, journalism, and youth spaces. Here are some things we know:

1. Young people have different concerns than do the adults around them. It's unrealistic to think that a sixteen-year-old is going to care about the same things that a forty-year-old does. So we should not be surprised that young people define "news" differently than do those who are older than they are.[11]

2. Many young people are happy to generate and share among their friends what they think of as "news."[12] The information that they draw from legacy media sources might come into play, but even then, the question of news for young people in the era of social media is no longer about where you get the news from, but who told you about it and whether or not you're going to share it.

3. "News" isn't what it used to be. Today's legacy media outlets are much leaner and operate under more tightly controlled corporate ownership than the media of the past. In order to survive, news organizations have had to appeal to the largest audience that is of interest to advertisers – namely, well-off adults – and as a result, many young people don't see their concerns addressed in legacy news.

The consolidated news media giants of today have crushed competition and eliminated smaller, localized, and diverse news voices, leaving a sanitized news perspective that may include pretty images of young people, but is not reflective of young peoples' perspectives and experiences. Twitter, Facebook, YouTube, and other platforms, on the other hand, are being utilized by young people to share interests and concerns in places that are outside of the legacy media's control. The owners of these social media platforms may not wish to recognize their role as news outlets, but social media networks are playing increasingly important roles in how "news" is defined.[13] News is no longer primarily understood as a product that's delivered, or even a profession that's practiced or an industry that disseminates a product. Today, news is something that informal communities think of themselves as engaging in *produsing* – as in producing + using, to use Axel Bruns's term – as they define for one another the information they deem worth discussing.[14] From a user perspective, news is defined, produced, and disseminated in relation to specific networks of people, with traditional distinctions between active production and passive consumption increasingly blurred. At the same time, social media platforms are being engaged by those in our society who wish to shape what "news" looks like, and this shaping takes place in ways that are often invisible from the news prod-user's perspective. Foregrounding the processes of youthful news production and consumption, then, creates a way for us to think about who we are as a community and as a public, and how we might want to go forward together. And that, as we will argue, is why it is worth further exploring the ways that young people are engaging in and learning about information-sharing of various kinds, across a range of digital platforms, and for a variety of purposes.

Instead of looking to the *New York Times* or CNN, many young people first encounter news of an unfolding event on Facebook or Twitter, when it is communicated to them from people or organizations they recognize, which in turn gives the telling legitimacy. We found this pattern again and again in our interviews, and it's something that others have found, as well.[15] When young people are asked about whether or not they seek out news from legacy media sources, they say something like, "I don't need to do that. If something is happening, it will show up on my Twitter feed, and then I can go to a CNN or something if I feel a need to follow up and get more information," as one student told us. Such statements raise new questions for us as we think about news. For instance, how does a person come to recognize an event, occurrence, or story as worthy of sharing with her friends? How do youth evaluate such information as credible? What is the tipping point at which young people will decide that sharing information is worth the possible social media backlash? And why might some people decide to limit what they share whereas others see themselves as opinion leaders who want to keep those in their networks informed about certain topics? Questions like these foreground the relationship between news and identity construction, or the ways that young people – and perhaps all of us – inevitably see things through a lens shaped by our own unique experiences of – and needs in relationship to – the larger world.

In this book, we report on ten years of ethnographic investigation into youthful practices with journalism, exploring how high school aged young people in the United States interact with, share, insert themselves into, and make news. We take what Ike Picone and his colleagues term a "radical user perspective" that is focused on the uses and users of news because we believe, with these authors, that "as control of media institutions over the news processes is in decline, we should take the news audience more seriously and try to improve our understanding of changing news use patterns."[16] We believe that a user perspective on journalism practices supports the development of a public-oriented journalism, in that it takes a practice-oriented approach that helps us to understand the roles of social media, informal social networks, and professional journalism in how publics are formed and sustained in a digital age.

News is widely recognized as "networked" and "ambient," and professional news is increasingly viewed as part of a much broader "news ecosystem."[17] And yet, while a growing body of research has been exploring the evolving relationships between professional journalists, audience members, and increased citizen opportunities within professional journalism, far fewer studies have considered evolving patterns in how journalism fits into peoples' everyday lives.[18] A few promising empirical studies have affirmed that despite dire predictions, news remains important as a central way in which people orient themselves in society. Irene Costera Meijer and Schrøder and Larsen have found, for instance, that as long as journalism industries deliver news that is considered "valuable" or "worthwhile," such news easily finds a place in people's lives, and Heikkila and Ahva's study of news consumers in Finland found that social networks are the central structure through which journalism is rendered meaningful for people.[19] But clearly, there is more to know about news in everyday life, particularly as it relates to concerns of youth and the public. The circulation of "false news" through social media is one such concern. During the final three months of the 2016 US presidential election, the twenty most widely circulated false election stories from discredited sites and hyperpartisan blogs generated more than 8.7 million shares, reactions, and comments. These stories were shared with much greater frequency than were the top circulating stories from major news sites.[20] Another concern relates to a dearth of what the Stanford History Education Group referred to as "civic online reasoning" among youth. In their study of 7,804 students from middle school through college, these researchers found that more than 80 percent of middle school students could not distinguish between an advertisement labeled "sponsored content" and a real news story on a website, while 40 percent of high school students judged a news story as credible based solely on pictorial evidence without questioning where the accompanying photo came from or if it was even related to the story's claim. Only a few college students in this study were able to recognize that data cited from a professional polling firm might strengthen the validity of claims made in a tweeted news story, and fewer than a third were able to articulate how the political agenda of the organization sharing the tweet might influence the content of the tweet. Their work, which comprises the largest body of data to date on how young people evaluate online sources of information in social media, demonstrates the great challenges of digital media literacy that young people, and by extension all of us, face in a social media era.[21]

Feelings of disenfranchisement among all ages also remain depressingly strong. In their study of media consumption and public engagement, for instance, Couldry, Livingstone, and Markham found that disconnection seems to be an overwhelming issue across the generations: there are few connection points between, on the one hand, the many who see themselves as disenchanted with public participation, and on the other, the communities or practices that might enable people to feel that they are capable of acting together to address what they perceive as their concerns.[22] The perceived and real sense of disconnection between youth and adult institutions enables various institutions and industries within society therefore to "suture" young people into civic and national identities, to use Murray Foreman's term, as part of the larger process of selling to, shaping, supporting, or containing youth.[23] Young people are aware of these processes, sometimes resisting them and at other times working within or reworking them to suit their own desires. Their lives, structured as they are by the school day, family expectations, juvenile justice systems, the military, social welfare policies, and even the media and entertainment industries, are also heavily regulated and under adult control. We argue that it is worth attending to their responses to these "suturing" efforts, then, as we consider questions of citizenship and participation, as well as the roles of information-sharing that inform them. As Picone and his colleagues have argued, we think that focusing on news users not only helps us to understand what journalism is, but what it could (or *should*) be in relation to the lived experiences of all of our young people.[24]

Some researchers have begun to focus on how people discuss politics within the realm of social media, with or without reference to journalism or the news media. Hightower, for instance, offers many examples of how social media become sites for mundane and personalized expressions of political commentary.[25] And any of the millions of young people who have seen Casey Neistat are aware of how news and politics can emerge in daily vlogs. YouTubers Schmoyoho and Weird Al Yankovich's "songify" version of the third presidential debate garnered over six million views by the election, and the activist organization The Other 98%'s screaming meme expressing frustration at the limited choice between Hillary Clinton and Donald Trump received more than 19.8 million views.[26]

Although they did not foreground news specifically, Henry Jenkins and his colleagues considered youth activism as it develops in relation to topics relevant to youth, exploring youth interest in and engagement with immigration reform, the DREAM act, racialized police violence, income inequality, and the legalization of marijuana, among other topics. They found an active "civic imagination" among young people, and an interest in working toward what a better world might look like and in creating media to move others toward that world.[27] Jenkins and his colleagues have been part of a larger initiative known as the Youth and Participatory Politics Working Group, which has looked at the ways in which people of various ages use social media to mobilize, help shape agendas, and exert greater agency by participating in the circulation of political information.[28] To determine the extent to which young people engage in participatory politics, Cohen and her colleagues conducted a nationally representative survey (in English and Spanish) of 15- to 25-year-olds.[29] They asked how often the study participants had done things such as forwarded or circulated funny videos or cartoons related to a political candidate, campaign, or political issues (20 percent had done this), forwarded or posted someone else's political commentary (17 percent had done this), or commented on a news story or blog post about a political candidate, campaign, or political issue (16 percent had done this).[30] Utilizing this definition of the actions associated with participatory politics, Cohen and her colleagues have reported that some 41 percent of young people have engaged in at least one act of participatory politics, and that 90 percent of these youth either vote or engage with institutional politics in some other way.[31] They note that in any form of political activity that includes participatory politics, institutional politics, and voting, engagement is most common among Black young people, possibly due to what's been termed the "Obama effect."[32] Their study also found that 45 percent of young people received news at least once a week from a family member or friend via social media such as Facebook or Twitter. When asked if they thought that they or their friends could benefit from learning more about how to gauge the trustworthiness of the news they encountered online, 84 percent of them said that they believed that they would.[33]

We believe that all young people have the right to have access to information that is relevant to their lives and that meets their needs and expectations, as articulated in the United Nations' Convention on the Rights of the Child.[34] This right is consistent with Vygotsky's argument that engagement in social activities is centrally important to the development of one's self-understanding as a civic actor who can comprehend and act upon the problems of society.[35] In this book, we therefore seek to develop a theory of the relationship between youth, journalism, and political development that is rooted in qualitative empirical evidence and that can inform current debates about how young people come to be members of publics and participants in political life in the social media age.

Our research began in 2006 and continued through 2016. While the bulk of our fieldwork took place on the East Coast (Boston, Philadelphia, and New Brunswick, NJ) and in the center of the country (Denver), we regularly drew upon the work of other researchers who were exploring related questions in Los Angeles, San Francisco, Chicago, and in the Washington, DC, area as well as in places outside the United States, including northern and southern Europe, Asia, Latin America, the Middle East, eastern Africa, and Australia. While we recognize that our own viewpoints and analyses are limited, our work takes place in conversation with the burgeoning research fields of youth and new media practices, youth activism, positive youth development, civic learning and engagement, and youth and participatory politics. Our particular contribution to this discussion rests in our closeup focus on the social interactions among young people themselves, as we look at why youth become involved in sharing information, and what it means to receive that information, within peer networks. We also focus on politics at the local level, considering how young people share, insert themselves into local news stories, and participate in making newsworthy stories meant to affect local policies and politics.

It will seem to some as if this "user-centered" way of approaching news completely loses sight of the political nature of current events-based and investigative news that have long been at the center of our models for why journalism matters in a democracy.[36] And yet, if you were to ask the students involved in the counter-protest mentioned at the beginning of this chapter, many would probably describe LGBTIQ rights as one of the most significant political issues of their time, along with climate change and globalization. Young people are not completely uninterested in what adults would define as "politics," but they engage in different ways today.

These new ways of engaging are best understood in relation to changing definitions of citizenship. Whereas in the past, citizenship was thought of as a duty that included voting, abiding by laws, regularly consuming the news, and participating in the armed services if needed, some argue that we now have to pay attention to other activities that are on the rise, such as participating in protests, environmental activities, boycotts, and civil court cases.[37] As political science and communication expert Lance Bennett has argued, participation in citizenship activities today comes about as a result of a desire for self-actualization, self-fulfillment, and personal expression rather than merely from a sense of duty.[38] The "dutiful citizen" and the "informed citizen" models have failed not because young people are no longer motivated or don't care. This has occurred as recent decades have seen the fragmentation of public institutions along with a rise in the number of highly educated yet underemployed young adults directly experiencing globalization's fluctuation of economic markets, both of which have contributed to a resultant crisis in the legitimization of democracy, as sociologist Zygmunt Bauman has pointed out.[39] As societal institutions continue to experience a decline in authoritativeness, young people increasingly find that governments are not addressing their needs. And students who live in families of lower socioeconomic status are even more likely to live in distressed neighborhoods and attend schools that have subpar technological equipment, few instructional opportunities linking digital media use to the fostering of political voice, and little encouragement to use these tools for civic or political engagement.[40] Young people who experience discrimination based on race, ethnicity, or religion express frustration and disillusionment with traditional political and media systems.[41] And youth who experience discrimination are more likely than others to voice concerns about surveillance and participate in self-censorship.[42]

Increased hopelessness contributes to the contemporary situation of contentious politics, and thus significant groups of young people have become increasingly critical of both public institutions and the global financial system, directly getting involved in demands for more representative democracy. The most notable examples include the *indignados* in Spain, a movement that had its beginnings when young adults boycotted elections to protest the high unemployment rate and the conservative government's economic austerity measures, and the *aganaktismenoi*, who followed suit in Greece. These movements brought to the forefront the ways that politics had become subsumed to economics, and this in turn raised questions about the gap between the political elite and the general population whose interests the elite did not represent.[43] While feelings that elected leaders don't represent their interests and anger over a lack of economic opportunity are expressed by US youth of all races and social classes, low-income and minority youth are especially disenfranchised. This has particular resonance in the United States as we become a majority minority country and as the #BlackLivesMatter and DREAM movements foster a heightened awareness of links between white privilege, elite power, racist systems of police enforcement, and exclusive college admissions. As such gaps between the elite and everyone else become unmistakable and coalesce into outrage and awareness about government failures, experts argue, what we've come to witness is a form of political life that isn't in decline so much as it is undergoing dramatic change.[44]

Some scholars, such as Philip Howard and Muzammil Hussain, have posited that digital media environments may provide sufficient and necessary conditions for both the toppling of nondemocratic regimes and the development of successful social movements, perhaps inaugurating what they have termed "democracy's fourth wave."[45] Others, less sanguine, have predicted that digital media and the "disruptive power" it affords to individuals and groups will continue to challenge the stability of the nation-state as a model for governance around the world, with the development of ever more invasive surveillance strategies to maintain order even in democratic societies.[46] And not all are enthusiastic about the effects of a 24/7 news environment and its concomitant increase in civic engagement, as the increased demand for news has correlated with increased polarization of opinion.[47]

The journalism of legacy and alternative media are not completely absent from these stories of political change, of course, as Adrienne Russell points out in her work on the ways in which activists and professional journalists influence one another's storytelling practices.[48] While it may be tempting for us to think that something entirely new is emerging in the youthful uses of social media, it's important to note that legacy journalism continues to play a role, even for youth. In the story that opened this chapter, for example, it's worth noting that for more than two decades before the protest and counter-protest event at East High School, the news media had covered the controversial actions of Westboro Baptist Church, producing stories on the group's protests targeting the LGBTIQ community and on the church's anti-gay protests at military funerals, at the funerals of hate crime victims, at the courthouses where same sex laws have been passed, and various free speech/hate speech cases in which Westboro Church has been involved.[49] Both conservative television commentator Bill O'Reilly and progressive documentary filmmaker Michael Moore had denounced the group.[50] The British Broadcasting Corporation (BBC) and several other organizations had produced documentaries on the group.[51] And in a well-publicized action, in 2012 the Anonymous community executed a distributed denial of service (DDOS) attack that shut down the church's website after Westboro announced their intention to picket the funerals of those who died in the Sandy Hook Elementary school shooting.[52] In short, if it hadn't been for the role of these traditional journalistic media in creating a space for public discussion about the controversial hate activities of Westboro Baptist, the students of East High School and the adults in their lives would not have been capable of recognizing what the church's protest at their school was meant to symbolize and what their own counter-protest might therefore mean, as well.

Some journalism advocacy organizations, such as the Newspaper Association of America, recognize the need for news organizations to pay more attention to the ways in which young people may develop interest in current events and politics. They recommend that news professions embrace a "life stage" approach that addresses news to particular generational segments rather than attempting to produce news for a "general" population that is usually of interest primarily to those over the age of thirty-five.[53] Those concerned about the future of news recognize that we need to know more about the ways in which young people come to find certain issues worthy of their attention, and we need to know more about why and under what conditions those issues are deemed worthy of sharing within their networks. At the same time, journalists are being encouraged to utilize social media to develop their contacts and to leverage their credibility within the communities that they cover.[54] Increasingly, journalists are recognizing the public's role not only as sources of news, but also as verifiers of the news that now comes from a variety of sources via social media.[55] And this means that journalists are rethinking their roles even as the various ways of thinking about journalism – the profession, its practices, and the cultural industries that have funded it – are undergoing dramatic changes in the digital age.[56]

All of these concerns translate into implications for the ways we think about politics, journalism, and young people. Clearly, political activities are no longer limited to voting, if they ever were. Journalism is no longer produced by professional reporters alone. And, as we argue along with many in the field of youth studies, youth can no longer be understood merely as a pleasurable biological life-stage that precedes the more "important" time of adulthood.

In spite of the fact that we all recognize these statements to be obvious, it seems as if our theories in political communication, journalism, and youth studies have not always kept up with one another. Theories in political communication have evolved to consider new concepts of citizenship, but these don't often find their way into the discussions of scholastic or youth journalism. Those interested in youth and politics aren't always attuned to or interested in changes in the formal and informal journalism industries, despite the fact that the field of journalism studies has been redefining itself in ways that those in politics are likely to find quite interesting. And little work in journalism and political communication is rooted in the lives of those outside of or younger than the four-year college experience, presumably because young people aren't interested in what has been the primary foci of those fields: legacy news and national elections.

This book seeks to address these gaps. Tracing young people's lived experiences with politics and journalism broadly defined, we specifically analyze the intersections of cultural practices, political aspirations, and sources of knowledge among youth. We foreground the experiences of disenfranchised, minoritized, and migrant youth who are under the age of twenty-one and who make up the fastest-growing populations in the United States, as we believe that understanding their experiences is vitally important to the development of new models for the study of youth, politics, and journalism.[57]

In this book, we argue that the young people who Tweeted, Instagrammed, texted, Facebooked, and later told the stories of their school's protests and counter-protests are participants in what we term *connective journalism*. By communicating with one another about what was going on in their school and by viewing these events as reflective of an urgent need to respond to current events as they impacted and sometimes threatened a collective view of themselves, the youth defined these various acts of civil disobedience as newsworthy. They engaged in journalistic practices, using social media to communicate their concerns to one another and to mobilize community members in response, and in doing so they created a story that later became important in the narrative about who they saw themselves to be *as* a community.[58]

We're not using the term "connective journalism" to suggest that these highly personalized practices are replacing the traditional news industries of CNN, *The New York Times*, Fox News, and the like, as we'll discuss. Yet it's clear that the most distinctive feature of this emergent form of journalistic practice is that from the user's perspective, the professions and the industries of legacy journalism are not at its center. For the young person engaged in connective journalism practices, traditional journalism is associated with the practices of building an accurate *story*, whereas connective journalism is associated with the practices of building a collective and individual *identity*. Thus, connective journalism is practiced as people engage in communicative acts that give voice both to their own distinctive way of viewing the world and to their views of how we ought to feel about what is happening in that world. Because the emphasis is on practices of sharing, there is a significant emotional dimension to the practices of connective journalism: young people share what *feels* important to them, and that is often determined through the emotions of outrage, anger, disgust, glee, anticipation, amusement, joy, or appreciation. These feelings are fleshed out as they are shared through communication with others.

Emotion has long played a role within traditional journalistic storytelling, of course, because professional practices, too, are rooted in the dynamics of how narratives come to be constructed. We tend to think about journalistic storytelling as somehow very different from other storytelling, and it is true that there are very real distinctions in access to power between media institutions and smaller groups of individuals. But constructing and controlling a narrative is part of the human need for creating meaningful frameworks for interaction. What connective journalism practices point to, then, are the ways in which structurally differentiated groups experience themselves as creating varying methods for navigating the social world.

It's true that an emotion-based approach to news has serious drawbacks, as we will discuss later in this book. But it's also important to note that sometimes, connective journalism can be actionable, in that the communication that is shared provides not only an emotion-tinged explanation about one's felt concerns but also a suggestion about what one can do in response. Moreover, what we have observed is that the practices of connective journalism can be understood developmentally, as the three practices of (1) sharing, (2) inserting oneself into the story, and (3) participating in the making of a story, all of which involve a willingness to embrace an ever-increasing level of interpersonal risk within the spaces of social media.

This book will therefore explore the differing connective journalism practices that are carried out among young people today, considering the potential that these practices hold for fostering political and civic engagement among youth. People want to share not just stories, but their *feelings* about those stories, and it is through this sharing that "affective publics" are formed, as Zizi Papacharissi argues. This is how young people "feel their way into politics."[59] As youth participate in connective journalism practices, then, they are laying claim to a political subject position: one in which their voice and views have value.

We hope to widen this discussion of affective publics to consider both the emotions that young people feel as they encounter news *and* the emotions they feel as they receive news that is shared in their friendship and family circles. Sometimes, as we will discuss, youth are discouraged from sharing news because they fear repercussions from others. Inserting oneself into a story by taking a photo or video of oneself at an event and posting it on social media is risky, and sharing a story about how one participated in addressing a problem by making and sharing original content is riskier still.[60] We argue that these three practices – sharing, inserting oneself into a story, and participating in making a story – are helpfully viewed as three steps on a ladder of political engagement that trace the ways in which young people come to move from interest to participation in a social media age.

In the next chapter, we begin with a discussion of contemporary youth and then introduce the various conceptual frameworks that inform our interdisciplinary analysis. These frameworks include research on youth and citizenship, politics and publics, journalism, and the news industries, all of which serve as a foundation for the development of our concept of connective journalism, which we elaborate on in Chapter 2. We then flesh out this concept by discussing the specific theories that contribute to its development.

Following this theoretical grounding, in Chapter 3 we focus our attention on the ways in which youth from disenfranchised, minority, and migrant populations express their disillusionment with the storytelling of legacy news as well as their hopes for how storytelling and journalistic forms could play a role in their communities in more productive ways. In particular, we explore four themes that emerged when we asked young people why they were not very interested in consuming and sharing news from legacy media: (1) problems associated with journalistic authority,

(2) problems associated with the imagined audiences for news, (3) problems with the business models of journalism in the US news marketplace, and (4) problems with news storytelling genres.

In Chapter 4 we turn to the news ecology in which young people today find themselves. Here we explore the possibilities and limits of youth-oriented news, considering (1) news produced by adults specifically for youth, (2) news programs produced for adults and young adults but for which high school youth are a substantial audience, and (3) news produced by and for youth with some support from adults. The chapter reviews several noteworthy digital media literacy programs that focus on empowering young people in journalistic storytelling. In Chapter 4 we also explore the ways in which neoliberalism shapes the school, after school, and other learning environments through which these programs are often understood, which, we believe, present some important limitations to their appeal and their ability to be reproduced and spread.

While Chapter 4 offers some insights into the media materials that are available for digital sharing, Chapter 5 widens the discussion to consider what happens when young people move from sharing stories to inserting themselves into the unfolding events and stories that they share with others. Chapter 6 foregrounds stories of young people who are given the opportunity to utilize media to make a difference in their communities – and to define the community, the difference they'd like to make, and the way they utilize media to make that difference. In that chapter we explore what happens as young people move from sharing to inserting themselves into the stories of ongoing events, and finally to participating in making a story that is itself newsworthy. Chapter 6 highlights several efforts to engender connections between the lived experiences of youth and to address the concerns of their communities, sometimes by partnering with grassroots organizing efforts. In Chapter 7, the book concludes with an argument that any model of the future of news must consider the following interlocking issues: (1) the emergent practices of young people in relation to social media connectivity; (2) the existing landscape of news-gathering and storytelling and young people's relationship to this landscape; (3) the cultural environment of neoliberalism that shapes and limits current understandings of schooling, citizenship, and participation; (4) the ways in which young people have nevertheless overcome a variety of barriers in order to participate in existing grassroots efforts for social change, and (5) the emergent infrastructure of digital media that requires greater transparency to facilitate truly democratic information-sharing in a social media age in which deliberation has been largely replaced by spectacle and performance.

Consistent with the nonlinear, hyperlinked way of consuming information that has become a familiar feature of everyday life, we've written this book so that it can be read in a variety of ways. For those who are interested in the relationship between democratic theory development and empirical research, we suggest that Chapters 1 and 2 will be of particular interest, as they set up a theoretical foundation that relates to contemporary debates in political theory. Readers less interested in theory may wish to skip to Chapter 3 to hear from students themselves. Those interested in positive stories of youth participating in social change may find Chapter 6 particularly useful.

Certainly, we're not suggesting that knowledge about isolated events like the protest/counter-protest that opened this chapter can substitute for the kind of in-depth knowledge generation that has long been recognized as important for democracy. What we are interested in, however, is how changes in news, technologies, and communities relate to one another, and what they tell us about citizenship and about the prospects for what John Dewey termed a "great community" that can participate in democratic decision-making. What can they tell us about the evolving roles of personal, legacy, and other forms of media in the lives of the publics that are present and emerging today? And what can they tell us about the future of news?

Our study of the emergence of connective journalism does not begin with an attempt to solve the crisis of legacy media, urgent as it is. We begin with the understanding that in order to better understand the current situation, we need a more expansive definition of journalistic practices, and a more precise understanding of the relationship between digital media literacy and participation in the storytelling that makes a difference to public life. In this book about youth, politics, citizenship and journalism, we foreground interpersonal peer relationships and relationality for one simple reason: we believe that it is in and through our private lives that we learn what it means to be part of a public. We draw together a framework for thinking about youth, journalism, citizenship, and politics by considering theories and concepts that have been well established across several disciplines. And that is the starting point for the first chapter.

* * * * *

I

Young People, Journalism, and Politics

"Come to a community meeting tonight to talk about locations for 10 new Hubway bike stations in East Boston!" read fifteen-year-old Alma's Facebook post. Alma hadn't started out interested in politics, journalism, or biking, for that matter. But as she experienced increased hope for change in her community, she got interested in all three. Part of that interest may have been sparked by stories she heard about positive changes in her neighborhood that were reported in the posts of her Facebook friend Mike, who lived in her neighborhood and frequently posted about changes taking place in the community where they both lived.

Two years earlier, sixteen-year-old Mike, along with other young people who were part of East Boston's Environmental Youth Crew, had been hired by a local non-profit community development corporation to identify and address environmental issues in their community. They had conducted a study that documented high nighttime airplane noise levels in the neighborhoods near Logan International Airport, where they lived, and highlighted problems related to those levels, including hearing loss, asthma, and increased interruptions in residents' sleep. Mike frequently shot and then posted on Facebook videos of airport-related traffic jams on his local streets as well his comments about noise, traffic, and air pollution from car fumes. He and other Environmental Youth Crew members shared their research with officials from the Federal Aviation Administration. In response, the officials agreed to alter nocturnal flight takeoff/landing patterns in ways that were less disruptive to sleeping residents, and the story was covered in the local community newspaper.[1]

East Boston is the fifth most environmentally burdened community in Massachusetts and borders the Chelsea Creek, the second-most polluted waterway in the state.² This working-class neighborhood, comprised largely of older Italian and younger Latino and Middle Eastern immigrants, has some of the city's lowest-income census tracts and has long struggled with pollution from industry, jet fumes, highways, three automobile tunnels, and vehicle traffic generated by Logan Airport. Alma's family, like Mike's, was directly affected by airport noise, traffic, and air pollution. So when the Environmental Youth Crew's organizing projects started to experience some success, Alma got involved. She joined the Environmental Youth Crew and became very active in research and social media efforts, sharing videos and photos about local environmental issues that were of concern to her neighbors and her peers. This led her to getting active in local efforts to expand public green space in her neighborhood that ultimately increased opportunities for residents to bike and do other forms of exercise. Eventually, both she and Mike were awarded citations of recognition from the Boston City Council for their organizing efforts, and Alma was invited to speak at the 2016 graduation of a local school to inspire other young people to get involved in their community.

Only a small number of youth have been actively involved in East Boston's environmental work, and few were involved in writing investigative stories for the local youth-run community radio station that covered the airport's environmental impacts on nearby neighborhoods. Still, Alma came to see herself as part of a larger collective that shared her concerns and that was involved in confronting the environmental injustices that afflicted her community after stories reached her through a hybrid media environment of professional, community, and citizen journalism and through her interpersonal contacts in social media. Eventually, both Mike and Alma engaged in journalistic practices, using social media to communicate their concerns to one another and their peers, and to mobilize other community members. In doing so, they created a story that later became important in the narrative about who they saw themselves to be *as* a community and as a public.

In this chapter, we explore the roles that storytelling and the emergent connectivity of social media are playing in changing the landscape of politics, political action, information sharing, and youth citizenship. In particular, we want to foreground the *relational* aspects of social media – or how social media afford different ways of interacting in relation with other people – so that we can better understand the ways in which the norms and practices of social media shape how information is experienced in young people's daily lives. Looking at journalism as a specific kind of communication, we want to highlight the ways in which news and information are shared through communication that takes place through differing interpersonal relations in socially mediated spaces.[3] We believe that looking at the actual practices of young people can be helpful in understanding not only journalism but its evolving relationship with politics, citizenship, and civic action as these are experienced in everyday life and as they inform the experience of youth and citizenship in the United States and around the world.

This chapter spells out the link between communication and politics, the particulars of youth in this equation, how social media can augment engagement, and how social media may be complicating engagement by undermining journalism. Chapter 2 then turns to the key theoretical approaches that inform this book, introducing the practices of *connective journalism* – a concept that draws upon current discussions about the role of information sharing in a democracy and fleshes out contemporary ways of understanding the relationships between youth, citizenship, media, and politics. Ultimately, we hope that these chapters make clear why we chose to foreground experiences of interpersonal relationships as mediated through social media in our efforts to better understand emergent user practices of journalism and politics, for we believe that it is by looking at young people's experiences within interpersonal relationships that we are able to better understand how some youth participate in the constitution of political talk and political action, as they move along a ladder of engagement toward greater participation in civic life, civil society, and in citizenship. We begin with a discussion of the relationship between communication and politics.

A RELATIONAL APPROACH TO COMMUNICATION

What does it mean to view communication as a set of relational processes and practices that are foundational to the constitution of society? To think of communication in this way, we have to begin by acknowledging with communication scholar James Carey that we have inherited contradictory notions about the processes and practices of communication.[4] On the one hand, the term communication brings to mind technological advances such as the printing press, television, computers, and mobile networks. But on the other, the term recalls ancient ideas about speaking and being heard.[5] In a book like this one that foregrounds practices of social media, one might expect that we would highlight the various ways that new media technologies are used to transmit journalistic messages to accomplish certain political goals, with *messages* thought of in terms of truth and accuracy and *goals* thought of in relation to an informed citizenry. Many of us are used to thinking about communication in this way, foregrounding how representations and stories shape our understanding of the world. But we must also recognize that communication, in its less technological and more ancient associations, brings to mind ideas such as sharing, participation, commonality, and the building of community. In this case, we might think about how those representations and stories are *products* of the social, economic, and political forces of our world and of the worldviews that we might share. This view of communication is, as James Carey wrote, "directed not toward the extension of messages in space but toward the maintenance of society in time; not the act of imparting information but the representation of shared beliefs."[6] This view of communication directs our attention to collective experiences, such as those related to the formation of publics, the practices of politics, and the exercise of power among all members of a group.

In the US tradition of democratic thought, we have often conflated the relational and technological approaches to communication, placing a great deal of hope in the possibility that technologies could help us to overcome distance and difference so as to strengthen the economic, political, and cultural unity of the nation. But we have feared that technology might undermine our goals of unity.[7] Indeed, while John Dewey long ago invested great hope in the possibilities that communication might bring about a "great community," he also worried that technological advances were responsible for the development of the more impersonal and distant relationships that he believed threatened to undermine democracy. Thus he wanted to see those in the United States steer technologies to align with the relational goals of society.[8]

In *The Public and Its Problems*, Dewey argued that being part of a public meant being part of a group of people who share common experiences, and he argued that they – or we – need communication to better understand those common experiences and to consider various alternatives.[9] As the United States was rapidly transforming itself from a rural to an urban society in the wake of industrialization, Dewey argued for the importance of communication to the formation and maintenance of a community that could sustain a democratic public. In 1922, he wrote:

We have physical tools of communication as never before. The thoughts and aspirations congruous with them are not communicated, and hence not common. Without such communication, the public will remain shadowy and formless, seeking spasmodically for itself...*Communication alone can create a great community. Our Babel is not one of tongues, but of signs and symbols without which shared experience is impossible.*

(emphasis added)[10]

For Dewey, the key to life in the great community is an awareness of common concerns, and communication is the necessary ingredient for the emergence of this consciousness. As he argued, it is only through communication that "...a scattered, mobile and manifold public may so recognize itself as to define and express its interests."[11] Community and acts of citizenship come into being through communicative practices, then, as it is through communication that people come to recognize themselves as being part of a community. Communication enables people to tell stories of who they are and to envision the consequences of actions, and so it allows people to consider how the future should be shaped.

Dewey argued that it is only when members of a community are faced with direct opposition to their interests that they become a public.[12] Once a community becomes aware of their collective power as a public, they can actively participate in democracy, he argued. Writing in the early decades of the twentieth century, Dewey also believed that mass media – in his day, newspapers – were key in helping people gain an understanding of the problems that faced the public and that "without such communication the public will remain shadowy and formless."[13]

Still, community is a word that tends to evoke ideas of a fixed group of people who are united either in a common geographic location or through a commitment to common values. And community, as communication scholar Raymond Williams noted, is a term that never seems to be used unfavorably, as we tend to have a great deal of nostalgia and sentiment that come to the fore in relation to the idea of community.[14] Yet, it's always worth remembering that even as community is a term that feels warm and inclusive, communities also exclude and prohibit as a means of maintaining their boundaries. In the current political landscape, numerous scholars have commented on the erosion of community and the need for a reconceptualization of the notion of community and its relationship to concepts of the democratic public.[15]

Approaching communication as a key to the building of community is the starting point for what is termed the Montreal School of communication.[16] This school of thought argues that communication is constitutive of organization and of organizations, in that it is not that people "use" communication as a vehicle for expressing ideas, but rather, communication is "the means by which organizations are established, composed, designed, and sustained."[17] In this sense, communication is always related to the political problem of democracy, as Dewey argued.[18]

The technological and the relational aspects of communication are not so much competing as complementary views of communication. But the relational aspects are more frequently overlooked when we focus on questions of technology or the transmission of information rather than on the role communication plays in holding societies together or enabling them to envision how they might be different. As we will see in this and in the following chapter, many scholars are challenging the simplistic technological or "transmission" view of communication that has tended to dominate the ways that some have approached news, information, and politics in the past. Instead, in this book we view communication as constitutive of reality. This is our starting point as we consider what "news" is as a form of story-based communication, and how both the relational and technological aspects of communication are implicated in the news and politics of a digital age. Technological and relational aspects of communication both play a role in how stories are told, how worldviews are shaped, and how societies therefore stay together or don't.

In order to consider how people interact with one another in a democracy, it is important to recognize that theories of democracy have long been concerned with two competing approaches to the concept of citizenship that suggest different paradigms of communication and interaction. The older, civic republican tradition of citizenship views citizenship as an active process in which people participate in addressing their frustrations and uniting in matters of common concern. This is the tradition that Dewey spoke of in his discussions of communication and the public. But the liberal individualist sense of citizenship, which arose in the late seventeenth and early eighteenth centuries, tends to view citizenship primarily as a legal marker. In this view, citizens are largely passive politically, with rights granted to them by the state and obligations placed on them to obey laws, pay taxes, and, if necessary, defend the nation during times of war.[19] Here, citizens might be understood as passive recipients of information from official sources rather than as participants in an active process. Both these traditions shape how we collectively experience the tensions of contemporary citizenship and our understandings of the role of news in relation to citizenship.

It's important to note that even within the liberal individualist approach in which participation may be deemphasized, concerns arise about how people should interact with one another in a democracy, which in turn raises questions about duties and rights. And questions of duties and rights are further complicated when we consider the questions related to age and generation. Thus, we need to discuss differing approaches to youth and citizenship that are prevalent today, exploring how these relate to assumptions about technological and relational communication. This will enable us to consider the role news has been imagined to play in relation to youth citizenship in the past, and how we might envision an emerging role for news in the digital era.

DEVELOPMENTAL APPROACHES TO YOUTH CITIZENSHIP

We argue that ideas of youth and citizenship in the United States have been shaped by three different concerns particular to youth. First, US adults, and in particular parents, worry that young people can be harmed in public spaces. Concerns about predatory adults result in warnings of "stranger danger" and mediated stories of abductions heighten these concerns to a level that is out of proportion to the actual dangers young people face in public.[20] Nevertheless, fears about potential dangers inform a cautious approach to how youth should be introduced to experiences in public spaces.[21] A second and somewhat contradictory worry is that young people gathered together in public spaces can *cause* danger, particularly for others.[22] Thus, youth – and black and brown youth in particular – are often perceived as threatening in public spaces. This concern, for some, informs a cautious approach toward youth in public, and a need for others, particularly parents of black and brown youth, to instill caution in their children regarding how others perceive them in public spaces. A third worry is more abstract: that "youth" is a social category linked with promotional culture. Young people are viewed as highly susceptible to the messages of advertising, and at the same time, youth is celebrated and fictionalized as products and services are made appealing for those who wish they were young.[23] "Youth" is therefore something that is imagined and articulated in public life in ways that do not fully represent the actual lived experiences of young people.

These three frameworks – youth as in need of protection, adults as in need of protection from youth (even when those youth are not dangerous), and youth as deeply embedded in consumer culture – inform our approaches to youth and citizenship. Youth are either positioned as not ready for citizenship, as potentially destabilizing and problematic to adult citizens, or included in the activities of citizenship primarily in a symbolic or token manner. As a result, even as representations of youth seem to be ubiquitous in public spaces, youth are rarely invited into the decision-making processes of public life.

These various concerns inform what might be termed as a developmental approach to citizenship. Within this perspective, adults need to provide young people with avenues that help them prepare for a gradual extension of rights and identification with the nation-state. Developmental approaches to citizenship presume that young people need to become informed about news, current events, and civic arrangements so that someday, as adults, they will be equipped to hold government accountable through voting and working in political campaigns.[24]

Many scholars and youth advocates have pointed out that it is not sufficient to define youth civic development strictly in relation to the need to become informed so as to participate in voting activities *at some point in the future*.[25] Such deficit-oriented views of the relationships between youth, citizenship, and political action do not adequately reflect and actually invalidate the many different ways in which young people are already coming to understand and act upon political issues throughout their years of childhood. As Maira and Soep have noted:

There is often an assumption in traditional work on youth and citizenship...that young citizens – to the extent that they have rights, which are often limited – must be socialized into adult norms of political involvement rather than being thinking agents who may express important critiques of citizenship and nationhood.[26]

Young people often feel that they are seen as trivial players in the decisions and movements toward globalization, even as they are experiencing the shifts of national and global forces in their lives in significant ways. They respond to the social conditions of their lives through new forms of political expression, yet their efforts are often dismissed, feared, or ignored altogether. They move across a variety of public and communal spaces, and yet they are infrequently asked to comment on their own experiences with globalization or on their own role in constructing knowledge about it.

Moreover, the developmental perspective on citizenship assumes that young people grow up in a context where their basic rights are assured and where they can look forward to a future in which their rights and responsibilities will expand.[27] Unfortunately, this does not pertain to many young people who have experienced marginalization due to disability, race, sexual orientation, lack of access to resources, or their parents' citizenship status.[28] For many young people around the world today, prospects for the future have never seemed dimmer.[29] Perhaps this is why Hava Gordon and Jessica Taft found that while "apathy" is a word that comes up among white teens, Black and Latino youth use the words "cynicism" and "hopelessness" to describe why their peers aren't involved in civic life.[30] From a critical perspective, then, hope for change becomes a key dimension of how youth citizenship must be reconceptualized. When young people cannot count on basic rights and are skeptical about whether or not they or others they know have ever had those rights, it is difficult to imagine why they would want to participate in the civic or collective life of a society.[31]

CRITICAL APPROACHES TO YOUTH CITIZENSHIP

Critical approaches to citizenship, in contrast, begin from the perspective that people of all ages should have access to the basic human rights of global citizenship, such as the right to clean water, education, health care, and a decent place to live.[32] This access to basic rights is what lays the groundwork for how young people learn about the greater responsibilities that are afforded to them at the age of eighteen or twenty-one. The need for change is certainly something that is central to the lived experiences of many of today's young people. And yet, in spite of the overwhelming evidence that many youth are in need of hope and support, it is often young people themselves who seem to be viewed as a problem to be contained. Black young Americans are particularly at risk, as a study by the *Washington Post* found that they were 2.5 times more likely than white Americans to be shot and killed by a police officer.[33] Rates of youth incarceration are higher than ever, with "tried as an adult" policies meaning that sentences are often longer than youth sentences and are accompanied by fewer opportunities for programs that seek to curb recidivism.[34] And even the most privileged of young people across various racial/ethnic backgrounds feel disempowered in that they are everywhere encouraged to emphasize individualism rather than the collective, and academic achievement over artistic expression, in order to compete in the increasingly cutthroat race to achievement that's believed to be the only route to their future economic security.[35]

In spite of all the problems young people face in the contexts where they find themselves, there are many who are not disengaged from citizenship and public life. Youth from around the world seek ways to share their experiences through music, dance, or creative works and strive to make a contribution to their communities. Alicia Garza, Patrisse Cullors, and Opal Tometi were in their late twenties and early thirties when they first started discussing the idea of Black Lives Matter and utilizing the #BlackLivesMatter hashtag in the wake of Treyvon Martin's death.[36] Thousands of students have called themselves DREAMers, signifying their solidarity with the many undocumented young people who are denied the opportunity to pursue a university education or a professional career, a discrimination based solely on the unlucky fact that they happened to have been born in a different country. Hundreds of thousands of youth have joined their parents and peers in movements protesting economic austerity measures impacting education, transportation, and social services in their cities, demonstrating their belief that things could be different, and their hope, if slim, that their own actions might be part of something larger that could actually bring about change.

It's important to point out that the developmental perspective on citizenship has also shaped ideas about youth and news. From at least the early nineteenth century on, most adults in the United States have believed that one of their primary tasks involves protecting children from harm, and many adults have expressed concern that viewing news from legacy media sources can be distressing for youth, especially for young children.[37] At the same time, a great deal of research has shown that news consumption enhances political knowledge, understandings of policy issues, and participation in national political campaigns.[38] How and when adults should allow youth to have access into the worlds of adults has long been in question and has been forever changed in relation to an always-on media environment in which young people have more access to information than ever before.[39] Thus, if broadcasting was the model for political socialization in the past, and if that model fit with the top-down orientation of the developmental model of citizenship, then what might the critical model of citizenship, along with information's role in political socialization, look like in the relational context of social media? Such an approach raises new questions, such as: how do youth socialize one another into political awareness and citizenship, and what is the role of social media in these processes? As social media platforms open up new spaces in which youth, rather than adults, may take the lead in public actions of citizenship, how and when do the legacy news come to play a role, if they do? And in this digital context, how might adults and news sources offer the legitimacy and resources that youth might need in their own efforts towards embracing critical citizenship? To address these questions, we need to consider how social media has been understood in relation to critical acts of citizenship.

HOW SOCIAL MEDIA CAN
AUGMENT ENGAGEMENT

Many scholars, journalists, and interested members of the public have viewed social media and other technologies related to the Internet as disruptive technologies, in that they are reordering both how we organize ourselves in social relations, and how we keep track of these relations over time. Many in the "disruptive technologies" school of thought view social media negatively as locations where narcissism and shallowness thrive, believing that these sites encourage self-focus and the building of relationships of instrumentality and voyeurism rather than of mutuality.[40] Some in this school of thought blame this narcissism for a purported decline in political engagement among young people.

On the other hand, others view these disruptive technologies as full of potential, exploring how new technologies can enable young people to harness creativity, boost resilience, and ultimately change the world.[41] Several governmental organizations, non-governmental organizations (NGOs), and youth organizations have taken this perspective, creating a range of youth-oriented websites and apps meant to encourage civic engagement.[42] Unprecedented experimentation is taking place among those who are designing apps and websites for youth voting, volunteering, and community involvement.[43] Meanwhile, numerous scholars are taking a more measured but still positive view, considering the ways in which youth are exposed both to positions that align with and diverge from their own perspectives in social media, and how young people are engaging in social media use to organize school walk-outs, join protests, and inform one another of ongoing efforts to enhance youth rights.[44] Such approaches seem to support the desire to allow young people to explore, experience, and expand democracy in a digital age, which is certainly a worthwhile goal.[45]

We appreciate the concept of mediatization, which, as Peter Lunt and Sonia Livingstone have argued, helps sensitize researchers to both a heightened historical awareness and to questions of how changes wrought in relation to communication technologies intersect with larger processes within modernity, such as individualization, globalization, urbanization, or commercialization.[46] We approach mediatization as a complex network of changes where media technologies, institutional and cultural practices, and individual actions all play a role in change, and we, thus, look for ways in which communication practices *augment* already-occurring processes of political or social change.[47] Along with Nancy

Baym and others, we believe that these technologies enable new forms of self-expression and serve to assist people who wish to strengthen bonds in ways that were not previously available.[48] In this sense, we aim to bridge the technological and relational aspects of communication in our approach to youth, news, and politics by moving away from a focus on either mass or interpersonal communication and instead toward a focus on social relationships, experiences, and processes.[49] This suggests that a close examination of practices, grounded in an understanding of larger social, economic, and political changes, can contribute to new ways of approaching questions of social media, news, and civic engagement, but also that social media may be complicating engagement, in particular by way of undermining journalism.

HOW SOCIAL MEDIA IS UNDERMINING ENGAGEMENT BY CHALLENGING NEWS AND INFORMATION

Today, many view the news, information, and truth itself as being under siege and relate this to the rise of new modes of how news is distributed, and how that distribution is rendered profitable. By 2016, social media had become an important location for news consumption among all age populations in the United States. About 44 percent of US adults surveyed by the Pew Research Center in 2016 said that they received news from Facebook, representing a dramatic increase from three years earlier.[50] In addition to Facebook, Instagram scored well in the same survey as a news source for young nonwhite adults between the ages of eighteen and twenty-nine.

Unfortunately, things shifted dramatically in the news world after Facebook changed its algorithms in mid-2016, when Facebook decided to favor posts from user's friends and family within news feeds and deemphasized stories from mainstream news media. Between the first and second quarters of 2016, some of the top news publishers in the United States saw traffic to their sites decline by double digits as a result of Facebook's decision.[51] *Newsweek* owner IBT Media saw its visits decline by 47 percent from the first to the second quarter of 2016, with the Gannett newspaper chain seeing a drop of 26 percent and the *New York Times* a decline of 25 percent. CNN traffic was down 33 percent, *The Washington Post* 26 percent, and Politico 38 percent, according to a study conducted by SimilarWeb.[52] The study also highlighted several relative newcomers to news publishing that saw increases in web page views in 2016. YoungCons.com (Young Conservatives), FiveThirtyEight.com (an opinion poll aggregation website), and TheHill.com (a website covering US Congress, The White House, and political campaigns) saw the greatest gains among the top 150 news sites as measured by web page views, while MSN.com, DrudgeReport.com, and Disney Media Networks remained in the top spots.[53] The impact of this de-emphasis on professional news was evident during the 2016 presidential campaign, where sensational fake news stories (including untrue stories such as the Pope endorsing Donald Trump and Hillary Clinton murdering a former colleague) circulated on Facebook far more than legitimate news stories,[54] causing many to blame Facebook for the outcome of the election.[55]

Some of the problems with today's journalism models existed before the Internet and continue to exacerbate difficulties in communicating information, particularly regarding access to news sources and the representation of different issues and people within the news, as we will discuss more fully in subsequent chapters. Despite the adoption of mobile devices throughout the US population, for example, discrepancies in the reception of online content remain. As Mossberger and her colleagues have pointed out, information technology use remains inequitable in American metropolitan areas, as many minorities and urban poor have limited access and dramatically lower levels of online activity.[56] Another enduring problem involves the comprehension of political messages made available in online spaces. Even with materials that are found to be more entertaining and accessible, a young person's general knowledge of politics is a strong predictor of whether or not she will comprehend the political message she sees.[57]

Other problems in traditional journalism relate to the failure of its financial models. Well-resourced news organizations invested first in experimenting with differing pay walls, then in learning the value of click bait, and later in the development of sophisticated metrics that measure scroll depth, time on page, and total time spent reading, all in an effort to increase reader engagement in their news product so as to monetize the time spent on their news site. Journalism organizations offered more content than ever before, utilizing aggressive social media strategies to compete for attention.[58] But at the same time, newsrooms experienced historic financial losses, which resulted in massive staff layoffs and greatly diminished investigative departments.[59] Today, some are experimenting with crowdfunded journalism, although most projects that reach their desired funding levels are those originating with individuals rather than from established journalistic organizations, and most of the funding goes to longer form projects like documentaries or in-depth reports rather than to daily news.[60] Crowdfunding for journalistic activities continues to trail significantly behind film, video, gaming, and art projects, pointing to concerns about the scalability of this model of funding.[61] Others place hope in garnering support from socially conscious local businesses that have a direct interest in the health of local communities.[62] The old financial models do not work, and thus we as a society have to figure out how we will pay for the professional journalism that we want and need, which is an issue that has been discussed in many other venues.[63]

Among the younger population surveyed in the 2016 Pew study noted above, most still seemed to get what Boczkowski and his colleagues term "incidental news," or news that they happen upon while they are online doing other things.[64] And as Facebook launches new and faster-loading features meant to make it more appealing to view news through their site rather than elsewhere, this may further reduce the chances of stumbling upon professionally produced news. Even Snapchat's recent improvements to its Discover option, featuring news from legacy media outlets such as the *Wall Street Journal*, suggest that Snapchat recognizes that its viewers are primarily interested in news about fashion or sports rather than political and current events.[65] These developments do not bode well for the future of news and information consumption among young people.

NEWS AND INFORMATION: WHAT'S WORTH PRESERVING?

In the last section, we suggested how social media practices have been undermining habits of professional news consumption. In this section, we explore how the affordances of social media align with societal goals of relationality, in that it can be within and through our relationships that we come to recognize the gap between what is and what ought to be. We therefore highlight two journalistic traditions that are taking new form in social media practices: investigative journalism and, relatedly, journalism's imperative of holding leaders accountable for their role in societal problems and in working toward solutions.

Often when we talk about the crucial role of media in illuminating the shared problems of a group of people, what comes to mind is the important tradition of investigative or "muckraking" journalism – a tradition that first emerged with the early twentieth century exposure of lynching, discriminatory laws, corruption, and other illegal and exploitive business practices occurring in the then-dangerously unsafe conditions of the US meatpacking industry and the oil and railroad companies. Such coverage resulted in litigation and improved legislation, curtailing monopolies and unfair labor practices and initiating laws that restricted child labor and implemented election reforms. That tradition regained prominence with the *Washington Post*'s investigation into the scandals of Watergate and was memorably popularized and romanticized as Robert Redford and Dustin Hoffman immortalized reporters Bob Woodward and Carl Bernstein in *All the President's Men*. More recently, investigative journalism's reputation has been further burnished in the exposure of Catholic clergy sex abuse scandals in the *Boston Globe* and in the subsequent portrayal of this exposure in another Academy Award winning film, *Spotlight*. Investigative journalism involves research practices that are thorough and it attracts people of passion and dedication. As Michael Schudson notes of this kind of journalism, "It is not a personal journalism and not a journalism of advocacy; if there is a personal element in it, it is not opinion or conviction but energy."[66] Investigative journalism is not a journalism of advocacy, but deep investigation may *lead* to advocacy when a monumental problem is revealed and when current political arrangements seem incapable of addressing the problem. Bill McKibben, for example, who started his career as a science journalist, became an environmental advocate after reporting for decades on the mounting scientific evidence and scientific consensus regarding climate change, having conducted deep investigations into the seeming intractability of solving the problems resulting from climate change.[67]

The decades of the 1960s through the 1990s marked the heyday of investigative reporting. But such reporting is resource-intensive and expensive, and the last couple of decades have witnessed large cuts in investigative journalism in news outlets around the world. In an earlier era, a team of investigative reporters would have generated stories about how the Massport Authority in East Boston initially opposed and forestalled addressing environmental impacts on the community. But in contemporary times, such investigative work, if it is done at all, happens and is communicated to others, in a variety of ways that may be at some distance from mainstream journalism. This is far from an ideal or complete direction for the future of news. But, as we are arguing, if we want to consider positive ways forward, it's worth exploring how these kinds of journalistic practices of investigation and watchdogging are gaining traction in the relational communication platforms of social media, and how they complement what is happening in the realm of professional journalism.

Investigative journalism is not the only kind of journalism that is believed to strengthen the economic, political, and cultural unity that we might wish to see within the US public (or, more accurately, within its various intersecting publics). Nor are daily newspapers and television news the only, or even the main, locations in which such productive investigations take place. The many and varied forms that professional journalism takes today remain an important part of democratic society because of professional journalism's role in articulating collective moral commitments, as Jeffrey Alexander writes:

The neutrality, the perspective, the distance, the reflexivity, the narrating of the social as understood in this time and place – all this points beyond the details of craft and the ethics of profession to the broad moral organization of democratic life. Even as the sacred codes of professional journalism reach downward into the practical production of daily, hourly, and minute-by-minute news, they reach upward into the more ethereal world of civic morals. When journalists make meaning of events, transforming randomness into pattern, they do so in terms of the broader discourse of civil society.[68]

The norms of providing neutral information in a fair and balanced way "contribute to a moral discourse that makes civil society possible," in Alexander's words.[69] In its varied forms, professional journalism remains a practice that is vital to a functioning democracy. How social media practices might play a role in the articulation of collective moral commitments is a central question for the future of news.

Not surprisingly, in today's era of declining professional journalistic resources, we are seeing a range of adaptations. Stories like those of Mike and Alma, who opened the chapter, offer signs of how some young people and their communities are adapting to this lack of investigative resources, even as the amount of work required and the slowness of the tasks in just one location are indicative of how much remains to be done. At the same time, we have seen the emergence of overtly partisan and ad-hoc practices of investigation that have arisen in place of professional journalism, as we will discuss further in the chapters to follow. It is in this troubling context that we must ask how we as a society are truly holding accountable those leaders and organizations we have entrusted to address our needs, consistent with a critical approach to citizenship.

Clearly, we are at a point where we need a new model for understanding the relationships between youth, journalism, and citizenship. And, we believe that looking at the actual practices of young people can be helpful in understanding not only journalism but its evolving relationship with politics, citizenship, and civic action as these are experienced in everyday life. In the next chapter, we introduce concepts of connective action and connective journalism that help to explain what we found when we studied the practices of young people, often as they encountered news, citizenship, and politics for the first time via social media.

* * * * *

2

Connective Journalism

The concept of connective journalism, which we introduced in the Introduction and will elaborate in this chapter, draws upon contemporary discussions about the role of information sharing and democracy in a social media age. In particular, we draw upon the work of Lance Bennett and Alexandra Segerberg. In *The Logic of Connective Action*, Bennett and Segerberg examine the ways in which digital media have opened up new possibilities for political action and organization.[1] They prefer "network" to "community," "public," or "social movement" because the term suggests the varied and flexible ways in which individuals and organizations are connected to one another. Movements are built on a collective sense of identity and the ideological negotiations that are worked out among coalition partners, whereas, they argue, networks are "decentered, distributed, and dynamic."[2] In addition to earlier forms of collective political action, then, which were centered around formal organizations that used communication technologies to broker information and manage mobilization efforts, Bennett and Segerberg propose that we are now seeing the emergence of what they term "connective action," or crowd-enabled networks through which people participate in political activities. Communication between people in these networks is central to the ways in which connective action can occur. As Bennett and Segerberg argue, "Beyond sharing information and sending messages, the organizing properties of communication become prominent in connective action networks."[3] Social network technologies enable people to personalize their connection with certain issues, Bennett and Segerberg argue, for individuals choose both what kinds of information they will share with those within their networks and how they will share that information.

The concept of connective action draws upon what is termed the Montreal School of the organizing properties of communication, or what we have referred to as the communicative constitution of organization.[4] This school of thought is related to the idea that communication is constitutive of organization and of organizations, as noted earlier; it is not that people "use" communication as a vehicle for expressing ideas, but rather, communication is "the means by which organizations are established, composed, designed, and sustained."[5] Because organizations are not fixed "things" but rather are continually realized as a result of sometimes precarious relationships that are experienced in communication processes, this school of thought is also interested in how "people 'tune in' to one another as they engage in coordinated activity."[6] Bennett and Segerberg were consequently making the argument that communicational events are not a mere afterthought in the processes of organizing for political change, a point that directs researchers to take seriously the ways in which language, discourse, rhetorics, narratives, and other communicative acts constitute relationships between people that, in turn, are constitutive of organizing for political change.

The concept of connective journalism that we are introducing in this book has a great deal in common with the concept of connective action. Both share a commitment to seeing communication as constitutive of organizations and of organizing; both take an approach to communication that is inclusive beyond texts and conversations and includes a variety of emotive ways in which people communicate; both are attentive to ambiguities and inferences in communication and are inclusive of human and non-human agency; both share an understanding of the ideational and material as co-constitutive in organizing; and both are interested in organizing and in organizations. (In this book, we are thinking about organizations specifically in relation to institutional actors like policy, city, and other political and community organizations as well as emergent social movement organizations.)

CONNECTIVITY AND INTERSUBJECTIVITY IN SOCIAL MEDIA

We wish to take this theory a step further in relation to the concepts of connectivity and intersubjectivity, for we see this as an important way to theorize the specific contributions of social media and journalism to processes of political information sharing and ultimately to the formation of publics. The concept of connectivity refers to the social practices that link together people and institutions through technologies and communicative actions. Jose Van Dijck and Thomas Poell bring attention to the infrastructure of connectivity, or the ways in which various social media platforms such as Facebook, Twitter, and Instagram are structured so as to encourage people to connect with one another in ways that generate profits for those platforms.[7] Twitter, Facebook, and other social media sites have also come to be incorporated into increasingly sophisticated efforts to mobilize constituents, raise funds, and garner new forms of power in the discursive battles that are waged through the digital realm. Thus, we want to discuss politics, news, and information in relation to how these things are experienced by people in their everyday lives and *in their relationships*, as mediated through social media. This is in contrast to other approaches to the study of politics that begin with either the actions of individual citizens (such as voting) or groups of citizens (such as political organizing).

The work of phenomenological philosophers Emmanuel Levinas and Hannah Arendt provide a foundation for this approach to considering intersubjectivity in relation to both politics and news. In phenomenology, scholars study the ways in which people perceive their experiences, recognizing that reality is always filtered through and constructed in relation to these perceptions, and that societal structures are revealed as we study them through the perceptions of others.[8] Key to the existential phenomenological approach of Levinas and Arendt is the concept of intersubjectivity, which affirms the idea that knowledge and shared meanings are constructed by people in their interactions with others. The concept of intersubjectivity became important in the work of social psychologist George Herbert Mead, who claimed that the self and society are irreducibly intersubjective.[9] Both social and natural reality are constructed through intersubjectivity, as later theorists in this school of thought such as Goffman, Merleau-Ponty, Berger and Luckmann, and Habermas would argue.[10] For this reason, we want to focus on what young people actually do as well as what they say about what can be widely understood as the political, particularly within their relationships mediated through social media.

Social media are usefully considered an intersubjective realm. The communicative meanings intended by the person posting, tweeting, or snapping are one aspect of communication that occurs in social media, but equally important are the meanings made by those who receive and, sometimes, pass along those communications and meanings to others. Listening, after all, is important in any new media discussion about contributing a "voice," as media scholar Kate Crawford has pointed out, noting that we all move back and forth between listening and disclosing online.[11] Moreover, any meaning communicated is also always already filtered through commonly shared understandings of language and culture. It might be wise to conceive of communication occurring in social media as consisting of layers upon layers of intersubjective communication. This is an idea to which we will return in the discussion of communication occurring in social media, that follows.

In our own analysis of social media, we find it useful to begin with Martin Buber's *I–Thou* philosophy, which brings attention to the interpersonal nature of all human existence. Buber argues that relationships are not based on the communication of information between beings, but rather on the I–Thou (or I–You) relationship constituted in *encounters*: encounters that may involve dialogue, mutuality, and exchange, but that are fundamentally different from I–It relationships. In I–It relationships, people and other beings are treated as objects used to serve the individual's interests.[12] I–Thou relationships are characterized by openness to the uniqueness of the other and are experienced in mutuality. Following Buber, we argue that the ways in which people communicate with others, in social media and in interpersonal relations as well as in organizations, vacillate between I–Thou and I–It relations. Buber contends that we as humans can recognize when we are in one kind of relationship rather than the other. We strive for I–Thou encounters, but often experience ourselves as "othered" or as viewed through another's thought categories.

Thus, one way in which we hope to contribute to the theory of connective action is by recognizing that while we share an interest in how communication is constitutive of order in the form of organizing, we are also interested in how communication is constitutive of *disorder* when relationships are not defined by mutuality. We believe that it is in this communicative construction of disorder that counter-narratives and questions are generated, and it is this disorder that is at the heart of tensions that arise within, outside of, or in relation to societal organizations. Communication contributes to the disorder of what Chantal Mouffe has termed the agonistic public, an idea to which we will return in our discussion of publics in Chapters 6 and 7.[13]

Here, we want to pay attention to how young people experience themselves as striving for I–Thou relations in social media. As noted earlier, we recognize that many view social media sites as locations where narcissism thrives, since these sites are believed to encourage self-focus, instrumentality, and voyeurism rather than mutuality.[14] But we also recognize that these technologies enable new forms of self-expression and serve to assist people who wish to strengthen bonds in ways that were not previously available.[15] Instead of eroding relations, social media such as Facebook, Instagram, and even texting may provide opportunities for people to connect with one another and to feel understood and accepted as a whole and unique self.

Buber notes the rarity of I–Thou relations. We don't often experience meaningful encounters with others anywhere, whether online or offline. And yet, we long for those experiences, and, as John Durham Peters has pointed out, communication is a registry of those longings.[16] Because human consciousness is a key part of the human condition, and because our consciousness is isolated from that of others, we are, in Peters's words, "hardwired by the privacy of (our) experiences to have communication problems."[17] He continues:

Communication...does not involve transmitting information about one's intentionality; rather, it entails bearing oneself in such a way that one is open to hearing the other's otherness...here communication is about the constitution of relationships, the revelation of otherness, or the breaking of the shells that encase the self, not about the sharing of private mental property.[18]

We are therefore interested in both the ways in which young people experience themselves as part of a mutual relationship within social media, and in the ways they find themselves *addressed* as subjects within these platforms. We know that as humans, we are driven to find connections with others, and research has demonstrated that we are more likely to experience prosocial rather than antisocial communication online.[19] The meanings that young people construct from the messages that show up on their Facebook timeline or in their text messages draw upon their relationship with and understandings of the person who is the author of the post. Thus, when they receive messages with some kind of political intent, these messages are weighed accordingly.

Posting such content is perceived as interpersonally risky. Political sociologist Nina Eliasoph's work is instructive on this point. In her 1998 study *Avoiding Politics*, she found that people in the United States often work hard to avoid speaking about politics – even in political and volunteer community organizations – because they want to avoid the confrontation that discussions of politics can provoke.[20] Like people of all ages, young people encounter difficulty in bringing politics into personal conversations, as such actions can bring about disagreements, feelings of discomfort, or even offense.[21] In Kjerstin Thorson's work exploring the uncertainties youth encounter regarding who might see their Facebook posts and how differing people might respond to them, she discusses "one collection of motivated, passionate youth [who] experiment with ways to 'do politics' on everyday Facebook and others [who] engage in protective strategies to avoid the possibility of offense or misinterpretation or an inaccurate presentation of self."[22] The second group – those who avoid politics out of fear of misinterpretation or a rupture of a mutual relationship – is much larger than the first.

When we communicate with others in social media spaces, we don't expect that what we see there will always be affirming of who we are. However, most of us do go to social media platforms with an openness to others that is not rooted in instrumentality, but rather is rooted in the hope that we will be seen and known. We are not seeking the secrets of another person's consciousness; rather, we want to take part in a collective world. But as we look for congruence that affirms our sense of a collective experience, we also notice discrepancies, and those become part of our relationship with the other person, as well. We must decide, consciously or not, to ignore, overcome, address, or negotiate these discrepancies in tending to our relationships. Or, we can choose to let that relationship go, which we are usually reluctant to do because it cuts off all possibilities for mutuality and even self-affirmation. This explains why some people are reluctant to disclose views about politics in online spaces, and what they have to overcome in order to do so. This also points to the fact that we are more likely to give someone we know a pass when we are not in agreement or in an experience of mutuality, because our interest is in at least maintaining the status quo of the relationship. The desire to take part in a collective world connects practices of social media with questions of democracy, following political theorist John Dewey's assertion that communication is always related to the political problem of democracy.[23]

INTERSUBJECTIVITY AND MUTUALITY IN DEMOCRATIC THEORY

An important aspect of the intersubjective in the work of both Arendt and especially Levinas has to do with the fact that the relations between the subject and one or more others raises questions about duties and rights. Arendt did not interact with Levinas during their most active work as scholars, but she shared Levinas's concern that too much of the work of political philosophers in the early twentieth century was focused on ideas and not enough on action. Arendt was interested in how people formed judgments concerning which actions were consistent with the exercise of political responsibility.[24] She was critical of the US approach to governance, contending that even though US citizens were protected from the arbitrary exercise of political power, they were not granted the means to actively participate in governance as moral agents.[25] Furthermore, Arendt distinguished between human rights, which are due to every person and the rights of the citizen, which are due by virtue of membership in a national political community in the liberal individualist approach to citizenship.[26] As a refugee who fled Nazi Germany, she argued that nation-states claimed to protect the human rights of all, but in fact the human rights of refugees are negated in favor of the interests of national sovereignty.[27] Thus, she observed that the nation-state sometimes had conflicting interests when it came to the rights and duties of those who lived within it, and this meant that human rights could be rescinded under national rights. Following Kant, she argued for the need to take the rights of "others" into consideration, contending that in a democracy, we are morally obligated to adopt a position that "thinks from the standpoint of everyone else," which is a position that requires government to support institutions through which the perspectives of others can be expressed.[28]

Arendt is helpful in our thinking about the contemporary situation for young people in several ways. The question of why young people may or may not share news with others directs attention to the ways in which people develop judgments consistent with a sense of political responsibility. How young people come to "think from the standpoint of everyone else" is a key question for our study, particularly as it is viewed as central to political theories of democratic deliberation and journalists have traditionally seen themselves as contributing to this enterprise.[29] Sometimes this idea of thinking "from the standpoint of everyone else" is discussed in the common assumption that journalism's mandate is to increase our understanding of those whose life experiences differ from our own.[30] In political theory, "thinking from the standpoint of everyone else" is also discussed in relation to the way in which people come to have empathy for those who are different from them, as we discuss further below. Arendt's analysis drew attention to the relationships between citizenship rights and human rights, raising questions that we still struggle with today regarding the sovereignty of the nation and the inheritance of laws within a nation that still does not treat all people as equals.

Levinas, like Arendt, was interested in the question of human rights, and both raised the issue of political responsibility in relation to those rights.[31] But unlike Arendt, Levinas did not put much hope in the idea that justice will emerge in the political realm as a result of deliberation. He came to this conclusion based on his belief that people operate out of indifference to ethical responsibility. Therefore, he felt that we cannot expect that justice will emerge; instead, we need to build ethical responsibility into the structure of our political institutions.[32] As he wrote:

The third party (le tiers) is other than the neighbor but also another neighbor, and also a neighbor of the other ... What am I to do? What have they already done to one another? Who passes before the other in my responsibility? What, then, are the other and the third party with respect to one another? Birth of the question. The first question of the interhuman is the question of justice. Henceforth it is necessary to know, to become conscious [se faire une con-science]. Comparison is superimposed onto my relation with the unique and the incomparable ... And through this, finally, the extreme importance in human multiplicity of the political structure of society, subject to laws and thereby to institutions where the for-the-other of subjectivity – or the ego – enters with the dignity of a citizen into the perfect reciprocity of political laws...[33]

In Levinas's work, politics and ethics are distinct, but also connected, as politics is the realm in which responsibility is regulated.[34] Justice is the foundational principle that is to guide how those regulations are to be constructed and maintained. This also raises questions related to our study, such as: How does our aversion in the United States to governmental regulation hinder our ability to take collective responsibility for the ways in which our society is structured? How does this aversion hinder our ability to develop a civic imagination that enables us to think of how society might be structured differently? And what role could media play both in fostering that civic imagination and in enabling the taking of collective responsibility?

CRITICAL CITIZENSHIP AND EXPANDED NEWS

In addition to our focus in this book on the interpersonal relationships that govern what is shared online and with whom, and our focus on I–Thou versus I–It relations, we also want to pay attention to how young people of color, in particular, evaluate the taken-for-granted ways of seeing and organizing the world that are often embedded in the journalistic storytelling of legacy media. We argue that young people of color often make evaluations of journalistic storytelling in relation to an ethical stance, one that the philosopher Emmanuel Levinas, building on Buber's theory of interpersonal encounters, has discussed in relation to a recognition of one's inevitable relationship with, and responsibility towards "the Other."[35] For Levinas, too, communication is about the proximity to or contact with the other, not about the communication of information.

According to Levinas, the relationship between self and Other must be premised upon respect and responsibility. As we will see in the next chapter, young people evaluate journalistic storytelling negatively when they view it as disrespectful of them, particularly when they see themselves and others they understand as part of their communities being "Othered." Sometimes they come to recognize storytelling itself as the location of the problem, such as in stereotypical representations of people of color in legacy media. At other times, they come to realize that the problem lies in the broader organization of society, as they see certain policies or practices that are reported on in the media as being disrespectful of them or their communities.

It is usually much easier for a person to let the relationship with a journalist go than a relationship with a person in one's social network. In fact, young people may not even notice a journalist's name or identify the story with the person writing it. It is thus easier for us to put that story into an I–It relationship than a story that comes to us in social media via a friend or family member. This is why connective journalism practices have the potential for democratic solidarity and public building that can seem to elude traditional journalism and the relationship between journalists and readers/viewers. When the story comes from a person in our social network with whom we have a relationship of some kind, both that relationship and the story participate in constructing the meaning that the person ascribes to the story.

In this book, we are interested in the role that journalistic storytelling and interpersonal communication in social media play in how young people come to recognize a problem *as* a problem, or how they come to question the taken-for-granted assumptions that give shape to the communicative actions of those in power. When young people do not accept but question the assumptions of those in power, the recognition of a problem can result in a "communication failure" or the constitution of *disorder* through communication, as discussed earlier.[36] Connective journalism is part of this process of questioning, then, as young people collectively "gatewatch" those in power and begin to assimilate, assemble, and share evidence that challenges the certainty, routine, and efficiency of the communicative processes of those in power. It is behavior that is proto-political in the sense that it is a precursor to connective action, since the concept of connective journalism recognizes how awareness of a problem comes to be constituted through communication. As this awareness is constituted through communication, young people come to see that things can and ought to be different than they are.

To address questions of the relationships between connective journalism and connective action practices, we have studied the connective journalism practices of today's youth as they become introduced to political matters through their social networks. We hope that such an examination will provide insights into how communicative acts in today's social media context are playing various roles in how young people establish and maintain relationships, formulate social movement narratives, channel resources, and participate in beckoning their peers toward participatory political action. As we noted in the Introduction, we understand connective journalism as the communicative practices young people engage in that give voice both to their own distinctive ways of viewing the world and to their views of how we *ought* to feel about what is happening in that world. The concept of connective journalism points to the fact that young people are always already situated in connective relationships with a variety of societal institutions, organizations, and individuals, and in the case of those young people from disenfranchised, minority, and migrant populations, they are also always already products of intersectionalities, or intersections of multiple systems of oppression or discrimination.[37] There are therefore both forces and counter-forces that shape the ways in which young people take part in creating, seeking, and sharing information, and that, in turn, affirm a sense of self or contribute to one's perceived community.

Following Nick Couldry's work on voice, we argue that connective journalism practices are political, as through connective journalism, people may draw upon a variety of communicative resources in order to convey their own belief both in the value of their own voice and in others' capacity to listen to that voice and, possibly, to cooperate with them.[38] Voice, understood as the sense of giving an account of one's life and conditions is, as Couldry argues, "an irreducible part of what it means to be human."[39] As such, an effort to consider an inclusive and plural concept of democracy and democratic action must embrace the importance of voice.

It is not that every communicative act is political, or that only communicative acts about political matters are important, but that all people want to speak and be heard on matters that affect their lives. And as people engage in efforts to speak and be heard among the communities that matter to them through social media, they draw upon the connective capacities of social media platforms and, sometimes, upon some of the classic concepts underlying journalism. Journalism practices, after all, are commonly understood as the gathering and sharing of accurate renderings of reality so as to enable participation in politics and culture of a society. In its ideal definition, journalism is seen as playing an integrative role in society. Thus, exploring connective journalism practices can provide a bottom-up means of understanding how people may be brought together in ways that can build a more contemporary view of politics and publics. In connective journalism, therefore, "news" is not defined by the industries or professionals associated with journalism, but rather it is defined, elaborated, and spread in relation to the interests and needs of networked groups of people: networks that can be comprised of people and groups who are more or less dynamically linked together at any given moment by their relationship to unfolding events and concerns.

Connective journalism is thus a term that builds upon Axel Bruns's concept of "gatewatching," which he writes is "the continuous, communal observation of the output gates of conventional news organizations, as well as the primary sources of news and information, for information which is seen to be of interest to the gatewatcher's own community."[40] Bruns was describing the process by which people come to contribute to citizen journalism sites. But following Andrew Chadwick, we suggest broadening our definition of journalism in a manner that recognizes what he terms the emergent, interdependent hybrid media system that brings together both old and new media, including traditional forms of journalism as well as political satire, YouTube commentary, Wikipedia entries, Wikileaks, tweets, and other experiments in critical inquiry and political journalism.[41] Further, with Adrienne Russell, we focus on meanings made not at specific news sites but among differing groups of people, including in our definition of journalism "the wealth of news-related information, opinion, and cultural expression, in different styles and from various producers, which *together* shape the meaning of news events and issues" (emphasis added).[42] As Clay Shirky observed, the pattern to this kind of news sharing reverses the traditional order of "filter, then publish" to "publish, then filter," leading to a crowdsourced means of evaluating and developing stories collaboratively. Those engaging in connective journalism practices similarly can either generate news as a professional reporter might, or they can simply share what they find interesting and worth

highlighting for those within their communities of interest. But in connective journalism practices, as noted in the previous chapter, the point
of sharing is less about building an accurate story, as is the case in citizen
journalism, and more about building a sense of collective and individual
identity, as reinforced in the telling of the story by and for a particular
group of people. In our work on connective journalism, we are interested in how it is that certain issues rise to a level in which people feel
it is urgent to address others so as to engage personally in what Jeffrey
Alexander terms the "civil repair" of something perceived as gravely
wrong with the way things are.[43]

Sharing, inserting oneself into the story, and making the story are
the phrases we use to describe three different practices of connective
journalism, and we will discuss these more fully later in this chapter. These practices represent different levels of investment in political identification, as evidenced in the ways in which they require
increasingly greater tolerance for interpersonal risk.[44] Our approach to
identifying these practices can be viewed as an alternative to existing
taxonomies of political identification, which have tended to focus on
political party affiliation and overtly political topics of concern. Our
approach also differs from studies focused on the amount of exposure
to news among youth, or studies that have sought to identify young
individuals as more or less informed.[45] Rather than attempting to char-
acterize individuals, our approach emphasizes modes of practice, following the model of analysis laid out in qualitative and ethnographic
research. In particular, we created our model following the influen-
tial study by Mizuko Ito and her colleagues that identified "hanging
out, messing around, and geeking out" as three related informal learning practices that occur in and through digital media spaces and that
represent increasingly stronger levels of engagement in learning.[46] We
turn now to these practices, which we have organized into three categories: (1) sharing the story; (2) inserting oneself into the story; and
(3) making the story.

SHARING THE STORY

As we noted in the Introduction, in a nationally representative study,
45 percent of young people reported that they received news at least once a
week via a social media site such as Facebook or Twitter.[47] Some 78 percent
of young people reported that they sent messages, shared updates, and

messaged people online, and more than half of all youth reported that they shared links or forwarded information at least once a week.[48]

Young people's online activities are largely "friendship-driven," as Ito and her colleagues have described them.[49] Youth report a sense of reward when they participate in sharing information within social network sites, and, as researchers such as danah boyd have argued, this sense of reward is closely related to the individual identity goals of the young people themselves.[50] However, youth are also cautious in what they choose to share and under what circumstances. If young people do not see a connection between their own self-narrative and a particular issue, they're not likely to feel that there is a reason to share information on that issue with their networks. Still, before the 2016 political campaign, one-fifth of young people had reported that they had forwarded political commentary created by someone else, or had shared news about a political campaign, issue, or candidate, or had passed along funny videos or cartoons that related to a political candidate, campaign, or issue.[51] As Henry Jenkins, Mizuko Ito, and others have observed, this rise in youth "participatory culture" is important because it means that social media provide contexts in which young people can practice sharing ideas and material with others, and it is in these contexts that they become familiar with how to interact and participate in various realms of life, including the political realm.[52]

Social network entities have seen the benefits of this aspect of participatory culture, as well. In an article on how Facebook has become the centralized place for online news consumption and the key location for political media, journalist John Herrman observed:

From a user's point of view, every share, like or comment is both an act of speech and an accretive piece of a public identity. Maybe some people want to be identified among their networks as news junkies, news curators or as some sort of objective and well-informed reader. Many more people simply want to share specific beliefs, to tell people what they think or, just as important, what they don't. A newspaper-style story or a dry, matter-of-fact headline is adequate for this purpose. But even better is a headline, or meme, that skips straight to an ideological conclusion or rebuts an argument.[53]

Thus, content providers have rushed to offer ever-more shareable content, a situation aided by evolutions within social media. In 2010, Facebook made it possible for publishers to invite readers to share their content, and publishers found that a widely shared link could substantially increase traffic to their sites. Initially, news organizations were enthused about these practices of sharing, as they served to attract more viewers to the stories they had produced and that they believed were valuable for political awareness and public discussion. Some, such as the *New York Times*, even entered into content-sharing agreements with Facebook.[54] Yet by 2012, Facebook had become the primary distribution hub for almost all information, and content providers seeking attention increasingly dealt directly with social media sites rather than with traditional news media outlets, cutting them out of the loop. With the turn to mobile devices, other social media sites similarly became portals through which people landed on content; by 2014, for example, Buzzfeed received 75 percent of its visitors from social media sites.[55]

This sharing of political content and news is the most common of the practices we refer to as connective journalism. It has also received a great deal of worrisome concern among those who compare these practices to the practices of professional journalism, because emotion and identity, rather than information sharing, are at its core. What is most likely to be passed on is not necessarily the most important information, but rather that characterized by what Terri Senft describes as "the grab," in that it grabs attention and demands a response.[56] One's own identity is affirmed as others choose to like or share it. There is not a great deal at stake if it is ignored, however, since the person who views the share can choose to ignore it or may not even view it as something with political import. Studies have shown, however, that males are more likely than females to post content that contradicts another post in order to assert their lack of agreement.[57]

Such sharing of material is interwoven into young people's everyday lives. Because many schools in the United States forbid the use of mobile phones during school hours, sharing becomes a part of the protean moments that occur as young people transition to and from school, and in between their other activities. "Hanging out" online is how young people socialize, and participation in connective journalism practices takes place within this context of hanging out.[58] In our study, we observed young people sharing video essays on racism, LGBT rights, the DREAM Act, youth activism outside the United States, and news about other current events, as well as excerpts from popular political satire programs like *Last Week Tonight with John Oliver*. Such material might show up in Facebook timelines following videos of pushup challenges and before memes of cats watching *Game of Thrones;* in other words, political commentary was seamlessly woven into young people's ongoing self-presentations online, sometimes eliciting likes or other emoticons and occasionally receiving an encouraging comment. At the same time, social media companies subject all such shared material to algorithms that are meant to predict and direct flows of this and future user-generated content, so as to maximize the profitability of the exchange by making it subject to future data mining.

In the next chapter, we discuss the factors that discourage young people from seeking out news that originates from legacy news sources, and in Chapter 4 we explore the news landscape from which shareable material is drawn. In Chapter 5, we explore what it means to be a "lurker," and how young people interpret and engage with news-related material that they receive from those in their social media feeds.

INSERTING ONESELF INTO THE STORY

Facebook has been especially attuned to this interest in inserting oneself into the story, developing and releasing widgets that allowed people to turn their profile photos into a rainbow in solidarity with the US Supreme Court's decision to legalize same sex marriage and working in concert with the Susan G. Komen Race for the Cure fund-raising efforts. But some young people take a further step in engagement as they participate more explicitly in sharing something that inserts them directly into a story of political import. They share what we term *artifacts of political engagement* that communicate their personal identification with and enthusiasm for a particular political position or way of seeing the world. Such artifacts of engagement may take the form of what John Durham Peters and Stuart Allan have termed "witnessing," in that they serve as evidence of the fact that someone in one's social network is able to provide an eyewitness account of unfolding events.[59] Photographs have become a new important currency for social interaction, as Jose Van Dijk has pointed out.[60]

While sharing information or commentary created by someone else can potentially result in negative comments from peers, it takes a willingness to embrace an even greater level of interpersonal risk to post a photo of oneself at a gay pride march on Instagram or on another social media site, just as it also takes courage to post a photo of yourself holding your hands in the air in reference to the "hands up, don't shoot" meme of #BlackLivesMatter. In our study, as we discuss in Chapter 5, we found that in general, young people were more reluctant to post photos of themselves engaging in activities like these that might be more clearly deemed political. The sense of risk was lower for those who believed that most in their social network on a particular platform would agree with their stance, but even in this case, young people were aware that engaging in this practice of inserting themselves into newsworthy political stories exposed them to greater possibilities for pushback from their peers and family members. Youth felt that engaging in such sharing of artifacts of one's engagement could be viewed as a form of preening, or posting with the intent to show that "something big happened, but the important thing was that I was there."

Inserting oneself into a political story risks misinterpretation, as evidenced in the story young people related to us of Lindsey Stone, the young adult whose friend posted a photo of her giving the middle finger at the Tomb of the Unknown Soldier. Stone's father, while demanding that she apologize, explained to the media that her pose was in reaction to the sign (asking for quiet and respect) and not to the place.[61] At one point, however, someone had created a Facebook page titled, "Fire Lindsey Stone" that garnered more than 19,000 likes, and Stone eventually had to hire a reputation management service company to rehabilitate her online image.[62] In taking and sharing an image of herself making what she claimed was a joke in a location others consider sacred, Stone seemed to have been focused on the "I was there" aspect of connecting rather than on the magnitude of the place within the civic imaginary. In our research, we learned of young people who were similarly criticized by their peers for posting images of themselves at important political moments. Such shares could be misinterpreted as preening even when the young person posting did in fact share the image out of a recognition of the magnitude of the political event. One of the risks of inserting oneself into the story as a connective journalism practice, therefore, is that what one shares can be misconstrued or misinterpreted as being "all about me" rather than about the political event or action itself.

Interestingly, few of the young people who engaged in these practices of inserting themselves into stories saw themselves as participating in "citizen journalism," although it's worth pointing out that thinking about recording an event as it occurs is an important step of recognition of an event's newsworthiness and its shareability. Nevertheless, professional journalists have seen the value in these citizen activities as they can be repackaged for a news audience and monetized in the name of giving citizens a "voice" in legacy media. We further discuss these practices of inserting oneself into the story in Chapters 5 and 6.

MAKING THE STORY

Although the connective journalism practice of witnessing seemed to gain traction during the student protest movements of 2015 and 2016, only 6 percent of young people during that time engaged in activities that called for creative activity (such as contributing an article, opinion piece, photo, or video about a political campaign, issue, or candidate), according to a Youth and Participatory Politics national survey.[63] However, that is roughly the same number of young people who, during the same time frame, said that they had participated in a protest, demonstration, sit-in, or in an event where young people expressed their political views through music, poetry, or some other form.[64] Thus, these online activities of creativity should be seen as existing in addition to rather than as a substitute for other forms of political engagement, as Cathy Cohen and her colleagues have pointed out.[65]

Social media invites creativity and replication, as witnessed in the rise of mashups, memes, vines, and other forms of commentary.[66] But young people also participate in creating stories that are much more traditional in form, whether as video essays, podcasts, printed reports, or Power Point slide shows. Additionally, students utilize journalistic research and storytelling practices to discover more about problems and to investigate how they might be addressed, as witnessed in the examples of Mike and Alma that opened the previous chapter.

The connective journalism practices of creating have been of particular interest to those who are concerned about youth citizenship and news.[67] In effect, professional journalists view young creators as those who have "self-nominated" to be a "source" (or to provide source material) for legacy journalism. Professional journalists, in turn, then may provide legitimacy to a story through their decision to cover a young person's creation of a meme, podcast, video, or printed report as the subject of a news story. And, once that story has been covered in legacy news, it can be shared again by young people as a renewed form of participation as well as a celebration of that participation.

Young people and the movements that work with them have become increasingly savvy about working directly within the recognized genres of newsmaking and commentary. Elisabeth Soep, building upon earlier work in the field of youth media such as that of David Buckingham, has argued that through participation in media creation, young people are cultivating new literacies that enable them to participate in public life.[68] Soep discusses five key strategies that we might say are necessary for youth engagement in connective action through participation in the connective journalism practice of making the story: pivot your public; create content worlds; forage for information; code up; and hide and seek.[69] Others, such Henry Jenkins and his research team, have explored how millennials seek to harness the stories of popular cultural heroes such as Harry Potter and Katniss from *The Hunger Games* to establish organizations that translate public policy issues into accessible opportunities for youth-led civic action.[70]

But it's important to note that young people themselves remain skeptical about the connection between the kind of information provided within traditional journalistic genres and outlets, and those that they believe are needed to bring about positive social change. Thus they sometimes hint at the differences they see between the kind of journalism practiced by those in the professional journalism industries and the kind of connective journalism that is practiced among peers through the circulation of artifacts that are displays of one's own political engagement. One student leader, for instance, who helped to coordinate one of the largest standardized test opt-outs in the country, replied respectfully when asked by an adult why she hadn't thought about taking her concerns first to the distinguished student media in her high school. She replied that she had served as the social media coordinator for her school's newspaper, and her friend was the editor of the paper, so the student media staff had frequently discussed their concerns about standardized testing among themselves and had run some editorials and stories on this issue. But she said that they ran into controversy when it came to what they could publish. They could cover the protests and opt-outs *after* they occurred, but the students were given a clear message by school administrators that the student media could not be seen as encouraging disruption in the school. "That would get us in trouble," she explained. And as this student leader pursued the path of working with others to organize the test opt-out, her own view of her role in relation to information dissemination began to change. She stepped back from her official role with student media to participate more freely in connective journalism practices. First, she utilized social media as she served as an organizer of activities, sharing the information that she felt compelled to downplay when working within the confines of student media. Later, she was able to utilize her abilities as a writer and researcher to explore what could be done and how others might be encouraged to participate. She set aside traditional journalistic approaches that focused on *making a news story*, embracing instead connective journalism approaches of making a *new* story for her community.

This focus on making the story, in turn, led her to become identified by her peers as a knowledgeable leader in the student test opt-out protest movement. Ultimately, as she pointed out, the opt-outs she and her peers orchestrated proved effective, as state legislators softened their language from promising consequences for schools where students refused to take the tests to agreeing not to penalize districts where large numbers of students opted out. She and other student leaders remained hopeful that student voices might be included in future decisions of the legislature and school boards, which they saw as a more promising alternative than either widespread news coverage or even the lowering of the legal voting age.[71] This student's story, like those of Mike and Alma, are of great interest as we think about the possible roles for journalists, journalism educators, and the journalism industries in relation to young people and the future of news. We therefore discuss this connective journalism practice of making the story more fully in Chapter 6.

CONCLUSION

Young people prefer to receive personalized messages to their posts and shares; they enjoy receiving a hearty response of likes and shares regarding content that they post. Yet, as we have argued in relation to the desire for I–Thou relationships of recognition and will argue in the chapters that follow, social media participation is about more than getting a boost for one's ego. Young people, like people of all ages, appreciate feeling that they are a part of something bigger. Sometimes, as recipients of stories that are shared or made by their peers, they are passively invited to feel a part of a larger collective. Yet, as we will argue, this feeling is an important aspect of developing a political will that can be mobilized through voting or public opinion. It is therefore worth exploring how and why young people send content and what happens when they are recipients of such content that is shared with them by their peers and family members. It's important to see these practices of connective journalism as intersubjective, then, as there is an implied communicative act in both the sending and the receiving of content shared via social media sites. This meaning can shift as recipients may be in a context, or may embrace a worldview, that differs from that of the sender. The point here is that young people are connected to one another and to others in a web of networks that have shaped and continue to inform their understandings of what it means to participate, or not, in a range of activities that we might think of as political, proto-political, or journalistic.

Connective journalism may bleed into connective action as young people begin to understand the counter-narratives that they have generated as a first, rather than as a final, step in the communicative process. This is what differentiates connective journalism from journalism as traditionally understood, for journalism focuses on the telling of the story as the final step in a communicative process, whereas at least some practices of connective journalism presume a pragmatic, solutions-oriented outcome to storytelling: now that we know this story, what should we do about it? In this way, connective journalism can move from the creation of the counter-narrative to engagement in action that is further supported by storytelling, and that can then be incorporated into collective or connective action. Connective journalism aims to recognize practices, actors, and contexts that may not be directly shaping young people's choices, and certainly aren't directly influencing legacy journalism, but may be contributing to the frameworks of participation and non-participation that are taken-for-granted in today's context, if only sporadically, and often unevenly, across youthful populations.

Incorporating the use of media into participation is not new, since community radio and community art projects have served as important precursors to today's practices of collaborative sharing and collective organizing,[72] as we will discuss more fully in Chapter 4. But social media extend the scope of these activities, enabling more people to participate, with greater possibilities for creativity, across a greater range of media outlets, and with different collaborators within one's social networks, in a manner not seen before.[73] The question for those interested in journalism is: in this quickly evolving social media environment, what are the appropriate roles for the professional journalist and for the legacy journalism industries? To begin to address this question for the future, we turn in the next chapter to how young people discussed their views on present-day journalism.

* * * * *

3

Hope and Disillusionment with Legacy News

"Journalism is dead," seventeen-year-old Yonas told a journalist who was interviewing him about social media.[1] He believed that with Twitter and other social media, he had access to many different sources of news, so he rarely looked to what scholars increasingly call the *legacy news*.[2] Legacy news is a term that refers to those news organizations that existed before the era of social media and that still exist in the form of websites, television and radio programs, and printed news. Yonas's statement reminds us that even as legacy news organizations have come to expect that their professional journalists will create recognizable identities in social media platforms, there is no guarantee that young people like Yonas will find them, choose to follow them, or even recognize a connection between the news that's retweeted on their feed and the news that originated from professional journalists or from legacy media outlets.

A number of other young people we interviewed expressed sentiments similar to Yonas about their approach to news. As José, aged seventeen, explained: "I don't really go out of my way to look for news stories. I just see whatever pops up. I have an app on my phone that has the top stories from different websites." Lissa, aged sixteen, agreed: "I don't watch the news too often…Twitter is almost like the news. I have it on my phone and if I'm holding my phone, it's like an instinct. I just go to it. If something's going on, everyone's talking about it on Twitter." Zuni, aged eighteen, said: "I'm not as apt to look up things or go out of my way because I know they are available on Facebook and places like that." Overwhelmingly, young people we interviewed expressed to us that if a story were important, it would find them. As Jenny, aged twenty, explained: "My friends are really tech savvy and they're always posting stuff on Facebook. I feel like I don't really need to read the news too much because they are always posting stuff I can see to keep me informed." Young people today feel that they can rely on those within their friendship circles to share news that is worth knowing, and they, in turn, give credence to the news that comes to them in this way, abandoning legacy news. Social media is now the main source of news, with one quarter of those in the United States saying they share news with others via social media at least once a week.[3] And research on youth and news finds that most people under forty consider newspapers to be impractical, inconvenient, environmentally unfriendly, and boring. Only one in twenty teens and one in twelve young adults read newspapers on anything close to a daily basis[4] and decreasing rates of news consumption among the young are echoed in studies done by the Pew Research Center in 2013 and 2015.[5]

In the last chapter, we introduced the concept of connective journalism – the practices through which people share information with an emotional punch that they think others should know about and that they share as a way of expressing their solidarity with others. Connective journalism draws attention to the changing contexts of youth interaction, illustrating how news (defined broadly) is circulated and discussed in online social networks. But it seems as if young people are rarely sharing news from legacy media with their peers. According to one study from the Pew Internet and American Life Project, only a third of those between the ages of eighteen and twenty-four said that they recalled seeing news on a social network site "yesterday."[6] In another survey, the Pew Center for People and the Press found that more than half of those surveyed could be considered news "grazers," those who checked in for news occasionally, but according to no particular pattern.[7] Young people may not know what news they are not seeing, and this is a fact worthy of concern. Why are they not more interested in sharing news from the legacy media with their peers? In this chapter, we explore this question in depth.

Political sociologist Nina Eliasoph's work is instructive as a starting point. In her 1998 study *Avoiding Politics*, she found that people in the United States often work hard to avoid speaking about politics – even in political and volunteer community organizations – because they want to avoid the confrontation that discussions of politics can provoke.[8] Today's social network sites function as "lifestyle networks," to use Lance Bennett's term, in which everything from fashion to politics may be discussed, and they've become places for interaction much as group associations were for older generations.[9] And like those of all ages, young people encounter difficulty in bringing politics into personal conversations, since such actions can bring about disagreements, feelings of discomfort, or even offense.[10] This may be one reason why many young people express reluctance about sharing politically oriented news with others on social network sites, as youth and journalism researcher Kjerstin Thorson has found in her research. Yet, as we will note in this chapter, we think that there may be additional reasons why young people do not share information from legacy news on social media sites.[11]

In her work exploring the uncertainties youth encounter regarding who might see their Facebook posts and how differing people might respond to them, Thorson discusses "one collection of motivated, passionate youth [who] experiment with ways to 'do politics' on everyday Facebook, and others [who] engage in protective strategies to avoid the possibility of offense or misinterpretation or an inaccurate presentation of self."[12] In the research conducted for this book, we also found distinct approaches to sharing news among the young people we interviewed and observed. Some of those we interviewed were similarly interested in "doing politics" online, and others were quite intent on avoiding political discussions to avoid misinterpretations or conflict. But when asked why they avoided talking about politics or news online, many of the youth also mentioned four problems that they attributed directly to the news industries themselves: first, problems they associated with journalistic authority and the voice of objectivity used to convey that authority; second, problems they associated with the imagined audience of the news, which they often saw as distinct from them and from the social groups with which they identified; third, problems with the business models of journalism as they structured and limited the US news marketplace; and fourth, problems with the storytelling genres common to legacy media's journalism. We believe that these four critiques are important in understanding the role journalism is coming to play in relation to politics as experienced among diverse youth today, and what this can tell us about the future of news. In this chapter, we review the ways that young people spoke of these four problems they associated with the contemporary news industries, and the ways these concerns are echoed in various places throughout our society. First, however, we have to consider the question: Why is it a problem if youth don't follow news? After all, as we noted in the previous chapter, young people have differing interests than older people do, and indeed, the problem of a "tuned out" youth population certainly isn't a new lament. We turn first to this question because it's an important one in relation to our vision of how information relates to democracy in Western cultures.

THE ORIGINS OF JOURNALISM AS A PUBLIC GOOD

It's a commonplace belief among news professionals and the general public that a free press and "accountability journalism" (investigative journalism that exposes corruption and keeps the powerful "accountable" to the public) are crucial elements of a successful democracy. Along with such "goods" as public schools, transportation infrastructure, clean air, and potable drinking water, independent reporting aimed at creating an informed citizenry is considered an indispensable public good in the United States. This idea goes back to Thomas Jefferson's famous and often-quoted statement:

> The basis of our governments being the opinion of the people, the very first object should be to keep that right; and were it left to me to decide whether we should have a government without newspapers or newspapers without a government, I should not hesitate a moment to prefer the latter. But I should mean that every man should receive those papers and be capable of reading them.[13]

Jefferson's belief in the importance of having information in order to participate collectively in decision making and to hold powerful decision makers in check has become an important part of US national identity. It's enshrined in the First Amendment to the US Constitution's freedom of the press, and with the increasing professionalization of the US news media in the twentieth century, the concept of the public good became an integral code of journalists.

Newspapers, of course, were not exclusively devoted to such high-minded ideals as the public good. They first began to publish broad coverage of business, political, and social news in the early 1830s, as a result of the drastically reduced costs and greatly expanded readership that came with the advent of the "penny press."[14] Prior to this, "newspapers" (which from colonial times until 1833 were usually newsletters directed at specific groups of paid subscribers) were mere voice pieces for the partisan trade associations and political parties that published them. The expansion of the news readership to a broader populace brought forth the concept of "reporters" who would go out into the world and "report" on events for the benefit of the general public.

The new ideals of journalism that emerged in the early twentieth century were, in a sense, a secularization of earlier religious notions of the public good. These earlier beliefs had emphasized the importance of subordinating individual self-interests in order to achieve the greater social good of a moral community.[15] Community members were obligated to address social injustices in order to achieve a harmonious and robust society and to hold government responsible for fair leadership. Newspapers thus took on a moral responsibility; they were to become the means by which, in the words of the Continental Congress of 1774, "oppressive officers are shamed or intimidated into more honourable and just modes of conducting affairs."[16] For newspapers that needed to operate in a commercial environment, such shaming and intimidating of leadership held the dual benefit of informing the public and providing entertainment for those who appreciated the moral comeuppance of individuals who wielded their power irresponsibly. Newspapers could, therefore, both fulfill a public good mandate and generate profits through sales of their product.

From the early twentieth century onward, journalists increasingly saw themselves as "watch dogs," exposing harm done to the public at the hands of monopolistic business corporations, corrupt political parties, and other forms of institutionalized power. "Muckraking" journalists Ida Tarbell (1857–1944), who exposed the unfair trust practices of the Standard Oil Company, Upton Sinclair (1878–1968), who exposed exploitative labor practices and dangerously unhygienic conditions of the US meatpacking industry, and many others, helped establish in the public imagination the crucial role of investigative journalists in holding government and business leaders accountable to society's moral expectations of integrity and justice.

By the late 1940s, the US Commission on Freedom of the Press articulated what came to be known as the "social responsibility" theory of the press.[17] Concerned with the increasing concentration of media ownership (even back then), the commission worried that the "marketplace of ideas" was in danger of having certain political viewpoints unpopular with media owners excluded from the public sphere. Thus, the commission called upon journalists to resist such pressures in favor of objective reporting, advising, "We suggest that the press look upon itself as performing a public service of a professional kind."[18]

Since the mid-twentieth century, the ethic of public service in US journalism has been a revered professional standard, whereby journalists are supposed to serve the public as a whole, rather than advance particular interests. The ideology of public service is a keystone of journalistic train-ing, along with the ideal of "objectivity" – the responsibility to report events from a non-sectarian perspective. Yet, with the present transfor-mations taking place in the world of journalism, this public service ideal has been challenged from a number of sides, for reasons related to both changing economics and technologies of the news media and to larger changes occurring in US culture and politics.[19] New forms of media have made it more difficult to maintain clear boundaries around what "counts" as news, as the "people formerly known as the audience" now become the ones who break news about political events and natural dis-asters on Twitter or other platforms.[20] This leaves professional journalists playing catch-up, as Dan Gillmor, Leonard Downie, Michael Schudson, and a host of others have pointed out.[21] A focus on shareholder profits has encouraged news outlets to remove the metaphorical "separation of church and state" between advertising and editorial, eroding the long-standing norm of keeping news content independent of business consid-erations. This increasingly flexible boundary between news and business has resulted in a major focus on entertainment, the slashing of current events coverage (and reporter positions), and the echoing of the exact same stories across media outlets rather than the exercise of journalistic creativity in watching over government and corporate leadership. All of this has had a dire result, as renowned journalists Downie and Kaiser have argued: journalism has turned its back on its public role.[22]

This move within legacy news outlets to embrace what is most likely to garner audience attention has left a large gap. And, as some have argued, it has also spurred opportunities for those interested in on-the-ground political actions to seek out new methods of communicating, through practices that utilize emergent social network platforms, in what Adrienne Russell calls networked journalism.[23] The rise in these "new journalisms" has denaturalized the authority of daily news, both in rela-tion to specific legacy news outlets and collectively for news organiza-tions as a whole.[24]

JOURNALISM, THE PUBLIC GOOD, AND THE PROBLEM OF AUTHORITY

Does journalism still serve the public good? This question is at the heart of the current crisis in journalism, because it questions journalistic authority, or the right of professional journalists to be understood *as* journalists who are doing what they consider to be their job. Journalism, as Lance Bennett and colleagues note, is guided by a "logic that determines who ought to be given public voice to say what kinds of things."[25] And yet, questions of who bestows authority and to whom it should be ascribed have been undergoing change since the beginnings of modernity, as sociologist Adam Seligman has pointed out.[26] Even those who affirm the importance of traditional sources of authority believe that *individuals* have the capacity to decide for themselves whether or not a particular organization or individual warrants authority. And this belief in the individual's power of reason is central to what Seligman calls "modernity's wager": the gamble or notion that a society based on reason is the only way in which people in a religiously and culturally plural society can live together peacefully. Individuals now look to themselves – rather than to God, nature, or church – as sources of moral authority, and this morally conscious self has become the foundation for the civic order.

Many of the young people we interviewed saw themselves as capable of making judgments regarding who they would deem to be authoritative on the current events of our day. They were unimpressed with the credentials of professional journalists and offered some biting critiques. Their concept of the morally conscious self came through in many of their comments about what they believed were the moral failings of journalists that, in turn, undermined journalistic authority. Some young people, for instance, suggested that news outlets presented the perspectives of the wealthy, shielding rather than exposing their wrongdoings. Sixteen-year-old George felt that journalists "were asleep at the wheel" before the 2008–2010 financial crisis, failing to expose immoral banking practices that harmed the American public. He spoke sarcastically about the concept of objectivity, implying that reporters used it to appear unbiased while glossing over wrongdoings: "In a news story, you can't say certain things. Like you can't point fingers and say, 'Well, *he* screwed up the economy by overpaying everybody and making stocks crash.' You have to be more 'objective' [sarcastic tone] about it, you have to say [mocking official voice], 'This company crashed because of the 'financial crisis.'" Journalists, in his opinion, hadn't "pointed fingers" and interrogated the people and policies responsible for the economic meltdown. He felt that moral judgment was lacking in journalistic reports. George preferred to turn to YouTube, Facebook, and other "non-news" sites for his information, as he felt he would be more likely to find truthful, unmediated reports, and exposés there that he could evaluate for himself. Yonas, aged seventeen, who had moved to the United States from Ethiopia with his family when he was a young boy, felt that the traditional journalist too often got between the viewer and the actual story. Like George, he believed that it was far better if a viewer could simply have access to a lot of raw footage on YouTube and disparate information from Twitter so that he or she could determine the truth for himself or herself. He felt this lack of trust in professional journalists explained why so many young people didn't even consider seeking out news as it was reported directly on official news websites and they often didn't follow reporters associated with the legacy news. Like Yonas and George, many youth we spoke with felt they got "truer" information directly from blogs and other social media sites. As Anthony, aged sixteen, explained: "A lot of bloggers capture things that regular media outlets don't," and thus he relied upon his own judgment to sort things out.

While we take these critiques seriously, we also believe that such a position underestimates the role that professional journalism continues to play in organizing and interpreting major events, not least because professional journalists continue to have access to institutions of power and [at least in theory] financial resources to devote to fact checking and independent research. But, it's clear that the Walter Cronkite days of an authoritative journalist who can speak with moral authority for and to a presumed united public are long gone. Struggles over journalistic authority are, therefore, indicative of the broader question of *who* gets to define what news is, and what news is *for*, particularly in relation to the existing multiplicity of publics in current US society.

JOURNALISM AND THE PROBLEM OF COMMUNITY

If modernity has inaugurated the morally conscious self as the foundation of the civic order, then it's important to reckon with the fact that the civic order itself is far from united and this, too, contributes to the problems of journalism and journalistic authority. In the context of increasingly fragmented audiences for news, as journalism scholar Chris Anderson argues, "previously simple notions of community, readership, and public suddenly become problematic."[27] Anderson points out that journalists tend to think of themselves as serving a geographically bounded community through their ability to uncover stories and create reports that would not otherwise be available to that community. Producing "original reporting...for the unitary public" describes journalists' self-understandings of their unique role in society, he argues.[28] The fallacy of a unified public was one of the most significant lessons of the 2016 presidential election, as the media establishment and political pundits who predicted victory for Hillary Clinton were spectacularly out of touch with large swaths of the US population. As veteran political journalist Alec MacGillis, who writes for ProPublica, noted: "The media are so, so far removed from their country...The media are all in Washington, D.C., and New York now, thanks to the decline of local and metro papers. And the gaps between how those cities and the rest of the country are doing have gotten so much larger in recent years."[29]

Journalists' self-understanding of creating original reporting for a unified public is even harder to maintain in the face of an ever-deepening pool of easily accessed online information that transcends geographic boundaries. And journalists themselves struggle with questions about whether or not incorporating information from the blogs, wikis, and other online sources that inform geographically diverse publics undermines their own ability to produce "original" reporting.[30] Added to this is the problem of inequities in ownership, as few media outlets are owned and operated by nonwhites and relatively few news organizations are dedicated specifically to the concerns of minoritized and working class communities, a subject we will discuss more thoroughly in the next section on the business aspects of the US journalism industry.

Many of the young people we interviewed do not experience themselves as part of the "unitary" public that they believe professional journalists are interested in addressing. In fact, sometimes they do not feel that their communities are addressed by legacy news media at all. Ana, aged sixteen, who noted that she found information on Facebook to be more up-to-date and informative than TV news or newspapers, relayed this story:

Yesterday there was a shooting on Falcon Street, a seven-minute drive from here. I saw it on Facebook. I got a notification. There was all kinds of comments. Some people had apps of police scanners, so you could hear stuff straight from the police. Then, before bed last night, I checked the TV news and there was NOTHING! So, I went back on Facebook and there were more updates about it.

Young people like Ana articulated a sense of feeling left out that we believe is particularly relevant when we consider the ways in which youth from minoritized communities think about news. In a society marked by stark racial and economic inequalities, young people's personal experiences become part of their understanding of themselves as citizens, influencing their level of faith in democratic institutions and processes.[31]

Many of the youth we interviewed felt that news focused on the frivolous and outrageous over stories that were "useful" or "relevant" to them. They felt that many reporters did not do a good job in protecting the public, a critique of the demise of the watchdog model also shared by adults. And, they observed that most mainstream news did a poor job of explaining complex issues or providing a variety of perspectives. As Eduardo, aged fourteen, noted, "You're supposed to explain every single side of a story, whether good or bad, so people can get the correct information and not be lured into risking their lives, or anything like that." Some young people suggested that journalists should be much more assertive in tracking the claims of politicians and corporations and take a clearer role advocating for the interests of "everyday people." As Trevor, aged seventeen, noted: "Journalists need to inform...the public about products' false claims. Like, if a company is lying to you about something in a product, like lead in toys and stuff like that." And as Mark, aged seventeen, emphasized, "The job of the journalist is to not only keep the people informed, but to be always checking up on the corporations and politicians."

Many teens agreed that journalism could serve an important role in relation to what they and members of their communities believed was the public good, but they felt that journalists often failed to meet this ideal. "A reporter's responsibility is to give the facts, although it doesn't happen nowadays...They should be reporting on issues that affect normal everyday Americans," said Óscar, aged sixteen, echoing the concerns with everyday people noted earlier. From the vantage point of these youth, the news media does not cover issues that their families deal with on a daily basis or, at least, does not cover them in ways that seemed useful. "Useful," for them, was coverage that explained issues in ways that everyday people could comprehend, so that they could appreciate how policies and events ultimately affected their lives. It also meant news that helped protect the public from danger. Discussing the types of issues he believed needed to receive more "understandable" news coverage, a ninth grader launched into a surprisingly detailed account of the unethical lending practices of mortgage companies:

Right now, the country is in a really bad situation. My family is actually in huge debt right now. My mom, she's gotten into a house that she was basically tricked into getting, because I mean she wanted to get a house for me and my brother so we could have a stable place to live. And right now the mortgage rate is extremely high and every single month my Mom is struggling to get the money to be able to pay and she's actually not even paying anything to the principal, she's only paying interest, which really gets me bummed out because she's paying so much but she's not actually paying anything. So the house basically isn't even ours. Many people are in that situation right now. (Eduardo, fourteen years)

Eduardo's statement implies that journalists had a role to play not only in reporting about the financial crisis that many families were experiencing at the time of this interview, but could also provide information that would be useful to family members as they attempted to deal with this crisis in their daily lives. This approach may raise questions for some regarding the extent to which news should be considered a provider of practical information. Yet if such information is not provided through neutral parties such as journalists, it is likely to come from sources with a vested interest in selling something, such as a new mortgage, a new financial plan, or escape from debt in the form of resale that might make money for a realtor. Precisely *because* they came from communities that were most in need of the sort of serious investigative journalism that keeps the powerful and predatory in check, these youth felt alienated from news media that failed to live up to their expectations.

We found that youth disillusionment in news media often coexisted with passionate opinions about political issues that interested them. For example, many young people stated that they enthusiastically followed the presidential campaigns of Barack Obama, in what they felt was an especially exciting election because of the candidate's relative youth, race, and idealism. Students from immigrant families followed ongoing debates on immigration reform and related news about factory raids, immigration laws, or immigrant bashing. Students with family members in military service overseas followed coverage of the wars in the Middle East, and so on. This complicates previous assumptions that young people don't follow news because they are apathetic about politics.[32] We found that when youth had opportunities to tell their own stories (whether via youth journalism initiatives or via posting opinions on social media sites), it helped counter a sense of nihilism, allowing them to feel part of a larger community for whom civic participation holds the possibility of bringing positive change.

When asked about what he thought of news, Anise, a sixteen-year-old who'd moved with his family to the United States from Somalia four years earlier, said that he didn't care for US news because "they edit it from their perspective." Anise observed that the genre itself made manifest the distance between himself and the representations he saw on news, and his ability to impact those representations. As he noted: "If news has a story, you know that story is not completely correct, or they aren't saying the whole truth, you can't just [go] to them and say 'oh you gotta change that,' 'cuz it takes more than one person to do that." Echoing Anise's sense that US news left out the viewpoints of the communities of which he felt a part, seventeen-year-old Karim, who moved with his family to the United States from Guinea just a few years prior to our interviews and was an English language learner, observed a tendency to rely upon a certain set of experts and to focus on the concerns of a certain public that is not inclusive of everyone. "I don't see people who look like me on news," he said, then switching to a narrative voice in which he positioned himself as one of many people of African descent who are seen in news under limited circumstances: "If we see ourselves in the news more – and I don't just mean sports coverage – then you know what? I'm gonna watch the news more because it's about me." Another African American male lamented that the only time he saw African Americans in the news was in crime stories: "I think it's kind of annoying that the major stories in the news are about people who get shot, usually people who have colored skin," said seventeen-year-old Tree. Karim and Tree's comments point to the ways in which journalistic expertise, as well as the selection criteria for "newsworthy" topics, both work together to construct boundaries of inclusion and exclusion. Karim felt that US professional news organizations didn't try hard enough to draw connections between diverse communities and the information they might need to know. He offered a specific suggestion in this regard, highlighting the need for journalists to spend more time in the communities they are supposed to represent:

In order to make people interested [in news], you or your organization has to go down and make them interested. You have to explain what you're about. Go down there.

The suggestion that journalism could more fully address the needs of underserved communities will be considered in this book's upcoming chapters, as we discuss the possibilities for greater service to the community that might be embraced as journalists think about not only how to provide stories, but how to engage communities in processes of identifying, producing, and sharing news in new ways. One of the greatest hurdles to such an endeavor, of course, is cost. And, as several young people noted wryly when they considered the shortcomings they associated with legacy news, journalism is a business.

JOURNALISM AS A BUSINESS

The past few years have been especially bleak for the news industry, with hundreds of daily and weekly newspapers folding each year. Venerable news institutions – such as Colorado's oldest newspaper, the *Rocky Mountain News*, which had published for 150 years, and Arizona's oldest newspaper, *The Tucson Citizen*, which had published for 140 years – have recently closed their doors forever. Other esteemed papers, like *The Christian Science Monitor,* now publish just once a week. In some cities, such as Detroit, daily papers have stopped home delivery while many other cities across the United States, such as New Orleans, Birmingham, Mobile, Syracuse, Harrisburg, and others, are left with no daily paper at all.[33] Nationally acclaimed papers like *The Chicago Tribune, The L.A. Times, The Boston Globe,* and even the country's most famous "newspaper of record," *The New York Times,* are now shadows of their former selves in terms of size and breadth of news coverage.

The print newspapers left standing have slashed the size of their newsrooms to cut costs, going from a high of 56,900 newsroom jobs in 1990 to just 32,900 in 2014.[34] US newsrooms have shrunk by about 30 percent since 2000, and many top news executives predict that this shrinking will only intensify.[35] Many US dailies have scaled down to web-only publications to save money, and this is a pragmatic move, since 85 percent of a newspaper's costs go to things like presses, paper, ink, trucks, and gas.[36] But, when newspapers go online to save money, they also cut staff – in some cases, quite severely. And, when print newspapers become exclusively online publications, the difference in staffing is generally a 1:20 ratio, or one online journalist for every 20 print journalists who used to work at a given paper.[37] For example, the award-winning *Seattle Post-Intelligencer,* a 146-year-old daily paper with a former editorial staff of 165, is now published online-only, with a web staff of just 21.[38]

The rise of online news has ushered in changes in journalistic work, as the business of online news publishing tends to be one of updating, monitoring, and repacking information, rather than of producing original news.[39] But given the fact that most online news sources repeat or discuss stories done by print journalists, this drop in newspaper staffs is significant in terms of the lower volume and depth of coverage that is possible.[40] The problem is further compounded when we realize that, historically, US television and radio news, as well as the vast majority of news found online, has depended on print newspapers for their content.

As print media reporting staffs are being decimated, then, the quality of *all* news is also diminishing.

What caused the crisis in today's news industry? Although declining readership is a part of the problem, it is advertising rather than subscriptions that has long supported the news industries. Experts ascribe the slide in newspaper profits to three things: (1) the emergence of Craigslist and Monster.com among other sites, which obliterated the need for classified ads, formerly the lifeblood of newspaper revenue; (2) the rise in online rather than print reading, which, combined with the rise in social media advertising, led to diminished demand for retail advertising space in daily newspapers; and (3) the decline in newspaper subscriptions, as people can now access news for free via a host of online platforms. This subscription decline makes newspapers less attractive overall for the investment of advertising dollars, which are then spent elsewhere to reach the would-be news audience.

The dependency on advertising dollars has long been a central issue in journalism's struggle to serve the public good. The media industries first became attractive to investors in the late nineteenth century, and newspapers soon came under the domination of what were then newly formed publishing companies. The establishment of national networks for radio and later television followed a similar path toward consolidation. Throughout the twentieth century, the managers of news companies saw themselves as competing against other news providers, and therefore during the second half of the century, news organizations either merged or sought to eliminate their competition in order to increase market share and profits. By the end of the twentieth century, the majority of news outlets in the United States were subsidiaries of multinational conglomerates. Dominant companies in the news industry in 2016 included Disney-ABC-ESPN, NBC Universal-Comcast-Telemundo, CBS Corporation-Simon & Schuster, Time Warner-CNN, and Rupert Murdoch's News Corp-Fox, although Viacom, Clear Channel, Gannett, Tribune, and the *Washington Post* continue to have significant holdings, and Google and Facebook have become major players in this realm, as well.[41]

The concentration of media ownership has long been a problem for those who favor a news landscape that includes diverse perspectives. As of 2016, women comprised 51 percent of the population, yet held fewer than 7 percent of television and radio station licenses. Blacks, Latinos, Native Americans, Asian Americans, and multiracial Americans comprised 36 percent of the US population, but people of color held just over 7 percent of radio licenses and 3 percent of television licenses.[42] This discrepancy in ownership has led Juan Gonzalez and Joseph Torres to refer to the problem as a "de facto apartheid media system."[43] As they argue: "Given that people of color are expected to comprise a majority of the [U.S.] population by 2050, control of virtually all the principal news production and dissemination by a white minority would be inherently undemocratic."[44] In their work tracing the evolution of race and media over two centuries, they found that a centralized system of news ownership correlated with setbacks for journalists of color. Although, at one time, people held out hope that the Internet might create a more equitable system for news creation and dissemination, today's patterns of concentrated ownership are unlikely to be disrupted unless we see significant changes in media regulations. Perhaps it's not surprising, then, that as the United States moves toward its future as a majority minority population, dissatisfaction with news will continue to increase among its growing numbers of people of color.

In their discussions about why they felt disillusioned by legacy news, many of the minoritized youth we interviewed mentioned the fact that journalism's business interests were a key problem. Several felt that journalists no longer were engaged first and foremost in serving the community, but rather, that they were serving the corporations that paid their salaries. They also observed that sensational and negative stories abounded because, as several students asserted, "that's what sells." In its efforts to appeal to the most profitable audiences, news relies upon rather than challenges stereotypes. And young people noticed that the positive aspects of the people and places in their communities were rarely shown in mainstream newspapers and television news. Instead, negative portrayals abounded: "Every time the news talks about [name of speaker's neighborhood], it's about houses burning down and cars getting stole and kids killing each other. It's not about anything positive," said Kia, aged fifteen. Michael, aged eighteen, stated: "The news doesn't cover these kind of places except to focus on bad things." While teens across racial and social class categories expressed disdain for "stupid" and "violent" commercial news, which they felt predominated television airwaves, minoritized youth were also painfully aware that people from other areas of their cities did not think highly of their neighborhoods and blamed the mainstream media, in part, for these negative perceptions.

News relies increasingly upon drama and conflict in order to compete in the crowded media marketplace, resulting in approaches that further turn off some young people. Eighteen-year-old Jay, the son of Turkish immigrants who regularly watched and read Turkish news, expressed disdain toward US news: "I try to watch the news on TV and I just can't take it. It's just people screaming at each other. It doesn't go anywhere." Conflict-driven and tragedy-oriented news was also identified as "depressing," such as the following quotes from Jackie (fifteen-year-old Cambodian): "I don't really like to watch the news. It's kind of depressing" and Marvin (seventeen-year-old Latino): "I stopped watching the news because ... every day I hear somebody died, some explosion, somebody else kidnapped. I couldn't really deal with that. I didn't want to be depressed." Tara (fifteen-year-old African American) felt similarly: "Everyday you read the paper, turn on the news, and it's always about a young person dying." Stefani, aged seventeen, similarly disliked the sensational content of the news, but admitted that she, like other members of the legacy news audience, often got swept up in the morbid details: "I think, for a lot of people, tragedy and crazy stuff is interesting. And then I'm thinking, 'Wow, I'm actually enjoying something bad happening!' It makes me feel like a bad person, but why do they glorify stuff like that on the news?!" Many of the youth we interviewed felt that grabbing the audience's attention by bombarding them with sensational, negative, and/or trivial stories failed to serve the news needs of everyday people. This model may earn profits for news companies, but it alienates many.

JOURNALISM AND THE PROBLEM OF THE JOURNALISTIC STORYTELLING GENRE

The young people we interviewed noticed that people like them and the communities of which they were a part were often not included in the stories told by the legacy news media, but there was also another way in which this problem found expression: the youth didn't have an appreciation for the style of storytelling found within legacy news media. In their desire to gain a more truthful and balanced understanding of current events, they preferred alternate forms of journalistic storytelling. In contrast to dry and disinterested observations of the political world found in mainstream news, the passionate, humorous, and acerbic current events commentary they found on social media "put things in context," gave "different opinions," and was "not afraid to tell it like it is." Seventeen-year-old Yonas lamented that journalistic storytelling took the life out of unfolding events and rendered them meaningless and separated from actionable community goals. Dennis, aged sixteen, noted the repetitive and uninspiring nature of official news: "ABC, CBS, NBC, FOX, they all have the same exact stories, even the same exact *order*. It isn't interesting or original. Everyone copies each other." Sopheap, aged fifteen, resented how the same images were repeated endlessly for drama: "My mom and dad watch the news...They just look at pictures of fires and be like, 'Oh, my God, there's another house burning up!' It could be a house burning up from three days ago, but they keep showing it and showing it." The feeling that news portrays negative events without helping make sense of issues gives young people a feeling of boredom mixed with inertia: "When we see the news, it doesn't pertain to us...It's just so boring!" (Manuel, sixteen years old).

And boredom is not the only lament; the frenetic pace of urgency that has become a part of the news landscape also comes in for criticism, and not just from youth. In 2013, for instance, Swiss novelist Rolf Dobelli asserted in *The Art of Thinking Clearly* that those who abstain from consuming what he terms "bite-sized news" see a rise in their personal creativity, insight, and level of concentration. In *The Guardian*, he shared his ten-point critique of news' negative effect on our collective health that reads like a stinging diatribe against professional journalism's claims of providing information in ways that enhance the public good: "Out of the 10,000 news stories you have read in the last 12 months, name one that – because you consumed it – allowed you to make a better decision about a serious matter affecting your life," he challenged.[45] It's not that we should be ignorant of current events, he argues. It's that the massive consumption of news across various media platforms, and the way that the news product has shrunk to fit into the lives of its distracted readers and viewers, encourages us to flit between bite-sized bits of stories. This undermines our ability to draw meaningful connections that would help us to better understand our world and the choices we face, a critique that echoes Yonas's concern that news does not provide a connection between storytelling and actionable goals. Dobelli's book became a bestseller first in Germany and Switzerland, and once translated from German to English it hit the best seller lists in the UK, South Korea, India, Ireland, Hong Kong, and Singapore.[46] Not surprisingly, while the argument against the hectic form of bite-sized news received praise from some people, journalists were eager to inveigh against Dobelli.[47] What is interesting, and echoes the youthful critiques we heard of the journalism genre, however, is that Dobelli isn't opposed to all forms of news information, but just the kind that happens to be most central to journalists' self-understanding of their role in creating interesting original reporting in a context of immediacy. "Society needs reporting – but in a different way," Dobelli writes. "Investigative journalism is always relevant. We need reporting that polices our institutions and uncovers truth. But important findings don't have to arrive in the form of news," he writes, speaking of the tendency for reporting to focus on immediacy and to arrive in the form of brevity. "Long journal articles and in-depth books are good, too," he argues.[48] Of course, Dobelli's words fly in the face of the current news consumption patterns that we noted at the beginning of this chapter, as young people seem inclined to wait for news to find them in its short-burst form rather than seeking it out in the longer formats that Dobelli advocates. And yet, there is some evidence of an interest in something that differs from the frenetic in the preferences that high school aged Yonas and his peers mentioned earlier. This is hinted at in the youthful mention of interest in blogs that provide greater information and insights than typically offered in the mainstream news; Twitter feeds that offer differing perspectives; books, documentaries, and audio commentaries that provide in-depth storytelling; and unedited raw footage on YouTube. All of these offer longer form opportunities for people to decide for themselves what is worth knowing for the kind of decision-making that they believe affects the public good.

All of us are familiar with the standardized genre of journalistic story-telling that we see today most frequently in televised and print news. The genre itself, which asks journalists to marshal visual or expert evidence that fleshes out the details of a story, is what often signals to us that we are to interpret the story as a balanced report of information rather than as a propagandistic attempt to appeal to our emotions. Michael Schudson explains today's journalistic genre in relation to the emergence of a particular narrative form that developed over more than 200 years, as reporters came to be seen not only as people who relayed events as they happened but also as interpreters who explored the political aims of the actors involved.[49] Mark Peterson, an anthropologist studying journalism, observed that, "As a practice, journalism involves recovering (or uncovering) referential meaning through an assemblage of 'facts' about an event that can be organized into a story."[50] Thus, we find that the very *style* of journalistic storytelling, like the sense of originality and the idea of the unified public, is closely tied to the self-conceptions of the professional journalists who assemble the stories. Robert Darnton further explained the ways in which news became conventionalized through a reliance on standardized images and clichés, which, in turn, made it possible for both professionals and consumers to recognize the final form as "news."[51] But the standardization that makes a story recognizable as "news" also renders certain images and narratives as more newsworthy than others, leading news stories to have the sameness in construction and in ordering that, as Sopheap noted, can engender repetition, boredom, and inertia, among those who do not appreciate the storytelling style.

Although the term "journalism" has long encompassed many different forms including opinion writing, feature writing, and human interest storytelling, most associate the concept with "hard news," or coverage that addresses political issues and events. The news genre is also understood in relation to what it is *not*, namely, advertising, public relations, or strategic communication. Currently, the journalistic non-profit venture ProPublica argues for a place for both "investigative journalism" and "explanatory journalism" in the pantheon of the genre.[52] The public's gravitation toward a panoply of storytelling "news" genres today underscores ProPublica's call for the respectful acceptance of these different forms, and for an even wider consideration of what might be included in the journalistic storytelling genre.

Young people's critiques of the news genre trigger some new questions – and some discomfort – regarding ways to widen the frame of what might be considered journalistic storytelling. For example, once, when Lynn and one of her graduate students were leading a high school class discussion on immigrant communities, they showed a news segment from the BBC on immigration that featured challenges of language and finances in the story of a recent migrant. The students present at the session, many of whom had come to the United States within the previous five years, had frequently discussed concerns about the very issues that were highlighted in the news segment. But, shortly after the segment had begun, the instructors noticed that the audience was becoming restless. Finally, one sixteen-year-old from Ethiopia blurted out, "Where is the music track? That would make it more persuasive." Lynn noted that "usually news doesn't have a music track" – but as quickly as the words were out of her mouth, several members of the class noted that the viral video KONY 2012 had a music track and had been much more effective in telling its story than the news segment they were being asked to watch, which seemed dull by comparison.

This interaction led to several subsequent discussions about whether or not the KONY 2012 video, which in the year it came out was named the most viral video ever, and which more than half of all US young adults had heard of within one week of its release, was, in fact, a form of "news."[53] Whereas some students readily agreed, others were more circumspect. Yonas, who was introduced at the beginning of this chapter, recognized the KONY 2012 video as a model for how information could be provided to people in a meaningful way, noting: "The KONY 2012 video [had] a pure, defined story...It's like, 'Who is this Joseph Kony guy?' " Yonas described the KONY 2012 video as being not so much like a story one would see on the evening news, but rather, "Like a movie, with a plot, and an ending." Yet, while he said that he preferred a narrative style of film to the standardized style of journalistic storytelling discussed earlier, he nevertheless expressed concern about the model of information campaigning that he felt KONY 2012 had unleashed into the social media news landscape. Having moved from Ethiopia to the United States with his parents in his childhood, he dreamt of starting a binational US/Ethiopian business, and this led him to pay close attention to the politics and economic issues affecting East Africa. Many of his friends also had ties to Africa, and like them, he too believed that Uganda's war lord Joseph Kony and his leaders were devastatingly corrupt. But, unlike his friends, Yonas found the KONY 2012 video problematic in its impassioned plea for the removal from power of the Ugandan warlord Joseph Kony. He recognized that the team that put the video together had successfully tapped into people's emotions, simplified complex historical problems, and produced a format that could be easily passed along, but he saw this as part of its manipulative potential. He found it frustrating that the video got many facts wrong and ignored the many organizations that had been working on the ground to stop Kony without an escalation of military presence in the area. He felt that what was needed was a regional political solution, not a US military attack that Kony's supporters could use to garner greater support in opposition to Kony's enemies. Given that the video did not come from professional journalists, Yonas also pointed out that too much rested on the individual behind the KONY 2012 efforts, so that when the life of the film's director, Jason Russell, seemingly unraveled very publicly after a video was posted on YouTube of him naked and engaged in lewd sexual conduct on a public street, it became easy for people to question the entire enterprise and subsequently dismiss concerns about the situation in Uganda. Yonas's objections echoed those voiced by numerous commentators in the weeks following the release and the subsequent virality of the KONY 2012 video.[54] Few of his high school aged colleagues voiced such a nuanced understanding of the situation in Africa or of the persuasive nature of the video. Over time, however, several other students eventually came to recognize that this fast-paced, hip form of storytelling, too, was not without its problems.

Interestingly, journalists who had long reported on Ugandan issues noted with some reluctance that the KONY 2012 video accomplished something within a journalistic function that they themselves had not been able to achieve (widespread awareness, concern, and an individual and institutional urgency toward taking action), even if it did so while violating several norms within the storytelling news genre. As the international commentator Lindsey Hilsum observed of the video:

> It may not be accurate. It may use out-of-date statistics. But it's struck a chord we never managed to strike…I think we could learn something from them about how to get a message across, and how to talk to a generation that has stopped bothering to read the newspaper and watch TV news.[55]

Based on his concerns about misinformation, Yonas noted that he hoped that KONY 2012 wasn't a sign of the journalism to come. However, he also agreed with Hilsum's professional analysis, observing that the video had accomplished something significant in relation to journalism's historic mandate to inform about wrongdoing.

WHAT NEWS IS AND WHAT NEWS IS FOR

Struggles over what "counts" as journalism are sometimes centered around discussions of whether or not a set of stories originates among professionals in legacy news media or among everyday citizens, although as Peter Dahlgren has noted, several variants of journalism have emerged that blend these distinctions.[56] Our use of the term *connective journalism* is not meant to suggest a new style of storytelling but, rather, the way in which facts, opinions, gossip, memes, visualizations, sentiment, narratives, commentaries, and urban legends may be called upon in differing settings as people pass along what they deem worth sharing with others in their communities. Rather than utilizing ideas of objectivity and immediacy when covering complex topics or when evaluating whether or not something "counts" as journalism, perhaps a better measure is suggested in Christopher Campbell and colleagues' book *Race and News: Critical Perspectives*. They argue for "clarity, value, and cultural significance" as a means of understanding the benefits that news, in whatever form, might bring to a community.[57] We propose that the "journalism" shared within connective journalism is therefore not confined to a certain genre or to endeavors that originate with professional journalists, and can be a space where lines are blurred between journalism and other forms of storytelling that may take on a journalistic function, but must meet these criteria of clarity, value, and cultural significance. And connective journalism may also include storytelling that is *actionable*. Such storytelling not only provides an explanation, but it also provides an interpretive context that explains how a story expresses the concerns of a community and what might be done to address them.

This embrace of advocacy and action is where many within legacy journalism part company with our concept of connective journalism. There is a deep discomfort with advocacy among journalists, even as professional journalists have viewed themselves as serving the public good of the community and providing the tools needed to advocate on behalf of citizens. Today, some advocacy is a necessary corrective to the highly commercialized environment that has rendered certain members of the public largely invisible, mostly because they are less profitable to reach as audience members and are underrepresented among the ranks of professional journalists. This has led to a further divide between those who are professional journalists uncomfortable with advocacy and those who align with advocates for historically underrepresented communities.

During the time when we were writing this book, for instance, a prominent group of scholars interested in media and politics began a large collaborative process of assembling articles for a 2016 publication called *Civic Media: Technology, Design, Practice*. From its earliest design, this volume had no plans to devote a chapter to journalism. The MIT Center for Civic Media involved in producing this volume performs interesting discursive work in the way that it distances itself from the journalism of the legacy media or even of citizen journalism. On their website, they write:

> We use the term civic media, rather than citizen journalism: civic media is any form of communication that strengthens the social bonds within a community or creates a strong sense of civic engagement among its residents. Civic media goes beyond news gathering and reporting…As with investigative journalism, the most delicate and important information can often focus on leaders and institutions that abuse the trust of the communities they serve. By helping to provide people with the necessary skills to process, evaluate and act upon the knowledge in circulation, civic media ensures the diversity of inputs and mutual respect necessary for democratic deliberation.[58]

Strengthening social bonds within a community and providing people with information about their leaders to ensure diversity and respect for democracy: that sounds a lot like the historical ideal of journalism developed throughout the early part of the twentieth century. And yet, news gathering and reporting – the backbone of journalistic storytelling – did not garner consideration as a form of civic media. The fact that journalism was not considered a form of civic media by those scholars *most* interested in studying media and politics in the early twenty-first century is indicative of the chasm that has grown between the historical ideals of journalism and the people engaged in the practices of the journalism profession. If there is indeed evolution of a publicly minded civic media that brings people together, informs them for public decision-making, and is separate from professional journalism, then we are left to wonder: what role is left for professional journalism?

As we noted earlier, we do not believe that it is appropriate, or even realistic, to dismiss legacy journalism in our own analysis of what we believe is emerging in the practices of connective journalism. We recognize that what people pass along to one another through connective journalism is often borrowed from or builds upon storytelling that originated in legacy news organizations. News produced by legacy media remains important, but is no longer the only form of storytelling that serves as a source of information for today's publics (if it ever was).

In today's age, professional journalists are not the only ones to lay claim to the cultural authority to tell the community's stories. Barbie Zelizer first illustrated this in her review of how Oliver Stone's feature film *JFK* contributed to reshaping a culturally authoritative story, giving credence to conspiratorial myths that, prior to the film, had been considered marginal by most in society (including the traditional journalists covering the assassination). Through Stone's use of narrative, imagery, symbol, and an ability to tap a deeply resonant theme of government conspiracy that had predated the Kennedy assassination, he was able to create a new version of history, much to the dismay of historians who understood the assassination's facts differently. This kind of cultural authority was interpretive and based on popular consensus, providing a narrative that differed from that of elites yet was popularly accepted and reinforcing of what people sacralized.[59] The example of the Stone film also illustrates that other forms of authority can contest the claims of journalistic authority, thereby calling into question the presumed connection between journalistic authority and the narrow confines of what we have come to think of as the "news genre."

Geoffrey Baym argues that rather than serving as the sole source of journalistic authority, professional journalists should help "to determine who should be given public voices." He argues that we must think instead of "multiple publics, shifting constellations of identities, affiliations, and voices."[60] In such an environment, journalistic authority must be constantly negotiated in relation to specific publics. And sometimes, those who are more familiar with the traditional newscaster or reporter form of journalistic authority will be surprised to find that celebrities such as Christina Aguilera and P. Diddy have been able to garner temporary journalistic authority as they've spoken about current events. Their journalistic authority draws together their life experiences with their celebrity fame and access to power and prestige, and is also tied to their own positions relative to differing publics, as they are able to symbolically give voice to discursive positions that have been excluded from journalism and journalistic authority in the past. Christina Aguilera, for instance, was able to speak authoritatively about domestic violence issues based on her personal experiences and served as a reporter for MTV on related campaign issues for the 2004 election.[61] Likewise, African American hip-hop artist P. Diddy served as an MTV correspondent from the floor of the 2004 Democratic National Convention, interviewing Jesse Jackson and Hillary Clinton about issues of race in America.

In a world where journalism is "dead," and where every individual must take on the mantle of journalistic authority to decide which information is worthy of her attention, we can no longer assume that people will recognize news based on the genre contours that have historically marked professional journalism. Youth often find that they learn more about happenings in their community from Facebook than from the stories of professional journalism, as Ana's comment about the shooting in her neighborhood illustrates. Or, they might find stories on social media that creatively rework journalistic genres more compelling than "straight" news reports.

This brings us back to the earlier questions of journalistic authority, the communities journalism serves, diverse storytelling genres, and business demands. What if part of the disconnect between the public good and journalism is really about changing notions of authority that are emerging in relation to a multiplicity of publics? What if there are other ways of thinking about how young people are creating publics that take on the functions of journalism, but not the trappings of its style? This leads to an argument for following young people as they rework the journalistic genre, which is the subject of the next chapter.

* * * * *

4

Young People "Produsing" and Consuming News

News is the information you need to have some engaging conversations with someone.
 – Marc, twenty-year-old Anglo-American from Washington state[1]

It's tempting to think that with the new media environment, young people will take it upon themselves to create and share news in ways that are completely separate from "adult" news. Yet, in this chapter, we argue that because youth operate within systems established and largely controlled by adults, it's important not to lose sight of how the news ecologies that youth create and participate in are inevitably reliant upon and shaped by the news they encounter via adults. Such news comes to young people frequently, although not exclusively, from "legacy" news: those sources that are associated with "old" media such as television, radio, and print journalism and that traditionally encouraged minimal participation in the creation of content.[2] Sometimes that news comes to young people in a way that we might say is twice removed – filtered not only through legacy news sources but also through such places as humorous satirical news programs on cable stations like HBO or Comedy Central, YouTube videos, or mentions by celebrities on social media sites, as this chapter will discuss. At other times, news seems to emerge directly from youth themselves, as we will discuss in the chapters that follow. But it almost always comes to them in the form of an informal invitation to conversation, suggested by a friend or acquaintance through a social media site. It thus has a strong social component, regardless of where the story originated. Given that youth often share what comes to them from non-youth sources, we need to better understand the different ways in which adults have conceptualized and provided news that young people consume, and the ways that they have created spaces for the development of youth voice for both the consuming and what Axel Bruns terms as the *produsing* (producing + using) of news.[3]

In the previous chapter, this book explored why it is that young people are not very interested in consuming and sharing with their peers the news from legacy media. We identified four themes that are related to this lack of interest: (1) problems of journalistic authority, as many young people are skeptical of the claim that those speaking from a position of journalistic authority represent their interests; (2) problems of the assumed audience for news, as many young people sense a discrepancy between themselves and the imagined audiences of legacy news organizations; (3) problems young people (as well as others) identify with the business models of journalism that structure and limit the US news marketplace, and (4) a dislike of the news storytelling genres that are common to legacy media.

Each of the reasons identified in the last chapter as to why young people are turned off by legacy media is relevant as we consider past journalistic storytelling efforts that have been created and shared for, with, and by young people. Some media specifically designed to reach youth and young adults have embraced experiments with journalistic authority, relying upon youthful news reporters and anchors as well as comedic, celebrity, or sports personalities. Other youth media efforts have experimented with youthful genres of storytelling. Many efforts have emerged in school settings in forms such as weekly or monthly student newspapers or student broadcasts. And other youth-oriented news forms, especially those emerging from established organizations such as public or community radio and television, have targeted age groups more narrowly, recognizing that journalistic storytelling differs greatly between eight- and eighteen-year-olds.

Because targeting youth as a specific audience has been generally viewed as unprofitable "niche" programming, it has long been assumed that youth-oriented news must rely upon funding models that differ from the profit-based business model of legacy news. Such efforts find funding from foundations, social service organizations, schools, and city or regional sources. As we will discuss further in the next chapter, some people assume that the creation of news *for* youth *by* youth should somehow emerge spontaneously from youth themselves, which is an exciting model, but one that faces particular challenges of sustainability and scalability that we will discuss. What this chapter will argue is that even though some efforts at youth news have been sustainable in the past due to their reliance on the financial health of the US legacy media, young people have particularly embraced models that encourage the development of youth voice that allows them to understand possible solutions to the problems they identify, so as to work toward those alternatives. In other words, as we will note, the most effective efforts in fostering the voice of high school aged youth have never been as well-funded or as easily sustainable as the programs that are closer to the US commercial media model. Still, it is worth considering what is possible given today's financial constraints, what is happening within those constraints now, and what is best from the perspective of youth.

This chapter considers some of the precursors to today's emergent practices of what we are terming *connective journalism*. As we noted in Chapter 1, we use the phrase connective journalism to refer to the ways in which young people draw upon the connective capacities of social media platforms and, sometimes, on the classic concepts underlying journalism (such as watchdogging or "gatewatching") to speak and be heard among the communities that matter to them.[4] Whereas traditional journalism is associated with the practices of building an accurate *story*, connective journalism is associated with the practices of building a collective and individual *identity*: practices that are reinforced in the telling of a story by and for a particular group of people. But, as we will see in this chapter, the identities built through connective journalism practices are not constituted in relation to a generic "youth audience" that responds consistently to a set of youth-oriented stories. Rather, in the new media context, we need to think differently about how young people are constituted into a "we" through ethical callings and moral imaginings mobilized through various forms of media, including narrative and humor, as Jeffrey P. Jones has argued.[5] Collective identities, or the sense of "we," emerges as media texts elicit feelings and as young people respond to issues through their emotions. As we will discuss, this means that when efforts to support or create youth-oriented news assume a homogeneous youth audience, they are likely to encounter problems. And, as we will note, this also means that young people are likely to continue to draw upon a wide array of information sources that reinforce, inform, or edify who they see themselves as being and becoming. This may mean that they're less likely to encounter information that disrupts or challenges them in ways that daily journalism might, which is an "echo chamber" or "filter bubble" concern related to news consumption practices of people of all ages in the new media environment.[6] But in this chapter, we focus on the information and journalistic storytelling that *does* come into focus for youth, whether through the intentional efforts of adults or through the serendipitous sharing that occurs on YouTube channels and other social media platforms.

We focus on youthful practices of news consumption and news sharing because, as we noted in the introductory chapter, we view connective journalism practices as a key precursor to *connective action*, a phrase that Bennett and Segerberg have introduced to describe crowd-enabled networks through which people participate in political activities.[7] Before people can choose to personalize their connection with certain issues, they have to become aware of the problem or issue in the first place. Connective journalism is part of this process, we argue, as young people become informed and as they collectively "gatewatch" those in power and begin to assimilate, assemble, and share evidence that challenges the certainty, routine, and efficiency of the communicative processes of those in power.

In a few (mostly isolated) cases, young people rely upon institutionalized sources for news that might be termed youth media, civic media, citizen journalism, or alternative media, as this chapter will discuss. But for the most part, young people rely on social media, on interpersonal relationships, and on news sources that were designed for older audiences rather than for them. For most youth, rather than coming to them directly from institutionalized sources, news tends to come to them second hand or via hearsay from their peers and family members, as a 2015 American Press Institute study found.[8] Traditional journalism outlets are often the original source of the topics discussed, but items arrive in the young person's news, Snapchat, Instagram, Twitter feed, or in other forms of interaction after sometimes passing through a variety of filters that might include school discussions, corporate websites such as Buzzfeed, Reddit, or Fusion that aggregate and discuss news, late night television shows, including adult-oriented animated series such as *South Park*, or commentary produced or passed along from one's peers. Young people also find out about topics of concern through a variety of sources that are at the outer reaches of journalism and include forms of expression such as art, graffiti, slam poetry, performance, and hip-hop. These forms are thus part of what we will term a broader *youth news ecology*, following Mizuko Ito and her colleagues' use of the term "ecology" to refer to the ways in which communication media constitute the environments in which young people live and learn.[9]

There is a long tradition of efforts, both formal and informal, through which current events and issues have been made more accessible for young people. This chapter will discuss three different approaches to the production of youth news: (1) news efforts produced specifically for youth by adults, (2) news efforts produced by adults for young adults but for which high school youth are a substantial secondary audience, and (3) news produced by and for youth. We will also discuss the outer reaches of news – forms of narrative and popular expression that introduce young people to current issues and concerns – acknowledging that most of these fall into the category of media produced by adults for young adults. Each of these approaches contributes to the news ecology that youth encounter today across an array of media platforms.

We argue in this chapter that news produced by adults for youth has tended to begin from what Nico Carpentier calls a "minimalist" approach to participation.[10] Such efforts have viewed young people from a developmental citizenship perspective that, as we discussed in Chapter 1, assumes that young people need to be protected and assisted as they prepare for adulthood, which is when they will be called upon to participate more fully in the political life of society. Following this protectionist approach to young people, many broadcast and print journalistic efforts designed by adults for youth have only minimally invited youth to participate in the life of society, primarily as audience members. After exploring a few examples of this approach to news created by adults for youth, we will then consider the news that youth consume that is produced for young adults, which positions high school aged youth at the periphery (even as high schoolers themselves may opt for greater participation as they share the critiques and social commentary of such programming with their peers through social media). These sources of news become important in the connective journalistic practices of young people as they "gatewatch" how problems are constituted in communication and then share evidence of problems with peers as part of their processes of creating performances of self-identification through social media. Finally, the chapter will consider the precursors to today's youthful "produsers" of news, which we view as falling into two categories. The first includes programs like high school journalism that have encouraged young people to be creators of news, but that are often controlled by adults through both the setting of the school and through various court cases that have limited student press rights. The second precursor to today's youthful "produsers" of news can be traced to a small but significant subset of efforts oriented toward fostering youth voice through the development of media competency/literacy. Some of these efforts have emerged spontaneously among youth themselves over the years. Yet, there are also traditions of adult involvement in creating spaces for the development of youth voice that have emerged among parents in formal and informal educational settings, as well as in critical youth media literacy and production efforts based in schools or after-school youth programs, as we will discuss. Many of these approaches have grown out of a critical approach to citizenship that challenges some of the more deficit-oriented assumptions of the developmental citizenship model that views young people only as "someday" citizens or as citizens in the making. Such critical approaches to youth citizenship have charted a way of thinking about the relationship between media consumption, production, and maximal youth participation in the life of society.

NEWS FOR YOUTH (FROM ADULTS)

Today, there are very few outlets that consistently strive to offer young people an age-appropriate review and interpretation of politics and current events, save youth sports news and the weekly children's insert that still comes with some daily newspapers. Perhaps the most outstanding example of a commitment to current event news created by adults for youth was the award-winning program *Nick News with Linda Ellerbee* on Nickelodeon, which was designed for children between the ages of eight and thirteen. The program aired on cable television in the United States every Sunday evening from 1992 until 2015 and was supported by advertising and subsidized by Nickelodeon. In 1993 through 1996, it also aired on the CBS network on Saturday evenings and continued to air on many CBS affiliates until 1999. The program received two Peabody awards recognizing its commitment to the public through its excellence in quality, one in 1992 and another in 1994.[11] It drew its largest audience with a 2002 program, "Nick News Special Edition: My Family is Different," which highlighted children discussing issues of child abuse, sexual harassment, and hate crimes. This program openly featured lesbian parent and comedian Rosie O'Donnell as well as members of conservative families that opposed same sex marriage.[12] Other special programs focused on fracking, living with a terminal illness, and school discipline.[13] In some ways, this program shared common ground with the commitments and orientation of the long-running Danish Broadcasting

Service's *News For Children* and the UK program *Wise Up!* which aired on Channel 4 between 1995 and 2000, the latter of which was also recognized by the Peabody awards.[14]

Channel One News similarly began as a broadcast entity in 1990 and continues to be available as a digital content provider today.[15] In its early years, its programming was made available in US public schools through a unique and controversial funding model in which schools were provided with satellite receivers and televisions in exchange for the promise that they would record and then air the daily advertising-sponsored program in classrooms. Although professionally produced, Channel One invited young people to report, produce, direct, and design one week's worth of programming each year during a Student Producer Week. Like *Nick News* and *Wise Up!*, *Channel One News* has been the recipient of numerous awards, and some research demonstrated that students with access to Channel One may have experienced some benefits in relation to current events knowledge.[16] However, unlike the other productions, this effort received continual criticism for product marketing and corporate-heavy content paired with a sensationalistic and lightweight approach to current events, as well as for its contribution to the incursion of commercialism into school settings.[17]

Children's Express was another interesting model that aimed to incorporate young people into the newsmaking process. Established by former Wall Street lawyer Robert Clampitt and former opera singer Dorriet Kavanaugh, in 1975,[18] this not-for-profit effort – which took place in the New York City area and then in Salem, Massachusetts, Washington, DC, Oakland, California, and several other major cities from 1975 to 1999 – teamed young people aged eight to eighteen with professional journalists. Professional journalists served as mentors, offering guidance while young people researched and conducted interviews, and together with the journalists wrote stories of interest to young as well as older audiences.

Children's Express (CE) first came to prominence when one of its thirteen-year-old reporters scooped the news that Walter Mondale would be Jimmy Carter's running mate as part of its 1976 reporting on the Democratic National Convention.[19] Then, after producing a segment about *Children's Express* in 1985 that aired on *60 Minutes*, CBS News reporter Harry Moses left *60 Minutes* to begin the children's news magazine series *CE News Magazine* with pilot funds from the Public Broadcasting Service (PBS). That program, broadcast on PBS during prime time, gained notoriety when one of its twelve-year-old reporters asked vice presidential candidate Dan Quayle if she should have to bring a baby to term if she were raped by her father, and he replied that he would not recommend an abortion even under those circumstances. The program, including that episode, went on to win an Emmy and a Peabody Award for 1988.[20]

CE stories were syndicated by United Press International and later they were self-syndicated. The work was taxing. As one thirteen-year-old participant told a reporter for *The New York Times*: "I'm burned out. Next year I'm going to do less television so I don't miss so much school."[21] Young television reporters for CE earned as much as $450 a week, although print reporters were not paid at all. The effort was successful in encouraging elementary and junior high students to participate in identifying and exploring youth-specific angles to current events. After Clampitt's death in 1996, several of the bureaus split off to form separate youth news organizations, including Y-Press in Indianapolis, Children's Pressline in New York City, and 8–18 Media in Marquette. It may be that such an effort could be revived in other markets with the enthusiasm of retired professional journalists, although increasing financial pressures on public broadcasting, after-school efforts, and on professional journalism remain a dominant concern for funding such an effort.[22]

Of course, the digital revolution has shaken up the financial models of all legacy media systems. News specifically written or produced for youth audiences was never consistently funded in the United States, and such efforts largely fell by the wayside with the loss in profitability of the commercial media systems in the early 2000s. If at one time some had hoped that a news-for-youth model funded by commercial media would catch on, in today's financial landscape, those hopes have largely evaporated.

NEWS FOR YOUNG ADULTS (WITH YOUTH AS A
SECONDARY AUDIENCE)

Although some of the young people we interviewed had experienced *Channel One News* earlier in their school environments, most had few recent encounters with or had never heard of the above-mentioned examples of news for youth. When asked how they learned about current events, many, however, mentioned late night television and satirical news shows like *The Daily Show* or *Last Week Tonight with John Oliver*, youth-oriented music, and comedic parodies.

Until the 2016 presidential campaign, the term "fake news" as used in popular US lexicon most commonly referred to humorous entertainment television programs that parodied network news, utilizing satire to discuss public affairs. While emphatically stating that they are entertainment rather than "news," programs such as *Last Week Tonight* with John Oliver, *The Colbert Report* (TCR), *The Daily Show with Jon Stewart* (TDS), and the "Weekend Update" on *Saturday Night Live* (SNL), have been widely popular among youth, with numerous studies reporting that teens as well as young adults rely on them as sources of news.[23] By the fall of 2016, however, popular usage of the term "fake news" more commonly referred to websites, usually coming from an extreme right-wing orientation and often connected with White supremacist groups, that knowingly published sensational false stories, not for the purpose of stimulating public discussion about genuine political issues, but rather for the purpose of generating click-induced advertising revenue or, more darkly, for the purpose of popularizing and legitimizing racist, sexist, homophobic, and fascist positions that have historically been rejected by mainstream news media. While the latter form of fake news and how it is influencing journalism and politics will be discussed in the concluding chapter, the earlier fake news shows, which we will refer to as satirical television "mock news" programs (to avoid confusion with the newer use of the term "fake news"), are examined in the current chapter for what they can tell us about young people and news consumption.

Young adults were arguably first targeted as a unique audience for a news product in the mid-1970s, with the introduction of Saturday Night Live's *Weekend Update*, which wove political commentary into humorous late night television monologues. Satirical mock news programming for young adults developed further with the rise of cable television programming in the 1980s through such channels as MTV, VH1, Comedy Central, and Current TV, and more recently in YouTube-delivered channels such as Vice News, and programs featuring youthful microcelebrities such as *The Philip DeFranco Show* and *The Young Turks*.[24]

MTV's partnership with *Rock the Vote* and its 2016 partnership with Tumblr and Change.org in its "Elect This" campaign and Robo-Roundtable series (using animation, talking robots, and animated plastic and stuffed animals to discuss political issues) stand out as exemplars in the news for youth area, particularly for the station's interest in foregrounding innovative genres of delivery and its efforts to encourage youth participation in politics. The channel has sought to reach young people by focusing on election-year issues such as gun legislation, LGBT rights, and climate change, with a big assist from music celebrities.[25] In their own pre-election survey of 2016, MTV found that 92 percent of their millennial-aged respondents agreed with the statement, "This election is like a bad reality show."[26] The online hub for "Elect This" featured in-depth information about issues, as well as lists of action steps and resources to enable young people to get connected with those working for the changes they wanted to support.

Political communication scholars Bruce Williams and Michael Delli Carpini have pointed out that due to the collapse of the broadcast "media regime" and the blurring of media storytelling genres, it is no longer possible to distinguish easily between information-centric media and entertainment media. They propose studying instead what they term "politically relevant media," and satirical television mock news clearly fits into this category.[27] Researchers have reacted with varying degrees of approval and concern to the public's growing reliance for news on shows that are not produced by journalists and that purportedly lack a commitment to professional journalistic norms of objectivity. Yet, according to national studies, viewers of such shows are better informed about national and international affairs than those who rely exclusively on mainstream news outlets. In particular, young adults who watched *The Daily Show* scored higher on campaign knowledge tests than those who watched network news or read newspapers.[28]

Scholars have considered satirical television mock news to be "knowledge-enabling" as opposed to merely "informational," in large part because such programs provide more context that enhances understanding for those new to certain issues or topics.[29] As communication researcher Geoffrey Baym has observed, while typical TV news reports the "facts" in rapid succession, switching topics with little or no contextualization, satirical mock news "places its topics in wider contexts, often providing background information and drawing historical linkages of the sort uncommon to television news."[30] Particularly useful for young people who are still learning about the workings of government, the in-depth discussions found on *TDS* and *TCR*, in particular, have provided information on institutional processes – such as how a bill becomes law or how the electoral college functions – that are mentioned but rarely explained in mainstream news. Thus, while official news increasingly resembles entertainment genres, various scholars note that satirical mock news provides the type of political communication that promotes public debate.[31] These programs also enact the classical watchdog role of journalism by striving, through satire, to hold the powerful accountable for what they say and do.[32]

Recognizing the hybrid nature of news information in our discursively integrated age, Baym, like Williams and Delli Carpini, urges us to move beyond mutually exclusive dichotomies of "entertainment or information."[33] Similarly, Borden and Tew have argued that since satirical mock news shows are free from the official constraints of gate-keeping and objectivity, they can offer the same kind of authenticity promised by bloggers and other online social media, in terms of drawing attention to lapses of journalistic integrity.[34] Jon Stewart's Socratic questioning technique on *The Daily Show*, for example, can be understood as "a rhetorical tactic to point out incongruities, inconsistencies and internal contradictions" in the public discourse of politicians and other powerful actors.[35] By purposely skewering the authoritative voices that are the hallmark of professional reporters, such shows critique the trivialization of news and superficial reporting that have become commonplace in professional broadcast journalism. They offer audiences a taste of what current events news could be, if stripped of its dependence on the authority of the presenter, focusing instead on the quality of arguments.

Learning from Satirical Television Mock News

Young people told us they often learned about current events for the first time by watching satirical mock news programming. Explaining how she first became aware of the 2008–2010 financial crisis watching *SNL*, one of our interviewees named Maneeya stated: "At first, when the economy was going down, they did a joke about it and I thought it was very funny. Then I saw the regular news and was like, 'Oh my God, it's true!' " Mike, aged sixteen, explained: "I watch *The Daily Show* and *The Colbert Report*. I actually find it a really interesting way to get news, because it's funny, but you learn from it." Mohamed, aged fifteen, watched *TDS* "every night before bed." Unlike many of his peers, Mohamed also sought out news from the ideologically opposite end of the scale, noting that he also watched the current events talk show *The O'Reilly Factor*, hosted by conservative political commentator Bill O'Reilly, which aired on the Fox News Network from 1996 until 2017. Although he held progressive views, Mohamed prided himself on being open-minded and tuned in to conservative shows to "hear the other side." He explained, "I'm very opinionated and quick to start an argument, but sometimes when you start an argument, it could lead to either yourself discovering something new about a topic or someone else discovering something new." Grouping *The O'Reilly Factor* with the other mock news programs he watched, Mohamed noted that he appreciated that the hosts of such shows provided unambiguous political opinions: "Jon Stewart criticizes people...he's sort of sarcastic about it. Satire. And, that's what I do when I argue with people."

Although it might seem as if these young adult-oriented programs emerged relatively recently, media scholar Liesbet Van Zoonen has argued that they are best understood within a long history of the blurring of politics and entertainment.[36] In the middle of the nineteenth century, for example, as Tony Kelso and Brian Cogan have reminded us, the Lincoln and Douglas debates were staged as a festival, complete with a spectacle of bands, flags, and banners.[37] Advertising also emerged in the nineteenth century, bringing a splash of color and entertainment to politics in a manner that tells us a great deal about how politicians imagined the nineteenth-century audience and what it would take to engage their interest in politics. One can observe an even longer tradition of entertainment rooted in casting John Adams as a "no-good monarchist" and Thomas Jefferson as a "vile atheist," in early election campaigns that were meant to appeal to people's emotions.[38] Current events have long been a source of entertainment, even if scholars have only recently begun to pay attention to the role these sources of entertainment play in political knowledge and, perhaps, mobilization.

Learning from Fictional Narratives

The previous eighteenth- and nineteenth-century campaign examples illustrate how politicians or their advocates have sought to harness the emotional power of popular culture and entertainment for their own ends. But with the rise of the entertainment and cultural industries beginning in the mid-twentieth century, corporations saw the benefits of this connection between emotional expression and politics, not only in terms of possible political engagement, but also in terms of profitability. This picture became more complicated as artistic expression, particularly fictional narratives, came to offer an important avenue for critiquing the impact of capitalism on everyday life in the postwar era, as Guy Debord has argued.[39] Scholars began to observe that fictional narratives served particularly well as a cultural forum through which people could explore differing and sometimes conflicting feelings, even to the point of challenging their own deeply held views.[40] Fictional narratives allow people to see themselves more clearly, and thus they are especially important for the development of a moral imagination, as Jeffrey Jones has argued.[41] He cites the philosopher Richard Rorty on fiction in relation to this point:

Fiction gives us the details about the kinds of suffering being endured by people to whom we have previously not attended. Fiction...gives us the details about what sorts of cruelty we ourselves are capable of, and thereby lets us redescribe ourselves.[42]

Fiction can elicit feelings, which in turn can contribute to the construction of a "we," or the construction of ourselves in relation to an affective public, to use Zizi Papacharissi's term.[43]

Fictional narratives are occasionally mentioned as a source of information about current events, particularly when such events are related to political and moral judgments. Over the past few decades, a number of fictional films and television programs have become sources of both information and identification for young people, serving as narratives that open discussion to broader contemporary issues such as poverty, racism, drug abuse, sexual harassment or abuse, homophobia, and the rights of members of the LGBTIQ community. Some of those mentioned among youth included *Precious, Boyz in the Hood, The Help, Orange is the New Black, Breaking Bad, Faking it, Degrassi High, The Boondocks, The Fosters, Glee,* and in northern European contexts, the popular Norwegian teen drama *Skam (Shame).* For specific references to contemporary political issues, US young people we interviewed also frequently mentioned the animated television series *South Park*, noting that they viewed the program on television, laptop computers, and mobile devices, with past episodes available on YouTube. Some noted that they shared links to especially popular episodes among their friends via social media. *South Park*, which is distributed by and is one of the most successful programs of the Comedy Central television network, debuted in 1997 and is slated to air through at least 2019.

While satirical mock news programs have been critiqued for their progressive orientations, *South Park* holds appeal among those who espouse center-right and libertarian beliefs, despite the fact that conservatives criticize the program's vulgarity.[44] The program has mocked anti-smoking activists, government-mandated diversity, sex education, and environmentalists, while also mercilessly skewering prominent left-wing celebrities such as Rosie O'Donnell, Jesse Jackson, Michael Moore, and Rob Reiner.[45] But *South Park* has also satirized America's interventionist foreign policy and conservatives, leaving some to view the program (and associated films) as largely reinforcing anti-political views.[46]

When asked to provide examples of political issues they learned about from the show, several youth such as Lucia enthusiastically recounted episodes:

They had a funny episode recently about Apple and iTunes and all that. [Laughing] You know how when you update things on your computer, it gives you pages and pages and pages of conditions or whatever, and you don't read it, you just click "agree." And, one day on *South Park*, one of the characters disappears and Apple takes him and turns him into a terrible science experiment because it was stated in the fine print. (Lucia, aged twenty)

Through this humorous animated program, Lucia considered for the first time the importance of reading website privacy policies – a topic of growing political importance. Meanwhile, Hermes, aged twenty, gained an understanding of civil rights violations occurring within US government spying operations:

South Park was making fun of the NSA spying on us, and the whistle blowers. There was an episode where Cartman was on his phone. He wanted to form a Meetup to fight the NSA spying on people, but then says, "The NSA found out about our meeting. They're reading my tweets." The NSA knows everything he's doing. Then, he goes to work for the NSA using the alias Bill Clinton. And it shows all these people in suits spying on everyone, observing the dumbest details, like what TV show they watch, and they're torturing Santa Claus. What I thought was really funny was how they showed the NSA is reading people's Twitter posts and emails. And, when Cartman tries to expose it, nobody cares. His own mother just says, "Yes, I know the government tortures people, honey, but they're keeping us safe." It was hilarious and also a depressing situation. (Hermes, aged twenty)

Alex, aged sixteen, first learned from *South Park* about Florida's "Stand Your Ground" law, made famous through the 2012 case in which unarmed teenager Trayvon Martin was shot in his own neighborhood by George Zimmerman, who was later acquitted of second-degree murder: "I can think of a recent episode where they were making fun of Zimmerman and the 'Stand Your Ground' rule. So, I looked up 'Stand Your Ground' to know what it meant," Alex explained.

Alex, echoing views of those who questioned traditional journalistic authority as noted in the previous chapter, observed that programs like *South Park* are useful in informing people about current events "because when people joke about things, I trust the source more. They're joking about bad things, things that are wrong." A program like *South Park* thus stands in a long tradition of humor and satire and shares a common literary tradition with the satirical mock news programs mentioned earlier.

Fictional narratives such as *South Park* not only exposed youth to current events, but also motivated them to seek additional information on politically relevant topics such as the "NSA" or "SOPA." And mobile phones made this process of secondary research highly accessible. Amanda, aged sixteen, who watched *South Park*, *The Daily Show*, and *Colbert* with her older brothers and cousins, appreciated the privacy and immediacy of her cell phone. "Sometimes they're all laughing at a joke and I don't get it. I don't want to let them know I don't get it, so I look it up on my phone," she noted.

Gleaning Knowledge from Mainstream News

We were continually surprised to learn that even youth who said they "don't follow news too much" had up-to-the-minute knowledge of news related to entertainment, celebrities, or sports. Some youth spoke passionately about sexism or racism in movies or songs, while others expressed views on the ethics of athletes taking steroids, illustrating that youthful gravitation toward popular culture is not mutually exclusive with developing political knowledge. A sixteen-year-old avid video gamer discussed a news story he learned about on Facebook: "There's this person from PETA wanting to sue Nintendo because of supposed animal cruelty on Nintendo video games, even though none of the animals are *real* on the games! It's so stupid! A friend showed it to me" (Manny, aged sixteen). Manny's interest in discussing video games with fellow gamers on Facebook led him to become aware of People for Ethical Treatment of Animals (PETA) and the animal rights movement. It also motivated him to develop his own political position regarding what he felt counted and didn't count as harmful behavior toward animals.

Even if they hadn't watched it on television, many students had heard about the winner of the September 2013 Miss America pageant, Nina Davuluri, on Facebook, Twitter, Tumblr, or YouTube, and nearly all mentioned the racist responses Davuluri received online as the first Miss America of Indian American descent. Nico, aged sixteen, said: "I learned about it on Tumblr. I remember someone reposting a few pictures and a story about how people were being outrageously racist about it. People made a lot of comments on Twitter and Steven Colbert also had a little skit about it. I mean, just because she's not white or blond or whatever, she's an American citizen and has a right to be Miss America." Julia, aged eighteen, who heard about the pageant on Facebook, Twitter, and *The Colbert Show*, echoed Nico's disapproval:

I thought it was terrible how racist people were and what people were tweeting about her. I was really upset by it. But, one of the good things about Facebook or social media is that I didn't necessarily look it up on my own, but scrolling through my news feed or scrolling through Tumblr, I saw more info about it... I saw a quote from her that said something like, "The girl next door is evolving in the US" or something like that. I thought that was a great quote.

Thus, a mundane popular culture event covered by the mainstream news and circulated on social media inspired online debates regarding race in contemporary US society, with youth able to view, critique, and express perspectives in the public sphere from the privacy of their phones, affirming in the process their own sense of identity as individuals opposed to racism. We found that social media, especially Facebook and Twitter, prompted youth to consider a variety of civic issues related to collective identity, national belonging, and the common good.

For example, David, aged twenty, the son of Colombian immigrants, was inspired via social media to consider an issue connected to notions of the common good – economic inequality. When a friend posted a video link of actor and comedian Russell Brand, on Facebook, David "liked" it: "He was talking about a revolution of the poor against the rich and talking about not voting and how the system is illegitimate." The YouTube clip was an interview on BBC's *Newsnight*, conducted by British journalist Jeremy Paxman. The ten-minute video showed Brand arguing that a revolution of the disenfranchised against the 1 percent was needed to achieve true democracy. The *Newsnight* interview, which most youth would not have seen otherwise, went viral, receiving more than 8 million hits and myriad comments on YouTube shortly after its release in 2013 and climbing to more than 11 million hits by 2016 due to its circulation on Facebook and Twitter.

Further illustrating how youth engagement with entertainment news via social media can introduce them to politics, Rafael, aged seventeen, gave the following response when asked whether he cared about a political issue, which he related to his love of video games:

Yes, the SOPA bill! There was a petition on the Internet against SOPA. The SOPA bill's, like, I watch a lot of video games on YouTube...but a lot of people do commentary over it and have their own experience with it. That's the difference between posting movies and posting video games. With a movie, it's the same experience whoever watches it, but with a video game, it's a different experience no matter who does it. And the SOPA bill would put a limit on that. Like movie companies could take a video down if they have a specific thing in it from that movie. The SOPA bill would, like, limit what you can poach from the Internet, and that's against free speech, against how people can express themselves. So, I signed the petition to make sure that doesn't happen.

A movie and gaming buff, Rafael first learned of SOPA (the Stop Online Piracy Act) from watching one of his favorite shows – a humorous online movie guide called *The Nostalgia Critic*. Unfamiliar with the term "SOPA," he later Googled it to learn more and began following the issue on Facebook and Twitter, sharing online posts with friends.

Ironically, while the students' comments and behaviors implied that they were uninterested in "objective" news, as we discussed in Chapter 3, it was, in part, their desire to gain a more truthful and balanced understanding of news that motivated them to view blogs, Facebook postings, YouTube videos, satirical mock news, and other "non-news" sources of news. This occurred as the youth encountered a connection between their own identities, including the things they cared about and identified with, and the contemporary issues that sparked their emotions. Such genres as YouTube, mock news, and other non-news sources do not simply *relate* the news, but also offer interpretations and judgments about current events that provide an emotional framework and a moral discourse through which young people can connect with current events. In contrast to disinterested observations about the political world, typical of "boring" professional news, the teens enjoyed the use of opinion and sarcasm employed in these media to expose lies and abuses. Kara, aged sixteen, expressed what many youth felt was a problem with professional news: "The regular news gives you one side and another side, but you don't really know which one is good or bad."

But, even these engaged young people cannot be viewed as "dutiful citizens" who are consuming news on a regular basis. Rather than follow "the news," young people tend to follow *issues* that are important to them because of this connection with identification. Kim, aged seventeen, is one such young person who was embedded in a community that cared a great deal about immigration. As she noted, she had "a lot of friends who are involved with the immigration movement. I get information from talking with them and from Facebook. I pay attention to news about immigration, because it affects my family." Kim knew that her friends and family members would be denied the opportunity to pursue college, which in turn would limit their employment opportunities, unless laws were passed to allow students born in Mexico but raised in the United States to pursue college at the in-state rate, with access to financial aid and US loans. She did not view knowing about immigration law as part of her civic duty to be informed, but rather as a pragmatic response to a set of rules that would either limit or make possible certain opportunities for her family and friends.

Other issues youth cared about included police brutality, racial profiling, reproductive rights, environmental issues, and news about their families' countries of origin. Eighteen-year-old Santos, the son of Brazilian immigrants, defined himself as "not very political," yet like Kim, he was also informed about issues that directly touched his life:

On Facebook, I've been hearing about all these demonstrations and protests all over the world, like there's tension in Brazil about the Olympics and all this money being invested to build buildings and brand new stadiums for this two-week event, when so many people in Brazil are living in very serious, sub-par conditions ... Also, there have been protests in Russia over gay rights. And of course there's the government shutdown here.

The fact that students like Kim and Santos followed some news stories and not others only further complicates the question of how news could be created and shared specifically for youth. These examples highlight the fact that there is no single "youth audience" who would choose to consume the same set of news stories, but rather a collection of audiences that more or less share interests with adults that center on issues.

Thus, when people share links to *South Park* or *Last Week Tonight with John Oliver* among their friends and family members, just as when they elect to talk about what Kara termed the "regular news," we argue that they are participating in practices of connective journalism. In the former case, they are sharing these programs because they are humorous, surely, but also because the program articulates something that allows them to claim an identification that is at once political and collective. We will return to this point, but first we turn to our final category in the contemporary youth news ecology: news that is created and shared by and for youth.

NEWS BY YOUTH FOR YOUTH

High School (Scholastic) Journalism

Nick News, Wise Up!, Channel One, Children's Express, various satirical mock news programs such as *The Daily Show, The Colbert Report,* and *Last Week Tonight with John Oliver*, as well as the fictional program *South Park*, were all relatively high-profile broadcast properties that were expensive to produce and featured content largely controlled by and aimed at adults. But more common models in youth news media, if less high profile, have involved locally supported efforts to engage young people, with some guidance from adults, in the reporting and analysis of current events.

The earliest forms of news produced by youth for youth date back to the 1930s, when high schools began to support newspapers meant to serve the student body. Following the introduction of the flash bulb at around the same time, high school journalism increasingly incorporated photojournalism, and by the 1950s and 1960s, both yearbooks and some high school papers aspired to take on a look heavily influenced by *Life* and *Look* magazines, which were the dominant publications of the time.[47] Yet, the printing quality of the high school press was often limited, as photocopy machines did not become widely available in schools until the 1970s and 1980s, so many mid-century high school presses relied on mimeograph machines. After the introduction of electronic video editing systems, which entered the commercial market in the mid-1960s, schools started to experiment with student broadcast news. Student news organizations began to go online in the mid-1990s, although many involved at the time were ambivalent about the fact that such publications could disseminate far beyond school boundaries, thereby opening schools up to a wider range of observers and critics.[48]

But the involvement of adults in the oversight of high school-related news publications has long been in debate. The 1969 Supreme Court case *Tinker v. Des Moines Independent Community School* established the constitutional rights of students to free expression and provided a test by which to judge whether or not a school's disciplinary actions violate First Amendment rights. The court held that students "do not shed their constitutional rights at the schoolhouse gate" and protected students' rights to express political views, in this particular case agreeing that students had the right to wear armbands protesting the Vietnam war.[49] The Student Press Law Center was established in 1974 to advocate specifically for student press rights, particularly the right to publish free of censorship by school administrators. California passed the first Student Free Expression Law in 1977 and Washington state passed a similar law that same year. However, in 1984 the US Supreme Court ruled that it was well within the authority of school administrators to determine the appropriateness of speech in classes and in assemblies, and in 1988 the Supreme Court ruled in *Hazelwood School District v. Kuhlmeier* that public school student newspapers that have not been explicitly established as forums for free expression are subject to a lower level of First Amendment protection. The court noted that a school could censor content deemed inconsistent with the school's "basic educational mission," and that rather than creating a public forum, a school newspaper was a "supervised learning experience" subject to extensive control by a faculty member.[50] *Hazelwood* became the standard for future student press cases, as it established that a school district could censor a student newspaper for a variety of reasons.[51] But as the Student Press Law Center notes, "the burden remains on the school to furnish a legitimate educational reason for censoring – and that cannot be simply protecting the school's PR image."[52] Courts and schools continue to debate student rights, most recently in relation to disciplining students in relation to Facebook content published off campus and about student writing that is deemed offensive and hateful rather than humorous and satirical, but involvement in high school journalism is related positively to voting, and to the development of civic competence.[53]

Although one might think that news by youth for youth would be youth-centered and youth-led, some youth journalism programs are extremely prescriptive, limiting what youth reporters can cover in order to fit with school policies. High school teachers and principals frequently discourage or prohibit student stories about war, teen sexuality, school policies, or other controversial issues.[54] Censorship has been found to disillusion student journalists regarding the viability of their political agency. In a study of high school journalism, David Martinson observed that censorship at school newspapers creates a situation in which "students fail to understand why it is important that they be engaged and committed citizens because they learn through the socialization process ... that the way to survive is not to raise questions but to go along."[55] Such dynamics instill in students a sense of irrelevance as political actors, curtailing their enthusiasm for journalism and civic engagement.

On the other hand, some programs that understand themselves as "news by and for youth" fail to provide sufficient guidance in helping youth understand what makes a story interesting and newsworthy. Sometimes, adult leadership is underprepared, such as in the case of high schools that thrust the English teacher into the role of newspaper advisor or recruit the physical education teacher for the task because she has a free period to fill. In other cases, funding sources dry up or volunteers leave before a system of cultivating interesting and newsworthy stories is developed. It is understandably harder to gather information on these programs, but it is nevertheless important to acknowledge that many such efforts are short-lived or fail to engender enthusiasm among youth.

Community Youth Media

Since the 1970s, news by and for youth can be further subdivided into news efforts that take place as part of a school's regular curriculum, such as the daily, weekly, or monthly school newspapers and broadcast initiatives discussed above and those that take place through extra curricular activities either advised by someone from the school or run completely apart from schools by community organizations.[56] The latter often are managed with funding support from foundations, corporations, local businesses, or local government, and range in purpose from "giving youth a voice" to "encouraging creative self-expression" and "preparing youth for a career in media," according to a US survey of youth media programs.[57] This same study found that the majority of community youth media programs serve modest income or under-resourced youth communities, and half of all of the programs surveyed operated with an annual budget of $100,000 or less, while 11 percent of them had no budget at all.[58]

When judged according to a program's ability to sustain youth interest and youth involvement, the most successful of the youth media program models allow young people editorial freedom to select their own story topics while teaching them how to tell their stories in ways that appeal to a wider public.[59] Some of the larger and more enduring examples of youth journalism programs include Zumix Radio in Boston, WHYY TV in Philadelphia, *Radio Rookies* and the Educational Video Center in New York, and Youth Radio in Oakland, California. Zumix Radio is a free after-school program in which teenagers are trained in journalistic interview and research skills and learn how to use radio recording and broadcasting equipment. Their stories are broadcast via community radio and on the web.[60] WHYY TV (Philadelphia Public TV) and the Educational Video Center (EVC) in New York City each teach high school aged youth how to create video news stories regarding issues happening in their neighborhoods. The stories from the first are aired on Philadelphia public television; with EVC, youth-produced documentaries make their way into the film festival circuit.[61] *Radio Rookies*, an initiative of WNYC (New York Public Radio), and Youth Radio in Oakland teach teenagers to use words and sounds to tell true stories about their communities. Upon completion, the news stories from these outlets are distributed worldwide via a variety of media outlets including public radio stations, CNN.com, iTunes, and the NPR programs *Morning Edition* and *All Things Considered*. All of these award-winning youth journalism models recruit youth from predominantly under-resourced neighborhoods where most high schools lack funding for school newspapers or journalism clubs. Operating within a youth empowerment model and run by staff with public television and/or community radio backgrounds (journalistic realms historically involved in "watch dog" journalism), these models allow teens to choose their own stories, even when these stories consist of controversial topics.

Because these examples are funded according to public broadcasting models of foundation, grant, and government support, they hold some things in common with the not-for-profit models now being widely proposed in response to the collapse of the for-profit commercial media industries.[62] This funding model is one to which we will return for further discussion in Chapter 7.

YOUTH MEDIA AND MEDIA LITERACY

Production Skills and Critical Analytical Skills

Most of the youth media programs listed above, as well as many other community youth media efforts, incorporate a significant component of critical media literacy into their work. According to Patricia Aufderheide and Charles Firestone, media literacy is generally defined as the ability to access, analyze, evaluate, and communicate messages in a wide variety of forms.[63] But, as we have observed about the differing levels of adult involvement in the production of news for youth, we also note different approaches that shape programs in media literacy. Some experts, such as Neil Postman, have argued that media literacy is important because young people need protection from a toxic culture. On the other hand, other experts such as David Buckingham have viewed media literacy differently. As media literacy expert Renee Hobbs has said of this "debate" between a protectionist, Postman-like approach, and a child-centric Buckingham approach to media literacy: "Maybe children and young people don't need to be protected at all, just invited to participate in the community's discourse about media."[64] Most who work in youth media adopt this latter approach to media literacy.

There are also debates in media literacy about the extent to which such efforts should be about directing young people toward concerns of social injustice. Whereas some, particularly in public education circles, view media literacy as an extension of what they view as a depoliticized process of "literacy," others, who prefer the term *critical* media literacy, think of media literacy as a tool for educational, social, and political change.[65] Those in critical media literacy also emphasize the importance of examining the role of various media institutions in the power relations of society.[66] As JoEllen Fisherkeller observes about the relationship between critical media literacy and youth media,

Often, but not always, youth media programs help young people to challenge the status quo and create change where necessary, and thus help youth to develop as powerful members of society, whether as workers, artists, citizens, activists, and/ or leaders.[67]

Several national US organizations, such as the Center for Media Literacy, the Media Literacy Project, and the National Association for Media Literacy Education, offer resources to assist in the incorporation of media literacy efforts in classrooms and after-school activities.

Some critical media literacy programs focus specifically on news. Paul Mihailidis's work with the Salzburg Institute is one example in which educators are encouraged to provide leadership in this area.[68] Ben Adler has noted that the News Literacy Project, which focuses specifically on helping young people evaluate the trustworthiness of differing news sites, is perhaps one of the more successful of the efforts addressing news, although even its reach of 10,000 students has been relatively limited.[69] Such news-focused efforts have been particularly interested in the ways that participation in the news selection and production process serve as a key part of a critical approach that can foster increased civic engagement among youth.[70] Hobbs and her colleagues, for instance, looked in-depth at an in-school news video production class to learn more about the outcomes of involvement in such programs. They found that having positive attitudes about news, current events, reporting, and journalism, attitudes typically developed in critical media literacy programs, were the best predictors for how young people would translate their experiences in youth media into civic engagement.[71]

While youth media and youth media literacy programs gained momentum with the ubiquity of television in the 1980s, 1990s, and 2000s, many programs now incorporate web and mobile app design and social media into their efforts.[72] Amy Stornaiulo and her colleagues, for example, have argued that efforts that utilize video conferencing technologies to bring together young people from various countries can help to humanize the struggles of one set of people for another, which can shift youth's self-understanding.[73] Youth media expert Lissa Soep has encouraged young people to develop and amplify techniques associated with citizen journalism, as they scan found footage and then attempt to create a larger narrative in which these can be placed to enhance a story's appeal among broader audiences.[74] Although we will return to a more fulsome discussion of the relationship between youth connective journalism practices and citizen journalism in the following chapters, it's important to note here that Soep's approach is a particularly promising way to assist young people in developing critical media literacy as well as production skills, since it asks young people to consider found footage as evidence that can then be placed into a larger interpretive context – something youth frequently do in connective journalism practices.

In our own research, we found that although some young people are critical of the business model of mainstream/legacy news, as discussed in the previous chapter, most are unaware of how the news they create and share on social media is mined, shared, and utilized for commercial profit and marketing purposes. This underscores the critical need for the teaching of digital media literacy to help youth think more about the business models and platforms of Facebook, Twitter, Instagram, and more. Young people need to have opportunities to consider whose interests are served and how algorithms work to give priority to different stories made available.[75] Such issues challenge the idea that just releasing one's youthful news stories or comments online will enable those stories to find an intended (or broader) audience. They also encourage those in leadership positions to question the celebration of social media platforms as "democratizing" and automatically enabling greater participation for all young people.

As prior research has found, many youth recognize and want this kind of critical media literacy education.[76] They realize that they can benefit from media literacy training and are appreciative when schools or after-school programs provide it. In the youth media programs we studied, we found that youth are adept at doing online searches for news on topics of interest to them and older teens, in particular, have some methods for evaluating the trustworthiness of information. These include scrutinizing a website's "look," checking multiple information sources, following links to determine a story's original source, and going to legacy newspaper sites.[77] One young person we interviewed named Jaime, aged eighteen, noted that when evaluating a news link, he tried to "make sure it's a primary source, not too far removed from the direct source. Also, usually in the web address if it says .gov or .com. or .edu, you can tell if it's coming from a university or government source or a commercial source." Susie, aged eighteen, also checked web addresses: "I usually look at the source, like if it's promoted by the government or by a business or some sort of legitimate source. I ask myself, 'Could I cite this source? Can I see a logo?' Does the website look nice?" Tito, aged sixteen, noted: "I go to ABC, NBC, those types of news sites, or CNN. Then, you can compare a story on each of them." Young people also noted that when they saw a story "all over the Internet," they tended to believe it. This speaks to the power of virality in verification practices of young people, which raises a number of issues that we will return to in Chapters 6 and 7. Amanda, aged sixteen, expressed this feeling: "If it's online and *everyone's* talking about it, it's probably true. You have to ask yourself, is this believable? Did someone make this up? But, there are some *real* things that are unbelievable! So, if I heard about it at first, I might think it's a joke. But, then I would check on a real, official thing like the *Boston Globe*." Because Amanda grew up with parents who followed the news and was involved in a youth media program, she may have been more attuned to checking legacy news sources than others. But, many youth, especially younger teens, were less wary and tended to trust online sources more easily.

As many leaders in youth media have affirmed in relation to the goals of their programs, youth need to learn to develop sophisticated ways of evaluating online sources of information, using techniques such as looking more closely at a website's mission, exploring an organization's funding model, learning about what types of people endorse it, and considering its history of accuracy. Interestingly, while many young people automatically trust big name news organizations such as CNN or Fox, we also found a tendency among some, particularly young people of color, to automatically consider larger news sites "biased" and smaller, purportedly "alternative" sites, as "reliable." This position is illustrated in the comments of Santos, aged eighteen: "I think that big media like NBC or Fox tend to have a bias...I like to go to smaller sites, like Jezebel.com...They tend to post a fair amount of unbiased and fair news." This kind of skepticism, also discussed in Chapter 3, is undoubtedly related to a long tradition of biased coverage of communities of color.[78] Still, when asked how they defined terms such as "unbiased" or "reliable," most youth have a hard time articulating criteria. Similar results were found in a national 2016 study of online youth civic reasoning, which noted: "Our 'digital natives' may be able to flit between Facebook and Twitter while simultaneously uploading a selfie to Instagram and texting a friend. But when it comes to evaluating information that flows through social media channels, they are easily duped."[79]

Being Informed in Immigrant Families

While media literacy is crucial in schools and universities for youth of all ages and races, it is especially important for immigrant youth, whose parents may have even less familiarity with US news norms and marketing tactics than US-born adults have. Immigrants, particularly those coming from rural areas of developing countries, are especially vulnerable to predatory lending, phone and mail scams, or other forms of exploitation. Because they usually speak English better and have greater technological skills than their parents, the children of immigrants often find themselves playing the role of "protector" and translator for their parents.[80] We found that those immigrant youth who had the benefit of civics or journalism classes noted that their parents were more trusting and less questioning of news sources than they were and credited their classes for making them more careful news consumers. Numerous immigrant youth noted that their parents had not finished high school and/or had limited English skills (some parents also had limited literacy skills in their native language) and most described their parents as having meager digital skills. In a reversal of traditional generational roles, the immigrant youth found themselves explaining US news to their parents.[81] For instance, Danny, aged twenty, who had recently won a scholarship to college, felt his educational attainment and technological savvy put him in a more advantaged position than his parents: "I like to think that the young generation is pretty smart. Smarter than the older generation, sometimes. Some of our parents never even graduated high school." He used the term "smart" to refer to higher levels of education and technological skill, but distinguished between "smarts" and "wisdom." Like most of the youth, he respected his parents' life experiences while recognizing that he was more up-to-date regarding US news. He continued: "We have that education and we think we're smarter, even though, you know, it's different because the older generation might be wiser. I know I get *my* wisdom from my parents."

Similar sentiments were repeated by others. Kim, aged seventeen, a senior in high school who lived in a single parent household, discussed the generation gap between herself and her mother, who was Peruvian and spoke little English:

I feel like my mother is less informed than me. She's working. She's busy. When she comes home she's tired and puts on the Spanish news, but she doesn't pay attention that much because she's cooking or doing other things…She reads the

Spanish newspaper, but…unless you are very tech savvy, and my Mom is very old fashioned, then you don't get up to date on what's going on. You don't have the chance to see lots of different opinions and debates…I think because of the energy that I put to find out information and the technology that is offered to me, that I'm better informed.

Kim noted two instances when she needed to explain current events to her mother. The first was news of a "lock down" (a concept her mother had never heard of) in relation to a shooting at a nearby school. The second was the Boston marathon bombing: "With the Boston marathon bombing, I had to inform her. I think my mom jumps to conclusions because she is so old fashioned. In school, these days, they teach us to be more open-minded and…they make us question a lot of things. I feel like my Mom doesn't question things…So, I often have to inform her of other sides of a story or more details than she normally gets."

Jaime, aged eighteen, said his parents "came through a lot, they've lived through things I wasn't around for…But, I'm more technology-wise and, in the online political world, I'm more informed." Hermes, aged twenty, whose Salvadoran mother cleaned office buildings, felt similarly: "I feel my mom is less informed, probably because we're definitely from different generations and she's not that Internet savvy. She works, she comes home and cooks, she watches a little bit of TV, but… she doesn't really care that much about it. I'm online, I'm more connected all day than she is, so I tend to hear about things before she does and have more information which I can explain to her." Tito, aged sixteen, summarized the type of exchanges that immigrant youth often have with their parents: "They're updated about what's going on in Colombia and I know more about what's going on in the English-speaking world. I tell them what's happening here and they tell me what's happening over there."

Just as immigrant children become translators for their parents in social service, medical, and legal situations,[82] their facility with digital media allows them access to more detailed, diverse, and up-to-the-minute news than their parents receive. Youth felt their parents were not *as* updated as they were about US news, particularly breaking stories. In a reversal of the usual parent–child relationship, young Latinos apprised their immigrant parents of US news developments and their meanings, including the DREAM Act, school policies, immigration laws, and hyperlocal crime news stories. The young people's proficiency with the Internet, near constant physical connection with mobile media, and fluent English skills underscored a generational digital divide that has technological, educational, and linguistic aspects.[83]

Social context is important here. While non-immigrant youth can also have parents who are less digitally skilled than they are, we found that much greater gaps exist between low-income Latino immigrant youth and their parents regarding formal educational attainment, English skills, and digital know-how. This is further complicated by the fact that many immigrant youth have parents who are undocumented residents. Because of precarious economic situations these parents may have faced both in their native countries and in the United States, many immigrant parents from developing countries lack high levels of formal education and find themselves working long hours at low-wage jobs with less time to focus on the news than more affluent parents might have. Many parents of the youth we interviewed were employed in manual labor jobs and did not have digital skills. While non-immigrant youth typically have parents and extended family members who can reinforce normative ideas regarding democratic rights and participatory processes, low-income Latino immigrant youth are less likely to have these ideals demonstrated or reinforced at home[84] and are the least likely of all US youth populations to discuss politics with their parents.[85] This combination of factors highlights the urgent need for critical media literacy programs for youth living in low-income immigrant and minority communities.

As the above section illustrates, youth media and critical media literacy programs face a variety of challenges that include but also extend beyond the issue of limited funding. Programs designed to encourage youth participation in media production and in critical media literacy must be designed with the specific contextual and cultural experiences of youth in mind.

CITIZENSHIP AND PARTICIPATION

As noted in the Introduction, we take a critical approach to youth and citizenship, and this forms the basis for how we suggest that readers think about the relationships between various elements of the youth news ecology and questions of political participation. Participation is sometimes viewed in a binary way, assuming that people either choose to participate in governance and politics, or they do not. However, some scholars have pointed out that the choice of whether or not to participate is usually shaped in advance by systems that foster either what Nico Carpentier[86] has termed as minimalist or maximalist approaches to participation. Although he discusses political systems only, we add that these two different approaches to shaping participation are found both in governmental systems and in other systems in which young people grow up. Dictatorships and nation-states with strong centralized leadership tend to take a minimalist approach to participation, as do authoritarian families. Similarly, schools that adopt a minimalist approach to participation focus on creating and maintaining order. In settings of minimalist participation, decision making remains centralized and participation is limited to elites. Politics is understood narrowly in relation to institutional politics, and political activities outside of official institutions are viewed as threatening.

Authoritarian households tend to operate with the same emphasis on centralized decision making and on containing threats from the outside. In political, family, and school systems of minimalist participation, then, participation is largely understood in relation to protection, obedience, and compliance. In such situations, there is little incentive for participation and choosing not to participate in decision making in these settings largely amounts to compliance with the existing arrangement of power and control.

Carpentier has explored what a minimalist approach means within the communication industries, arguing that those media systems that have embraced a *minimalist* approach have envisioned a single, homogeneous public that is to be won over, persuaded, or punished when out of compliance. He notes that minimalist forms of media participation therefore provide a potent support system for institutionalized politics and make it difficult for those deemed "outsiders" to be heard. In minimalist approaches, media professionals keep a strong grip on processes of production and dissemination and, as Carpentier writes, "participation remains unidirectional, articulated as a contribution to the public sphere but often mainly serving the needs and interests of the mainstream media system itself, instrumentalizing and incorporating the activities of participating non-professionals." This results in the disconnection of the audience from media as well as from other societal fields. Clearly, the minimalist approach to participation aligns with a broadcast media model, in which power is centralized in the hands of the few and non-elites are generally discouraged or barred from access.

In contrast, a maximalist approach to participation, as suggested by the term, seeks to maximize participation on the part of all people. This approach, Carpentier argues, embraces a broadly defined notion of the political, considering many sites of decision making. Moreover, a maximalist approach to participation is concerned with the continuous role of participation in decision making, rather than merely in the election of representatives.

Those who advocate a maximalist approach to participation tend to emphasize communication rights not only in relation to institutionalized politics, but also in relation to a variety of other social realms in which consensus and collaboration are deemed important aspects of collective decision making. Some in the fields of media studies therefore focus on democratizing the media sphere itself.[87] Others similarly highlight the importance of community, citizen, and alternative media to overall processes of informing and equipping people for collective decision making.[88] A maximalist approach to participation allows for the possibility that participatory actions will bring about change within political systems as well as in arrangements of power and resources.

In the United States, families and schools that embrace a maximalist approach to participation are in minority. In most families, a parent retains primary responsibility for supporting children financially and emotionally, and it is not until children are financially and emotionally independent that arrangements in power relations truly change. But in families as well as in schools and in other settings that aspire to maximalist participation, young people are encouraged to participate in family decision making, and such participation can result in dramatic changes to the ways in which families interact as family members, and the ways in which students participate in the life of their schools and beyond.[89]

We have observed this same approach in relation to news provided for and with youth. Some youth media programs presume that young people are passive audiences, or understand youthful expression as subjugated under the rights of school administration. In contrast, others envision youth as participants who co-create and distribute news, sometimes with the assistance and financial support of adults. These latter kinds of programs do not "empower" young people so much as they create a space for young people to identify a problem, explore how that problem is constituted in communication, and then provide resources that amplify practices of connective journalism that would otherwise reach only a very small number of peers. It is this amplification that we believe is an essential aspect of the news of the future. We therefore do not advocate that adults view the practices of connective journalism as somehow apart from the context of "adult" life, news, and citizenship, or as something that could survive as developed serendipitously among youthful populations. That kind of unplanned activity can be viewed instead as a first step. In order to truly involve youth in processes that link their concerns with the changing of policies that shape their lives, it is going to take resources and vision. Many youth media programs provide evidence of these kinds of hope-filled activities that can change youthful life trajectories, and they therefore deserve more attention among those who question the future of news and the role of young people, and participatory citizenship, in that future.

Satirical mock news programs and references to fictional narratives seem to lend themselves well to youthful connective journalism practices because young people are able to utilize the sharing of such items as a means of starting a conversation, illustrated by Marc's quote about news at the very beginning of this chapter. A key part of this conversation rests on the fact that sharing such items communicates something about the person who is doing the sharing. And, since the person receiving the communication indicates agreement with a "like," retweet, or snap, the item can play a role in reinforcing a shared sense of identity. To the extent that either the sharer or any of the recipients interpret the item through the lens of contemporary political concerns, the communicative act of sharing becomes proto-political because it is interpreted, and hence constructed in shared meaning, by those who participate in the communication. It is not easy to determine whether or not a particular proto-political connective journalism practice is part of a larger political process that leads to action – a subject to which we will return in the next two chapters.

CONCLUSION

As we argued in the previous chapter, young people who come from low-income and minoritized communities are exactly the people most in need of the kind of investigative journalism that reveals abuses of power that will affect their lives and the lives of their families, peers, and community members. When people take note of the fact that youth are not frequent news consumers, we argue that it's not that young people do not care about the issues reported, but rather that many seem to feel that most of the mainstream news sources available to them fail to live up to their expectations of what journalism should do, as was discussed in Chapter 3. However, this does not negate the fact that young people deserve to be informed about issues that affect their quality of life.

In this chapter we have argued that maximalist and minimalist participation occurs in how youth are situated in relation to the youth news ecology that surrounds them. Those news efforts produced by adults for youth have often begun from a minimalist participation perspective, focused on protecting youth and preparing them for adulthood in a way that echoes rather than questions the developmental approach to citizenship. These efforts have largely fallen out of favor, as financial models within the legacy media have rendered this approach unsustainable. But, as we have observed, although these efforts may have informed youth of relevant current events in genres that were meant to appeal to youth, they remained at best on the periphery for most young people. Much more familiar to youth were the satirical mock news efforts designed for a young adult rather than an early or mid-adolescent population. Because youth are only peripherally considered a part of this audience, to some extent, even the popular mock news programs largely end up positioning adolescent (and younger) people as outsiders who watch and share the shows. Only a small minority of youth actually create and share their own critiques, although such efforts open spaces enabling young people to envision a journalism with fewer ties to the journalistic authority that they tend to resist or question.

Some youth-oriented media efforts exist within a similarly protectionist and minimalist participatory framework, as school administrators and courts question student rights to free expression. Such a protectionist approach cannot be seen apart from the underfunding of schools that make it necessary for them to serve more frequently as places of containment than as places of encouragement, learning, and empowerment. Other youth media efforts have successfully experimented with a maximalist orientation to participation that is youth-centric and creates a space for young people to find their way into participation. However, as this chapter has pointed out, there is a need for much greater exploration of what maximalist participation for youth could mean.

With a focus on how structural forces enhance or impede youthful participation, we have also highlighted issues beyond the questions of what happens when youth encounter, create, or share news. We argue that if we, as a society, want to see greater engagement of young people in news and in the larger life of our society as engaged citizens, we need to examine the structures that shape and limit youthful life experiences. The future of news for youth is not only about encouraging youth. It is also about partnering with them in rethinking and reimaging a society that better assures human rights for all.

Therefore, in the next chapter, we will discuss how young people embrace connective journalism practices that move beyond simply sharing information within the youth news ecology, to inserting themselves directly into the stories that are unfolding around them. In recent years, with the rise of youth movements related to #BlackLivesMatter, LGBT rights, The DREAM Act, public transportation, or school funding, administration and standardized testing, youth have participated not only in sharing news, but in reshaping how we think of what news *is*, and how practices like witnessing events and expressing shared outrage factor into the evolution of connective journalism.

* * * * *

5

Connective Journalism and the Formation of Youthful Publics and Counterpublics

Inserting Oneself into the Story through Witnessing and Sharing Outrage

In March 2016, students at Ponderosa High School in Colorado staged a protest against what they believed was unusually high teacher turnover that they attributed to the poor educational policies of their school board. The students wanted to amplify their teachers' dissatisfaction after an independent evaluation had found that morale among teachers and staff had fallen and that there was little support for top-down reforms initiated by the district leadership.[1] But before the student protest took place, Grace Davis, the sixteen-year-old sophomore who organized the protest, was called into a ninety-minute private meeting with the Douglas County school board president and a school board member to talk. "I felt they were trying to scare me out of it," Davis later said. Davis recorded that conversation and shared it with her parents.[2] Then, a month later, she shared the recording with local news media, in advance of a board meeting in which Davis called for the board members' resignation, articulating her view that the school board members had bullied her. On the recording, one of the board members can indeed be heard telling Davis that "if things go sideways for some reason," at the protest, the responsibility could "land squarely on you or your parents' shoulders." The board members also asked if Davis was willing to bear the cost of police protection for the event if it was needed. Davis's parents noted that they sent the district a letter in which they accused the board members of "threatening and intimidating" their daughter.[3] This led to an internal investigation that ultimately found no wrongdoing on the part of the board members, although one of the board members resigned from her volunteer post as a Girl Scouts leader under pressure.[4] Community members who united under the hashtag "#IstandwithGrace" continued to call for the board members' resignation.[5] In a possibly unrelated move, within two months of the original protest and one month after the investigation was launched, the district superintendent left to head a smaller school district in a different state.[6] Perhaps this is why one of the area's local alternative weeklies began a story about these unfolding events with the lead, "We wouldn't advise messing with Grace Davis."[7]

Surely, not every high school student is interested in confronting her school board members about their policies. However, a small but significant number of students do have an interest in engaging in political action, as noted in the previous chapter. But what is it that motivates peers to join in with youthful leaders like Grace Davies? And what is the role of social media, and the practices of connective journalism, in providing either support for or discouragement from participating in such youthful forms of political action? Addressing these questions brings us to the subject of youthful publics and counterpublics.

In Chapter 4, we considered the youth news ecology that young people are immersed in. We noted that much of the news that youth gather and share originates from adult sources, and that while some of those sources include the journalism associated with "old" media such as television, print, or radio journalism, other sources, particularly those produced for a young adult audience, include satirical "mock news" television, YouTube videos, or celebrity advocates who share their views through social media sites. Even fictional narratives from books or movies can play a role in helping young people to formulate their views and their identifications with differing societal groups.

In this chapter, we want to consider what happens among political newcomers when young leaders like Grace Davies utilize social media to share their outrage and witnessing of injustice. We employ the concept of *connective journalism* introduced in the previous chapters to argue that connective sharing practices that take place among peers through social media like Snapchat, Twitter, Facebook, and Instagram can serve a catalytic function in this process of activating political newcomers. In fact, by utilizing social media to share with their peers what we will term *the artifacts of political engagement,* we argue that young people have effectively countered what has come to be known as "the spiral of silence," a phrase that refers to the tendency for people to remain silent when they believe that their own views differ from the dominant view.[8]

POLITICS, THE PUBLIC, AND SOCIAL MEDIA

Scholars theorizing about the public are often in conversation with those who write about what social theorist Jurgen Habermas termed "the public sphere."[9] The public sphere is understood as a space where people can share information and opinions in order to form a public will that influences political action. It is also understood as a space in which political officials are held accountable for political action. Habermas is recognized both for having created a story of how the journalism of modernity evolved into central importance in the maintenance of the public sphere, and for having articulated the norms of how journalistic efforts should therefore be judged according to whether or not they contribute to or detract from the life of the public. In Habermas's view, the purpose of journalism is to stimulate the conversations that need to happen so that people can form opinions, rationally debate their views, and then come to a consensus about what should be done. As Peter Dahlgren notes in a critique of the Habermasian approach to professional journalism, "This deliberative view gels neatly with traditional views on how citizenship should be enacted and how discussion should take place."[10] In other words, Habermas's idea of the public sphere rests on some of the same assumptions of developmental citizenship that we discussed in Chapter 1, in that it assumes citizens must somehow be "ready" to discuss and deliberate the issues that affect them.

Of course, not all members of society enjoy the same level of access to conventional public realms of decision making, as several of Habermas's critics subsequently pointed out.[11] In the United States, only white male landowners were initially granted the right to represent everyone else in political decision making. After the women's and African American suffrage movements extended voting rights to more diverse populations in the late nineteenth and early twentieth centuries, the legacy of historical inequities continued to structure life in the United States. Today, political power remains overwhelmingly in the hands of a white wealthy male elite.[12] Furthermore, people do not enter into the public sphere on equal footing in order to debate rationally, because the very ability to participate in deliberation is contingent upon a host of other factors that include education and access. Groups within society that traditionally have not had access to public decision making have therefore gathered in spaces far removed from mainstream media discourse and state-approved spaces in order to discuss and work toward their shared political interests.

Youth, in particular, have a complicated relationship with public spaces. As we noted in Chapter 1, there are two contradictory concerns at work in relation to youth in public spaces. First, there is a tendency for adults to worry that young people can be harmed in public spaces, as they are believed to be subject to "stranger danger." But second, young people gathered together in public spaces are also a cause for concern because they are perceived to threaten social order and create danger for others.[13] Another problem in relation to youth and public spaces was implied in the previous chapter: youth goals often require young people to interface with institutions that have been created and maintained by adults. Youth are not often invited to be participants in public life and do not feel welcomed if they attempt to insert themselves into discussions that adults think of as "political."

In response to Habermas's description of a singular public sphere, Nancy Fraser and others have argued that there are actually multiple publics and that marginalized or "subaltern" groups have created and become a part of *counterpublics* in response to the exclusionary politics of the dominant publics.[14] Chantal Mouffe's concept of "agonistic democracy" is relevant here, as she has pointed out that identities are formed through political struggle in what is inescapably a contentious political landscape comprised of heterogeneous populations and conflicting interests.[15] Rather than deliberation, Mouffe argues that what happens in public space is *embodied participation* that is an expression of political agency and that can emerge in contentious ways. Political change therefore occurs not only through deliberation but also through communicative action, as Dahlgren has pointed out:

Political innovation often builds on (or begins by) forming new publics, breaking up established modes of discourse, challenging prevailing perceptions of social reality, and formulating new issues and strategies that confront entrenched ideological positions. This involves a variety of communicative strategies, including rhetoric, irony, and aesthetic interventions.[16]

Dahlgren argues that these communicative actions place the emphasis on *performance* rather than *deliberation*, an important turn in recognizing that deliberative political discussion can quickly become arcane and uninteresting, whereas political performance can be spontaneous and emotionally engaging. A different way to describe entrance into public spaces, then, is in relation to embodied participation, and particularly in relation to counterpublics and social movements.

People do not "join" counterpublics so much as they are hailed into them by finding their own emotions and viewpoints validated by a collection of others. This hailing occurs in relation to texts and their circulation that, again, emphasize embodied political performance rather than deliberation, and that stand at some distance from the mainstream. Indeed, Michael Warner makes the key point that counterpublics exist not out of intentional creation on the part of would-be members, but by virtue of *being addressed*.[17] As people are able to recount their experiences and feel that those experiences are heard and matter in relation to public policy, they experience themselves as *actors* within those counterpublics, and they come to see counterpublics as the "nucleus for an alternate organization of society," in the words of John Downing and Natalie Fenton.[18]

Often, these experiences of action and voice occur primarily, or only, within diasporic public spaces, thus limiting the ability of those at some distance from dominant political subject positions to speak and be heard by larger publics.[19] But sometimes, given the right circumstances, grievances are so widely shared that they can come to challenge dominant discourses through communicative performance and help give birth to new social movements. The concepts of publics and counterpublics take "the political" beyond the realm of institutionalized contexts for political discussion and policymaking. They recognize that politics can emerge anywhere, independently of the formal political processes in which elites engage.[20]

Social media such as Facebook and Twitter have been found to enhance or enlarge counterpublics.[21] Dimitra Milioni suggests a site-based definition of online counterpublics, arguing that some sites can be identified by the fact that people visit those sites for information, self-determination, interactivity, and delocalized network (inter)action.[22] Dahlgren broadens his definition of online publics and counterpublics beyond single sites, suggesting that a public or counterpublic may be understood as "a constellation of communicative spaces in society that permit the circulation of information, ideas, and debates, ideally in an unfettered manner," where political *will* may be constituted.[23] It is this definition that we embrace here. Beyond websites, apps such as Snapchat can also become a part of this constellation, particularly because it is easier for newcomers to communicate their agreement with a smaller subset of people that they intentionally select for receipt of sensitive communications. Snapchat is therefore a site where micro-publics may form, providing a venue for sharing that is relatively protected yet can be a foundation for "hailing" individuals into larger counterpublics, as we discuss below.[24]

COUNTERPUBLICS AND AFFECTIVE PUBLICS

Social media, as Zizi Papacharissi has argued, provide new locations through which people can express themselves and participate in what she terms the "soft structures of feeling" that help people feel that their views matter and are worthy of expression in a particular moment.[25] "Affective publics," as Papacharissi terms them, are "networked public formations that are mobilized and connected or disconnected through expressions of sentiment."[26] First, as she notes, we *feel* like we're a part of the developing story, and then, as we contribute our own emotive declarations online through our words, photos, and videos on Twitter, Facebook, or in other social media venues, we *become* a part of the story.[27] Her explanation of affective publics shares some common ground with our description of counterpublics, although it also may differ in some ways, as we will discuss. Nevertheless, Papacharissi brings current debates about social media's ability to facilitate emotional feelings of belonging into the realm of debates about political engagement. This is an important intervention at a time when scholars such as Warner, Mouffe, and Fraser have been challenging the deeply rooted assumptions of deliberation and reason that inform the idealized Habermasian public sphere, and fleshes out the role of affect, or the potential for emotional response, in the formation of publics and counterpublics.

In many ways, Papacharissi's work shares common ground with Bennett and Segerberg's argument that social media have brought about what they term *connective action*, referring to the ways that networked communication enables individuals to personalize expressions of a movement's goals outside of the bounds of traditional social movement organizations, as discussed in Chapter 2. But while Bennett and Segerberg wish to contribute a new means of understanding this Internet-assisted phenomenon of political organization, Papacharissi is particularly interested in bringing theories of affect into the conversations about how people come to "feel their way into politics."[28] Her work therefore provides an important foundation for what we have introduced here as the practices of *connective journalism*, particularly those that are emotionally fraught, such as the witnessing and sharing outrage.

One of the analytical challenges to both the concept of affective publics and to connective journalism involves parsing out the relationships between publics, counterpublics, social movements, and the role of affect in each of these. In order to clarify these relationships, we might begin by considering the affect that was central to the following frequently retweeted dispatch initially composed and shared by a young adult during the contentious U.S. political primary season of spring 2016:

> *"Every time Bernie and Hillary fans start fighting it's like my parents are getting divorced all over again and Hitler might be my new stepdad"*
> – @Kaylaris, posted on Twitter March 14, 2016; Retweeted more than 5,000 times by summer 2016.

By the spring of 2016, the campaign of Bernie Sanders had not only gained momentum but had also begun to offer unflattering critiques of his adversary for the Democratic nomination, the by-then presumed Democratic candidate Hillary Clinton. Young people were overwhelmingly supportive of Bernie Sanders, with Clinton garnering lukewarm support in spite of her historic role as the first female nominee to the U.S. presidency. Young people were also overwhelmingly opposed to Trump's candidacy, and like many of their older counterparts, dismayed by what they believed that the extent of his support said about the limits of tolerance and acceptance in US society.[29] By some estimates, more than half of those under eighteen in the United States have experienced the divorce of their parents, making the emotions of this tweet immediately recognizable and humorous for the way it connects familial and political feelings.[30] Such messages are imminently shareable as they are expressive of the feelings of many. One could argue that this particular tweet played a role in the constitution of a counterpublic whose members recognized themselves as alienated from all politics. However, as the results of the election proved, the dismay and frustration expressed in this tweet represented a *dominant* rather than a counter-narrative of political alienation in the United States, especially among young people, who could have elected Hillary Clinton by a landslide if more young citizens had felt inspired to vote.[31] The tweet is certainly less expressive of outrage at the overall political system than the following tweet, circulated widely as #BlackLivesMatter was cohering into a widespread social movement:

> *"Whites torch cop cars and destroy property after baseball games: rowdy. Blacks torch cop cars and destroy property after cops get away with murder: savages."*
> – Observation attributed to a comment in worldstarhiphop.com and circulated via blogs, tweets, Tumblrs, and Instagram, December 5, 2014.

The first tweet is an example of how affective publics might coalesce around common emotional experiences of frustration with contemporary politics and may invite young people to "feel their way into politics," as Papacharissi has noted. But the second tweet also invites young people to see themselves as part of an emergent counterpublic, and, in turn, a social movement that is rooted in a critique of the way things are. The second tweet thus engenders both affect and solidarity in a way that can then play a role not only in mobilizing people to act within a political system, but to question that political system altogether. That questioning is key to the formation of a counterpublic and, in turn, to the formation of a social movement. The fact that both tweets were retweeted thousands of times among young people provides evidence that youth were ripe for participation in the practices of connective journalism, in which young people pass along emotion-laden messages that express something of themselves and their views about what is wrong with the world. We propose that it may be helpful to further differentiate between affective publics and counterpublics in our theorizing of connective journalism. With the contemporary junction of politics, journalism, emotion, and social media, perhaps all publics constituted through communication are now affective publics.

But, we have observed that practices of connective journalism hinge on the role of emotion in suturing people into a collective identity. Such practices can have the potential for political engagement, but may also be expressions of commonly held emotions that are conjured in relation to the events or occurrences of the moment. What a study of connective journalism practices can do is to draw attention to a continuum of communicative action so that we can better understand how people might actually move from first considering whether or not to express themselves, to the point at which they share meaningful stories, and finally to a point at which they are willing to involve themselves in the more arduous work of actual political agitation or policymaking. Scholars in social movement theory have explored how people migrate from the sidelines into a recognition of themselves as hailed into a counterpublic and then perhaps into participation in transformative action, noting that this progression often takes place much more slowly, more ponderously, and much less thrillingly than we might wish.[32] It is this process of moving from observer to newcomer in political participation, and the role of social media in this process, that we now wish to explore further.

CASE STUDIES: COUNTERPUBLICS AND
SOCIAL MEDIA IN #BLACKLIVESMATTER AND
NO EASTIE CASINO

The above discussion of affective publics, counterpublics, and social movements offers an important foundation for understanding the roles that social media spaces can play, illustrated when we observed young people engaging in the national social movement #BlackLivesMatter, and in a local movement that emerged in Boston's "Eastie" neighborhood. Unfortunately, none of the students with whom we interacted explored any of the open source information sharing projects and platforms such as Ushahidi or Freenet that have been utilized by adult protesters who are more seasoned in political action.[33] Rather, they relied on ubiquitous commercial tools that are easily accessible: social media platforms such as Snapchat, Twitter, Facebook, Tumblr, and Instagram. These tools share certain characteristics: they are easily accessed through smartphones, laptops, or tablets; they allow for instantaneous and real-time postings that can consist of quick reports, shared photos, or short replies; and they offer users a way to measure their own status by considering the number of followers, friends, retweets, comments, and @replies they receive.[34] But, they are also distinct from each other in certain ways. Facebook serves as a "social lubricant" that allows people to broadcast life occurrences and to seek support or useful information. Twitter encourages playful performances and creative improvisation within its 140-character limit and also allows for instant validation of the quality of one's public contribution. Snapchat allows users to communicate with a select group of recipients, to control how long those recipients have access to the message that a user sends, and to learn instantly whether or not the recipient has opened the "snap." It is therefore less public than other social network sites and also more likely to garner an immediate response because of its time limit. The processes of connectivity facilitated across social media sites create opportunities for differing kinds and levels of identification, belonging, and support that energize collective resistance to oppressive power, illustrated in the cases we consider here.[35] We begin with a discussion of the early days in the formation of the #BlackLivesMatter counterpublic.

In August 2014, an unarmed African American teenager named Michael Brown was shot to death by a Ferguson, Missouri, police officer, leading to widespread expressions of public outrage and protests in the streets of many US cities. As protests continued, some observers speculated that this was the beginning of a new social movement decrying not only racial bias in law enforcement, but also the wider social and economic system that disadvantages young people of color in the United States.[36] Online conversations and live protests were initially reported on as if they had erupted suddenly and spontaneously on social media.[37] But what was articulated in social media spaces aligned with the African American community's long-standing rage about injustices in relation to the treatment of blacks by members of law enforcement. Conversations about #BlackLivesMatter later birthed a countermovement of sorts with the introduction of the phrase #AllLivesMatter, and later #BlueLivesMatter, each of which were meant to counter the narrative of the #BlackLivesMatter counterpublic and reinforce the dominant arrangements of power and authority as appropriately left in the hands of a police force presumed to be accountable to their communities and deserving of respect. As the discourse became strained, fewer and fewer people felt themselves to be completely outside of these positions, which is what it means to be hailed into the emergent counterpublic or into the dominant view of the public. Even as some sought to move forward a dialogue, these competing positions were in need of negotiation and shaped all spaces for public conversation into potentially fraught contested spaces, as we will discuss.

In our ethnographic study, we observed that although many young people of color did seek out information from the mainstream news media, these networked youth also experienced identification with others as they came across information and expressions on social media that echoed their own conflicted feelings about law enforcement. Many of the students of color with whom we interacted found that their feelings and experiences of injustice in relation to law enforcement were validated through the emotional expressions about #BlackLivesMatter that they read and viewed on Snapchat, Twitter, Facebook, and in other social media.[38] But it wasn't until they felt compelled to take a stand (or not) that they were truly hailed into the #BlackLivesMatter counterpublic and had to make a choice about whether or not to be a part of a nascent social movement.

In her analysis of multiple publics and counterpublics, Catherine Squires has noted that there is a key distinction between groups engaged in "idle talk" and those that have the potential to *act* as counterpublics, noting that what she terms a Black public sphere must offer space for the critique of the dominant order and must also enable participants to engage in action that can challenge and change that order.[39] She proposes a definition of a Black public as "an emergent collective composed of people who a) engage in common discourses and negotiations of what it means to be Black, and b) pursue particularly defined Black interests."[40] She notes that this definition allows for heterogeneity and also allows for coalitions, including those who do not self-identify as Black but who identify with similar issues.

According to the Pew Research Center, 73 percent of African American Internet users participate in social media, and nearly one quarter of African Americans online utilize Twitter.[41] The Internet, as Andre Brock has argued, "maintains Western culture through its content and often embodies Western ideology through its design and practices," and is therefore not "value-neutral" but rather mediates racial and cultural identity.[42] This has led to the emergence of what some have termed "Black Twitter," which Brock identifies as the "mediated articulations of a Black subculture."[43] Black Twitter thus becomes a space for what Henry Louis Gates terms "signifyin,'" which is the articulation of a shared worldview expressed through references to Black culture and Black idioms.[44] According to Brock, Black Twitter calls into question the whiteness of online public space, as it disrupts the way in which White experiences are taken as normal and invisible, whereas racialized populations are visibly marginalized. Black Twitter is not a counterpublic, but is rather a space in which counterpublics may form as people find and follow one another, engage in discussions about the meanings of Blackness, and discuss strategies for engaging in political action that arises from those meanings.

Hashtag memes, snaps, Twitter @replies, and retweets flourish among densely connected clusters of people, as is the case among young Black social media users.[45] From August 2014 onward, key voices on Ferguson[46] emerged in Twitter and other social network spaces. Some of these emergent leaders, like Ta-Nehisi Coates, were also affiliated with traditional media outlets like *The Atlantic Monthly*. Others, such as Ashley Yates, Tory Russell, Johnetta Elzie, and Deray McKesson, along with organizations such as the Ferguson Response Network and Millennial Activists United were active on Twitter and elsewhere and came to be identified as activists by the mainstream media after assuming organizational roles in the protests and responses.

But even with the emergence of Black Twitter, young people from historically underrepresented communities do not experience themselves as members of a singular community, nor do they uniformly choose to follow or interact online with elites or those who have emerged as political leaders. This is, in part, because political activism is understood among youth in these communities in ways that differ from their more

privileged middle class counterparts, and schooling shapes these differences in profound ways. In the United States, privilege is correlated with
higher parental educational levels and better schools, both of which are
predictors of participation in political activism.[47] In privileged communities, schools may be understood as locations where young people are
encouraged to draw connections between civic engagement and personal empowerment.[48] In contrast, as we noted in the previous chapter,
young people from what Sandrina deFinney and colleagues refer to as
"minoritized" backgrounds are more likely to attend high schools that
are underfunded and undersupported.[49] These schools are more likely
to espouse minimalist forms of youth participation, where students are
expected to follow orders and not question authority. At the same time,
students in such schools are aware of the negative judgments rendered
against their schools by outsiders, and many believe that the quality of
their education suffers due to discriminatory practices and policies that
shape their school experiences. Rather than viewing the school setting
as a place for empowerment, they may experience it as an extension of
a national discourse that emphasizes the containment of youth and the
embedding of young minoritized "Others" into racialized constructs that
privilege whiteness.[50] It is from these points of departure that minoritized
young people express skepticism about participation in large-scale collective action and do not necessarily see themselves as part of what they
perceive to be a "White" public.

Our research indicates that online social networks can function as
spaces for the formation of counterpublics and, in the following, we discuss two examples to illustrate how young people navigate those spaces
as they encounter and consider political participation in relation to an
unfolding political movement.

THE DIGITAL MEDIA CLUB AND FERGUSON
PROTESTS AMONG HIGH SCHOOL STUDENTS

As part of a larger ethnographic project exploring how minoritized young
people become engaged in utilizing media to make a difference in their
communities, Lynn and colleagues in Denver, Colorado, created a context
in which such youth would have an opportunity to work together within
a process that involved, first, a critical examination of our places in and
the relationship of media systems to existing hierarchies of power, and
second, a consideration of how various media might be used to organize
for social change. They led an after-school group called the Digital Media

Club in one of Denver's most culturally diverse high schools. Discussions in the weekly interactions included one-on-one consultations as well as group conversations. Students discussed how social media had played a role in the ways they and their peers had learned about and shared views regarding events related to both Ferguson and to local law enforcement.

During the weeks following the Ferguson grand jury decision, the youth in this after-school group reported that they, along with most of the students they knew, first learned about the protests happening around the country from face-to-face communication with friends, peers, family members, or teachers. Students then encountered news about the protests secondarily through Facebook. Consistent with what is already known about social network sites, the students said that many more young people had read about than had posted about the happenings.

Students reported that many of their peers had chosen to engage in online discussion about the protests in a somewhat tentative way, viewing a Tumblr, tweet, comment, or photo and then tagging or @tweeting a friend or family member they knew to be sympathetic with the views of the protesters, thereby identifying themselves as supportive to someone else they believed to be equally supportive. Others chose to "like" or "favorite" a message they encountered on someone else's feed, thereby leaving a more public declaration of how their views comported with those of the protesters.

Even more courageous students chose to repost, retweet, or otherwise share a curated message more broadly through their own Facebook, Twitter, Tumblr, or Instagram feeds, either with or without commentary. The students reported that a few young people they knew had gone so far as to create their own Tumblr on the issue. When students engaged in the reposting of curated content, they risked receiving negative comments or feedback from those in their social networks who disagreed with them. Responses could take the form of "microaggressions."[51] Sometimes, these curated reposts, retweets, or shares were effectively silenced after receiving negative comments. One student who re-posted a curated message supportive of the Ferguson protesters noted that while some peers "liked" his post, another peer enacted a form of microaggression by tagging him without comment in a post that denigrated the protesters. The student who'd been tagged felt embarrassed, but also seemed to believe that by publicly voicing support through his Facebook page, he was "taking a stand." Even questions about safety were interpreted as potential microaggressions meant to express a difference of opinion about unfolding events. One student noted, "I got a lot of texts from family members and friends asking if I was safe, but who's asking if the black men who live in this city are safe every day?" Students who chose to express opinions about the protests and walkouts occurring at various schools experienced themselves as entering contested social spaces.

News of the non-indictment of police officers in the Michael Brown and Eric Garner cases had occurred when students were out of school during the US Thanksgiving holiday. On the second day back in school, the city's largest urban high school staged a walkout. One news report, giving voice to the dominant frame of police as public servants who protect all members of the community equally, quoted a member of the police union who labeled the walkouts "unlawful," complaining that they cost taxpayers money and restricted the police's ability to pay attention to other issues as they were charged with keeping students protected during their walkouts.[52]

The following day, three other urban high schools joined in staging walkouts. On that day, conversations about Ferguson and about the protests in the urban high school where the digital media club was located were tense. Students interviewed seemed to feel that the majority of students in their school were listening rather than commenting on the protest activities and tensions at other schools. As a group, the students in the after-school program that day were reticent and tentative. Whereas many teachers had offered general support for participation in the walkouts, only a few teachers discussed the protests in the class. The students said that these few teachers attempted to place the frustration and rage behind the protests in a larger historical context, noting that many in the African American community did not feel that the police were there to protect them and the courts were not, either. One student in the club volunteered that maybe this was because of the US legacy of slavery, noting that the law during that time was used against the interests of minority communities to protect the interests of slaveowners rather than slaves. All of the students in our after school club recognized the contentiousness of the issues involved and were reluctant to enter into the contested public spaces of online discussion about the unfolding events. One student noted her reluctance about participating in discussions about the Ferguson protests because, as she said, in "heated situations," people can become "targets" for the aggression of others, and she didn't want to put herself in a position of becoming such a target.

Later on, however, the same student reported excitedly that she had just received a text from another student about the possibility that her school would be organizing a walkout. Her enthusiasm was palpable as she frantically texted others in her social circles, seeking more information about where and when the walkout would take place and then reporting to others in the room on what she was learning: "they're trying to decide if it's going to be tomorrow or the next day," she said to no one in particular. But this interaction, witnessed by the other students, changed the tone of the discussion from a conversation about what others had done, to what this particular group of students might or might not do. Seated in one of the school's computer labs, students quickly found official and alternative news images online of students at neighboring schools who had participated in a walkout that day, sharing and discussing them with one another. When an adult mentor then asked another student whether or not she would attend her own school's walkout if, indeed, it were to take place, the student was hesitant. Her parents would not want her to miss school, she said. Another volunteered to say that he had heard that the walkouts at one school had led to a disciplinary lockdown, in which no one was allowed to leave the school building. That student did not want his school to receive a "bad reputation" and was concerned that participation in a walkout during the school day might cause that. Finally, several students noted that they did not think that they understood all the facts related to the protest. "What if someone asks me what I'm protesting for and I can't really explain it?," one wondered, giving this as a reason for hesitation in participating.

However, by the next day, many more students had received word of the possibility of a walkout through in-person and text conversations. A student organizer had set up a Facebook event page that quickly circulated throughout the student body. Another organizer stopped in to the school's front office to discuss the protest with the high school administration who, in turn, alerted local law enforcement and parents: their school was going to stage a walkout in solidarity with the other protesters. Together, student organizers and teachers decided on a plan to walk around the nearby park, hold a rally, and then return to classes.

On the day of the scheduled protest, students from that high school held handmade signs reading, "Respect," and chanted, "Hands up, don't shoot," using the mantra associated in the media with Michael Brown's arrest. They shared photos with their friends primarily through Snapchat. But during the protest, the group split, with some students following the original plan to walk and then rally at the school while others elected to walk downtown to the grounds of their rival high school, where the first local school protests had taken place. Much to the chagrin of the student organizers and school administrators, the rogue student protesters shut down a major thoroughfare, snarling traffic for more than an hour. Some reportedly shouted profanities. They were all eventually bussed back to their school.

"Come back!" students who had remained with the protest organizers had texted their friends. Many sent snaps with photos so that those who had begun the trek downtown would realize that not all students were heading downtown. These instantaneous communications were important during the chaos of the moment, as the school's principal used a bull horn to try to stop the impromptu rogue protesters and as the protest's organizers continued back toward the school. Students also texted and exchanged snaps with their friends at the rival school downtown, alerting them that some had chosen to take the protest to their school grounds. That school went on lockdown, and students in the school texted and exchanged snaps with friends they saw outside, reportedly telling them to go back to their own school. The split colored the experience for many and became central to the narrative students later told about their involvement in this protest activity. Perhaps it is ironic that in the midst of all of the personalized communication through various social media, students later articulated the problem as a lack of centralized communication.

Still, many students saw the participation in the protests as valuable. One student at another school expressed to a journalist the feeling that seemed to be experienced by many of those engaged in the walkouts. Responding to some of the criticisms he and others had heard about the walkouts, he noted, "Some people were like, why is walking out of school even going to help anything? To me it was like, we're students, and this is what we can do. A grievous injustice took place in our nation and it's continuing to take place!" And then, this student noted the emotional significance he felt in recording the event as it was happening: "As I was filming, I was getting a shot of everyone's feet coming down, and I just got goosebumps."[53]

ARTIFACTS OF ENGAGEMENT

Why was it that this particular student had "goosebumps" when filming the activities of his school's walkout? A great deal of research has already focused on the fact that being involved in the action through protesting, as well as by photographing and texting about it, enhances a person's sense of emotional identification with a movement and its aims.[54] But what was especially of interest in this case was what happened when those on the margins of political action, including students who had been unsure about the walkouts, encountered firsthand evidence of others in their peer networks who had decided to walk out. It is worth focusing not on the smaller numbers of creators and circulators of most of the protest's video or texts, but on the larger numbers of recipients and viewers of that material.

Not all of the students in the Digital Media Club after-school program decided to join the walkout as soon as they learned that others their age had been similarly involved, and many expressed hesitation even when they learned that those in their peer networks were going to participate. But, the conversation noticeably shifted as they encountered more and more images, texts, and other forms of evidence of how people they knew were becoming involved in these activities. It became difficult for them to remain indifferent to or isolated from the protests and the many discussions that took place about them.

The *recording* of these activities through video, photos, and messages, thus, had a particular salience, not just for those who created and shared, but also for those participants at the margins who viewed themselves at a greater distance from the core of the movement's activities. The comments, photos, videos, and stories were no longer simply the stories of unknown individuals. As they became artifacts shared online, these stories spoke of a form of political action with recognizable actors in the narrative. These *artifacts* provided evidence of their peers' *engagement,* not only in political activities like the walkout, but in the act of sharing stories about their engagement with a wider audience. The sharing, for which we have coined the term *artifacts of engagement* – comments, photos, videos, tweets, and news stories that were found or created and then passed along largely via Snapchat, Facebook, and Twitter, as well as through texts – may not have been on the same order as other political activities, but they provided an avenue into what Dahlgren calls the "proto-political," or the important step whereby young people come to be aware of the collective limits of their situation and the possibility that things could be different as a result of their own involvement in the action at hand.[55] The artifacts of engagement that peers and others created and shared sutured young people into emergent counterpublics coalescing around the perceived injustices in Ferguson and elsewhere. These artifacts thus became part of a non-linear chain of causality that contributed to the ways in which the less-involved students came to see participation as not just something that *others* did, but as something in which they themselves might also engage. Artifacts of engagement thus functioned as personalized expressions of a collective counterpublic that propelled people toward connective action.

NO EASTIE CASINO:
A COUNTERPUBLIC WINS THE DAY

We witnessed other examples of young people gradually moving from being onlookers, to sympathizers, to actors in politically contentious movements. In her fieldwork in the largely Latino neighborhood of East Boston, Massachusetts, Regina conducted periodic ethnographic research from 2007 to 2015 to explore how low-income young people of color learned about and responded to political events happening locally in their communities, as well as citywide, nationally, and globally. During the months while she was conducting one-on-one interviews and observations with young people aged fourteen to twenty-one at a local youth center, an alternative high school program, and a community radio station, she had an unexpected opportunity to observe and speak to minoritized youth who were teenagers or, in some cases, in their early twenties, while the No Eastie Casino movement, an initiative to prevent the construction of an enormous gambling complex in East Boston, emerged and grew in 2013.

Suffolk Downs racetrack was an early favorite to win voter approval of its $1 billion casino proposal. It outspent opponents nearly 50 to 1 – $2 million versus $40,000. But the long-shot opponents, a coalition of churches and grassroots community organizations, rallied for a come-from-behind victory, defeating the proposal.
    – WBUR, Boston, National Public Radio, November 6, 2013[56]

No Eastie Casino was a multi-racial coalition of residents from East Boston, Massachusetts, spanning the age spectrum from teenagers to octogenarians. But, it is the involvement of Latino young people, who are nationally among the *most* avid users of social networks, that is highlighted in this section.[57] Early in 2013, the Las Vegas company, Caesar's Entertainment Corporation, proposed the construction of one of the largest casino complexes in the Western Hemisphere, a billion dollar project with two towering hotels, numerous chain restaurants, retail shops, and other entertainment facilities, to be built in the working class residential neighborhood of East Boston (known citywide as "Eastie"). The casino was to be situated on 163 acres of East Boston's famed Suffolk Downs, once New England's grandest thoroughbred horse racing track, which was planning to close due to the dwindling popularity of live horse racing. The neighborhood of East Boston – a community of 40,000 residents over 50 percent of whom are Latino, making it Boston's largest Latino community – is one of the most heavily populated areas of the city, with a high density of schools, significant levels of poverty, and the city's highest per capita percentage of children. The casino's proponents touted the anticipated creation of thousands of construction and service industry jobs and claimed that the casino project would generate more than $32 million of annual tax revenue for the city. Meanwhile, East Boston parents, teachers, youth groups, churches, and community-based organizations were against the casino, alarmed that an industry known to increase gambling addiction and poverty among low-income individuals and correlated across the United States with increased alcoholism, depression, and crime in communities abutting casinos was being hailed as "positive development." However, community opponents faced powerful adversaries, including then Mayor of Boston, Thomas Menino and Massachusetts Speaker of the House, Robert DeLeo, most other elected city and state officials, all of the local labor unions, and the big business community who collectively spent more than $2 million to promote a "Yes" vote in the public referendum scheduled for November 5, 2013. According to all of the mainstream news reports, the casino proposal was considered a fait accompli.

With transportation analysts predicting an increase of 25,000 cars per day on East Boston roads if the casino were built, Eastie residents were concerned by anticipated traffic and health impacts on their already congested local streets. Also of great concern were national studies indicating that when casinos were constructed next to residential communities, levels of addiction-related crime, particularly car theft and home burglaries, rose significantly in abutting neighborhoods. The vast majority of casino opponents were low-income and working class residents, many of whom lacked high school or college levels of education and none of whom had political clout. East Boston is predominantly comprised of immigrants or the children of immigrants from Italy, Latin America, South-East Asia, and the Middle East, and many adult immigrants did not speak or write English fluently. However, their children did, and the young people's bilingual skills, together with their social media connectivity, proved to be key in turning the tables in this David versus Goliath battle.

What the mainstream media and powerful politicians didn't see was the communication occurring under the radar across racial, ethnic, and religious lines. Organized through word of mouth and via social media, the multi-racial, multi-lingual interfaith No Eastie Casino coalition was formed to discuss the anticipated impacts of a casino on the neighborhood, along with strategies to oppose it. Comprised of members of the community's Catholic, mainline, and Evangelical Protestant churches, its Buddhist temple and its Muslim community, together with local civic and activist groups, the coalition brought together residents who may not otherwise have closely interacted. Many young people learned about the casino issue from their parents, teachers, youth workers, or religious leaders, and many others learned about it via social media contact with those who were actively involved. While people over forty years old focused on making phone calls, pamphleting, and going door knocking to spread the word house by house, people in their teens, twenties, and thirties utilized Facebook and Twitter to promote and support these efforts. User generated videos of community meetings and protest marches were posted on YouTube and Facebook and it became popular among young people to substitute their Facebook profile photo with the "No Eastie Casino" logo, making this issue the first thing fellow Facebookers would see on their Facebook page. Some of the high school and college-aged youth involved were affiliated with a local non-profit youth arts center that had run a youth-led community radio station and an after-school radio journalism program for nearly a decade. The site of much of Regina's research, these programs had taught young people in the area how to tell their stories on the radio and via blogging. While a small percentage of youth were actively creating radio stories, blogging and tweeting about the anti-casino organizing efforts and protests, a much larger number of their peers followed them as protest actions unfolded on Twitter and Facebook, including calls for volunteers to phone bank, pamphlet, attend marches, and do language translation work. It became popular for Facebookers to "like" the No Eastie Casino webpage along with related posts from friends, and the social media presence of the protest encouraged other young people to feel connected, attracting more volunteers and supporters.

Like many of the local youth organization's alumni, twenty-year old Raz, who had participated as a high school student in the after-school youth journalism program and radio station, stayed connected to friends and staff via the youth organization's Facebook page, even when he went away to college. When a Facebook friend of his posted a link to the "No

Eastie Casino" webpage, Raz liked it. "You can like a page or not," he explained. "You can go on a page without liking it and you can see all kinds of strong opinions that can influence you one way or another." Recognizing the risk inherent in taking a stand, he said: "Once you like a page you're bombarded with things" (posts and comments from other people who may be hostile or supportive). Nonetheless, he felt it was important to support his friends and family in Eastie. Gabriela, aged eighteen, described how her priest spoke against the casino during Sunday mass at the Most Holy Redeemer Church, the largest Catholic church in East Boston with a Latino population of more than 2,000 attendees each Sunday. She noted that her parish was active in organizing an anti-casino protest that took place directly after mass one Sunday. "People walked out of church and joined the protesters who were waiting outside, handing out signs. My parents and I walked with the marchers for a while." Yet, Gabriela didn't immediately mention the protest on her Facebook page until she later saw a link on a friend's page to a YouTube video of the march. On seeing the YouTube video, which was filmed and posted on YouTube by a Latino No Eastie Casino coalition organizer that she personally knew and admired, Gabriela realized more fully the importance of the march and felt more comfortable claiming participation in it. "When I saw us all marching in the video, it made me feel kinda proud. Like, I couldn't believe how many people were marching." At that point, she also posted the YouTube link on her Facebook page and began to follow the issue more closely on Facebook and Twitter, garnering additional "likes" and followers. As in the Ferguson example, these Facebook posts, tweets, and YouTube videos were artifacts of political engagement that helped young people like Raz and Gabriela connect with a sense of collective identity, shared community grievances, and willingness to take a stand.

On the night before the November 5, 2013, referendum, most mainstream news media were confidently predicting a win for casino advocates. The *Boston Globe* referred to the anticipated voting results as a "lock," while one of the city's most prominent politicians stated publicly that the casino was a "slam dunk" and "unstoppable." To everyone's great surprise, however, there was a *landslide* vote against the casino.[58] A community of immigrants and other low-income people, who mainstream political operatives did not consider a threat because of their "low" (i.e. marginalized from the mainstream) status, succeeded in developing a counterpublic and exerting political agency in a stunning upset of dominant political forces. Election pollsters, political pundits, and the mainstream media drastically underestimated the impact that online *connectivity*, coupled with old-fashioned grassroots organizing, could have.

In both cases discussed here, it was young people's anger and passionate feelings of perceived injustice against their communities that motivated them to express support for the Ferguson and casino protesters, respectively. Communication about political action within social network sites has become an important "open channel" associated with the mobilization of newcomers, particularly in locations where civic infrastructures are weak.[59] As the young people we observed shared their artifacts of engagement on social networks, their activities and perspectives became visible to other members of their communities who might not otherwise consider such actions to be appropriate for their group. This is important, as we know that strong collective identities, as well as strongly felt shared grievances, can play a central role in mobilizing members of one's extended social networks to consider political participation for the first time.[60] Knowing that others in one's social circle are expressing their concern through action is a strong predictor of future participation.[61] This makes *artifacts of engagement* that signal a possible connection to an emergent social movement something worthy of further investigation as we strive to understand the role of social media in fostering connective action. It also reveals the significance of more immediate and less public forms of communication that are a part of Snapchat, as we found that young people at the margins who may have been reluctant to voice either support or opposition on Facebook or Twitter found the participation barriers to be much lower in communication among a select circle. Through Snapchat, youth could express their views or call on their peers to act, thus signaling their membership in a nascent counterpublic in a less public yet still social setting that demanded attention and response.

RETHINKING THE SPIRAL OF SILENCE IN
THE DIGITAL AGE

"Spiral of silence" is a theory of public opinion formation that posits that people are silent when they fear that the group of which they are (or aspire to be) a part, will isolate or shame them when it's learned that the individual's views diverge from those of the group. The spiral is further narrowed as people fear that these social practices of isolation or shaming could result in material consequences, such as the loss of a job or of status within the group.[62] Noelle-Neumann has argued that the "mass media" of her day – what today is called the "legacy media" of television and radio broadcasting and print journalism – play a prominent role in promoting self-censorship, as the media reinforce certain views as acceptable and dominant while others are framed as marginal or aberrant. Dietrich Scheuferle, who observed that the spiral of silence works in relation to issues with a moral or value-laden component, noted that "it is the *perception* of opinion distribution rather than the real opinion climate that shapes people's willingness to express their opinions in public."[63]

With new media, scholars have reexamined the spiral of silence theory. Some, such as Shirley Ho, have posited that because people can retain greater anonymity online, it may be that those holding minority opinions are more likely to speak out.[64] And indeed, some have found that the affordances of social media act as a counterweight to the spiral of silence. In her study of LGBT communities living in rural areas, for instance, Mary Gray found that social media provides LGBT persons with the means to communicate with those who share common experiences, providing a form of solidarity and sense of critical mass that is often elusive in less populated rural areas.[65]

Yet while this may be true in forums related to health or other issues that bring together people who do not know one another, other scholars have noted that social media sites may actually encourage self-censorship, in that they invite people to speak to large and disparate groups of people with whom they are acquainted. Pew Research Center's Internet and American Life Project found this to be true in their study of why people are reluctant to post political views on Facebook. Their study found that 86 percent of Americans were willing to have an in-person conversation about whether or not they believed that Edward Snowden, the National Security Agency (NSA) contractor who leaked massive data files revealing the breadth of the US surveillance system, was justified in his actions. However, only 42 percent were willing to post about it on Facebook or Twitter. And, consistent with the spiral of silence theory, Pew researchers found that in both personal and online settings, people were more willing to talk about their views if they believed that their audience agreed with them.[66]

Nevertheless, there is a "root for the winning team" phenomenon that takes place in relation to political involvement.[67] And, indeed, when young people in this study encountered evidence that others agreed with their stances or actions, they became more willing to consider greater involvement themselves. However, digital activism, like activism occurring in the streets, is not without costs.[68] Youth were aware that the open-ended nature of platforms such as Twitter and Facebook meant that they were more likely to encounter resistance when they expressed views or engaged in actions related to contentious politics.

This chapter has argued that as students encountered evidence through social media of how their peers and others in their communities participated in political dissent, they may have been able to overcome fears and find the courage to participate themselves as members of counterpublics. Students in this study utilized different social media platforms for different actions. They used Facebook groups to organize and talk about protest events, Twitter to send messages to their followers about their activities, and Snapchat when events were immediately unfolding, particularly if they wanted to target a select group of people. However, once the protest events passed, conversations returned primarily to the sharing of broader commentary through Twitter, Instagram, and Facebook. The affordances of differing platforms combined with the political and cultural contexts to shape how students negotiated their desire or reluctance to participate in the unfolding political action.

By exploring participants at the political margins and their relationships with other communities and networks outside the realm of a particular political action, we seek to broaden thinking about the ways in which political awareness may transform into political action, and how we might conceptualize the role of social media and specifically the practices of connective journalism in this process. Our findings confound prior theories that presumed that casual online and largely observation-only participation might be dismissed as merely a form of "slactivism." In contrast, we suggest that such casual observation may serve an important role as a form of early participation that is made possible through digitally networked communication. In other words, even participation at the margins and its representation in social media matters; it just may matter to different groups, and on a different time frame, than prior theories have invited us to pay attention to.

* * * * *

6

Youth Citizen Journalism

The Connective Journalism Practices of
Participation and Making the Story

You mean what we did – researching, writing it up, and telling the story to get people to recognize what is wrong with our public bus system – THAT's investigative journalism? Then I want to do more of that!
– *Amran, sixteen-year-old Somali American from Colorado*

When the 2015 film *Spotlight* won the Academy Award for Best Picture and Best Original Screenplay, it reinvigorated the public's interest in the role of investigative journalism in uncovering corruption. The film depicted a team of reporters at the *Boston Globe* working through reams of research to reveal the systemic patterns of child sex abuse and coverup among the Boston area Roman Catholic priests and hierarchy, and it did this while drawing its audiences into an emotional tale of the search for the truth. Josh Singer, co-writer of the script with the film's director Tom McCarthy, said that he wanted to "tell the story accurately while showing the power of the newsroom – something that's largely disappeared today. This story is important. Journalism is important."[1]

Even with the popularity of this film, many young people we interviewed and worked with knew very little about this side of journalism, as we noted in earlier chapters. Amran, who is quoted above, had conducted in-depth research into the city administration's decision-making processes about public transit after she had learned of negative impacts those decisions had on her community. But she did not realize until after the fact that by telling stories about those impacts, she and her peers were involved in investigative journalism. And yet, the work that she conducted with her peers, as this chapter will detail, resulted in immediate changes while also contributing to a long-term political effort to rethink city government accountability structures. She and young people like her have demonstrated time and again that youth are capable of telling stories that make a difference in the lives of their communities, and that they can marshal these skills for political participation and action.

In the previous chapter we discussed the significance of what occurs when young people insert themselves into the stories of the moment, detailing youth who took it upon themselves to chronicle their involvement in student protests via social media. In that chapter, we pointed out that whereas much of the research literature has focused on youth who have taken on a role within activism, there has been much less attention paid to the young people who are on the receiving end of the youth activists' messages. This is important for, as we noted, those receiving are participating in the intersubjective creation of meaning about those activities. And when those activities and the stories about youth involvement in them echo the concerns of a larger group of young people, those who are activists are engaging in activating a public (or counterpublic) through their articulations. As they circulate the artifacts of their own engagement in politics, they provide a personalized message that links those from their own network with a broader narrative of social change. And this, as we argued, opens the way for others to consider themselves as members of that public who, either directly or indirectly, participate in the construction of the public will.

In this chapter we revisit some of the ideas presented in Chapter 5 to consider another way in which young people insert themselves into the stories of the day. But the youth in this chapter embrace the journalistic dimension of what they do in a slightly different way from those who are witnesses of the moment. We, therefore, look at young people who are more intentionally involved not only in inserting themselves into the story, but in *making* the story. The connective journalism practice of making the story begins much earlier than what happens when young people pick up cameras and create narratives. As we will note, much like professional journalists, the practice of making the story begins with identifying the story and then researching it. Rather than primarily being in the right place at the right time, making the story begins with the goal of political action, with creating a news story about that action as a secondary rather than a primary goal. In other words, rather than focusing on those who attend and tweet the protests, it focuses on those who organize the protests or other activities that seek to influence political outcomes.

In Chapter 4 we introduced the idea that much of the news that was produced specifically by adults for a youth audience in the print, television, and radio era tended to assume a minimalist approach to participation, meaning that young people were largely conceived of as passive audiences, rather than presumed to be actively engaged in political action. This assumption of minimalist youthful political participation was particularly clear in cases of youth-produced news in school settings, as under US law, such youthful expression has long been subjugated to adult authority. Thus, although engaging in story selection and production can help some young high school journalists gain a sense of themselves as citizens and decision makers, not all of the news that youth produce for their peers necessarily leads to enhanced political participation among its target audiences, nor does it even seem intended to do this.[2] We argued that this minimalist approach to youth media and participation comported well with a tradition of understanding youth as being in need of protection, as they were rewarded for obedience and compliance.

Another media tradition has existed for many years and has demonstrated some promise when it comes to encouraging greater political participation among youth – the tradition of media produced by youth and for youth, usually in after-school settings and in association with existing legacy or community media organizations. Sometimes, the resultant youth-produced programs are broadcast on community radio or television, although some high-profile programs also air on national media outlets and on larger regional public broadcasting systems, as we noted in Chapter 4. Many of these programs incorporate critical media literacy, providing young people with the means to access, analyze, evaluate, and communicate messages in a variety of forms.[3] For the most part, these youth media programs embrace an approach to media literacy that views youth as capable of participating in and contributing to conversations of local, national, or even international import. Moreover, research into youth media programs has found that as young people participate in the processes of selecting and researching stories and making production decisions, they gain important competencies in civic engagement.[4] Thus, these programs have provided some important models for maximizing youth political participation.

In this chapter, we consider youth-created journalistic storytelling as a form of youth citizen journalism, an idea first introduced in Chapter 4 and elaborated on in Chapter 5 in relation to critical youth media and media literacy efforts. While we have discussed how young people are engaging in what we have been calling the socializing practices of connective journalism, as they share links to humorous political satire and commentary, and have also noted how youth sometimes engage in sharing videos or photos of the events unfolding around them, we want to share our observations about young people who make intentional efforts to link investigative research techniques with storytelling intended to make a political difference in their communities. First, however, we need to discuss the tradition of citizen journalism and its relationship to politics, so as to better conceptualize the role of media in student organizing and the role of student organizing in relation to youth media efforts.

CITIZEN JOURNALISM

Bowman and Willis have offered a definition of citizen journalism as "citizens playing an active role in the process of collecting, reporting, analyzing, and disseminating news and information."[5] Equated with user-generated content and often made manifest in relation to what we have termed the connective practices of witnessing and sharing outrage, some have identified early moments of citizen journalism with the ways in which information circulated outside of formal news media channels during the December 2004 Asian tsunami, the July 5, 2005 bombings in London, and during and after Hurricane Katrina in the United States in August 2005.[6] Perhaps the most ambitious citizen journalism project to date is Global Voices (GlobalVoices.org), an initiative that brings together more than 1,400 citizen journalists from around the world who report and translate what is happening in the blogosphere. It was the first large-scale translation project of the Web, and still offers trending news stories from 167 countries, with translations into 35 languages.[7]

Many other citizen journalism initiatives exist at the local level, setting out to forge connections between public and political agencies and populations that have been underserved due to ethnic and linguistic barriers. One example of this is The Alhambra Source, a local news outlet set up in a suburb of Los Angeles, where the population is 53 percent Asian, 33 percent Hispanic, and 11 percent Anglo, and where 75 percent of the population speak a language other than English at home.[8] With more than 90 contributors, reports on the site are available in many languages, although English still remains the dominant language for both contributors and readers. The Source also coordinated efforts to ensure that the local law enforcement agency launched a Sina Weibo account (a Chinese microblogging site resembling a hybrid of Facebook and Twitter), which enabled the Alhambra police department to attract more than 5,000 Chinese followers on this community's preferred social media platform within its first week, and more than 11,000 within its first four months. The police department saw a significant uptick in the number of requests for translation into Cantonese and Mandarin, as well as more tips to help solve crimes.[9] New Jersey Spark is a social justice citizen journalism lab at Rutgers University that brings students and community members of diverse races and ethnicities together with media makers and journalists to create media for and with underserved communities. With a focus on stories of working class, immigrant, and impoverished populations, NJ Spark highlights organizations supporting these groups and points to the inequality and injustice in society as well as to potential solutions. Believing that when citizens come together, they can "spark" change, NJ Spark encourages people to "steal our stories" in order to republish and recirculate them on the Web.[10] Stories have exposed toxic waste sites and other environmental hazards in New Jersey, as well as labor and housing abuses. In Philadelphia, everyday citizens are empowered to do journalistic work as participants in the award-winning Media Mobilizing Project (MMP). Since its founding in 2005, MMP has trained hundreds of youth, immigrants, low-wage workers, and others to use strategic media, arts, and communications to intervene in critical human rights struggles related to public education, transportation, health care, media reform, and public services. Trained in media collaborations, narrative development, audio/video production, digital literacy and human rights, local Philly residents tell the stories affecting their lives with the aim of inspiring political organizing and action to improve their lives.[11]

Despite these and other prominent examples, some scholars and professional journalists have expressed skepticism about citizen journalism's importance within the larger news ecology, noting that not all user-generated content is citizen journalism, and that what is sometimes termed citizen journalism is better understood as "superficial observations rather than considered judgment."[12] However, others have pointed out that citizen journalism has strengthened reporting during times of crises, as citizens around the world who have found themselves in extraordinary circumstances have taken the initiative to report on those events, often providing crucial information before professional journalists arrive on the scene.[13] Some have even argued that the contributions of citizen journalism may represent one bright spot in an otherwise dark time for professional journalism, since citizen reporting has emerged during what many have claimed is an all-time high point for the falsification of information from politicians and corporations.[14]

Peter Dahlgren has argued that debates about citizen journalism's worth would be helped tremendously through the development of a more nuanced approach to the differing forms that citizen journalism can take. He posits that there are five variants of citizen journalism: (1) amateur-assisted journalism, in which ordinary citizens contribute to the efforts of formal news organizations; (2) community and grassroots journalism, which emerges somewhat spontaneously as citizens take the initiative in identifying common problems, communicating among themselves, and proposing solutions; (3) advocacy journalism, in which interest groups seek ways to connect the concerns of ordinary citizens with the efforts of political parties so as to mobilize people to participate in controversial issues that impact a community; (4) activist journalism, which is the "news arm" of political organizations; and (5) alternative journalism, which refers to the independent news organizations that are anchored in professional journalistic norms but are positioned to challenge the dominant news representations of mainstream news.[15] In our own schema of connective journalism practices, we want to focus on Dahlgren's category of *community and grassroots citizen journalism*, as we are interested in the occasions when young people take it upon themselves to identify problems, communicate them among themselves, and propose solutions. We are also interested in the ways that connective journalism can intersect with *advocacy citizen journalism*, in that some student-led organizing efforts and youth media efforts have begun to emphasize the development of media skills as a means by which to connect young people and their interests with political or civic organizations that are already working on the changes that youth would like to see. We like the fact that Dahlgren widens understandings of citizen journalism beyond the witnessing and sharing of events, as we believe that his approach signals that investigation can play a role in the journalism young citizens create when they seek to work on community and grassroots efforts toward particular ends, and when they partner with other social organizations or movements in ways that amplify their own efforts to engage in political advocacy. Both these approaches to youthful citizen journalism are aspects of what we have termed the connective journalism practice of *participating*, as we will elaborate further in this chapter.

PARTICIPATING, ORGANIZING, AND
YOUTHFUL CITIZEN JOURNALISM

As Checkoway and Gutierrez have observed, youth participation is "a process of involving young people in the institutions and decisions that affect their lives."[16] They note that such initiatives can address educational reform, juvenile justice, environmental quality, or other issues, and can take place on local, regional, national, or international levels. Specifically, we follow the work of those who write about participatory politics, defined as "interactive, peer-based acts through which individuals and groups seek to exert both voice and influence on issues of concern."[17] In the actions of participatory politics, young people may utilize digital media to investigate issues, raise awareness, participate in dialogue with their peers about these issues, or mobilize their networks for fund-raising, protests, and other activities. This has led some to argue that digital media do not replace traditional modes of political participation, but enhance the repertoire of practices through which youth can participate in political activities.[18] Studies of participatory politics have explored how young people have understood political messages and how youth have sought to add their voices to issues of concern.[19]

But the research into participatory politics has also revealed unevenness in how digital tools are taken up among differing groups of young people. There is considerable evidence demonstrating that economic differences are predictive of what young people do, or do not do, online.[20] Moreover, students who live in families of lower socioeconomic status are more likely to live in distressed neighborhoods and to attend schools that have subpar technological equipment, few instructional opportunities linking digital media use to the fostering of political voice, and little encouragement to use these tools for civic or political engagement.[21] Young people who experience discrimination based on race, ethnicity, social class, or religion express frustration and disillusionment with traditional political and media systems.[22] And young people who experience discrimination are more likely than others to voice concerns about surveillance and to participate in self-censorship.[23]

In spite of these barriers, some young people have used digital tools to agitate for access to education and to counter negative stereotypes among their peers.[24] Yet research suggests that little work has been done exploring how young people from diverse backgrounds might become prepared for lives of inclusive and participatory politics.[25] Specifically, there is little analysis of the role of digital media in projects in which young people from urban lower socioeconomic backgrounds use mediated storytelling to gain access to those wielding political power, and how young people might adjust their own messages and goals in the process of seeking influence. This chapter aims to address that gap.

Several efforts around the world have sought to involve young people in youth citizen journalism, although as noted in Chapter 4, many initiatives come and go as they are dependent on grant support and volunteer labor. POPPYN (Presenting on Perspective on Philly Youth News) was a half-hour news television program produced jointly by university and high school students in Philadelphia as part of Temple University's University Community Collaborative. Distributed on the community access channel and screened in several high school and university classrooms, the programs, which addressed issues that the students selected, also circulated via social media.[26] Puget Sound Off was a blog focused on providing Seattle area young people with an online platform on which they could publish their views about issues affecting them.[27] The Iindaba Ziyafika project in South Africa, funded by a Knight Foundation grant, was successful in encouraging high school students from poor communities to contribute to their local newspapers by sending text messages about current events, but ultimately the researchers found that "providing technological access, skills training, citizenship awareness, and even a small financial incentive is not on its own sufficient to mobilize a major investment by young people into citizen journalism."[28] However, they did note that a great deal of youthful citizen journalism was produced by a small number of contributors, thus supporting their claim that they had given "sustainable skills" to a small group of key young citizens.[29]

One of the central challenges in such youthful citizen journalism efforts, as Peter Levine has observed, comes in assembling the right audience to hear that youth voice.[30] Levine points out that in youth media programs, a great deal of energy is devoted to teaching young people how to use the tools of digital media to produce a news story or documentary film that expresses their experiences of the world. Yet ultimately, as Levine notes, important as it is to foster voice, "rich and meaningful political discourse cannot be achieved by asserting, 'we are making films.'"[31] When youth media products fail to reach the audiences that can actually play a role in changing the lived situations of the young producers, young people can get a sense of dissatisfaction and disillusionment about the end result of their efforts.

Whereas youth citizen journalism efforts have tended to emphasize the development of technological as well as storytelling skills while leaving the actual selection of storytelling up to individual young people, efforts that begin from a student organizing perspective are focused on assisting young people in collectively determining a change that is worthy of pursuit and that will, it is believed, have a positive impact on the community as a whole. Rather than being shaped around the expectations that the desired outcome lies in the completion of a particular media product, therefore, youth organizing efforts focus on working with and listening to young people as they think about the publics with whom they want to communicate and about how those publics might be constituted and addressed. In this approach, digital media resources and productions can be decided upon after the larger goals of desired policy change are specified, and after the audiences, and avenues for reaching those audiences, have been identified. This aligns well with what has come to be known as "solutions-oriented" journalism. Solutions-oriented journalism starts by identifying a shared problem and then seeks to identify potential solutions to that problem by conducting in-depth research and identifying the various decisions that have been made or are being made that affect a community's well-being.[32] People sometimes disagree about the proposed solution, and discussing those disagreements becomes part of the journalism process and "the story." The goal of this form of journalism is to help people move forward as a society by addressing common problems through a democratic process of engagement, discussion, negotiation, and action.

In the past, youth organizing efforts had a model of media involvement rooted in the assumptions of professional journalism. The aim of young organizers was to stage events that attracted the attention of professional journalists, who would then write about the event, thereby bringing attention and publicity to the cause. This had its shortcomings when it came to youth political organizing, however. As sociologist and youth organizer Hava Gordon has pointed out, "adultism," or the tendency to think that adults are at the heart of any political organizing activity, has shaped the way that these activities have been covered in the mainstream media. She observed:

For Youth Power (the youth student organizing group she studied), the raised fist symbolized collective resistance and the power that comes from multiracial unity. However, adultist mainstream media coverage of Portland student activism rarely spoke of student organizing in political terms, or even in terms of collective student anger as resistance. To recognize student anger, dissent, or political frameworks would have required the media to reconceptualize teens as highly cognitive, critical, reflective, and legitimate political beings – conceptions not in line with dominant images of youth."[33]

Mainstream media tend to depoliticize student organizers by constructing them as "innocents," which is presumed to be a more palatable (and less threatening) representation for their adult audience.

Yet, in today's era of citizen journalism, young people can not only orchestrate the event and contact the mainstream media, but can participate in telling their own stories of why they are organizing. They can then participate in sharing those stories with their peers through social media, rather than primarily relying on the mainstream media to "get the word out" about their activities. In addition, they can create messages of youthful citizen journalism with very specific audiences of policymakers, leaders, educators, or other adult decision-makers in mind.

STORIES OF YOUTH CITIZEN JOURNALISM

The students who would become active in designing several participatory youthful citizen journalism interventions in Denver did not initially think of their work as journalism at all. Youth organizing was a much better framework, because the first part of their effort involved discussing what they felt were common problems that they shared with their peers. The students were participants in an after-school program that had experimented with youth-led participatory action research in the past, roughly following a curriculum developed by community engagement expert Cara DiEnno that invited students to (1) identify a problem, (2) conduct research on the problem as well as on the governmental, school, or civic offices and policies that inadvertently exacerbated the problem, and then (3) devise a plan of action for addressing the problem in a manner that could be presented to those who had the authority to change those policies deemed problematic.[34] To this design, Lynn and the after-school Digital Media Club of Denver's South High School added a media-rich dimension that included utilizing the latest information and communication technologies in both the conducting of research and in the production of a series of messages that comprised a fourth step: (4) designing a communication plan that would present evidence in support of the proposed plan of action developed by the youth in step three. This communication plan would include differing messages, formats, and distribution outlets specifically designed to motivate and persuade a series of differing audiences that might include policymakers, fellow students, members of the public, or all of these.[35] Each of these messages took the form of what Dahlgren had described as *community or grassroots citizen journalism*, as young citizens took the initiative in identifying common problems, communicating about those problems among themselves, and proposing solutions to those problems. But as the projects developed, several of them also evolved into what Dahlgren described as *advocacy citizen journalism*, in that students were introduced to adult members of interest groups, civic and political organizations, and social movements who had been working on addressing the issues that the students had identified and had, therefore, already played a role in both articulating the controversial issues that impacted the community and mobilizing people toward specific political solutions.[36]

The process of developing youthful citizen journalism efforts with the Digital Media Club took place during the school year over the course of six consecutive years, with the goal of completing the production of messages in the communication plan and holding a meeting with relevant constituents in the middle of May prior to the release of the students for summer vacation. Rather than working within deadlines established by media outlets, therefore, this effort worked on the timeline of the school calendar, with adult leaders primarily assisting in facilitating the timely completion of various tasks that the students had identified for themselves.

More than one hundred students participated in the club's efforts over the course of its first six years. Each year, the club attracted from between 8 and more than 20 high school students, most of whom were from new immigrant communities and had been in the United States for five or fewer years. Student participants had come to the Denver area from Somalia, Ghana, Ethiopia, Eritrea, Kenya, Thailand, Bangladesh, Vietnam, China, Mexico, Iraq, and the United Arab Emirates. Other student participants were members of domestic minority groups, including several who identified themselves as Latinx, Asian American, African American, Native American, and multiracial.

Padres Y Jovenes Unidos

The first youth citizen journalism effort that this particular group of students engaged in followed a curriculum outlined by critical media literacy expert Benjamin Thevenin, who was especially interested in developing in students an ability to explore the ways in which portrayals in popular media could help young people to think about their world *as it is*, and *as it ought to be*.[37] Benjamin and Lynn worked with four groups of high school students to reflect on the media they consumed and wanted to create in order to make a difference in their communities. One of the groups introduced the rest of the students and adult leaders to a local organization named Padres Y Jovenes Unidos (Parents and Youth United, or PJU), a group that started in Denver and that was engaged in a campaign that PJU called "End the School to Jail Track."[38] Their target was the "zero tolerance" approaches to discipline that disproportionately affect low-income students of color in schools across the United States. As part of the campaign, PJU produced a report demonstrating that (1) police involvement in high school discipline had resulted in an increase in school suspensions; (2) there was a link between increased suspensions and increased high school dropout rates, which (3) in turn related to higher rates of incarceration. PJU wanted to turn this around by limiting police presence in schools and by offering support for more effective in-school disciplinary policies so that vulnerable populations would stay in school and out of jail. With funding to implement pilot projects, they developed alternatives to the "zero tolerance" approach, establishing several restorative justice[39] programs in urban high schools that encouraged students to assume responsibility for repairing the damages that they caused. PJU regularly coordinated with student leaders at local high schools to hold rallies so as to increase support for their efforts statewide.

When Ezana, one of the students in the South High group, learned that students in another high school had developed a skit to illustrate the differences between punitive and restorative approaches to discipline, he and his peers sought to create a similar skit for their own school, working with the Digital Media Club to help film it. The student leaders cast fellow students in the roles of fighting students, stern security officers, a traditional principal who embraces first a punitive and then a restorative justice approach, and a restorative justice counselor who works with the students to discuss what each can do to address and be accountable for the consequences of their actions.

The students took great joy in writing and filming the skit. While filming the fight scene, lots of laughter ensued as the school's security guards actually showed up to see what all the noise was about. Several students spent hours editing the video footage. Once the editing was complete, the students circulated the video widely across their social media networks. They also shared it with teachers and with the school's principal, who – much to the students' delight – showed it in a teacher/training event to demonstrate the value of embracing a restorative justice approach in their school. This was only possible because their work was linked to the wider efforts of PJU that had already gained a place on the school's agenda.

While the students were planning and filming the skit, the larger PJU organization continued to work with the Denver Public Schools to craft a new discipline policy that limited the police presence in schools and that outlined protections for students and their families. They also worked with the state senate to craft what came to be known as the "smart discipline" bill that aimed to expand the policy into a statewide law. As the bill moved through the state senate, the students involved in the Digital Media Club followed the news and kept their friends updated. When the state senate passed the bill at the end of the school year, the students were overjoyed. They knew that they had expanded PJU's work in their own school, and so experienced themselves as participants in the larger political action and felt a great deal of ownership in the bill's success.

A year after many of the students involved had graduated from high school and two years after creating and circulating among their networks their skit about restorative justice, President Obama suggested making "smart discipline" a national priority. And those students who had worked on using media to envision "what ought to be" could feel pride in knowing that their efforts had joined with many others to bring about political change that would affect their communities for years to come. Through their direct involvement, they experienced themselves as participants in the public will that brought attention, and then widespread change, to the issue of school discipline. Many of their friends and other members of their social circles participated only marginally or not at all. Nevertheless, they also experienced themselves to be part of this public, even if their own participation had been by proxy through following their more active friends online.

Bridging the Gap: Kids and Cops

In August 2014, when the students in the club were discussing the possible focus of that year's project, protests were erupting in the streets of several cities in the aftermath of the death of Michael Brown, an unarmed African American teen who was shot and killed by police officer Darren Wilson. Students in this particular high school likewise participated in protests, as did those in several high schools and universities throughout the area.[40] Students in the club decided they wanted to use media to make a difference in the relationships between students of color – including students from new immigrant communities – and members of law enforcement. Once they had selected this goal, following the success of working with PJU, Lynn made contacts with various community organizers in the city to find out about ongoing efforts that might connect with the students' goals. The young adult liaison with PJU introduced Lynn to a project that was being directed by the Office of the Independent Monitor (OIM). The OIM is the City and County of Denver's independent civilian oversight agency which monitors the Denver Police and Sheriff Department and had been working to develop a program that would improve relations between students of color and members of law enforcement. The students agreed to invite the staff members from OIM to a meeting to discuss mutual interests, and students then decided to form a partnership with OIM.

The OIM Youth Outreach Project (YOP) was particularly interested in collaborating with these students because of their experiences and expertise as members of new immigrant communities. The OIM YOP believed the students could add their perspective in informing program and curriculum development, particularly regarding rights and responsibilities when youth are involved in encounters with police officers. Over the course of the year, OIM YOP made arrangements for the high school students to visit a district police station, and meet with and digitally record interviews with police officers. Students also attended and recorded a Citizens' Oversight Board public forum in which data about police body cameras were shared. The OIM YOP staff also arranged for police officers to visit the high school, allowing the students to conduct follow-up interviews with the officers. In the meantime, the students also conducted interviews with their peers about their own interactions with police officers, held discussions among themselves about racial/ethnic identity and law enforcement, and met on several occasions with the Student Resource Officer assigned to their high school. Professor Margie Thompson, a colleague of Lynn's, invited her university research methods class to design their own project that related to the high school students' exploration of police–youth relations, which the university students then presented to the high school club members. This effort created an opportunity for the high school and university students to have an in-depth discussion about the role of race, ethnicity, and national origin in differing experiences with law enforcement, which highlighted concerns of institutional racism and white privilege. These interactions, too, were digitally recorded as video.

Over time, the high school students' views of the difference they wished to make in the community evolved. Initially, many of the students wanted to teach their school peers about how to de-escalate situations between police officers and students of color, and their goals were thus aligned with the OIM YOP's program on students' rights and responsibilities. However, other students became especially interested in countering the negative images of police officers that were flooding the media at the time, and based on their one-on-one experiences with police officers, they wanted to seek out ways in which others could have similar productive experiences with police so that both youth and police officers could foster a more balanced view of one another. A few young people were especially interested in efforts to increase the accountability of police. The host school's administration expressed nervousness about this latter goal, however, fearing that it could draw negative publicity to the school. The co-leaders and OIM staff went out of their way to address her concerns, and the club decided to focus its investigative interests on how to foster "positive" interactions between police and youth, a focus that, perhaps surprisingly, was embraced enthusiastically by most of the students.

As students were given opportunities to interact directly with members of law enforcement, they came to appreciate the importance of developing relationships of understanding and respect between members of law enforcement and students of color and thus came to be aligned with OIM YOP's mission. The students wondered about how to foster such relationships and considered how video recordings could help one group to understand the experiences of the other group. Some became very enthused about the prospects of creating a documentary out of their videotaped footage.

By early May 2015, the high school students of the Digital Media Club involved in the effort had amassed a significant amount of digitally recorded material and had identified a number of somewhat similar pilot projects about teaching rights and responsibilities that were underway in Boston, Philadelphia, and in other US cities. Because of the voluntary nature of the club, not all students nor co-leaders of the club were involved in all aspects of the project. Rather than create a documentary with insufficient time, skill, and resources, club members opted to work with a university student to curate the materials on a website that the students and others could access. As the students in the club reviewed and organized these materials for the website, they and the adult leaders identified patterns that became the basis for a list of findings that would organize the website.

At this point, the OIM YOP was anxious to see and share the website with additional community stakeholders and curriculum developers, but the site was not yet finalized. Lynn then wrote up a draft of a research brief that she presented to the student group, who then further developed it for distribution to the OIM YOP partners. The final version of this research brief included nine findings and was coauthored by the adult co-leaders, university student participants, and the 22 high school student participants.

The finding that proved to be most useful for the OIM YOP in strengthening their project's goal of community-lead facilitation between youth and law enforcement was this: "Usually when students interact with police, the police do the talking and the students do the listening. Students would like to flip this script and feel heard by officers."[41] Students further fleshed out this finding in the report, noting that police often came to their school to speak at school assemblies, addressing topics such as cybersafety and bullying, and police also addressed them when it came to explaining expectations or reiterating rules in school. The report observed that *none* of the students could recall a time when police officers had come to listen and learn from them. This point had been reinforced when students had interviewed police, who assumed that because "[they] were teenagers once," they did not need to listen to or receive "training" about youth development or youth lived experiences. This had never been part of the policy of police training in the past, and even those police officers who had participated in conversations with the students expressed a lack of consideration as to the value in receiving such training.

This lack of insight about the experiences of students only reaffirmed the club members' views that police could benefit from such training. Several students discussed the need to "change the dynamic" and "give students the power and the voice." They spoke of "youth voice" and of the desire to "be heard," and felt that officers did not understand their varied life experiences. They also wanted to create opportunities to talk to officers about their concerns. This aligned well with the OIM YOP's project which creates opportunities that would bring together youth and officers for both joint and separate trainings that could take place on the same day.

Initially, the joint efforts of the OIM YOP and the club, which brought together members of law enforcement and students of color, were uniformly met with suspicion from students, members of law enforcement, school officials, and parents. However, as the year progressed, the adults and students involved assumed leadership positions in establishing an environment of respect, trust, and curiosity. In other words, those holding hostile views were invited to express those views, but in ways that were framed in relation to developing mutual understanding. This model confirmed that the direction of the OIM YOP curriculum was valid and helped to shape the messaging as the curriculum was being finalized.

The curriculum, which the OIM YOP named Bridging the Gap, was then tested among students and members of law enforcement who participated in forums on a voluntary basis during the 2015–16 academic year. Students received training on their rights and responsibilities and on implicit biases they might bring into their encounters with police officers, while officers received training on youth development, implicit bias, and the effects that experiences of trauma leave on young people. Young people and officers then came together to share a meal and engage in facilitated dialogues. With an adult and youth facilitator in each small group, youth and officers were encouraged to ask questions of each other, helping to mitigate blame, shame, or defensiveness. All were invited to answer questions personally rather than speaking about or on behalf of "all" officers or "all" young people. By the end of the 2015–16 academic year, more than 200 high school aged young people had participated in the forums and more than fifty Denver police officers had been trained in adolescent development and de-escalation techniques.

When the OIM YOP interacted with the club's students and later with its youth advisory board, they did not speak of policy change but rather of *culture* change. They knew that as an outside entity, OIM YOP did not have the authority to compel police officers to receive training about youth development, youth trauma, or implicit biases, nor did they have the authority to release officers from a day's work to interact with young people, some of whom might harbor hostilities toward them. The OIM YOP began its initiative with the desire that youth could be trained to better understand their rights and responsibilities, hoping that such training could lower rates of arrest and juvenile justice system involvement as well as keep youth and officers safe as young people and officers learned and practiced de-escalation techniques. The voices of the student participants in the club, as expressed in personal interactions with OIM YOP staff and especially in the coauthored research brief during a year in which a great deal of media attention was devoted to negative interactions between students and police, gave the Bridging the Gap program an important source of credibility. This credibility in turn provided the impetus for leaders among the police to encourage officer participation in the city's Bridging the Gap program. Leaders among the city's police have now committed to training more than 100 officers per year. Thus, the student project succeeded in having an impact on how Denver police now organize training and, perhaps more importantly, in contributing to a police culture in which interactions with youth of color are perceived as worthwhile. Notably, this was not a citizen journalism project that involved the production of media messages for a public. Students utilized video recordings as a form of data to be shared only among themselves and ultimately communicated their message primarily through a black and white photocopied and academic-looking "research brief" that carried legitimacy as it included voices of both university professors and student researchers.

However, once the students came to recognize their experience and their role in policy change *as* a story, they enthusiastically spoke with several reporters from local and national news organizations who elected to cover it. They then participated in re-circulating the story among their own social networks, thereby reinforcing their own role as participants in the change that they had wished to see.[42] Thus, they were participating in practices of connective journalism, first by involving themselves in efforts aligned with community and grassroots citizen journalism as they researched and developed ways to talk about community concerns, then by partnering with the offices of local government to participate in working toward cultural change as their own narrative of what needed to happen took shape, and finally by celebrating their successes as they utilized social media to share stories in mainstream media that had provided legitimation for their involvement in political activities.

RTD AND THE CHALLENGE OF CONNECTING DATA
TO DECISION MAKING

In the 2015–2016 school year, the Digital Media Club considered continuing its work in the Bridging the Gap program, and several students were trained to serve as youth facilitators in the youth/officer forums designed to bring together young people and members of Denver law enforcement. However, they also wanted to consider other possible issues for their focus. Seraphina, a ninth grade biracial teen who was new to the club but had been involved in youth media production efforts in the past, mentioned transportation as a possible issue to explore. She had discussed the problems of overcrowded buses and slow transportation routes to city schools with other peers who attended a different high school, and the students in the club enthusiastically agreed that this would be something worth looking into. As she noted:

I brought up the idea of transportation. It was a bigger issue for us because all of us take the bus. And so we decided that we would investigate it a little bit more. We went to check out the bus stops, and interviewed people off-camera, and we watched the buses pass people, and thought, wow, there are issues!

The students then decided on a general plan of action, following a youth organizing framework. First, they decided that they would conduct a survey of their fellow students to determine exactly how well-served students were (or were not) by the current offerings made available through Denver's Regional Transportation District (RTD). Based on their own experiences of an admittedly small and unrepresentative sample, they knew that they and their peers often spent a great deal of time waiting for buses to arrive and were sometimes refused service if a bus was already filled. They therefore began with the idea that they would simply want to present RTD officials with information on which routes were most overcrowded. They were also interested in learning about whether or not a large number of their fellow students were inconvenienced by existing bus routes that required them to take two or more buses to attend school.

The project quickly took on an investigative thrust with its emphasis on data collection among students and on the processes through which transportation issues were decided within the region. A galvanizing moment occurred when students were discussing the fact that RTD offered all students a discount for monthly bus fares. Rather than paying the $40 monthly fee expected of adult riders, students only paid $20 each month, or a total of $180 each year. The students thought this was a "good deal" – until they started to do research into the amounts that students in other school districts paid to get to school. A sister urban school, they learned, had negotiated an even lower monthly rate for its students. But what really surprised them was when they learned that the school district that served many of the wealthiest neighborhoods in the area offered bus service to students completely subsidized by local taxpayers. It was at this point that their project took on the tenor of a social justice issue. "Why is it that they get bus service for free when we have to ask our parents to help us pay for each sibling's ride to school?," they asked.

Because the school did not want to take up class time for the distribution of the survey, the students themselves arranged to invite students to take the survey using mobile phones in times before and after school and during the lunch hour over the course of several weeks. As the students introduced their fellow peers to the survey, they took the opportunity to inform their peers of what they had discovered about discrepancies between the bus service they received and the services that were available in other areas of the city.

As had occurred in earlier youth citizen journalism efforts of this group, the students invited several not-for-profit organizations to come and talk with them about citywide initiatives to improve transportation, particularly for underserved populations, including Denver's not-for-profits Mile High Connects and Transportation Solutions (broad-based groups of people and organizations committed to fostering transportation equity in the region). They learned that Denver Public Schools had drastically cut most of its subsidized bus services some twenty years earlier as a cost-cutting measure. This move had placed the responsibility for transporting students with the area's RTD, which oversaw all bus and light rail lines throughout the city.

Several students continued to do research on how students across the city got to school, while others focused on analyzing the data from the nearly 400 surveys they collected from their high school peers. Many of the students attended a monthly board meeting of the RTD, to the surprise of the bureaucrats and adult citizens in attendance. Several attendees offered to introduce students to those who worked in scheduling for RTD, and students learned more about how and to whom to make an effective presentation. The students decided that they wanted to make a presentation to decision makers who could be influenced by the information they desired to share, as they wanted to offer alternative proposals to current arrangements. This presentation, they decided, would be most effective if it included both data from their survey and a short video that conveyed the problem of bus overcrowding so that decision makers would have a better feel for the student experience with public transportation.

In recent years, RTD had been investing heavily in improving the infrastructure that would provide transportation for Denver's burgeoning population to get to the airport, located some twenty miles from the downtown area. In fact, in 2016, much fanfare accompanied the announcement of a new rail line that would link the southern suburbs, which contained many of the city's wealthiest neighborhoods, to the airport far to the northeast of the city. Another new line would link the downtown area directly to the airport, travelling through an area to the north of the city. But unfortunately for those living in the east neighborhoods, which are where many of the area's most impoverished citizens and new immigrant communities live, neither rail line improved their transportation to the city center, which is where most of the city's employment opportunities existed. For the time being, those in the east neighborhoods were going to remain reliant on overcrowded and unreliable bus service.⁴³ To make matters worse, even some of those bus lines had to be cut for "cost-saving measures," according to RTD, as the city had to locate funds for the larger rail projects. No one would be without service, RTD promised, as they focused on cutting redundancies and poorly utilized lines.

The student survey found that many of the students from the high school lived in these east neighborhoods. There had been a school that was located closer to where the students lived, but that school had closed some five years earlier due to poor test scores and a reputation for problems with drugs and violence.⁴⁴ Thus, most of the students in these neighborhoods had been redirected to the school where the club was located. The survey of transportation needs found that a majority of students travelled thirty minutes or more by bus to get to and from school each day, and many took two buses to get there. Moreover, the survey also found that the bus line most frequently used by English language learning students was among those for which service would be drastically reduced. According to an estimate based on the survey, some one hundred or more students would now need to take three buses to get to school. Cesar, a junior who had moved with his family from Mexico to Denver, noted that he took a first bus shortly after 5:00 a.m. because he wanted to ensure that he arrived at school on time and knew that if that bus line or either of the other two buses he needed to take were overcrowded, he would risk being late to school.

As it happened, thanks to arrangements made by Transportation Solutions, the RTD scheduler and RTD commissioner had agreed to meet with the club students on an arbitrary day in April – and that date turned out to be four days after the proposed bus service changes went into effect. While a great deal of mainstream media attention had focused on the opening of the rail lines to the airport, very few reporters had looked into the effects of curtailed bus lines.⁴⁵ This made the student meeting with RTD officials of particular interest to local journalists, and the largest community-based newspaper in the area covered the meeting, giving extensive coverage to students' concerns and placing the story on its front page a few days later under the headline, "South students now commuting longer."⁴⁶ The club's Facebook page linked to this article as well as to the humorous yet poignant video the students had put together illustrating bus overcrowding and frustration over curtailed bus lines. Although nervous, the students had prepared their presentation for the RTD officials by putting together and rehearsing a PowerPoint that included the three-minute video on bus overcrowding.

The RTD scheduler who watched the video and listened to the students' presentation immediately agreed to reinstate the line that affected the large number of students, as documented in the student survey, and the students were very pleased with their success. But we also learned in that meeting that RTD did not receive any data from the schools about where their students lived. Such information would of course be useful to RTD for planning routes. As the students looked into this further, they learned from Transportations Solutions officials that the data would need to be anonymized before it could be given to RTD, and this was part of the problem: no one at the school district had the time to anonymize the names and addresses of the 40,000 students who were a part of the Denver school district.

The commissioner adamantly noted that they needed such data in order to make good decisions:

Some of the complaints I get sometimes are, "your buses are running around empty." There's a good reason for that. In the middle of the day, people are not going to and from work. So, we have to figure out how to balance the resources we have as best we can, to serve everyone... So again, if we have more data, then (the scheduler's) office can crunch the numbers and figure out what we have to spend. And the money we get, by the way, is mostly from tax money. And we have to allocate fairly according to where is the greatest demand. So, organizing yourselves, if you can provide more data for them to do that, then you're likely to get the best result.

This prompted one adult participant to ask: "So, what was the data that made it seem possible or important to cancel the 73 line? It seems like 100 or so bus-takers would be a significant amount," to which the scheduler replied, "It's all driven by trying to maintain the budget on the one hand, limited resources, where do people have alternative services." He went on to explain that those students had the option of taking a different bus. But Cesar, the student who was affected by this service change, noted that without the reinstatement of the bus service that had been cut, his alternative route would add not only a third bus but also another fifteen minutes to his walk to and from the bus. At this point, the scheduler reiterated that he would "check" to ensure that the bus service he had earlier promised to reinstate would, in fact, be reinstated. He also promised to look at adding more buses during the times when bus service is most in demand in order to alleviate overcrowding. He added, "I can't promise, but it's something else we can look at."

Wilfred, a student who had moved with his family to the United States from Ghana several years earlier, then asked, "Didn't one of you say that you live in (the wealthy school district where the students had earlier learned that bus service was fully subsidized)? I'm just curious. How do your kids get to school?" To which the scheduler noted that in the school district where his children attended, "they provide school buses." "Oh. Ok..." Wilfred replied, allowing the exchange to hang in the air. Returning to the subject of the lack of buses in Denver, the scheduler noted, "It was a budget thing. DPS had to put what they had into education instead of transportation. That's a whole different thing." "It's related, though," Lynn replied, adding, "Because it's about offsetting the costs. So that now instead of transportation being paid by taxpayers, it's being paid by the students and their families." The scheduler responded by stating, "Some schools will charge a fee."

As the meeting time was drawing to a close, the RTD commissioner praised the students for their efforts, noting:

> This is a beginning. This is a great idea to have a group like this that represents the school, and it might be good for other schools to have something like this. Because RTD can do its job better if it has more information. So, finding facilities for information to be gathered and organized well, so that they can use it to make good decisions that will serve, and don't have to wait a half an hour, or so that the bus will go to the places at the right times. So, learning from this, doing more of it, maybe talking to other schools. It's a good idea.

The RTD officials expressed gratitude for the opportunity to hear from the students directly, and once the news reports about the students' efforts came out, the local news outlets continued to follow the story. It was at this point that the students told their peers about the project through connective journalism practices, sharing links to the story via their Twitter and Facebook pages. Interestingly, students did not share information with peers as the story was unfolding, such as when they were completing preliminary analyses of the data or when the video was completed and shown to several of the school's teachers.

Other students did learn about the project as it was unfolding however, although often this happened inadvertently. Students involved reported that news of the project was greeted with overwhelming support. When students and adult co-leaders were recruiting survey participants, more than one student asked, "Are you from RTD?" Upon learning of the students' project, their peers offered their own hopes for more bus lines, better service in their home neighborhoods, or lowered prices.

On one occasion in the school's computer lab, Seraphina and Lynn were editing the video that we had designed with the intention of showing to the RTD commissioner in charge of the area. The video highlighted the ways in which the demand for after-school buses far exceeded bus availability, which in turn was forcing some students to wait for two or three buses to pass by before there would be available seats on a bus. Another student in the computer room who was working on a different video project overheard the talk about RTD and began a conversation with her friend about the anticipated change in bus service that she'd heard about. As they talked in an animated way, Lynn turned to the girls and said, "Are you concerned about RTD service? Because that's what we're making this video about." When she pointed out that Seraphina had worked with several of her fellow students to produce the survey about RTD bus service that she and her friends might have heard about, the students immediately looked impressed and began to speak in animated tones about the then-upcoming bus changes that would inconvenience them as well as others they knew. Lynn asked if they'd be willing to be interviewed so that they could be included in the video, and they agreed. Seraphina got the camera and, after a brief discussion about the questions she wanted to ask, interviewed the young women while Lynn operated the camera. One of the young women interviewed provided the closing statement for the video when she observed that it seemed unfair that students from new immigrant communities were likely to be particularly negatively affected by the changed bus lines. As she noted, "English is already a barrier. Don't make transportation a barrier."

These young women, who had had no direct involvement with the larger youthful citizen journalism effort, were nevertheless willing to participate in the youth citizen journalism activity because they shared a passion for the issue at hand. They were happy to have an opportunity to speak about their experiences and were enthusiastic that some of their peers had taken the initiative to address a problem that they, too, had also experienced. And this instance raises an important point about youth citizen journalism and youth publics. Professional journalists may still play a key role in providing legitimacy to the events and activities that are covered in youth citizen journalism efforts, as they always have in relation to youth organizing projects. But professional journalists are no longer the only storytellers. Nor are they the only ones who can provide legitimacy to student organizing, as stories passed along by peers through connective journalism practices now also garner legitimacy. This can happen when the students involved have some recognition among their peers as leaders, or when, more commonly, as was the case in this instance, those who are creating and telling the stories are sharing stories that resonate with their peers. Transportation was an issue that many students saw as a problem. As they recognized their own concerns in the story of youthful citizen journalism, many young people felt that they, too, had been given a voice in the political activities that affected them. They experienced themselves as part of a public in that they were being addressed, as Michael Warner notes in the previous chapter in relation to the formation of publics.[47]

It is important to point out that these cases share noteworthy similarities with a number of "participatory politics" efforts taking place in relation to digital media literacy programs in that they involve following young people as they (1) define political issues of concern to them and as they (2) decide upon the strategies they would like to embrace.[48] What was particularly unique about these instances was that each situated individual political agency in the context of larger and more longterm organized efforts to bring about positive social change, and each effort focused on changes that were deemed important within the context of disenfranchised communities. The students' work in creating a story of "what ought to be" and circulating it among their communities helped them see themselves as communicators who were part of an effort to address injustices in their community – an effort that had begun before them, and that would continue long after their own direct involvement was to end. Through their ability to connect youth organizing with youth citizen journalism and connective journalism activities, they came to see the value of working with organizations like Padres Y Jovenes Unidos, Denver's Office of the Independent Monitor, and the not-for-profits Mile High Connects and Transportation Solutions offices, each of which was already involved in serving as a watchdog in connecting community concerns with political initiatives. And the students' work both in their local situation and in relation to a much broader information campaign therefore enabled them to draw a connection between their own stories and concerns and those of people throughout their communities. Through their involvement in a youth citizen journalism effort that incorporated both grassroots efforts among their peers and work with advocacy organizations, the students came to see themselves as engaged in a much broader effort of political reform toward "what ought to be" in our public schools, in relations with law enforcement, and in our communities. A final point to be made is that by working on these projects, young people were given opportunities to see connections between youth citizen journalism and more traditional forms of investigative journalism found in legacy news.

CONCLUSION

This chapter has argued that youth citizen journalism is something that can be encouraged in tandem with the efforts of youth organizing efforts. As suggested by Dahlgren, citizen journalism is something that occurs as people work with community and grassroots groups to identify problems and to come up with ways of discussing possible solutions to those problems. Citizen journalism can also encompass activities that bring citizens together with civic, not-for-profit, and political organizations or movements that have already established a track record in articulating a community's concerns and working toward specific policy outcomes. And, as we have noted here, youth citizen journalism can incorporate some of the practices associated with traditional investigative journalism, as young people employ the tools of digital media to conduct original research about identified community problems and to create compelling storytelling that probes the injustices they have discovered.

We realize that it is only a relatively small number of young people who are so actively engaged in youth citizen journalism practices. But this chapter has offered these examples as illustrations of the kinds of stories emerging today in the youthful news ecology that provide evidence of how young people participate in political activities, and how they share their involvement in those activities with their peers through connective journalism practices online. They become partners with professional journalists as they learn that they, too, can participate in making the story. In the process, they are also reshaping expectations regarding what journalism can do, and what news is for.

The stories in this chapter also illustrate that adults can become meaningfully involved in facilitating connections between students, community organizations, and journalism. Many of today's young people are keenly interested in the future of their communities, and through programs supportive of youth citizen journalism, young people can be encouraged to move from thinking of themselves as *creating a news story* to *creating a new story* for their communities. Such story-making can and does occur without adult support, of course. But the fact that such efforts *might* occur does not excuse adults from the responsibility of supporting the conditions that make these efforts possible. For young people to become politically involved through the making of connective journalism, then, the question remains: how can those involved in professional journalism, journalism education, and the future of news help to support the conditions that will foster greater youth involvement and nurture youth voices in the creation of youth publics? We explore this question in the next and final chapter.

* * * * *

7

Moving Forward

What We Can Do

I don't follow the news. But, Twitter is almost like the news. I have it on my phone and if I'm holding my phone, it's like an instinct. I just go to it. If something's going on, everyone's talking about it on Twitter.

– *Lissa, aged sixteen*

The comment above reflects the reality of how today's youth experience news stories, as this book has explored. But, what does it mean for the future of news and democracy when young people are not following the news in intentional ways, but mostly "happen" upon it through their relationships within social media? To explore this question, this book has placed journalism industries in the background to focus on the ways in which US young people encounter, share, insert themselves into, and make stories that they feel are newsworthy, using the platforms of social media to do so. By discussing the ways in which young people can become members of communities by telling and sharing stories, we have aimed to illustrate how the personal identity construction and risk-taking involved in increasingly greater levels of online sharing can lead not only to the recognition that one is part of a certain community, but also to the realization that one can initiate or join efforts to address injustices facing that community. Drawing attention to the deficit assumptions regarding youth that have framed earlier approaches to citizenship and civic engagement, we've questioned traditional notions of the relationships between news and the youthful "not-yet-citizen," advocating for an understanding of young people who are deserving of rights, respect, and responsibility. We have foregrounded the intersubjective role of social media in order to bring into focus the fact that "information" is not the only form of communication that is necessary within democratic relations, setting forth an approach to news and citizenship rooted not in information and duty but in the *mutual listening and shared obligation that brings publics into being*. And drawing upon research on the increasingly blurred lines between journalism and emergent forms of remix storytelling, we have introduced the concept of connective journalism as a means of understanding young peoples' online practices of (1) consuming news, (2) sharing information, perspectives and emotions, and (3) participating in storymaking that allows them to take greater responsibility and ownership in political actions in the context of their interpersonal relationships. We begin this chapter by reviewing what this book has found about young people and news, and we then offer insights into what we believe needs to happen in order for news and the practices surrounding its online sharing to better foster political engagement among young world citizens.

In this book's introduction and in Chapter 1, we explained how the concept of connective journalism foregrounds identity and intersubjectivity in relation to the youthful online sharing of information, emotions, and viewpoints. Exploring the practices of connective journalism through a relational rather than primarily a technologically oriented perspective, we suggested, clarifies how young people may become "hailed" into publics or counterpublics and ascend the "ladder of engagement" as they take greater and greater interpersonal risks with regard to what they share with others and what they encounter in social media. Thus, connective journalism takes seriously the everyday media sharing practices of young people that have largely been dismissed as trivial, self-absorbed, or politically disengaged, in an attempt to rethink concepts of citizenship and "publics" in the twenty-first century. We argued in the Introduction that when the Colorado high school students began sharing photos on Facebook and tweeting about the anti-gay protests they staged at their school in opposition to the Westboro Baptist Church (a story that hadn't been mentioned in local news), they were not only sharing their identity and values with each other, but through social media they called into being a latent public of peers who supported LGBT rights. This occurred as they communicated with one another through the intersubjective spaces of social media in ways best understood through the lens of critical approaches to citizenship. They shared not only information but a collective outrage, which in turn revealed their desires to connect with their peers as a collective entity and with the broader world, as well. We argued that understanding the future of news rests in discerning not just what journalism industries do or what individuals do, but in how these interrelate in social practices. As members of society engage in social practices across a variety of settings and institutions, these practices give shape to the roles technologies come to play in our lives – which, in turn, shapes our collective lives. This interrelatedness between humans, technologies, and practices led us to explore theories of intersubjectivity in political relations in Chapter 2 in order to flesh out the concept of connective journalism practices as proto-political actions that can lead young people into collective and connective actions.

Chapter 3 explored reasons why many young people feel disinterested and disillusioned with legacy news media, examining their critiques of mainstream news storytelling genres, content bias, and commercial interests while noting that today's youth, like previous generations, recognize and appreciate the watchdog role that journalism should ideally play in safeguarding the public good. As Mark, aged seventeen, noted: "The job of the journalist is to not only keep the people informed, but to be always checking up on the corporations and politicians." Yet, many youth felt that legacy news was dull, racist, irrelevant to their lives, biased toward the wealthy and powerful, and unconcerned with stories happening in the "less newsworthy" communities of color where many of them lived. While they retained historic ideals of journalism and the public good, namely, that journalists should "stand up for what's right" and "protect everyday people," many youth we spoke with felt that legacy news journalists were "asleep at the wheel." These young people preferred getting news on social media because they felt it was more truthful, relevant, up-to-date, and diverse in its perspectives. The youths' comments revealed the complicated nature of the concept of "community," illustrating that legacy journalism's history of producing news for a unitary, geographically based public has left the younger, geographically dispersed and culturally diverse generation feeling left out. The chapter pointed out that youth do not experience themselves as part of a unitary public, but rather as participants in various publics, and journalists of the future need to both provide stories that engage diverse communities in processes of identifying and sharing news, as well as engage diverse communities in becoming makers or co-creators of those stories. To do this would require journalism to move away from the sensationalistic, profit-obsessed model of reporting that dominates today's corporate-owned media markets, and embrace a wider array of creative journalistic storytelling genres, partnerships, and funding models. Thus, our findings imply that what is needed in the news of the future involves more than journalistic training that would increase diversity or even increase connections between the citizen journalism efforts of community leaders and the legacy media. Our work suggests that what is required is the rethinking of a concept of journalism that currently views people as revenue sources rather than as citizens. We will discuss this further in what follows.

Tracing the history of today's youth news ecology, Chapter 4 discussed precursors to contemporary connective journalism practices, reviewing three main types of news production that were traditionally aimed at youth and exploring how they relate to theories of democratic participation. Following research illustrating that online interest-driven activities correlate with higher levels of youth civic and political engagement,[1] the chapter demonstrated the fluid nature of how young people draw upon various personal and popular cultural reference points, developing their own political consciousness and opinions as they share content with one another. And, even as we recognize that young people will continue to interact with news that is produced by legacy media sources aimed primarily at an adult audience, we argued in that chapter that news *produced* by and for youth (as opposed to news produced by adults for youth) in contexts where young people are able to select and create their own stories, unfettered by adult censorship, is most conducive to what Carpentier termed as a "maximalist" model of democratic participation. This kind of participation embraces consensus-oriented processes of democracy, collaboration, and decision making, as we elaborated in the chapter.[2] We also observed that the most successful youth journalism programs provide resources that amplify practices of connective journalism that would otherwise reach only a very small number of peers. It is this amplification that we believe is an essential aspect of the news of the future. The chapter argued that while young people do not need adults to tell them what problems are worth exploring or which stories to research and cover, youth can benefit from partnerships in which adults are conscious of their roles as connectors to resources and powerful allies in adult spaces.

Chapter 5 included a discussion of theories and critiques of the public sphere, where we argued that hope for change is an important yet overlooked aspect of what it means to be a citizen. This, we argued, is especially true for young people from under-resourced communities whose experiences with poverty, discrimination, and violence have alienated them from mainstream political and media institutions. Chapter 5 also offered examples of connective journalism practices, as teenagers spontaneously shared the "artifacts of engagement" of their involvement in the then-emergent #BlackLivesMatter and No Eastie Casino movements on social media. As we noted, this led to the unintentional formation of youthful counterpublics that demanded substantive local political change.

To further illustrate how connective journalism practices can lead to civic participation, Chapter 6 provided examples of young people using social media not only to tell their stories and connect with each other, but to do so in tandem with larger organizing efforts of established community organizations working to address issues of injustice. This chapter contextualized these practices in relation to evolving ideas regarding citizen journalism, specifically related to communities and advocacy, and introduced the concept of solutions-oriented journalism. Through this research, we have come to believe that encouraging youthful storytelling that connects with young people's concerns and communities engenders the type of collective identity formation and connective action that fuels political change. We have seen that as youth gatewatch how problems are constituted in communication, share evidence of problems with peers, and define their own stories through social media, they create their own performances of self and performances of their relations with others that are political in nature. Both Chapters 5 and 6 thus highlighted the importance of teaching young people techniques of investigative journalism and helping them to connect their passionate interests and personal stories to relevant research data in order to analyze social inequities and tell meaningful stories that can influence local policymakers.

The impressive numbers of young people involved in recent change movements from Occupy Wall Street to #BlackLivesMatter to the Bernie Sanders's presidential campaign and the Standing Rock protest of the Dakota Access Pipeline illustrate that today's youth are not complacent. They have the desire and capacity to transform themselves into engaged, articulate citizens. So how can we, as a society, develop the capacity to support them? This is the question that we wish to address for the remainder of this chapter.

WHAT JOURNALISM ORGANIZATIONS AND JOURNALISTS COULD DO

Based on our research into the relationships between young people and the existing journalism legacy news outlets, we believe that there are five possible paths that news outlets could take as they seek to address the most glaring challenges noted in the previous chapters and to buttress the most promising of the connective journalism practices we have illuminated. Legacy journalism outlets, such as local newspapers, radio and television stations, as well as emergent digital journalism outlets, can

1. focus on engaging youth as citizens, not profit generators,
2. cultivate connections with local community youth as sources for news,
3. partner with local community and school news efforts,
4. train young people as makers of news and new stories about their communities, and
5. train local youth in investigative research, and partner in story production for differing audiences with the aim of solutions-oriented journalism.

Focus on Engaging Youth as Citizens, Not Profit Generators

As noted in Chapter 4, many local initiatives that once sought to address the needs of young people were discontinued in cost-cutting measures and, in today's frantic economic environment, there is little appetite and few resources available to consider the issue of youth engagement in news. Given the context of commercially driven news organizations, youth engagement is generally viewed by journalism organizations as "not our problem." Of course, opting to view youth disengagement in this way has not served journalism as a cultural institution very well in the past, as we now have communities that are extremely alienated from all forms of legacy journalism. As journalism continues to struggle to retain its legitimacy as an institution that plays a crucial role in US culture, we argue that continuing to ignore youth, and particularly youth from low-income and immigrant communities who are among the fastest growing communities in the United States, is no longer an option.

Cultivate Connections with Local Community Youth as Sources for News

Many local news organizations have made strides in cultivating connections with members of communities that too often have been underserved, underreported, or stereotypically reported. Sometimes, this occurs through the work of enterprising reporters who build connections with local community leaders. It is much more difficult, however, to connect with those who do not hold leadership positions in communities, particularly people experiencing frequent moves necessitated by rising costs in rents (as in the gentrification of formerly affordable urban neighborhoods), unstable employment, and unreliable transportation situations. Some have argued that Twitter can fill this gap, while others look to initiatives that seek alternative voices through online platforms such as the American Public Media's Public Insight Network. While this is a challenging path for journalism outlets to pursue, they need to think more about ways to engage with these overlooked communities. In addition to connecting with youth from under-resourced urban communities, it is crucial for journalists to connect with youth in rural areas, many of whom are from low-income backgrounds and geographically isolated areas. The shock waves radiating among the US mainstream news media following the 2016 victory of Donald Trump in the presidential election illustrates how out of touch mainstream media have been with the problems and frustrations of these rural populations. However, connecting with rural youth as sources of news will require investments in bringing back journalism to the many small cities and towns that have lost local newspapers and radio and television stations in successive waves of media consolidation since the late 1980s.

Partner with Local Community and School News Efforts

For a long time, partnerships have existed between journalism outlets and community and school news efforts. Sometimes these partnerships have consisted of little more than the offer of free newspaper delivery to schools or tours of the local broadcast stations. Other partnerships involve the sponsorship of local events, which engender goodwill for journalistic outlets. These are starting points for relationship building between journalists and community members, although too often these efforts rest upon the performance of partnerships rather than on engagement designed for supporting the development of a public will. Perhaps the most well-known model of media partnering with local schools and communities is Radio Rookies, New York City Public Radio's initiative that trains teenagers to create radio stories about issues affecting their communities and the larger world. To do this, WNYC works with local New York high schools, immigrant organizations, social service agencies, and other community-based organizations throughout the city's boroughs to train youth in storytelling that is eventually broadcast on National Public Radio. Similarly, WERS radio at Boston's Emerson College, the nation's highest rated college radio station, collaborates with Zumix Radio, the afterschool youth community journalism program in Boston, discussed in Chapter 4. And, WHYY, Philadelphia's public TV station, also mentioned in Chapter 4, trains high school students in radio and TV production, helping them tell their stories for broadcast audiences. All of these award-winning initiatives are undertaken by non-profit media organizations with missions to produce original, high-quality public affairs programming. In theory, for-profit media organizations could connect with local schools and communities in a similar manner.

There are a number of creative ways in which news media from diverse and geographically isolated communities could be funded. In early 2017, the Federal Communications Commission (FCC) auctioned off nearly $20 billion dollars worth of unused broadcasting spectrum in the second-highest grossing spectrum auction in FCC history.[3] These airwaves were the public's and have always come with public interest obligations. States, communities, universities and public broadcasting affiliates that sold licenses and underutilized spectrum could use the money generated from the auction to invest in an exciting array of public interest initiatives, including digital news sites, blogs, podcasts, YouTube channels, and public data sites devoted to providing stronger community news coverage and watchdog journalism in underserved areas. Freepress.org and other media advocacy organizations have partnered with philanthropic foundations to encourage this, and in some states, such as Virginia, Connecticut and Massachusetts, public broadcasters have already announced plans to invest auction proceeds into strengthening public and community media through new journalism pilot projects, educational initiatives and foundations to promote civic media. For example, the Commonwealth Public Broadcasting Corp. in Virginia announced that it will invest $182 million it earned from the auction to fund expanded community service and a foundation to promote public media, while Connecticut Public Broadcasting will invest $32.6 million in similar initiatives.[4] Boston's WGBH website states that it will use a portion of the $219 million in proceeds it received to strengthen efforts in local journalism.[5]

While public-TV license holders across the United States made huge amounts of money from the auction, most haven't yet committed to investing that money into improving local journalism or community programming. Many administrators would prefer to use these revenues to fill short-term holes in state budgets or increase university and station endowments. However, citizens in states across the country are pushing their elected leaders and public stations to invest current and future spectrum auction profits in strengthening local journalism. New Jersey, one of the most underserved states in the nation when it comes to local news coverage (due to severe budget cuts, acquisitions, and the fact that the state is overshadowed by the major metropolitan news markets of New York and Philadelphia), received the prodigious sum of $332 million in proceeds from the auction.[6] Citizens and advocacy groups such as Free Press and its "News Voices"[7] initiative are urging local lawmakers to invest a significant portion of the proceeds into the newly created New Jersey Civic Information Consortium, which would issue grants to benefit the state's civic life and meet the information needs of New Jersey's underserved communities by partnering with local universities, media outlets, technology companies, and community groups to increase original, investigative reporting that would fill New Jersey's news gap. Widescale public involvement and activism will be needed to accomplish such goals in New Jersey and across the country.

Train Young People as Makers of News and New Stories about Their Communities

This is a path that offers promise, and through initiatives such as the Knight News Challenge, several large university journalism programs have engaged in efforts that train high school and college students to fill in news gaps left by layoffs within local news organizations. In smaller markets and where large university journalism programs are not available, this path has been much less frequently pursued. Since 2007, the Knight Foundation has "challenged" media organizations, universities, community organizations, Internet entrepreneurs, and others to generate innovative "breakthrough" ideas for news stories. But, it is rare that the young people who are trained to generate news come from the neighborhoods and communities that are most underserved within local markets. This approach therefore does not address a fundamental disjuncture between communities and news organizations. More problematic is the fact that this approach can fall into the trap of viewing community partners as sources for the extraction of value, in that community partners are asked to generate stories for no remuneration (and, in some cases, students are relied upon to provide free labor for this extraction), while those within the industries benefit financially and even personally from the extraction of those stories.

It is possible that a win-win scenario could be developed in which community organizations partner with universities and news organizations to provide cultural sensitivity training and to jointly design pathways for all parties involved. Members of the community could mentor college students and news media organizations in community issues, and university students or news reporters could then work with community members in the development of journalistic storytelling that meets the varied goals of communities and that may serve as career paths into journalism for young community members. Such an endeavor is time-consuming and resource-intensive, however, and it also calls upon news industries to make a commitment to hiring local talent cultivated through this process. We have seen few initiatives of journalism outlets that have brought this level of commitment to a community, although in the wake of the 2016 presidential elections, there has been a vigorously renewed public dialogue among news organizations, universities, and non-profit organizations concerning how to "fix" journalism.

Another possibility, which could include many of the "win-win" aspects mentioned earlier, would be to develop a journalism version of "Teach for America," where newly minted university journalism graduates could do one- to two-year internships while living in urban and rural underserved areas and working at community newspapers/websites, TV stations, or radio stations to help forge connections with and provide news stories from under-resourced communities.

Train Local Youth in Investigative Research, and Partner in Story Production for Differing Audiences with the Aim of Solutions-Oriented Journalism

This is an elaboration of the previous path for journalistic outlets, and one that is equally resource-intensive, but deserving of greater consideration. As we have noted in this book, several after-school community youth programs have already embraced techniques of action research in ways that guide young people through the processes of identifying community concerns, researching ways to address those concerns, and developing a plan of action that brings youth together with decision makers who hold the power to effect changes. What we proposed in Chapter 6 is that such an approach, coupled with the development of a plan that incorporates media messaging designed to provide data to decision makers, could provide a template for what we, along with others, have termed solutions-oriented journalism. In this model, training in storytelling comes much later in the process than is usually the case in models embracing community members or students as news generators. This is because in general, whereas journalists and journalism educators feel competent to train young people in journalistic storytelling genres, they are much less prepared to address the cynicism and outrage that is often a starting point for discussions of community concerns. In other words, it is rare for those in journalism to have received training in democratic processes of mutual listening, or to approach these processes as an important aspect of story development. And yet, as our research has found, the rise of connective journalism foregrounds the need to reconceptualize journalism's role in democratic processes, as we must bring greater attention to how publics form *in and through* interpersonal relationships and consider what is needed to facilitate these processes. This is an issue to which we will return in the final section of this chapter. First, however, we look at another area that shapes the experiences of young people: education.

WHAT YOUTH JOURNALISM EDUCATORS AND PARENTS COULD DO

Advocate for High School Journalism Programs

As we discussed in Chapter 4, school-based journalism programs are perhaps the most prevalent form of news that is created by and for youth, but they are not necessarily oriented to fostering youth voice and civic engagement. When we consider what is needed in relation to young people and the future of news in a social media era, it's worth beginning with these programs, as they represent an existing infrastructure with representation in many schools across the United States. However, the recommendations outlined in what follows can also be implemented in after-school youth programs with a focus on media and journalism and some of the discussions we suggest can be initiated by parents, as well as teachers and youth workers.

Journalism programming in high schools is a crucial element in encouraging youth citizen journalism and civic participation. However, economically strapped urban schools, with student bodies comprised largely of low-income, minoritized youth, have historically experienced a paucity of high school journalism programs, tending to have weak, infrequently published newspapers, if any at all.[8] Because of drastic cuts in public education in recent decades that have disproportionately affected those school districts serving low-income, immigrant, and minoritized youth, the relatively few high school journalism programs that previously existed in low-income school districts have been further reduced. In Boston, for example, the vast majority of the city's 128 public schools (with a population that is 78 percent low-income and only 13 percent White),[9] lack journalism courses or afterschool journalism clubs. Low-income school districts across the United States face similar realities. Thus, there needs to be a dramatic re-funding of such programs at the school and afterschool levels, ideally encouraging collaborations with public or community-based radio and television stations or citizen journalism websites such as the examples we've noted in this book.

Protect Free Speech for Youth

For youth fortunate enough to have access to journalism programming, censorship is a factor preventing many from feeling free to express themselves, as noted in Chapter 4. In contrast to the ideals of free speech implied in typical high school journalism program mission statements, restrictions on the free speech of youth journalists are common. High school teachers and principals frequently discourage or prohibit student stories about war, drugs, teen sexuality, school policies, and other controversial issues and such censorship has been found to disillusion student journalists regarding the viability of their political agency.[10]

With the advent of the Internet and media's sensationalistic coverage of youth cyberbullying and sexting, the national conversation about student freedom of expression grew heavily focused on how schools could further curtail it online. While student hate speech and cyberbullying are serious issues that must be thoughtfully addressed, many schools have abused newfound anti-bullying authority to suppress lawful student criticism of school policies and personnel.[11] However, momentum toward legal protections for student speech has been growing. Working with advocates in law, education, civics, and journalism, young people are currently organizing for the same free speech rights accorded to adults,[12] and the issue is being decided on a state-by-state basis until the Supreme Court revisits the topic. Students in North Dakota fought for the John Wall New Voices Act, a landmark measure signed into law in April 2015, which ensures the free-speech rights of journalism students in

North Dakota public schools and colleges. Similar measures were signed into law in Maryland (April 2016), Illinois (July 2016), Missouri (August 2016), and Vermont (May 2017) and are being introduced in other states as part of the nationwide New Voices campaign.

Meanwhile, free speech struggles continue regarding the rights of students to express political opinions online about school policies. When the University of Missouri football team announced a boycott through Twitter in November 2015, vowing not to participate in any football activities until the university president resigned due to his inaction in addressing an inhospitable racial climate on campus, the issue of student censorship again received front-page attention. While the University of Missouri students were able to act without disciplinary consequences, dozens of National Collegiate Athletic Association (NCAA) Division I athletic programs restrict student athletes' speech on social media.[13] In order to foster a sense of political agency in young people, we need to support ongoing efforts that protect youth free speech in high schools and universities, not only in the realm of student newspapers, but also on social media.

Advocate for Partnerships across the Curriculum

Journalism programs and classes are sometimes, but not always, viewed by schools as holding some relationship with media literacy and civic education programs. But, too often, these programs are structured to be in competition with one another for students. We think that this is unfortunate, for our research suggests that the development of critical digital and media literacy skills is key to fostering civic agency in the current era, and opportunities to teach these skills exist in a number of high school courses. In our experience, those engaged in school journalism programs are often the best-positioned to build relationships across the curriculum in order to bring media into conversation with other curricula of relevance for youth citizenship, particularly civics, social studies, and English classes.

Provide Training in Social Media as Part of a Broader Focus on Critical Media Literacy

According to the 2013 Annual Survey of Journalism Graduates conducted by the University of Georgia's Cox Center,[14] journalism school graduates get *most* of their news from social media and other online sources, rather than from newspapers, magazines, and traditional news formats predominantly taught in high school journalism programs. Additionally, a study by the Poynter Institute for Media Studies found that most professional journalists now use social media for newsgathering and story research.[15] Yet, despite this reality, most journalism curricula still do not offer a critical focus (or in many cases, *any* focus) on social media, whether at the university level[16] or the high school level.[17]

At both levels, journalism curricula have been slow to include instruction on social media and, when included, there has generally not been a critical focus. When incorporated into journalism curricula, social media are most often discussed in terms of the utilitarian benefits they afford reporters in publishing/promoting stories and in creating their own personal "brand," rather than in terms of using social media to teach responsible journalism practices and effective modes of civic engagement. Even professional journalists receive little guidance regarding such ethical issues as reusing material they find on social media, for example.[18] Therefore, we advocate for the importance of teaching young people *critical* news literacy, a branch of media literacy defined by Howard Schneider, founding dean of the School of Journalism at Stony Brook University, as "[t]he ability to use critical thinking skills to judge the reliability and credibility of news reports, whether they come via print, television or the Internet."[19]

As noted in Chapter 5, most youth today are very savvy at using social media, but ill equipped to evaluate the credibility of online news sources. We feel that educators should use social media as a *starting point* with youth (rather than an afterthought) to discuss journalistic concepts such as credibility, reliability, bias, and other ethical concepts related to journalism.[20] Critical news literacy includes not only helping youth develop the ability to judge the reliability of online information, but also the ability to understand the legal and ethical considerations involved in online storytelling in both personal and professional contexts. While youth recognize that social media can be unreliable, they tend to automatically trust online information when it is sent to them from a familiar person or website. This phenomenon is not limited to youth, but highlights the urgent need for frank discussions about social media as sources of and distribution points for news.

With the prodigious rise in 2016 of blatantly deceptive fake news websites and the proliferation of false news stories being shared on social media (before, during, and after the 2016 US presidential election), critical news literacy has never been more important. While from the 1990s through the first fifteen years of the 2000s, the term "fake

news" commonly referred to news satire TV shows or parody websites such as The Onion (United States), Private Eye (Britain), Faking
News (India), and others that humorously critiqued the mainstream
news media's coverage of political issues as a way to encourage public
discussion of current events, the term "fake news" took on new meaning in 2016 and is now most commonly associated with websites that
spread purposely misleading and false stories for sheer economic profit.
Whereas satirical mock news shows such as *The Colbert Report, The
Daily Show with Jon Stewart*, or *Last Week Tonight with John Oliver*
openly identified themselves as entertainment (yet regularly used fact
checkers regarding the stories they discussed), today's fake news websites, which have a predominantly far right (or "alt right") perspective,
are not transparent about their fakeness, instead going out of their way
to make deceptive headlines and photos appear legitimate. Rather than
political satire, their goal is the purposeful spreading of sensational and
inflammatory hoax stories designed to get mouse clicks that generate
thousands of dollars per day from advertising. Whereas news parody
websites offer clues about their fakeness via purposely silly headlines
and other indications (for example, the banner logo of the site News
Biscuit reads: "News Before It Happens"), "alt right" fake news sites
look real, with legitimate-sounding names such as The New Observer,
The National Report, or DailyNewsPolitics.

The result has been that stories with paranoid, racist, sexist, xenopho-
bic, or White nationalist perspectives, which, in earlier times, would have
had miniscule audiences and would have been dismissed as fringe con-
spiracies by most people, are wielding previously unimaginable influence
on the public, and particularly on youth, due to their wide circulation
on social media. As an example, the following false story "FBI Agent
Suspected in Hillary Email Leaks Found Dead In Apparent Murder-
Suicide," published on a fake news site called DenverGuardian.com
was shared on Facebook over half a million times.[21] And according to
the 2016 Stanford University study reviewed in the Introduction and in
Chapter 1, young people are more likely than adults to believe fake news
stories because youth focus more on a story's content than its source and
are unaware of basic conventions for verifying digital information.[22] The
study found that high production values, links to sites with reputable-
sounding names, and polished "About" pages were able to easily convince
college students to trust false information. Noting that democracy may
be in danger because of the ease with which false information about civic
issues is flourishing online, the study also noted that most of the media

literacy curricula used in US middle schools and high schools are "stuck in the past."[23]

The growth of fake news websites has created confusion regarding what is true or false in the news, actually calling into question the validity of real news.[24] The extensive social media circulation of untrue stories regarding the 2016 US presidential candidates, coupled with the fact that these sensational false stories were shared more widely online (especially by young people) than the more subdued accurate stories that corrected and disproved them, have been blamed for significantly influencing the election results.[25] In response, Facebook, Twitter, Google, and other social media platforms announced in the weeks following the election that they would implement algorithms to help identify false news stories. While algorithms may be helpful, it is social media users who share material online, so a crucial line of defense should be to teach users to better evaluate digital information.

Discuss How Codes and Algorithms Structure the Social Media Young People Use

Social media discussions need not be limited to what happens in relation to use. While there are hopeful developments regarding the potential for civic engagement that have been realized in the "front end" of social media platforms (applications that users interact with directly), we want to emphasize the need for greater diversity, accessibility, and transparency at the "back end" (servers, programs, and applications that support front end activities) in order to ensure that young citizens will continue to encounter digital platforms amenable for the development of connective action. More attention needs to be paid to how Internet infrastructure and platform designs constrain certain types of ideas and actions. Science and technology scholar, Langdon Winner, has noted that the functions and intentions of technology are intimately connected with the self-understanding of those who design them.[26] The Internet and social media networks are predominantly designed by and reflect (consciously or unconsciously) the perspectives of the upper-income, profit-oriented, White, and Asian males who hold the lion's share of decision-making power in the digital technology landscape. Popularly dubbed "brogrammers" in reference to a primarily male, macho computer programming culture that has been hostile to women, the "brogrammer effect" has been blamed for the shrinking proportion of women in programming over the past two decades.[27] In major tech companies such as

Google, Twitter, Yahoo, Facebook, eBay, Apple, Pinterest, LinkedIn, Intel, Cisco, and Hewlett Packard, women comprise fewer than 30 percent of employees in leadership and technical positions, and historically under-represented populations such as African Americans, Hispanics, Native Americans, and Hawaiian/Pacific Islanders comprise fewer than 10 percent of such employees.[28] This lack of diversity translates into fewer diverse ideas around design intent with respect to how platforms and infrastructures could function.

While front end online user activities appear open and egalitarian, back end social media mechanisms reflect the priorities and assumptions of the non-representative sector of the US population who design and run them. Exemplifying a recent aspect of this problem, even before the 2016 election, Facebook had been accused of manipulating its back end algorithms to reflect certain political perspectives and marginalize others, impacting the news and views that front end users were exposed to without users even being aware of it.[29] In addition to concerns about the marginalization of political viewpoints on social media are concerns regarding the ways in which algorithms can perpetuate stereotypes and social divisions based on gender, race, or social class. Most websites recommend articles that are similar to those a reader has previously read so, for example, a woman may be primarily recommended articles on childrearing or diet because she has read articles on these topics in the past. To enhance the Internet's potential to serve as a forum for democratic public debate, coders should experiment with developing algorithms that also direct readers to articles to which they might not otherwise be exposed.[30] All of these issues deserve more open public discussion and input, and a place to start such discussions would be in interdisciplinary media literacy conversations with students in high school and college. While most of us never think about it, algorithms have social implications. They don't just reflect reality; they help shape it.

Technocratic decisions regarding the design and uses of social media, made behind the scenes without input from the general public, ultimately affect the public sphere. As Jürgen Habermas has noted, "If the discourse of experts is not coupled with democratic opinion and will-formation, then the experts' perceptions of problems will prevail at the citizens' expense."[31] Without public input through democratic channels, advancements in technology will likely serve privileged interests rather than the public interest. We need mechanisms to diversify and monitor the management, design and infrastructure of social media companies that have heretofore been exempt from the types of public monitoring and transparency historically applied to traditional news outlets and tele-com companies. In this way, we can attempt to ensure that de facto censorship does not occur regarding ideas deemed unprofitable or not in keeping with elite technological gatekeepers' notions of acceptability. The undemocratic demographic composition of those designing and running social media companies and the Internet is only a more concentrated version of the undemocratic power distribution in the larger US society, so policies enacted to address the latter would help ameliorate the former.

Discuss and Support Policies to Address the Digital Divide

Another issue that stands at the intersection of media and numerous social issues is that of unequal access to technologies and skills. Given the historic and growing socioeconomic inequality in the United States,[32] particularly between White populations and racially minoritized populations (i.e. African Americans, Latinos, and Native Americans), the "digital divide" or unequal access to new communication technologies, is a concern regarding news and the future of democratic participation. Early digital divide concerns focused on people's ability to purchase and learn how to use new media technologies;[33] however, contemporary concerns center on connectivity rather than ownership or proficiency, since people cannot participate in social media if they lack reliable Internet access.

While the vast majority of youth we interviewed owned cell phones, including youth whose families lived below the federal poverty level, many individuals said that the cost of monthly cell phone providers was a significant burden for their families, with some students reporting that their cell phone service had been cut off more than once due to their family's inability to pay the monthly bill. Youth also noted that the less expensive Internet service providers commonly used by low-income families were less reliable. As Jose, aged seventeen, said: "If you have an iPhone and you are covered by a large franchise like AT&T or Verizon, then you won't lose connection to the Internet. But, if you're covered by a cheaper company, like Metro-PCS, it can sometimes become difficult to stay connected." A national study found that while nine out of ten low and moderate income families have home or mobile Internet access, nearly half have speeds that are sluggish, intermittent, and too slow to be useful, while 29 percent of surveyed families living in poverty reported having their service disconnected due to failure to pay.[34] The economic instability faced disproportionately by low-income minoritized populations illustrates the fragile and undemocratic nature of digital access.

While the FCC has mandated a lifeline policy since 1985 to ensure that qualifying low-income families can apply for discounted telephone service, there was no such policy for the Internet until 2016. Under pressure from public interest groups and consumer advocates, the FCC decided on March 31, 2016, to reform the lifeline policy to include broadband. The new rates, which went into effect in December of 2016 and offered a modest 500 minutes of 3G speed for $9.95 per month, were fought by conservatives in Congress who attempted to block the subsidies.[35] Although they were not successful at the time, conservatives vowed to continue opposing the subsidies and, under the Trump administration, have moved towards dismantling them. In February of 2017, the new Trump-appointed Chairman of the FCC, Ajit Pai, dealt a blow to the lifeline program by announcing that nine companies previously approved to offer subsidies to low-income families would no longer be able to do so.[36] Such policies that undercut companies' ability to provide low-cost Internet to the poorest Americans will deepen the digital divide, if the public is not outspoken in its support for universal broadband access. As part of critical media literacy curricula, young people need to be made aware of these types of legal battles so that they can participate in the political organizing and advocacy work necessary to win them.

Discuss Media Reform and Regulation

Educators, youth workers, and parents need to have discussions with youth regarding the non-egalitarian aspects of social media because the general population, including youth, must work in support of more democratic media reform and regulation. We must keep in mind that initiatives designed to ensure democratic access to the Internet for *all* have repeatedly been attacked and thwarted by for-profit Internet providers and the elected officials who they economically support. For example, "Wireless Philadelphia," a 2004 initiative by Philadelphians to become the nation's first municipality with free and low-cost Wi-Fi across the entire city, was thwarted by telecom giants Verizon and Comcast, a situation faced by other cities across the country that have tried similar initiatives. This will continue to be a crucial issue in the future.

Net neutrality[37] – the principle that Internet service providers and governments should treat all data on the Internet equally, not discriminating or charging differentially by user, content, site, platform, application, type of attached equipment, or mode of communication – has repeatedly been under attack (most recently in the years 2010, 2012, 2014 and

2017) by Comcast, AT&T, Verizon, and other massive telecom industry affiliates who stand to make far greater profits if they are allowed to charge premium rates for faster download speeds. While the concept of net neutrality was upheld by the US Supreme Court in 2015, the telecom industry immediately announced that it would appeal the Court's decision. Committees in both the US Senate and the House of Representatives subsequently introduced bills in support of the telecom industry's goal of dismantling net neutrality. Donald Trump and his FCC appointees are vocal opponents of net neutrality, so if this democratic concept is to be saved, young people will have to become very involved in the fight.

Bills such as SOPA (Stop Online Piracy) and PIPA (Protect IP Act) are other examples of legal battles that have been fought around issues related to Internet access, content sharing, and freedom of expression. Supported by media companies and industry associations such as the Motion Picture Association of America, the Recording Industry Association of America, and the Entertainment Software Association, these bills were introduced in 2011 by both the US Senate and the House of Representatives purportedly to enforce copyright infringement, colloquially known as "online piracy." However, the bills contained measures that free speech advocates, artists, scholars, and Internet websites such as Google, Wikipedia, Facebook, Twitter, Tumblr, Reddit, and a host of others felt would greatly curtail online freedom of speech, significantly limiting what could be shared online, and ultimately harming websites and Internet communities. While both bills were defeated in 2012, largely due to the power of citizens to use social media to inform and organize the public, the powerful forces behind these bills continue to push for individual states to pass similar domestic laws and are pursuing international trade agreements that would force signatory nations to comply. These and other concerns related to open access and expression will continue to need the advocacy of an informed and active public. But how do we make young people feel passionate about seemingly obscure and dry political issues such as media policies and regulations? Some have found encouragement for this in satirical social commentary that illustrates important political issues in ways that are easily understood by everyday people.

Discuss Alternative News Sources: Consider Satire and Pastiche as Educational Tools

To foster a more informed and active public, news of the future will need to be disseminated in ways that help people understand the relevance of current events to their own lives. In our interviews, young people repeatedly told us that some of the sources they found most informative regarding political issues were satirical mock news shows such as *The Colbert Show* and *The Daily Show with Jon Stewart*. These shows place political topics in broader socio-political contexts, providing background information and clarifying what is at stake in ways that promote public debate.[38]

An example of this was the June 1, 2014, HBO episode of *Last Week Tonight with John Oliver*, in which host John Oliver spent thirteen minutes discussing net neutrality (which he relabeled "cable company f_ckery"). With an audience of 4.6 million weekly viewers,[39] many of whom are under forty, the half-hour show is a satirical weekly review of news, politics, and current events. Before the episode aired, most Americans knew little about net neutrality. However, the segment explained what was at stake in such a direct and compelling manner that it went viral, launching more than 45,000 new comments to the FCC website and giving a greater boost to the net neutrality movement than advocacy campaigns had previously been able to achieve.[40] HBO uploads the weekly episodes of the show to YouTube and this clip received more than 12,219,367 online views.[41] As net neutrality faced the chopping block once again under the Trump Administration, Oliver did a second segment on the topic on May 7, 2017, garnering 2,957,981 views on YouTube in just the 48 hours after it aired.[42] The video was widely shared online and reignited public interest in this issue, with the FCC receiving 100,000 public comments in the twenty-four hours following the show.[43] Oliver's segments on other contemporary topics such as Facebook privacy, gun control, the death penalty, the US prison system, student debt, corruption in FIFA (the entity that organizes the World Cup), and other political issues have also gone viral on social media, illustrating young people's interest in political issues when they are portrayed in an interesting and relevant way.

Alternative media shows and websites that combine news parody, humorous banter, ironic recaps of current events, and political discussion, such as *The Daily Show with Trevor Noah* (2015 to present, which was formerly *The Daily Show with Jon Stewart* from 1999 to 2015), The Onion (1988 to present); *The Philip DeFranco Show* (2007 to present); *The Young Turks* (2002 to present), *Full Frontal with Samantha Bee* (2016 to present), and numerous others are extremely popular with youth and young adults. Similar humorous news formats have appeared in countries around the world, garnering large youthful audiences. These include such shows as *CNNNN* and *The Roast* in Australia, *This Hour Has 22 Minutes* (Canada), *31 Minutos* (Chile), *The Week That Wasn't* (India), *Stiscia la notizia* "Strip the News" (Italy), *PowNews* (Netherlands), *7 Days* (New Zealand), *Banana News Network* (Pakistan), *Wazzup Wazzup* (Philippines), *The Noose* (Singapore), *ZANEWS* (South Africa), *El Intermedio* (Spain), *Mock the Week* (UK), and dozens of others. The appeal of these formats has not been lost on legacy news establishments such as the *New York Times*, which has started incorporating some humorous videos in its coverage of political topics. Examples include a *Times* video of the Gregory Brothers musical mash-up of governors Chris Christie, Andrew M. Cuomo, and other politicians arguing to reform drug laws[44] and a *Times* video juxtaposing jump cuts to illustrate the similarities (and alleged plagiarism) of Melania Trump's 2016 Republican Party Convention speech to Michelle Obama's Democratic Party Convention speech eight years earlier.[45]

But, while alternative media formats like these can be effective in helping younger audiences engage with otherwise "dull" political stories, they are no substitute for in-depth investigative and local journalism. In fact, these shows *depend* on the existence of professionally trained print journalists, as pointed out on August 7, 2016 by John Oliver in his twenty-minute comedic defense of print journalism on *Last Week Tonight*. In a spoof of the Academy Award-winning investigative journalism drama *Spotlight*, portraying a future in which overloaded reporters have their serious ideas dismissed in favor of coverage of viral "raccoon-cats," Oliver emphasized the crucial need to fund quality journalism, stating: "The media is a food chain that would fall apart without local newspapers."[46]

Taking a lesson from the playbook of such popular news satires, students can similarly be encouraged to research political issues and then satirize them. In our role as educators, we need to be open to various forms of creativity and playfulness in approaches to teaching young people about journalism and news literacy. They can certainly be made to reproduce traditional genres of news they don't like, but for many of today's students, this will not inspire them to take an interest in news and public affairs. The popularity of ironic takes on the news illustrates our earlier point; stories that hit people at an emotional level are the ones that are consumed, liked, and shared most often online. Touching people in ways that engender feelings of anger, passion, joy, fear, sorrow, frustration, urgency, etc. is a key aspect of connective journalism. However, it is crucial that the stories being told and shared are based on reliable data and responsible reporting in order to avoid manipulating people's emotions for ideological objectives. In today's splintered media markets, news storytelling that is not based on facts or reliable sources has grown exponentially, further dividing society and promoting blame, fear and hate in place of public dialogue and democratic deliberation.

Discuss Ideological Polarization

While future news will need to convey stories in ways audiences can feel engaged and passionate about, we need to teach young people to recognize writing and programming that irresponsibly play on people's emotions in a one-sided way – spreading lies, stirring up fear, and engendering hostility. Earlier, we discussed the need to teach young people how to define journalistic concepts such as bias, accuracy, transparency, credibility, avoiding conflicts of interest, and minimizing harm. It is crucial that young news consumers be able to distinguish quality reporting from inflammatory fear mongering. Nationalist, racist, and sexist media offerings are on the rise and thriving in the United States, Europe, and throughout the world, supporting the growth of far right-wing and neo-fascist candidates and platforms that were relegated to the extreme fringe in earlier times.

The Internet is a place where fear and hate can be openly promoted and many of its misogynistic, racist, and homophobic discourses are recycled from one-sided "shock jock" radio and TV commentary shows that are also available online. In their book, *Shock Jocks: Hate Speech and Talk Radio*, journalists Rory O'Conner and Aaron Cutler profile "America's 10 worst hate talkers" (among them Don Imus, Rush Limbaugh, Bill O'Reilly, Glenn Beck, and Sean Hannity), arguing that their vitriolic messages have had significant political consequences such as thwarting immigration reform, gun control laws, and publicly funded national health care.[47] Non-profit media watchdog organizations such as Fairness and Accuracy in Reporting and Media Matters have similarly argued that Fox News contains conservative editorializing in its stories. Examples of this include Fox's active promotion of the conservative Tea Party Movement, the station's avid denial of global warming, its tirades against President Obama's Affordable Health Care Act, and its portrayal of the #BlackLivesMatter activists as "cop killers."

Independent research organizations such as the Project for Excellence in Journalism and the Pew research centers have concluded that Fox News is the most politically ideological news program in the United States,[48] as the station goes far beyond conservative advocacy based on facts to routinely urge viewers to write letters, make phone calls, or attend rallies in support of conservative and libertarian causes. While most people associate Fox News viewers with an older demographic, a 2016 national survey conducted by Suffolk University and USA TODAY found that people of all ages, including those aged thirty-four and under, who represented slightly under a third of people surveyed, listed Fox as their single most trusted source for television news.[49] This would seem to confirm what young people told us in Chapter 3 about a growing disregard for the journalistic norms of objective news reporting, but it may also speak to a lack of youth training in how to recognize credible and trustworthy journalistic sources, as discussed earlier. As parents, educators, and youth allies, we need to help youth recognize the difference between fact-based reporting and unfounded assertions, as well as the difference between political critique, on one hand, and hate speech or fear-mongering, on the other. This is essential in order to move beyond ideological polarization to engage in the types of fruitful discussions and debates needed in a democracy.

This brings us back to our discussion in Chapter 2 of agonistic democracy, which recognizes that identities are formed through political struggles within an inescapably contentious political landscape. Rather than striving for a Habermasian ideal of consensus that has proven elusive, we point to the value of online identification, performance, and display for the expression of political positions and democratic action. While the ideals of democracy affirm that all individuals deserve the same rights and respect, the intolerance and hate proliferating in a lot of talk radio and social media indicate that these democratic ideals are not shared by everyone. Significant numbers of people in the United States believe that certain individuals (such as Whites, males, "birthers," Christians, and heterosexuals) deserve more rights and privileges than others. We need mediums for encouraging and exploring our mutual responsibilities and obligations to each other as fellow citizens. Connective journalism is one way that this can happen, allowing people to explore the differing political directions of potential policies.

Discuss the Growing Role of Sponsored Content In News Spaces

Critical discussions about social media are crucial at the high school level, given that relatively few teenagers are aware of the fact that writers are routinely paid by corporations and political groups to post links and comments on social media platforms or to blog about issues in ways that appear to be a "natural" sharing among friends and followers. "Sponsored content" (stories, videos, or podcasts that look and feel like journalistic content but are sponsored by advertisers to promote products and services) is common and actively solicited by Facebook, Buzzfeed, Vice, and many other social media sites, with legacy news media such as *The Atlantic* and *The New York Times* now depending on sponsored content for as much as three-quarters of their digital ad revenue.[50] Likewise, most young people are unaware of "astroturfing" – the practice of masking the sponsors of politically relevant messages in order to give the impression that they originate from grassroots groups of everyday citizens when, in fact, they are created by public relations firms hired by individuals or groups to promote specific (and often undemocratic) political agendas.[51]

Use Social Media Discussions to Initiate Conversations about Privacy and Surveillance

Of additional ethical and legal concern, most young people are unaware of the ways their privacy and personal information are compromised and exploited through their participation in social media networks. As Lucia, aged twenty, said in Chapter 4, "When you update things on your computer, it gives you pages and pages and pages of conditions or whatever, and you don't read it, you just click agree." Many young people are shocked to learn that once they post content on social media sites (i.e. photos, artwork, videos), they grant the sites license to use that material in any way they want *for free*, while also granting these sites the right to let their client companies use the material as well. For example, by posting photos or videos on Facebook, individuals (most of whom do not read the fine print) give the company "a non-exclusive, transferable, sub-licensable, royalty-free, worldwide license to use any [IP] content that you post on or in connection with Facebook ("IP License")."[52] This means that sites such as Twitter, Twitpic, and Facebook not only utilize people's personal content for their own ends (which in other circumstances would be a copyright violation), but also make profits by licensing such images to others for commercial use. While there is a growing policy discussion about how government should act in a social media environment where personal information about youth is widely collected, analyzed, and shared as a new form of currency in the digital economy, young people need more opportunities to consider and discuss the ramifications of sharing information on social media. These include issues related not only to privacy and copyright, but also to identity theft, cyberbullying, and cyberstalking that can be discussed in journalism and digital media courses. For example, as part of a class activity, students at the University of Denver's Emerging Digital Cultures course formulated a list of strategies for protecting oneself online, including how to trace and block online trackers, maximize social media privacy settings, and utilize encryption and virtual private networks (VPNs).[53] In addition, youth along with their parents, teachers, and allies should be encouraged to contact media companies and public policymakers to express their concerns around privacy and surveillance.

Raise Awareness about Who Shapes Online Conversations of News and Politics

Young people across all of these programs and others must also be encouraged to reflect upon *which* voices and perspectives are most prominent on social media and which are underrepresented, examining the ways in which gender, race, sexual orientation, social class, age, and other factors affect online expression. White middle class males have historically dominated the US political, economic, and media landscape – a dynamic that continues today. And while females of all backgrounds are participating in public life in higher numbers than ever before, they are still a small minority of the country's political, business, and media leaders. This unequal representation is also reflected in political discourse online. While women use social media sites in roughly equal proportions to men, males make up the majority of those discussing, commenting on, and posting news online.[54] Moreover, while White males comprise the majority of news and opinion writers at most news organizations, including *The New York Times*, *The Washington Post*, *The Guardian*, and other high-profile national and international news generators, articles and comments written by women of differing backgrounds attract more abuse and dismissive trolling than those written by men, further discouraging the expression of female perspectives online.[55] These gender differences have profound implications for media, gender equality, and our democracy.

When certain segments of the population are underrepresented in online discussions of news and politics, the views that are *held* by the public are not the views that are *heard* by the public, resulting in skewed public debates. In an example from the research of computer scientist, Emma Pierson (who analyzed over one million posted comments in *The New York Times* and found that women wrote only a quarter of them), while women nationally favored the Affordable Care Act (ACA) in much larger numbers than men did, females were significantly underrepresented in comments sections on the topic in *The New York Times* and other online news sites.[56] This gave the impression that the ACA was less popular than it actually was. Similarly, Pierson found gender gaps in online comments regarding the topic of sexual assault, a divide that other researchers have also noted.[57] For example, women's comments were overwhelmingly sympathetic to a *Times* blog posted by Dylan Farrow, Woody Allen's stepdaughter, in which she accused Allen of sexually assaulting her. In contrast, male responses to the post were evenly split between sympathetic and dismissive.[58] Males and females have different experiences and views on a variety of issues (such as reproductive rights, public funding for education, social services, day care, and gun control, to name just a few). The underrepresentation of the perspectives of females (and other historically marginalized populations) in online news discussions means that views held by these citizens get less public visibility, influencing which opinions are favored by the public and ultimately supported by policymakers.

Discussing and analyzing social media in high school classes, student newspaper clubs, or after-school youth media programs presents opportunities to teach youth about the ways in which historical disparities based on gender, race, and other factors continue to influence who speaks in the public sphere and what types of views are expressed. Such discussions offer opportunities to teach youth about the norms of democratic deliberation, helping them acquire skills to respectfully disagree in public forums and encouraging them to think about how online anonymity can permit people to spread untruths, hurt others, withhold opinions for fear of occasioning offense and retaliation, or withdraw altogether from conversations when differences of opinion emerge. Including complex discussions of social media in high school journalism curricula and after-school youth programs can help young people within a variety of school and after-school programs to learn and apply the practices of responsible journalism (such as truth seeking, transparency, fairness and accuracy, minimizing harm, acting independently, avoiding conflicts of interest, and being accountable)[59] to the technologies and platforms they use every day.

While many high schools either lack critical news literacy programming or have not updated their offerings to include social media, there are some excellent resources available for discussing social media with youth. These include the *Social Media Toolbox: A Resource for Student Journalism Programs,*[60] developed by Marina Henricks.

Another helpful resource is SchoolJournalism.org, which has links to Social Media and Digital Tools Lesson Plans as well as links to a Poynter Institute website with useful information on teaching critical news literary. Students are taught how to check the "social history of the source" and "seek official and social corroboration" by asking questions such as "Does the person posting have a history of publishing reliable information in the past?" "Was the source a firsthand witness?" "Was the source in a position to know what he or she claims to know?" Other helpful materials include the high school journalism curriculum created by the Journalism Education Association, which includes a "Truth in Social Media" unit,[61] as well as the scholastic journalism criteria provided by The Learning Network Blog of the *New York Times*.[62]

Include Critiques of Current News as Well as Visioning Exercises That Invite Young People to Imagine What Kind of News Might Exist Instead

Taking into account how citizen-subjects are constituted and contained in the context of public schools that are marked by racial and economic disparities, we believe that if our society is to achieve greater democratic participation through political action, educators, youth workers, and activists must help young people critically consider and re-imagine the types of stories they currently tell and the types of stories they *might* tell. We need to help them recognize the elements that comprise a compelling story, inspiring them to see that their own communities are full of vital stories that deserve to be told. We also need to encourage them to resist the individualistic, narcissistic, and competitive tendencies that are encouraged in today's social media landscape, drawing inspiration from everyday stories of *collective* heroism and successful collective action that can extend young people's interests into community involvement. This is something that could be linked with the next proposal, which seeks to enrich partnerships between youth journalism and other efforts in young people's local communities.

Connect Youth Journalism Programs with Grassroots Organizations and Community Media

As we discussed in Chapter 6, efforts to teach young people lessons in civics and journalism are much more effective when connected to real-life collective problems faced by youth populations. Having youth journalism programs, whether organized by high schools or after-school agencies, collaborate with established political advocacy groups and community media outlets infuses young people with the recognition that what they create and share on social media can have concrete political consequences. Such connections encourage the development of citizenship for social reconstruction (changing the world for the better) rather than social reproduction (reproducing the status quo).[63] This approach also dovetails nicely with the earlier suggestion that partnering with local legacy media organizations might open new pathways for developing research and storytelling tools that can benefit the communities and issues concerning young people the most.

YES, BUT HOW REALISTIC IS ALL OF THIS?

Are the pathways to the future described here likely to be undertaken by journalism organizations, educators, and community groups? Perhaps, perhaps not. But rather than blame these groups and individuals for a failure to pursue these lofty goals, we wish to raise a broader series of questions that we gestured to earlier in this book but have not yet addressed. First, how does US individualism and our aversion to governmental regulation hinder our ability to take collective responsibility for the ways in which our society is currently structured? And on a related note, how does this hinder our ability to develop a civic imagination that enables us to think of how society might be structured differently? And finally, what role could media play both in fostering that civic imagination and in enabling the taking of collective responsibility?

In order to address these questions, we must begin with a recognition that we are living in a time in which US public schools have been chronically underfunded while community enrichment opportunities have been drastically defunded, particularly in low-income communities. In fact, almost everything in our public lives has been reconfigured according to the values of profitability. In our high stakes, "casino capitalism" society, individuals who are elderly, developmentally delayed, chronically disabled, or otherwise unable to work can suffer from discrimination as a result of their inability to serve as "productive" members of society, which says a great deal more about our collectively impoverished view of humanity than it does about the individuals themselves.[64] This tendency to believe that some lives matter more than others has pervaded our labor and our social welfare systems, as well, and continues to exacerbate the already entrenched systemic racism in US society. As a key example, when the globalization and deindustrialization of the late 1970s and 1980s led to the moving of factories overseas and the loss of manufacturing jobs in the United States, crime rates rose and cities and small towns throughout the country became sites of urban decay and joblessness.[65] But rather than investing in rebuilding our urban cores that were disproportionately home to African American, Latino, and Asian immigrant communities, every US president since 1980 has contributed to mass incarceration through ever harsher policies of arrest and extended confinement, which has, in turn, contributed to higher rates of joblessness, particularly among Black males.[66] The reform of social welfare in the 1990s imposed limits on welfare assistance and saw an overall plummeting of public funding by some $54 billion, which, in turn, doubled the number of families living in extreme poverty in the United States.[67] Cuts in public housing, including a law restricting former inmates from living in federally assisted housing, combined with cuts in Pell grants for prisoners seeking education, made rehabilitation after imprisonment almost impossible.[68] These policies affect a surprising share of the US population, particularly young people, and disproportionately affect people of color. According to one national survey, 44 percent of black women and 32 percent of black men have a family member in prison, compared with 12 percent of white women and 6 percent of white men.[69] Nearly 10 million children in the United States have had a parent incarcerated at some point in their lives. One out of 57 white children, one out of 28 Latino children, and one out of every 9 African American children have an incarcerated parent.[70] Today, the United States has the highest rate of incarceration in the world.[71] In fact, while our seeming inability to enact higher taxes on the wealthy or legislation to regulate either the financial industries or free market trade seems to signal a national aversion to regulation, our policies of mass incarceration reveal our willingness to impose regulations on non-white and non-privileged persons.

In order to address any questions of the possibility for greater civic engagement among *all* people living in the United States, therefore, we return to our earlier conviction that hope for change must be a starting point for a critical understanding of citizenship. And what will it take to ignite hope? Reinvestment in alternatives to mass incarceration and in programs that prevent recidivism would make an important start, as would reinvestment in public schools and in programs that support young people from disadvantaged communities. Ultimately, what has to be rebuilt is trust, and this has to begin on a local level, which is why we feel it is crucial for media organizations and journalism programs to connect with local communities, and particularly with young people, in storytelling, research, and advocacy collaborations that help people believe that their stories (and their lives) matter. The emerging practices of connective journalism are one way that young people are telling and sharing stories that can not only engender a sense of community, but also help cultivate trust in the idea that collective expressions can lead to connective actions that can bring about change.

As a society, US trust is at an all-time low. This is a concern because economists have found that countries with low levels of trust fall victim to enacting policies that benefit one's own family or community rather than seeking opportunities that would be economically beneficial for the collective population. Along similar lines, as Ana Swanson observes, when there are low levels of trust, people "might be more inclined to pursue Ponzi schemes or other frauds in the business world, or pay off an official to secure a lucrative government contract."[72] But, as economist Alex Tabarrok has noted, when people believe that their financial situation will improve in the future, they "become much less concerned about black vs. white, foreign vs. domestic, immigrants vs. nonimmigrants. They become much more open to the world and their fellow citizens."[73] Trust and economic peace of mind seem to go together.

We are convinced, therefore, that one key to a rebuilding of trust lies in reconceiving of humans as persons rather than as revenue streams. Whether we are viewed as revenue streams for the massive prison complex, for the low-wage positions in the emergent service economy of globalization, or even as audience members whose participation in the news ecology is viewed as advertising revenue, we are, in a certain sense, placed into what Martin Buber termed an I–It rather than an I–Thou relationship. We are too often reduced to objects that are understood in relation to the benefit we bring to others. And this returns us to questions of the role of news and young people in relation to democratic theory, a discussion that we began in Chapter 1. What role might media play both in fostering civic imagination and in enabling the taking of collective responsibility?

THE ROLE OF MEDIA REPRESENTATIONS IN
FOSTERING OR UNDERMINING EMPATHY

The question of how people of all ages develop empathy in an increasingly diverse democratic society has become important for moral philosophers, theorists of citizenship, and those interested in questions of media messages. Some, such as communication theorist Roger Silverstone, posit that with the globalization of media, we are all capable of becoming immediately aware of the suffering of others around the world, and this can contribute to the growth of compassion for the Other.[74] He and others argue that what is needed among young people today is a cultivation of a cosmopolitan world view that is open to finding points of commonality across difference, following Ulrich Beck's argument for the fostering of an authentic European openness to otherness and Luc Boltanski's suggestion of the transformative potential in the viewing of others' suffering.[75]

Yet as Shani Orgad and Irene Seu have pointed out, a weakness in Silverstone's analysis is that his work is framed normatively, in relation to how people *ought* to respond rather than how they *actually* respond to media images of the Other.[76] In contrast, some, such as Susan Moeller, have argued that as legacy media rely upon grisly images of war and suffering to attract and retain attention, they contribute to generating widespread indifference toward others due to "compassion fatigue."[77] This, in turn, leads some to avoid consuming news altogether, as we saw among some of the young people in Chapter 3 who discussed tuning out news due to the way it generated negative feelings for them.[78] Lilie Chouliaraki further argues that historical change in humanitarian appeals reveals that their mediation and appeal to a North American and European audience has transformed moral conviction into a lifestyle choice, leading those of us in the West to become "ironic spectators" of the suffering of others.[79] Far from opening up opportunities to foster cosmopolitanism, then, this research suggests that young people today may be more likely to view distant stories of suffering with indifference.[80]

The notion that moral convictions and civic engagement are "lifestyle choices" has also been taken up Kjerstin Thorson, who notes that youth today see civic engagement as a choice rather than a duty to the larger society (in what she coins "do-it-yourself-citizenship," the notion that people should seek out news across multiple sources, becoming their own researcher, fact checker, and policy expert).[81] Thorson notes that this runs the risk of setting the bar of informed citizenship so high that many people won't bother trying to achieve it, adding to public apathy or inertia. If civic engagement or political participation is motivated only by personal interest, as critics of this phenomenon note, then there is seemingly little pressure to adhere to a particular "right way" to be a good citizen, since the tolerant "everybody should do what they want" attitude of today's youth has replaced earlier notions of civic duty. Similarly, Christian Smith, Director of the Center for the Study of Religion and Society at Notre Dame University, argues that this creates a "debilitating effect," making it impossible to discern what is socially shared or to consider "how the public might need to pull together to achieve common goals."[82]

However, like Thorson, we believe that in our fast paced age of new media, where it is no longer possible to develop a set of unified abiding norms about civic engagement to be handed down to future generations, contemporary citizenship characterized by choice, openness, and uncertainty are leading to new forms of political engagement, which can co-exist with and build upon older forms. Contrary to having a debilitating effect, we believe that youthful practices of connective journalism are an important avenue through which individuals can recognize what is socially shared and decide when, how, or whether to pull together to achieve collective goals.

Meanwhile, in terms of media representations, we support the continued advocacy for fair representations of all persons in the media, recognizing that education is necessary for fostering critical viewing. Political and media discussions deserve to take place in relation to one another. Exploring the role of pedagogical interventions in the development of empathy has led to an interest in varied ways that empathy might be taught and learned.[83] Some, for instance, have argued that through pedagogical efforts, young people can come to have a sense of "embedded cosmopolitanism," or an identification with a community to which they have a commitment.[84] But, again, what if there is a distance between the empathy we wish we could engender among youth and the reality of a fractious, agony-filled or "agonistic" political environment in which young people feel that their lived experiences are disrespected?[85]

THINKING THROUGH DISCORD

I'm not respectable. I'm not your gentle pacifist queer telling myself that love will win. Love isn't winning. Prepare accordingly. – Zoe S. tweeted June 13, 2016, after the Orlando nightclub shooting, the largest mass shooting in US history

The above quote is illustrative of the sense of frustration and impatience some young people feel when encountering the normative call for cosmopolitanism and empathy. When more than one hundred people were shot on June 12, 2016, at an LGBT Orlando nightclub on Latin Night, responses from then-presidential candidates Clinton and Trump differed dramatically, although neither initially called for the reevaluation of US gun regulations, as President Obama did. In this case, the victims and many members of their communities were participants in an LGBT subculture that had experienced multiple state-supported oppressions and sufferings in the past. However, the shooter also allegedly acted out of outrage at his perceived experience as being oppressed by a state that allowed LGBT freedoms that he himself did not condone.

Here, it is useful to turn to the argument of Geoff Boucher, who, consistent with our discussion in Chapter 2, suggests a turn to intersubjectivity, so as to pay greater attention to the ways that members of differing thought communities share social experiences that differ vastly from members of other thought communities.[86] Boucher argues that it is helpful to begin with the observation that capitalism is no longer working and that we need to find new compromises by which our societies can operate.[87] His approach is rooted in Althusserian Marxism, as he tries to address why it is that sometimes a set of social relations takes on a configuration that makes social reproduction, or the continued stability of a system, impossible.[88] We like this approach because it presents a macroeconomic theory that draws together history, political science, and sociology to better understand the ways that institutions and institutional relations are created, sustained, and broken apart. This approach helps to reframe the questions that emerge in relation to the agonistic public that Mouffe suggests and, therefore, helps us to address a question that has threaded throughout this book: namely, how do we, as a society, go about reimagining democracy and the media it needs in an agonistic situation in which passions are high? While some have suggested that the answer lies in an empathy viewed as a characteristic of cosmopolitanism, others are not so sure that the development of empathy is sufficient.

In his critique of what he terms "thin cosmopolitanism" in which people can feel compassion but still leave power arrangements intact, Andrew Dobson has argued, instead, for a "thick cosmopolitanism" that takes into account "the material ties that bind" and that "prompt obligations of justice in a globalizing world."[89] He argues for a starting point of political obligation, noting that we feel obligated as we feel implicated: "Causal responsibility produces a thicker connection between people than appeals to membership of common humanity, and it also takes us more obviously out of the territory of beneficence and into the realm of justice. If I cause someone harm, I am required as a matter of justice to rectify that harm."[90] Arguing that climate change discussions are a helpful illustration of cosmopolitanism, Dobson notes that marshaling facts about the ways that consumption in one part of the world exacerbates climate change and, hence, the suffering of people in another part of the world, can foster "cosmopolitan emotions." Examples include "shame when humans harm other humans and non-humans, and guilt when little or nothing is done to alleviate distant suffering," writes another advocate for political obligation, Andrew Linklater.[91]

Helpful also in this turn to thinking about obligation is Kwame Anthony Appiah's argument that "conversations" that signal a depth encounter across difference do not need to involve consensus. The main goal is to learn to live with one another. Cosmopolitanism, he notes, is constituted in "unity plus difference," in which our obligations to one another are balanced with the affirmation of all particular lives. Drawing upon one aspect of Ulrich Beck's view, Appiah argues that cosmopolitanism is not the solution, but the challenge.[92] A robust view of cosmopolitanism through the lens of political obligation would suggest that we must also recognize the material inequities that shape how people experience the political system and why they want change.

As Adam Smith pointed out back in the mid-eighteenth century, we all have a tendency to be much more concerned about our own lives than the lives of others.[93] This is why it is productive for those working with young people to not only work toward engendering empathy or beneficence, but to also help them recognize the need for compensatory justice. Postcolonial and feminist critiques offer helpful intersectional frameworks for understanding difference and evaluating claims of privilege, oppression, and justice.[94] Throughout this book we have argued that such a critical approach is important both to how we think about citizenship and how we might begin such discussions of citizenship from a standpoint of hope.

CONCLUSION

This book has discussed a variety of ways in which young people are expressing themselves via online social networks, in what we have coined "connective journalism." We have shared examples of how youth encounter politically relevant issues in their day-to-day online activities related to socializing, identity formation, entertainment, and hobbies, and how they can develop political consciousness and start to express their own political positions via these activities. Some may wonder whether connective journalism results in citizens being alerted to important issues *only* if they find those issues immediately relevant to their own life circumstances, missing out on other important stories in the news. This is a concern that is not new to social media, of course, and one that does not have an easy answer. People's political engagement needs to start somewhere, and starting with taking interest in an issue of personal importance can lead to developing larger political awareness about not just what is happening in one's own neighborhood, but about what is going on at a national or international level. Moreover, while there have been concerns regarding echo chambers and filter bubbles on social media, in which people are purportedly exposed online to only those articles and ideas amenable to them, there are also recent studies finding that people report being exposed to diverse and ideologically opposing opinions and issues on social media.[95]

Many young people want to be part of political conversations and this book has offered examples of ways they are already doing this. Our research on youth, news, and civic engagement over nearly a decade has convinced us that youth are not as apathetic and disengaged as older generations believe. We need to conclude by observing that it was incredibly inspirational to work alongside the young people we studied and learned from while conducting the research that formed the basis for this book. We were often struck by the fact that we were working with youth who, in spite of their skepticism about traditional media and political systems, nevertheless were willing to expend a great deal of effort in conducting research, considering media strategies, and working to bring publics into being. We are convinced that there is no shortage of young people who want to make the world better. The question that this chapter raises, however, is: how committed are *we* to supporting them in this endeavor?

In the last section of this chapter, we have expressed concerns about US society's commitment to fostering greater civic engagement and political participation among all of our young people, based on our belief that not all have been granted the respect and rights that everyone deserves. And despite our attention to the interpersonal realm and questions of ethics, many of the media trends we have identified in this book only exacerbate the ability of Facebook and other social media sites to exert ever-greater control over the media landscape in the future.

However, we believe that the connective journalism practices that we have outlined in this book – that favor emotionally driven sharing; that shed light on how feelings of outrage can provide motivation for inserting oneself into the story; and that highlight the resource-demanding nature of participating in making one's own story – offer useful insights into the directions in which citizen journalism, democratic deliberation, and political participation can develop in the future. We do not wish to erase or downplay the dire situation of contemporary journalism. Our hope is that by highlighting the creativity and drive of young people and their social media practices, and the potential for concerned adults and organizations to work with youth by engaging with them in relationships of mutuality, we can redirect concerns away from worries about apathetic young people and toward concerns of fixing the systems that seem most apathetic toward them. Adults have to trust that young people engaging in the participatory practices of connective journalism are creating a story, not just telling one. And if we focus on that, the result will be a story worth telling.

* * * * *

Methods Appendix

The research that formed the basis of this book took place between 2006 and 2016 and included ethnographic research and in-depth interviews in major urban areas of the United States. Employing qualitative methodologies of interviews, participant observation, and participatory action research, we were interested in understanding the processes through which young people come to engage in political acts, and the role that journalism and the practices of social media – including sharing, inserting oneself into stories, and making stories – play in these processes.

We are aware that there is a great deal of research that has been conducted on young people and citizenship, as well as on young people and their media use. Because we wanted to understand young people and their agency – or the processes through which they come to be informed, aware, involved, and in some cases engaged in acts of resistance – we felt that qualitative research was necessary for grasping the nuances that shape how young people respond to social situations. Inspired by the work of thoughtful youth researchers such as Hava Gordon, Vikki Katz, Heather Horst, Mimi Ito, Michelle Fine, Maria Torre, Julio Cammarota, Sunaina Maira, Lissa Soep, Sonia Livingstone, and many others, we wanted to engage directly in talking with and observing young people so that we could understand their experiences with politics, journalism, and social media.[1] Such work, we recognized, would depend upon what anthropologist Clifford Geertz termed "deep hanging out," and so we needed to immerse ourselves in the everyday social experiences of high school aged young people. But we also recognized that we, as older White female adult educators, needed to take on roles in those experiences that were recognizable and comprehensible from a young person's perspective.[2] In the earliest days of this study, therefore, we spent a great deal of time contemplating access and relationships: who did we already know in the worlds of youth, media, and politics, and how could we deepen our own relationships with young people to learn more about the ways that activities related to these worlds emerged and converged in their lives? Because in the past each of us had conducted interview-based research with young people (Lynn) and community activists and artists (Regina), we were fortunate to have many points of connection with young people and those who work most ardently with them, including teachers, parents, community organization leaders, pastors, rabbis, and coaches. Following Tim Ingold's assertion that anthropological insights often emerge from experiences in joint activity, we initially sought out ways to interact with youth while also providing some kind of payment or service to them in return.[3] We continued to ask adults we knew for introductions to young people and interviewed willing volunteers in exchange for a small payment usually in the form of a gift card. But as university professors, we also offered workshops and mentorship in school and in after-school activities, deepening our initial contacts with high school journalism teachers and community media organization leaders and finding our way into more relationships with adults in the sites that young people frequented. We discovered that our focus on digital and mobile media and on youth media-making provided an initial entrée into several sites, as we were each invited to serve as guests in high school classrooms devoted to discussions of Internet safety and as guests in after-school media production efforts where we were invited to informally share expertise in writing, message design, digital platforms, and communication planning.

We found that we came to be viewed by both staff and students in a manner similar to the many other White female educators in and outside of the schools where young people spent most of their days: we were seen as both authoritative and helpful, and, sometimes, as suspect or naive. As outsiders, we were sometimes viewed as adults giving something of added value to young people, such as our time and our linkage to digital knowledge, but we were also viewed as adults who needed to earn the trust of those with whom we interacted, and who were less consequential than other adults in the school. Greg Dimitriadis and Vicki Mayer have made similar observations about the entrance into their fields of study with diverse communities.[4] The students with whom we interacted in the early days of this study recognized that we were researchers, but given our repeat presence and our occasional work as volunteers, we also came to be viewed by some young people more broadly, as a digital media instructor; a sometimes-advocate for the students, the school or the after-school program; someone with connections to the local universities; or sometimes even as a mentor.

Over the course of the next several years, our participant observation research included attending and participating in public and private school and after-school events, observing and leading youth media-making activities such as high school journalism, high school broadcast, and community-based media programs, and attending community gatherings as well as continuing education events for educators and parents. We each took field notes and kept journals of our evolving thoughts about our experiences with young people and those who spent a great deal of time with them. Data were also gathered while attending and observing political rallies, protests, marches, and educational events.

Although we began our work with studies of high school journalism, we quickly hit upon several concerns that made it necessary to extend our work. First, even in schools that had high levels of racial/ethnic diversity, those young people who self-selected or who accepted invitations to participate in high school journalism were overwhelmingly white and/ or middle class. We came to observe that an important form of social reproduction was going on in these programs, as privileged and talented young people came to feel that they had an important voice within their communities, while less privileged youth did not. Second, we found that experienced high school journalism advisors largely saw their role as replicating the culture of professional newspaper journalism, with its focus on truth-telling, facts, deadlines, and good balanced writing that generally appeals to the frameworks of middle class readers. While these are admirable goals that research suggests may engender a lifelong interest in news and politics among high school journalists, we were concerned that a tendency to focus on the concerns of the (mostly White and middle class) involved students reproduced rather than interrogated differences between those students and others in the student body, unintentionally rendering invisible those whose lived experiences were quite different from those of the newspaper staff. Furthermore, in some low-income communities where we did research, local high schools had no journalism clubs or courses, which pointed us toward after-school media programs serving these youth populations. The kind of social reproduction mentioned earlier was far less observable among those involved in the community radio programs we studied, which were rooted in urban locations and led by activists who saw their role less as journalists per se than as adults charged with empowering disadvantaged young people for self-esteem and leadership. These initial insights led us to more general considerations of how some young people became involved in youth media production and in youth activism. Moreover, throughout the time period of our study, social media was taking root in the everyday lives of youth, changing not only the practices of high school journalism but the spread of information more broadly, with increased interest in the role of social media in youth civic participation and political organizing.

After the initial years of the study, Lynn developed a relationship with a high school in the Denver area that houses one of the region's largest English language learner programs, and Regina developed a relationship with a youth-run community radio program in Boston. We also became immersed in relationships with other people engaged in youth media work and in educational and political activist efforts among disenfranchised, immigrant, and minority communities. Ongoing participation in after-school community media and arts activities and the long-term relationships established through this participation formed the core of the research for this project. These lived experiences provided rich opportunities to witness the complex ways in which diverse young people aligned and clashed with one another and with adults in positions of authority over contentious political issues and their representation in a variety of media.

The research also included slightly more than 200 semi-structured in-depth interviews with high school students, along with close to two dozen interviews with parents, youth workers, and educators. In-depth interviews explored young people's perceptions of journalism and of politics as well as their concerns about racial inequalities, school discipline, relations between students of color and law enforcement, and first-time participation in political and proto-political activities, as we discuss further in the following.

METHODS OF INTERVIEWING

One routinely hears from commentators inside and outside the news industry that the youthful generation is key to the future of news media. So, we began our work by asking young media producers about their thoughts on journalism, what participating in a youth journalism program meant to them, and their notions regarding the concept of public good. We focused largely on teens involved in high school and after-school journalism programs because they are more connected to journalism and arguably more interested in the news media than most of their peers. While the youth we interviewed included individuals from a variety of socioeconomic backgrounds, we chose to focus largely on working class, low-income, and immigrant youth for a number of reasons. These include the fact that this population has been largely understudied in the existing research on youth and media. The need to study this sector becomes even more evident as recent research has found that immigrant and minoritized youth (particularly African Americans, Latinos, and Asians) constitute the heaviest users of mobile devices and social media. Finally, we chose to pay special attention to this group of youth because both historically and currently, they are a sector of society that is least represented by and least included in mainstream media efforts. Today, minority and immigrant youth constitute the fastest growing sector of the US population and will constitute the *majority* of the national population by 2040, according to the most recent US Census Bureau estimates. We feel that studying how these young people feel about journalism and how they utilize social media can provide important insights into how the media industry and journalism should develop in the future.

Regina and her research assistants interviewed over 115 young people, including 90 high school students in Boston, Massachusetts, 10 high school aged video documentary journalists from WHYY in Philadelphia, and 10 high school students from New Jersey who wrote for their high school newspapers. In total, the racial breakdown of the youth that she interviewed was about 35 percent Latino, 25 percent African American; 25 percent White; 5 percent Southeast Asian, 5 percent Middle Eastern, and 5 percent multi-racial, with the interviewees being roughly 50 percent male and 50 percent female.

Lynn and her research team conducted semi-structured interviews with more than 80 young people, including 55 high school journalists from 18 high schools and 32 high school participants in media after-school programs, and she observed and briefly interviewed an additional 25 young people involved in various community, school, youth activism, and religious organizations. The racial breakdown of the youth she interviewed was about 35 percent African and African American, 25 percent Euro-American or White, 15 percent Southeast Asian, 10 percent Latino, 10 percent Multiracial, and 5 percent Middle Eastern.

Over the six final years of this study, more than 80 young people were involved in the after-school media program that Lynn co-led in

Denver, with a little less than half participating in interviews. The school that houses the program is one of the most culturally and economically diverse schools in the area. It has a strong English language learners program that serves a school with more than 70 countries and more than 40 language groups represented in the student body. More than 70 percent of the students in the school qualify for the free or reduced price lunch program made available through the US National School Lunch Act for those who qualify based on household income eligibility. A former staff person at the school invited Lynn to co-create the after-school group known as the Digital Media Club, which, as described in Chapter 6, aims to work with students who want to use digital media to make a difference in their communities. The after-school program has drawn about one dozen regularly attending students for each of its six years, and students involved have included those who were born in the United States, Mexico, Ghana, Ethiopia, Somalia, Eritrea, Guinea, Jordan, Iraq, Russia, Taiwan, and Vietnam. Students born outside the United States have had varying levels of English language proficiency and have been in the United States from between two months to twelve years. Through this core group of students and club leaders, Lynn met many other students, teachers, and administrators in this and in other area high schools. Through these connections she has been invited to serve as a guest speaker in classes, has served as host for students from area high schools who visit her university, and has participated in numerous school-related instructional, sports, arts, career, university prep, scholarship review, and cultural activities as well as informal picnics, parties, and get-togethers over coffee or pizza.

About a third of the ninety Boston youth who were interviewed worked at a teen-run community radio station. They were participants in an after-school program called "Zumix Radio," which trains teens to research, write, and produce current event stories.[5] The program is rather unique among youth journalism efforts in that it encourages students to regularly attend local community meetings in order to develop a better understanding of the socio-political issues facing their neighborhood, such as air pollution, gang activity, and the gentrification that is starting to price working class families out of the area. These journalists ranged in age from fourteen to nineteen, and all of them attended a one-semester radio journalism-training course and worked at the radio station for at least six months before being interviewed. Coincidentally, about a quarter of the teen radio journalists who were interviewed were also members of their respective high school newspaper staffs, and were able to speak of their

experiences as both radio journalists and high school newspaper reporters. Over nearly a decade, Regina not only interviewed young people
involved in this radio station, but also periodically observed them in
action as they held meetings, discussed story ideas, worked in the recording studio, and attended community meetings. She also interviewed six
radio staff members who trained and supervised the teen radio journalists, and eleven parents of the young radio journalists.

In addition to interviewing the teen radio journalists, constituting one
of the only recent studies based on in-depth, individual interviews with
high school aged media makers, Regina also interviewed forty young
people in Boston who were regular participants in a non-profit community center serving youth from throughout the city. This youth center,
which celebrated twenty-five years of operation in 2016 and has won a
variety of national awards for its successful youth engagement (including the 2011 National Arts and Humanities Youth Program Award from
President Obama), offers low-cost music lessons and free arts programming (dance, chorus, theater, song writing, video production, audio
recording and engineering, technological equipment repair, and more)
to youth aged nine to twenty-one. This center was chosen as a research
site because it attracts young people from a diversity of age, socioeconomic, racial, and ethnic backgrounds, although the large majority are
from working class and low-income families. Nearly half of the youth
interviewed from this center were from immigrant families, with parents
working in the informal and service sector, and some of these students
were undocumented or had family members who were undocumented
immigrants. Because it served youth of varying ages, religions, races, and
ethnicities from across the city of Boston, this center provided an excellent opportunity to interview a broad range of young people about their
thoughts on journalism, the news media, and social media practices.

Regina also conducted focus group interviews and surveys with
twenty-seven students from the City Roots Alternative High School in
Boston. Most of these students were African American and Latino and
ranged in age from sixteeen to twenty-one. Administered by the Boston
Public School system from 1981 to 2013, City Roots served students
who, for a variety of reasons often related to poverty, had dropped out of
high school but wanted to pursue a high school diploma in an alternative
school setting. These students did not participate in journalism programs
and many of them were "older than their years," in that they had experienced hardships such as teen pregnancies, gang life, homelessness, incarceration, drug addiction (or were dealing with addicted parents/family

members), and other issues that made it difficult for them to finish high school, much less participate in afterschool youth programs. However, their feedback about their social media practices and their thoughts on journalism and the news media provided insights from an at-risk youth population that is hard to reach and largely excluded from research on youth and media.

After receiving Human Subjects approval, all interviews were audio recorded and transcribed, with participant names changed to protect their confidentiality. In Boston, interview participants were recruited in a variety of ways. Paper posters were hung in both the youth center and radio station and Regina visited the after-school youth programs and the alternative education site to speak about the research project and ask for volunteers. Youth signed up for interviews via sign-up sheets that were kept in the youth center office or, in the case of City Roots, kept in the office of the program director. Regina then did follow-up phone calls and e-mails with the young people and their parents to confirm interview dates. All interviews for the radio journalists and other youth center participants were conducted in the conference room or in music rooms at the youth center and were scheduled for directly before or after an interviewee's regularly scheduled program activities. The City Roots focus group interviews took place in the City Roots classroom in South Boston. The WHYY interview participants were recruited via personal contact with Rutgers graduate student, Christine Schneider, who had previously worked with the program, and were interviewed at WHYY's youth video program site in Philadelphia. The New Jersey high school newspaper journalists were recruited by Regina's undergraduate student research assistants, Cristabel Cruz and Carina Sitkus, who had previously participated as high school students in the school newspapers involved and still had contacts with the teachers who were the newspaper advisors.

YOUTH PARTICIPATORY ACTION RESEARCH

We both worked with young people between the ages of fourteen and twenty-one in the context of a Youth Participatory Action Research (YPAR) framework that embraces a view of youth that "acknowledges the structural constraints in their communities … but also views them as active participants in changing debilitative neighborhood conditions."[6] In practice, the YPAR framework means that when we used the phrase, "using media to make a difference in our communities" to describe digital media literacy activities, the young people involved at any given time get to define which media they would like to use, which communities they hope to work with, and how they hope to make a difference within those communities. Our desire in this book has been to explore the ways in which this openness to youth-defined means of utilizing various forms of media for storytelling both for and within their communities can shed light on the emergent ways young people are not only engaging in connective journalism, but also in how these practices might develop and shape collective understandings of democratic action in the future.

After relationships with young people had been established, whenever possible, Lynn and Regina triangulated interview and online data by asking students to show and describe their online and mobile activities with social media platforms including Facebook, Twitter, and Snapchat, although we did not "follow" or "friend" our research participants until they had completed their high school years and had given us their permission to do so, or had asked us to follow them.[7] Permission for youth participation was attained when both parental consent and teen assent forms had been received. We also received permission to conduct this study and collaborated with high school principals, teachers, journalism advisors, community liaisons, community program directors and community activists.

DATA ANALYSIS

Over the course of the period of data-gathering, Lynn and Regina spoke with one another every few months to discuss field notes and interviews so as to develop analytical categories. We employed what Lindlof and Taylor have referred to as a constant comparative method that involves reexamining and confirming, discussing excerpts, and then selecting cases that illustrated our evolving analysis and insights.[8] As we worked, we followed an approach of grounded theory that includes the three steps of (1) exploring our data in relation to preexisting theories, (2) iteratively constructing theories that are grounded in empirical data (mainly obtained through an inductive approach), and (3) ensuring that our emergent theories had what Goldkuhl and Cronholm term "internal grounding," or an internal coherence and consistency between our data, the existing theories reviewed, and the theory that we, as analysts, were ultimately developing.[9] Rather than concluding a study with a list of findings, grounded theory provides a conceptual account of how the participants in a study resolve their main concern.[10] In this way, grounded theory results in a practice of *naming*: specifically, naming the processes that have been observed, but also naming the main concerns of the study's participants, and the core categories that explain how participants solve those concerns. As described in earlier chapters, we became aware that young people's engagement in political activities through social media needed to be understood in relation to the pressures they felt as young people. Namely, most young people have heightened concerns about how they are related to and understood by their peers, which is a developmentally appropriate response to social situations. We thus came to focus on the different patterns in how young people utilized social media in relation to political information and activities. We came to recognize the significance of "lurking," or of observing how young people responded when they came into contact with posts or text messages that suggested that peers they knew were involved in or were sharing political information. We then came to see that there were differing levels of engagement implied in the social media practices of young people, observing that whereas many had observed the online activities of more active peers, only some chose to share political information with others, and most frequently when such information was shared in an expression of outrage. Fewer still chose to insert themselves into stories of political action, sharing what we came to term the artifacts of engagement with their peers. And fewer still emerged as leaders who were willing not only to share but also to participate in making a new story for their communities. We were especially interested to find that those in this select latter category seemed to view social media as well as legacy media coverage as a means of leveraging their political activities, even as many of these young people continued to express skepticism about mainstream media and about their peers' propensity for civic involvement.

Once we had deduced that differing levels of engagement existed and were imbricated with the practices of social media, we returned to our data to consider again what we had learned through our interviews and observations. We also began to gather information about similar activities undertaken by young people elsewhere in the United States through both interpersonal connections with other researchers and youth workers and through data collected via national surveys and through coding of youthful political activities appearing in various journalistic venues, thus deepening and extending our analysis.

Additionally, we have had opportunities to discuss our research and findings not only with research colleagues working in areas similar to ours, but also with the young people with whom we worked during these many years. Some have participated in conversations about this analysis long after their initial interviews and activities, lending the perspective of distance and age to their high school experiences, while others read and commented on drafts while they were still in high school. We are thankful to all of those who worked with us and let us into their lives and shared their journeys with us. We hope that they recognize some of their own experiences in this book, and we hope that this book is expressive of the hope and inspiration they have given to us as, in various ways, they have sought to use media to make a difference in our communities.

Notes

Introduction: Young People and the Future of News

1 Michael Roberts, "Westboro Baptist Protest at East High Champions Love over Hate," *Westword* blogs, November 7, 2011, accessed January 15, 2014, http://blogs.westword.com/latestword/2011/11/westboro_baptist_church_east_high_photos.php. A note to readers from outside the United States: "high school" is the US term for grades 9–12, often referred to as "secondary school" in Europe and elsewhere in the world. The US term borrows from the French, *haute école*.

2 Allie Bidwell, "Opt-out Movement about More than Tests, Advocates Say," *USA Today*, accessed March 10, 2015, www.usnews.com/news/articles/2015/03/10/as-students-opt-out-of-common-core-exams-some-say-movement-is-not-about-testing; Steve Almasy and Holly Yan, "Protesters Fill Streets across Country as Ferguson Protests Spread Coast to Coast," *CNN*, November 26, 2014, accessed March 10, 2015, www.cnn.com/2014/11/25/us/national-ferguson-protests/

3 Noelle Crombie, "Forest Grove High School Students Walk Out over 'Build a Wall' Banner," *The Oregonian*, May 19, 2016, accessed June 17, 2016, www.oregonlive.com/forest-grove/index.ssf/2016/05/forest_grove_high_students_pla.html; Tawnell Hobbs, "150 Spruce High Students Walk Out in Protest over Conditions," *The Dallas Morning News*, April 29, 2016, accessed June 17, 2016, http://educationblog.dallasnews.com/2016/04/over-100-spruce-high-school-students-walk-out-in-protest.html/; Josh Logue, "A Broader Protest Agenda," *Inside Higher Ed*, April 19, 2016, accessed June 17, 2016, www.insidehighered.com/news/2016/04/19/student-protests-year-broaden-beyond-issues-race; Daniel Funke, "Here's Where the Sanctuary Campus Movement Stands," *USA Today*, December 19, 2016, accessed May 13, 2017, http://college.usatoday.com/2016/12/19/heres-where-the-sanctuary-campus-movement-stands/; Ashley Cleek, "Weighing the Risks of a

Sanctuary Campus," February 16, 2017, Public Radio International, https://www.pri.org/stories/2017-02-16/weighing-risks-sanctuary-campus, accessed May 13, 2017.

4 Emanuella Grinberg, "Ending Rape on Campus, Activism Takes Several Forms," CNN, February 12, 2014, accessed May 13, 2017, www.cnn.com/2014/02/09/living/campus-sexual-violence-students-schools/.

5 Kristen Bellstrom, "The Stanford Rape Case Shows Social Media Doesn't Have to be Bad for Women," *Fortune*, June 7, 2016, accessed June 17, 2016, http://fortune.com/2016/06/07/stanford-rape-social-media/; Kim LaCapria, "Brock Turner Rape Controversy," *Snopes.com*, June 8, 2016, accessed June 17, 2016, www.snopes.com/2016/06/08/brock-turner-rape-controversy/.

6 Lydia O'Connor, "London Vigil for Orland Victim Draws Thousands," *Huffington Post*, June 13, 2016, accessed June 17, 2016, www.huffingtonpost.com/entry/london-orlando-vigil_us_575f1632e4b0e4fe51435b1b.

7 "Stand with Standing Rock," Standing Rock Sioux Tribe, accessed December 11, 2016, http://standwithstandingrock.net. Also see: "Thousands Unite in Solidarity with Standing Rock," ECOWATCH, November 16, 2016, accessed December 11, 2016, www.ecowatch.com/day-of-action-dakota-access-pipeline-2095669637.html, and Christopher Mele, "Veterans to Stand as 'Human Shields' for Dakota Pipeline Protesters," *New York Times*, November 29, 2016, accessed December 11, 2016, www.nytimes.com/2016/11/29/us/veterans-to-serve-as-human-shields-for-pipeline-protesters.html

8 *How Millennials Get News*, A Report of the API and AP-NORC Center Media Insight Project, 2015, www.mediainsight.org/Pages/how-millennials-get-news-inside-the-habits-of-americas-first-digital-generation.aspx; Reuters Institute for the Study of Journalism, *Digital News Report: Social Networks and Their Role in News*, 2016, www.digitalnewsreport.org/survey/2015/social-networks-and-their-role-in-news-2015/.

9 Thomas Patterson, *Young People and News*, A Report from the Joan Shorenstein Center on the Press, Politics and Public Policy, 2007. Also see: David Mindich, *Tuned Out – Why Americans Under 40 Don't Watch the News* (New York: Oxford University Press, 2005).

10 Roberts, "Westboro Baptist Protest."

11 Young people have long been disaffected in relation to legacy news. See, e.g., a Pew study from nearly twenty-five years ago: *The Age of Indifference: A Study of Young Americans and How They View the News*, A Report from the Pew Research Center, Washington, DC: Times Mirror Center, 1990, www.people-press.org/1990/06/28/the-age-of-indifference/

12 See, e.g., Sandra Oshiro, "Future of News Audiences: What's Next as Young Fail to Become Strong News Consumers," *Poynter*, January 27, 2014, accessed December 16, 2017, www.poynter.org/latest-news/top-stories/237055/future-of-news-audiences-whats-next-as-millennials-fail-to-become-strong-news-consumers/

13 News is now portable, personalized, and participatory, as Kristen Purcell and her team argue. See Kristen Purcell, Lee Rainie, Amy Mitchell, Tom Rosenstiel, and Kenny Olmstead, *Understanding the Participatory News Consumer: How Internet and Cell Phone Users Have Turned News into a*

Social Experience, A Report of the Pew Internet & American Life Project, Washington, DC, 2010, www.pewinternet.org/2010/03/01/understanding-the-participatory-news-consumer/.

14 Axel Bruns, *Blogs, Wikipedia, Second Life, and Beyond: From Production to Produsage* (New York: Peter Lang, 2008).

15 Jesse Holcomb, Jeffrey Gottfried, and Amy Mitchell, *News Use across Social Media Platforms*, A Report of the Pew Research Journalism Project, Washington, DC, November 14, 2013, www.journalism.org/2013/11/14/news-use-across-social-media-platforms/; Mary Madden, Amanda Lenhart & Claire Fontaine, *How Youth Navigate the News Landscape*, A Report from Data & Society and the Knight Foundation, February 2017, www.journalism.org/2013/11/14/news-use-across-social-media-platforms/.

16 Ike Picone, Cedric Courtois, and Steve Paulussen, "When News Is Everywhere: Understanding Participation, Cross-mediality and Mobility in Journalism from a Radical User Perspective," *Journalism Practice* 2014, 9(1): 35. Couldry makes a similar argument; see Nick Couldry, "The Necessary Future of the Audience…and How to Research It," in Virginia Nightingale, ed., *The Handbook of Media Audiences* (Malden, MA: Wiley-Blackwell, 2011), 213–229. See also S. Elizabeth Bird, "Seeking the Audience for News. Response, News Talk, and Everyday Practices," in Virginia Nightingale, ed., *The Handbook of Media Audiences*, 489–508.

17 C. W. Anderson, "Journalistic Networks and the Diffusion of Local News: The Brief, Happy News Life of the 'Francisville Four,'" *Political Communication* 2010, 27(3): 289–309. doi:10.1080/10584609.2010.496710; Alfred Hermida, "Twittering the News: The Emergence of Ambient Journalism," *Journalism Practice* 2010, 4(3): 297–308. doi:10.1080/17512781003640703; Adrienne (Cambridge: Polity Press, 2013); Pablo Boczkowski, Eugenia Mitchelstein, and Mora Matassi, "Incidental News: How Young People Consume News on Social Media," presented at the 50th Hawaii International Conference on System Sciences, University of Hawaii at Manoa, January 4, 2017, doi: hdl.handle.net/10125/41371.

18 See, e.g., David Domingo, Thorsten Quandt, Ari Heinonen, Steve Paulussen, Jane B. Singer, and Marina Vujnovic, "Participatory Practices in the Media and Beyond: An Online Comparative Study of Initiatives in Online Newspapers," *Journalism Practice* 2008, 2(3): 326–342.

19 Irene Costera Meijer, "Valuable Journalism: A Search for Quality from the Vantage Point of the User," *Journalism* 2013, 14(6): 754–770; Irene Costera Meijer, "The Paradox of Popularity: How Young People Experience the News," *Journalism Studies* 2007, 8(1): 96–116; Kim Schrøder, "Audiences Are Inherently Cross-Media: Audience Studies and the Cross Media Challenge," *Communication Management Quarterly* 2011, 18 (6): 5–27; Heikki Heikkila and Laura Ahva, "The Relevance of Journalism: Studying News Audiences in a Digital Era," *Journalism Practice* 2014, 9(1): 50–64. See also Jacob Linaa Jensen, Mette Mortensen, and Jacob Omen, eds., *News Across Media: Production, Distribution and Consumption* (New York: Routledge, 2016) and Chris Peters and Marcus Broersma,

"The Rhetorical Illusions of News," in Chris Peters and Marcus Broersma, eds., *Rethinking Journalism Again: Societal Role and Public Relevance in a Digital Age* (London: Routledge, 2016), 188–204.

20 Craig Silverman, "This Analysis Shows How Fake Election News Stories Outperformed Real News On Facebook," *Buzzfeed*, November 16, 2016, accessed December 18, 2016, www.buzzfeed.com/craigsilverman/viral-fake-election-news-outperformed-real-news-on-facebook?utm_term=.olV2602PDv#.idwRa7R8Gp.

21 *Evaluating Information: The Cornerstone of Civic Online Reasoning*, A Report of the Stanford History Education Group, Stanford University, November 2016, 1–29, https://sheg.stanford.edu/upload/V3LessonPlans/Executive%20Summary%2011.21.16.pdf

22 Nick Couldry, Sonia Livingstone, and Tim Markham, *Media Consumption and Public Engagement: Beyond the Presumption of Attention* (London: Palgrave Macmillan, 2007).

23 Murray Foreman, "Straight Outta Mogadishu," in Sunaina Maira and Elisabeth Soep, eds., *Youthscapes: The Popular, The National The Global* (Philadelphia, PA: University of Pennsylvania Press, 2005), 3–22.

24 Picone et al., "When News Is Everywhere." Peters and Broersma similarly argue for taking an audience perspective to news; Peters and Broersma, "The Rhetorical Illusions of News."

25 Tim Highfield, *Social Media and Everyday Politics* (New York: Polity 2016).

26 Statistics based on reported YouTube views, November 10, 2016.

27 Henry Jenkins, Sangita Shresthova, Liana Gamber-Thompson, Neta Kligler-Vilenchik, and Arely Zimmerman, *By Any Media Necessary: The New Youth Activism (Connected and Digital Futures)* (New York: New York University Press, 2016).

28 Cathy Cohen, Joseph Kahne, Benjamin Bowyer, Ellen Middaugh, and Jon Rogowski, *Participatory Politics: New Media and Youth Political Action*, Executive Summary, a Report of the Youth and Participatory Politics Research Network of the MacArthur Foundation's Digital Media and Learning Initiative, 2012, ypp.dmlcentral.net/sites/default/files/publications/Participatory_Politics_Report.pdf

29 Cohen, et al., *Participatory Politics*. For full details on their thoughtful methodology, which included oversampling of minority populations to yield significant findings by racial/ethnic demographic groups, see their full report. A total of 843 young people completed the survey, conducted on behalf of Knowledge Networks at Mills College in northern California. After another round of surveys after the 2012 election with the sample size increased to nearly 3,000 young people, the findings remained largely consistent with those reported in the initial report, according to Jenkins, *Confessions of an Aca-Fan Blog*, June 17, 2016, accessed July 19, 2016, http://henryjenkins.org.

30 Cohen, *Participatory Politics*.

31 Cohen, *Participatory Politics*. Other items they measured included: started or joined a political group on a social network site (11 percent), engaged in "buycotting" (11 percent), written an email or blog about a political

campaign, candidate or issue (7 percent), and contributed your own article, opinion piece, picture, or video about a political campaign, candidate or issue to an online news site (6 percent). These numbers are slightly higher when compared with other "offline" political activities in which young people reported that they engaged, including participating in a boycott (10 percent), participated in an event where young people express their political views (such as a poetry slam, musical event, etc.) (7 percent), or taken part in a protest, demonstration, or sit-in (6 percent).

32 Cohen, *Participatory Politics*. Just 25 percent of Black youth report no engagement in political behavior, whereas 33 percent of whites, 40 percent of Asian Americans, and 43 percent of Latinos report no engagement. On the "Obama effect," see "African American Youth: Political Engagement Trends," CIRCLE (Center for Research on Civic Learning and Engagement) blog, accessed April 11, 2017, http://civicyouth.org/african-american-youth-political-engagement-trends/

33 Cohen, *Participatory Politics*.

34 United Nations, Convention of the Rights of the Child, General Assembly Resolution 44/25 of 20, 1989, www.ohchr.org/en/professionalinterest/pages/crc.aspx. See also Sonia Livingstone, "Children's Digital Rights," *InterMEDIA* 2015, 42(4/5): 20–24.

35 Lev Vygotsky, *Mind in Society: The Development of Higher Psychological Processes* (Cambridge, MA: Harvard University Press, 1978); Lonnie Sherrod, Constance Flanagan, and James Youniss, "Dimensions of Citizenship and Opportunities for Youth Development: The Who, What, Why, Where and How of Citizenship Development," *Applied Developmental Science* 2002, 6(4): 264–272. Michael Delli Carpini and Scott Keeter, *What Americans Know about Politics and Why It Matters* (New Haven, CT: Yale University Press, 1996).

36 See Fred S. Siebert, Theodore Peterson, and Wilbur Schramm, *Four Theories of the Press* (Chicago, IL: University of Illinois Press, 1963).

37 Russell Dalton, *The Good Citizen: How a Younger Generation Is Reshaping American Politics* (Washington, DC: CQ Press, 2009); Cliff Zukin, Scott Keeter, Molly Andolina, Krista Jenkins, and Michael Delli Carpini, *A New Engagement: Political Participation, Civic Life, and the Changing American Citizen* (New York: Oxford University Press, 2006).

38 W. Lance Bennett, "Changing Citizenship in the Digital Age," in W.L. Bennett, ed., *Civic Life Online: Learning How Digital Media Can Engage Youth* (Cambridge, MA: MIT Press, 2008), 1–24. See also Hava Gordon, *We Fight to Win: Inequality and the Politics of Youth Activism* (New Brunswick, NJ: Rutgers University Press, 2009); Brian Loader, ed., *Young Citizens in the Digital Age: Political Engagement, Young People and New Media* (New York: Routledge, 2007).

39 Zigmunt Bauman, *Liquid Times Living in an Age of Uncertainty* (Cambridge: Polity Press, 2007). See also Zigmunt Bauman, "Downward Mobility Is Now a Reality" *The Guardian*, May 31, 2012, accessed May 11, 2017, www.theguardian.com/commentisfree/2012/may/31/downward-mobility-europe-young-people

40 Lucinda Gray, Nina Thomas, Laurie Lewis, and Peter Tice, *Teachers' Use of Technology in U.S. Public Schools* (NCES No. 2010040) (Washington, DC: National Center for Education Statistics, 2009); Regina Marchi, "From Disillusion to Engagement: Minority Teen Journalists and the News Media," *Journalism: Theory, Practice and Criticism* 2011, 13(8):1–16; Regina Marchi, "With Facebook, Blogs, and Fake News, Teens Reject Journalistic 'Objectivity,'" *Journal of Communication Inquiry* 2011, 36(3): 246–262. Beth C. Rubin, "'There's Still No Justice': Youth Civic Identity Development amid Distinct School and Community Contexts," *Teachers College Record* 2007, 109: 449–481; Beth C. Rubin, Brian Hayes, and Keith Benson, "'It's the Worst Place to Live': Urban Youth and the Challenge of School-Based Civic Learning," *Theory Into Practice* 2009, 48(3): 213–221; Peter Tatian, G. Thomas Kingsley, Joe Parrilla, and Rolf Pendall, "Building Successful Neighborhoods," *What Works Collaborative*, 2012, March 16, 2016, www.urban.org/sites/default/files/alfresco/publication-pdfs/412557-Building-Successful-Neighborhoods.PDF

41 Sunaina Maira, *Missing: Youth, Citizenship and Empire after 9/11* (Durham: NC: Duke University Press, 2009); Brian O'Loughlin and Marie Gillespie, "Dissenting Citizenship? Young People and Political Participation in the Media-security Nexus," *Parliamentary Affairs* 2012, 65(1): 115–137. doi: 10.1093/pa/gsr055

42 Alice Marwick, "The Public Domain: Surveillance in Everyday Life," *Surveillance and Society* 2012, 9(4): 378–393.

43 See, e.g., Marina Prentoulis and Lasse Thomassen, "The Legacy of the Indignados," *Open Democracy*, August 13, 2013, www.opendemocracy.net/can-europe-make-it/marina-prentoulis-lasse-thomassen/legacy-of-indignados

44 Dalton, *The Good Citizen.*

45 Philip Howard and Muzammil Hussain, *Democracy's Fourth Wave? Digital Media and the Arab Spring.* Oxford Studies in Digital Politics (New York: Oxford University Press, 2013). Similarly, Karine Nahon and Jeff Hemsley argue that virality can increase demand for more transparency from governments. See Karine Nahon and Jeff Hemsley, *Going Viral* (London: Polity, 2013).

46 Taylor Owen, *Disruptive Power: The Crisis of the State in a Digital Age*, Oxford Studies in Digital Politics (New York: Oxford University Press, 2015).

47 David Tewksbury and Jason Rittenberg, *News on the Internet: Information and Citizenship in the 21st Century* (New York: Oxford University Press, 2012).

48 Adrienne Russell, *Journalism as Activism: Recoding Media Power* (New York: Polity, 2016).

49 Michael Paulson, "Fred Phelps, Anti-Gay Preacher who Targeted Military Funerals, Died at 84," *New York Times*, March 20 2014, www.nytimes.com/2014/03/21/us/fred-phelps-founder-of-westboro-baptist-church-dies-at-84.html; Ray Lane, "Anti-Gay Hate Group Targets Seattle Churches," *KOMO-TV*, June 13, 2009, www.seattlepi.com/local/article/Anti-gay-hate-group-targets-Seattle-churches-1304527.php; Reed Williams and Chris I.

Young, "Opponents Rally against Westboro Baptist Hate Group," *Richmond Times-Dispatch*, 2010, http://web.archive.org/web/20100305025103/; Stephen Mikulan, "H8ters LA Vacation: Fred Phelps' Antigay Baptists Come Out on Oscar Night," *LA Weekly*, February 25, 2009, www.laweekly.com/2009-02-26/columns/h8ters-l-a-vacation-fred-phelps-146-antigay-baptists-come-out-on-oscar-night/; Bay City News, "Lowell HS Students' Counter-Protest to Crazy Religious Attention Seekers," *San Francisco Appeal*, January 28, 2010, http://sfappeal.com/2010/01/lowell-hs-students-counter-protest-of-crazy-religious-attention-seekers-successful/

50 Rick Cohn, "Students Support Targets to Oppose Westboro Baptist Church," Nonprofitquarterly.org. https://nonprofitqu/arterly.org/index.php?option=com_content&view=article&id=6871:students-support-targets-to-oppose-westboro-baptists&catid=155:nonprofit-newswire&Itemid=986; Sarah Miller, "Out Comes the Sun and the Anti-Semites, in Honor of the New Orleans GA," *Haaretz*, November 8, 2010, www.haaretz.com/jewish-world/out-comes-the-sun-and-the-anti-semites-in-honor-of-the-new-orleans-ga-1.323647

51 http://topdocumentaryfilms.com/brainwashed-westboro-baptist-church/; www.bbc.com/news/magazine-12919646; www.imdb.com/title/tt0977649/

52 www.huffingtonpost.com/2012/12/17/westboro-baptist-church-hacked-anonymous-protest-newtown-shooting-victims-funerals_n_2315070.html

53 Newspaper Association of America, *Common Threads: Linking NAA Foundation Research to Today's Young Media Consumers* (Chicago, IL: NAA Media Management Center, Northwestern University, Newspaper Association of America Foundation, 2010).

54 Madison Gray, "Spreading the Gospel of LinkedIn for Journalists," *Poynter*, May 26, 2014, www.poynter.org/latest-news/top-stories/253445/spreading-the-gospel-of-linkedin-for-journalists/

55 Alfred Hermida, "Twittering the News: The Emergence of Ambient Journalism," *Journalism Practice* 2010, 4(3): 297–508.

56 Here we borrow a definition of journalism offered by Barbie Zelizer, *Taking Journalism Seriously: News and the Academy* (Thousand Oaks, CA: Sage, 2004).

57 U.S. Census 2012. See "Asians Fastest-Growing Race or Ethnic Group in 2012, Census Bureau Reports," United States Census Bureau, June 2013, www.census.gov/newsroom/releases/archives/population/cb13-112.html

58 Mohammad Yousuf was also working on developing the concept of connective journalism, as we learned after writing this. In his conceptualization, he similarly foregrounds social network services and their democratic nature as well as the continuation of journalism's traditional norms and values as they are played out in new ways. See M. Yousuf, "Positioning Journalism Within Networks: Conceptualizing and Operationalizing 'Connective Journalism,'" presented at the Conference of the International Communication Association, London, June 2013.

59 Zizi Papacharissi, *Affective Publics: Sentiment, Technology, and Politics* (New York: Oxford University Press, 2015). See also Zizi Papacharissi and Maria de Fatima Oliveira, "Affective News and Networked Publics: The

Rhythms of News Storytelling on #Egypt," *Journal of Communication* 2012, 62(2): 266–282; Alfred Hermida, "Social Journalism: Exploring how Social Media is Shaping Journalism," in Eugenia Siapera and Andreas Veglis, eds., *The Handbook of Global Online Journalism* (Wiley-Blackwell: Oxford, 2012): 309–328.

60 Cohen et al., *Participatory Politics*. This is evident when considering the YPP data on sharing, inserting oneself into the story, and making the story, as noted earlier and as will be explored in the chapters to come.

1 Young People, Journalism, and Politics

1 John Lynds, "FAA Heeds Youths Findings to Restore 'Head-to-Head' at Logan," *East Boston Times*, January 14, 2015, accessed January 10, 2016, www.eastietimes.com/2015/01/14/faa-heeds-youths-findings-to-restore-head-to-head-at-logan-airport/

2 Daniel Faber and Eric Krieg, *Unequal Exposure to Ecological Hazards*. A Report by the Philanthropy and Environmental Justice Research Project of Northeastern University, 2005, accessed August 24, 2016, www.northeastern.edu/nejrc/wp-content/uploads/Final-Unequal-Exposure-Report-2005-10-12-05.pdf. In January 2015, the author of this study stated that he had not seen significant changes in the situation. See Heather Goldstein, "Massachusetts Has an Environmental Justice Problem," NPR affiliate WCAI, January 20, 2015, accessed August 25, 2016, http://capeandislands.org/post/massachusetts-has-environmental-justice-problem#stream/0

3 James Carey, *Communication as Culture* (Boston, MA: Unwin Hyman, 1989).

4 Carey used the phrase "ritual approach to communication" to contrast with the "transmission approach to communication" when discussing how communication played a role in relation to identity and community. Although our approach is very similar, we prefer to use the term relational as it captures the character of communication in a social media era while also maintaining the interest in communication's role in ideological, social, economic and political processes.

5 Carey, *Communication as Culture*.

6 Carey, *Communication as Culture*, 18.

7 Carey, *Communication as Culture*, 18.

8 John Dewey, *The Public and Its Problems* (New York: Holt Publishers, 1927).

9 Dewey, *The Public and Its Problems*.

10 Dewey, *The Public and Its Problems*, 143.

11 Dewey, *The Public and Its Problems*, 144.

12 Dewey, *The Public and Its Problems*.

13 Dewey, *The Public and Its Problems*, 142.

14 Raymond Williams, "Community," in *Keywords: A Vocabulary of Culture and Society*, revised edition (New York: Oxford University Press, 1983).

15 Robert Putnam, *Bowling Alone: the Collapse and Revival of American Community* (New York: Simon & Schuster, 2000); Benedict Anderson, *Imagined Communities: Reflections on the Origins and Spread of Nationalism*

(New York: Verso, 2006); Michael Warner, *Publics and Counterpublics* (New York: Zone Books, 2006); Ulrich Beck, "Cosmopolitanism as Imagined Communities of Global Risk," *American Behavioral Scientist* 2011, 55(10): 1346–1361.

16 Francois Cooren, *The Organizing Property of Communication* (Amsterdam/Philadelphia: John Benjamins, 2000); Francois Cooren, Timothy Kuhn, Joep Cornelissen, and T. Clark, "Communication, Organizing and Organization: An Overview and Introduction to the Special Issue," *Organization Studies* 2011, 32(9): 1149–1170.

17 Cooren et al., "Communication, Organizing and Organization," 1150, 1152.

18 Dewey, *The Public and Its Problems*, 18.

19 Derek Heater, *A Brief History of Citizenship* (New York: New York University Press, 2004).

20 David Finkelhor, "The Internet, Youth Safety, and the Problem of 'Juvenoia,'" Paper from the Crimes Against Children Research Center, www.unh.edu/ccrc/pdf/Juvenoia%20paper.pdf

21 This protectionist approach has grown gradually over time and is unique to the last century; see Vivianna Zelizer, *Pricing the Priceless Child: The Changing Social Value of Children* (Princeton, NJ: Princeton University Press, 1994).

22 Gill Valentine, "Children Should Be Seen and Not Heard: The Production and Transgression of Adults' Public Space," *Urban Geography* 1996, 17 (March): 205–220. See also Mats Lieberg, "Teenagers and Public Space," *Communication Research* 195, 22(6): 720–744.

23 Juliet Schor, *Born to Buy: The Commercialized Child and the New Consumer Culture* (New York: Scribner, 2004); Alissa Quart, *Branded: The Buying and Selling of Teenagers* (New York: Basic Books, 2004).

24 Lonnie Sherrod, Constance Flanagan, and Jerome Youniss, eds., "Growing Into Citizenship: Multiple Pathways and Diverse Influences," a special issue of *Applied Developmental Science*, 2002, 6(4).

25 Michael X. Delli Carpini and Scott Keeter, *What Americans Know about Politics and Why It Matters* (New Haven, CT: Yale University Press, 1997).

26 Sunaina Maira and Elisabeth Soep, "Introduction," in Sunaina Maira and Elisabeth Soep, eds., *Youthscapes: The Popular, the National, the Global* (Philadelphia, PA: University of Pennsylvania Press, 2005), loc 360 (Kindle).

27 Martin Gardner, *Understanding Juvenile Law*, 3rd ed. (New York: Matthew Bender & Co., LexisNexis Group, 2005).

28 Embedded within the developmental view of citizenship are certain heteronormative assumptions of a developmental trajectory that would lead young people to heterosexuality and gender complementarity as they grow into full civic recognition, as the "ideal citizen." At the end of the nineteenth century, "citizenship" was a universalized and abstracted idea even as, according to Nancy Fraser and Linda Gordon, the citizenry it celebrated was largely "male-led (and female supported), white, middle class, procreative, and normatively gendered Protestant." Nancy Fraser and Linda Gordon, "Civil Citizenship against Social Citizenship? On the Ideology of Contract-Versus-Charity," in B. Van Steenbergen, ed., *The Condition*

of Citizenship (London: Sage, 1994): 98–101; Don Romesburg, "The Tightrope of Normalcy: Homosexuality, Developmental Citizenship and American Adolescence, 1890–1940," *Journal of Historical Sociology* 2008, 21(4): 417–442.

29 Estelle Sommeiller, Mark Price, and Ellis Wazeter, *Income Inequality in the U.S. by State, Metropolitan Area, and County*, Report of the Economic Policy Institute 2016, accessed August 18, 2016, www.epi.org/files/pdf/107100.pdf

30 Hava Gordon and Jessica Taft, "Rethinking Youth Political Socialization: Teenage Activists Talk Back," *Youth & Society* 2011, 43(4): 1499–1527; Christine Griffin, "Challenging Assumptions about Youth Political Participation: Critical Insights from Great Britain," in Joerg Forbrig, ed., *Revisiting Youth Political Participation: Challenges for Research and Democratic Practice in Europe* (Strasborg: Council of Europe, 2005), 145–154; Anita Harris, "Dodging and Waving: Young Women Countering the Stories of Youth and Citizenship," *International Journal of Critical Psychology* 2011, 4(2): 183–199.

31 Flanagan argues that civic identities form in adolescence and are shaped by their personal experiences and accord with the experiences and views of their closest family members. Constance Flanagan, *Teenage Citizens: The Political Theories of the Young* (Cambridge, MA: Harvard University Press, 2013).

32 Sharon Detrick, *A Commentary on the United Nations Convention on the Rights of the Child* (The Hague: Martinus Nijhoff Publishers, 1999).

33 Wesley Lowery, "Aren't More White People than Black People Killed by Police? Yes, but No," *The Washington Post*, July 11, 2016, accessed August 18, 2016, www.washingtonpost.com/news/post-nation/wp/2016/07/11/arent-more-white-people-than-black-people-killed-by-police-yes-but-no/?utm_term=.53230885ce9c

34 "Keep Youth Out of Adult Courts, Jails, and Prisons," *National Juvenile Justice Network*, accessed August 18, 2016, www.njjn.org/about-us/keep-youth-out-of-adult-prisons

35 Karyn Lacy, *Blue Chip Black: Race, Class, and Status in the New Black Middle Class* (Berkeley, CA: University of California Press, 2007); Michael Kraus, Paul Piff, Rodolfo Mendoza-Denton, Michelle Rheinschmidt, and Dacher Keltner, "Social Class, Solipsism, and Contextualism: How the Rich Are Different from the Poor," *Psychological Review* 2012, 119(3): 546–572.

36 Deen Freelon, Carlton McIlwain, and Meredith D. Clark, *Beyond the Hashtags: #Ferguson, #BlackLivesMatter, and the Online Struggle for Offline Justice*, Report from the Center for Media & Social Impact, 2016, http://cmsimpact.org.

37 Karyn Riddle, Joanne Cantor, Sahara Byrne, and Emily Moyer-Guse, "People Killing People on the News: Young Children's Descriptions of Frightening Television News Content." *Communication Quarterly* 2012, 60(2): 278–294.

38 Tom P. Bakker and Claes H. de Vreese, "Good News for the Future? Young People, Internet Use, and Political Participation," *Communication Research* 2011, 38: 451–470. doi:10.1177/0093650210381738; Delli Carpini and Keeter, *What Americans Know about Politics*; Dan G. Drew and David Weaver, "Voter Learning in the 2004 Presidential Election: Did

the Media Matter?" *Journalism & Mass Communication Quarterly* 2006, 83: 25–42. doi:10.1177/107769900608300103; Bruce W. Hardy, Jeffrey A. Gottfried, Kenneth M. Winneg, and Kathleen Hall Jamieson,"Stephen Colbert's Civics Lesson: How Colbert Super PAC Taught Viewers about Campaign Finance," *Mass Communication and Society* 2014, 17: 329–353. doi:10.1080/15205436.2014.891138; Raymond Pingree, Roseanne Scholl, and Andrea Quenette, "Effects of Post-Debate Coverage on Spontaneous Policy Reasoning," *Journal of Communication* 2012, 62: 643–658.

39 Meyrowitz foresaw this in relation to television's widespread availability in 1985. With digital and mobile media, the boundaries between adult and youthful sources of information have only eroded further since then. See Joshua Meyrowitz, *No Sense of Place* (New York: Oxford University Press, 1985). For an update of Meyrowitz for the digital age, see Lynn Schofield Clark, *The Parent App: Understanding Families in a Digital Age* (New York: Oxford University Press, 2013).

40 Sherry Turkle, *Alone Together: Why We Expect More from Technology and Less from Each Other* (New York: Basic Books, 2011).

41 Jane McGonigal, *Reality is Broken: Why Games Make Us Better and How They Can Change the World* (New York: Penguin Books, 2011).

42 Shankuntala Banaji and David Buckingham, *The Civic Web: Young People, the Internet, and Civic Participation*, The John C. & Katherine T. MacArthur Series on Digital Media and Learning (Cambridge, MA: MIT Press, 2013).

43 Shankuntala Banaji and David Buckingham, *Young People, the Internet, and Civic Participation: Key Findings from the CivicWeb Project*. IJLM MIT 2010, 2013; Eric Gordon, "Beyond Participation: Designing for the Civic Web," *Journal of Digital and Media Literacy* 2013, 1(1), accessed on May 13, 2017, www.jodml.org/2013/02/01/design-for-civic-web/

44 danah boyd, "Myspace, HR4437 and Youth Activism," Zephoria.org, 2006. www.zephoria.org/thoughts/archives/2006/03/28/myspace_hr_4437. html; Sasha Costanza-Chock. *Youth and Social Movements: Key Lessons for Allies*, Kinder and Braver World Project: Research Series (danah boyd, John Palfrey, and Dena Sacco, eds.), 2012, http://cyber.law.harvard.edu/sites/ cyber.law.harvard.edu/files/KBWYouthandSocialMovements2012_0.pdf; Sasha Costanza-Chock, *Out of the Shadows, Into the Streets! Transmedia Organizing and the Immigrant Rights Movement* (Cambridge, MA: MIT Press, 2014); Joseph Kahne, Ellen Middaugh, Nam-Jin Lee, and Jessica T. Feezell, "Youth Online Activity and Exposure to Diverse Perspectives," *New Media & Society* 2011, 14(3): 492–512.

45 W. Lance Bennett, "Changing Citizenship in the Digital Age." *Civic Life Online: Learning How Digital Media Can Engage Youth* 1 (2008): 1–24.

46 Peter Lunt and Sonia Livingstone, "Is 'Mediatization' the New Paradigm for Our Field? A Commentary on Deacon and Stanyer (2014, 2015) and Hepp, Hjarvard, and Lundby (2015)," *Media, Culture and Society*, 2016, available via LSE Research Online: http://eprints.lse.ac.uk/view/lseauthor/ Livingstone,_Sonia.html See also Stig Hjarvard, *The Mediatization of Society* (London: Routledge, 2013).

47 Lynn Schofield Clark, "Exploring Religion and Mediatization through a Case Study of J + K's Big Day: A Response to Stig Hjarvard," *Culture and Religion: An Interdisciplinary Journal* 2011, 12(2): 167–184, doi: 10.1080/14755610.2011.579717. This is similar to Leah Lievrouw's definition of mediation as comprising "an ongoing, mutually shaping relationship between peoples' use of communication technology (reconfiguration) and their communicative action (remediation) that produces social and technological change." See Leah Lievrouw, *Alternative and Activist New Media* (London: Polity, 2011), 231.

48 Nancy Baym, *Personal Connections in the Digital Age*, 2nd ed. (New York: Polity, 2015). See also John McCarthy and Peter Wright, *Technology as Experience* (Cambridge, MA: MIT Press, 2004); danah boyd, *It's Complicated: The Social Lives of Networked Teens* (New Haven, CT: Yale University Press, 2013).

49 Sonia Livingstone, "The Participation Paradigm in Audience Research," *Communication Review* 2013, 16: 1–2, 21–30; see also Alice Mattoni and Emiliano Trere, "Media Practices, Mediation Processes, and Mediatization in the Study of Social Movements," *Communication Theory* 24(1): 252–271; and Lievrouw, *Alternative and Activist New Media*.

50 Jeffrey Gottfried, and Elisa Shearer, *News Use Across Social Media Platforms*, report of the Pew Research Center, May 26, 2016, accessed June 24, 2016, www.journalism.org/2016/05/26/news-use-across-social-media-platforms-2016/. Meanwhile, a 2016 report by Reuters found that 58 percent of people surveyed internationally got news from social media: http://reutersinstitute.politics.ox.ac.uk/sites/default/files/Digital-News-Report-2016.pdf. Accessed May 15, 2016.

51 Matthew Ingram, "Facebook Traffic to U.S. News Sites Has Fallen by Double Digits, Report Says," *Fortune*, August 16, 2016, accessed August 17, 2016, http://fortune.com/2016/08/16/facebook-traffic-media/

52 Joseph Schwartz, "U.S. Media Publishers and Publications – Ranked for July 2016," Report from DigitalVision (SimilarWeb), August 14, 2016, accessed August 17, 2016, www.similarweb.com/blog/us-media-publishers-july-2016

53 Pablo Boczkowski, Eugenia Mitchelstein, and Mora Matassi, *Incidental News: How Young People Consume News on Social Media*, presented at the Proceedings of the 50th Hawaii International Conference on System Sciences, January 4, 2017, accessed May 6, 2016, www.academia.edu/28652218/Incidental_News_How_Young_People_Consume_News_on_Social_Media; Schwartz, "U.S. Media Publishers." Also among the top ten news sites as measured by desktop and mobile page views in July 2016 were Yahoo, Google, Time Warner, Fox Entertainment Group, Advance Publications, Gannett Company, and NBC Universal.

54 www.vox.com/new-money/2016/11/16/13659840/facebook-fake-news-chart

55 www.nytimes.com/2016/11/20/business/media/facebook-considering-ways-to-combat-fake-news-mark-zuckerberg-says.html

56 Karen Mossberger, Caroline J. Tolbert, and William Franko, *Digital Cities: The Internet and the Geography of Opportunity*. Oxford Studies in

Digital Politics (New York: Oxford University Press, 2012). Also see Vicky Rideout and Vikki Katz, *Opportunity for All? Technology and Learning in Low Income Families. The Joan Ganz Cooney at Sesame Workshop*, 2016, www.joanganzcooneycenter.org/publication/opportunity-for-all-technology- and-learning-in-lower-income-families/; Regina Marchi, "News Translators: Latino Immigrant Youth, Social Media, and Citizenship Training," *Journalism and Mass Communication Quarterly* 2016, doi: 10.1177/1077699016637119 2016: http://jmq.sagepub.com/content/early/2016/03/09/1077699016637119.abstract

57 Benjamin J. Bowyer, Joseph Kahne, and Ellen Middaugh, "Youth Comprehension of Political Messages in YouTube Videos," *New Media & Society* 2016, doi: 10.1177/1461444815611593

58 Danny Funt, "A Compulsive Audience and a Complicit Media," *Columbia Journalism Review*, August 16, 2016, www.cjr.org/special_report/news_media_health_screens_brain_cost_business.php

59 PaperCuts is a site that documents newspaper layoffs and closings around the United States. See: http://newslayoffs.com.

60 Nancy Vogt and Amy Mitchell, Crowdfunded Journalism: A Small but Growing Addition to Publicly Driven Journalism," a report of the Pew Research Center, 2016, accessed June 24, 2016, www.journalism.org/2016/01/20/crowdfunded-journalism/

61 Vogt and Mitchell, "Crowdfunded Journalism."

62 Larry Greene, Unpublished document on socially conscious businesses supporting community news, 2016.

63 Pablo Boczkowski and Eugenia Mitchelstein, *The News Gap: When the Information Preferences of the Media and the Public Diverge* (Cambridge, MA: MIT Press, 2013).

64 Boczkowski, Mitchelstein, and Matassi, *Incidental News.*

65 Nicole Ortung, "Will Snapchat's Redesign Make the App a Go-To News Source?" *Christian Science Monitor*, June 8, 2016, www.csmonitor.com/Technology/2016/0608/Will-Snapchat-s-redesign-make-the-app-a-go-to-news-source?cmpid=gigya-tw

66 M. Schudson, *Discovering the News: A Social History of American Newspapers* (New York: Basic Books, 1978), 189.

67 See, e.g., Russell, *Journalism as Activism.*

68 Jeffrey Alexander, "Introduction: Journalism, Democratic Culture, and Creative Reconstruction," in Jeffrey Alexander, ed., *The Crisis of Journalism Reconsidered: Dramatic Culture, Professional Codes, Digital Future* (Cambridge: Cambridge University Press, 2016), 10.

69 Alexander, "Introduction."

2 Connective Journalism

1 W. Lance Bennett and Alexandra Segerberg, *The Logic of Connective Action: Digital Media and the Personalization of Contentious Politics.* (Cambridge: Cambridge University Press, 2013).

2　See also Peter Dahlgren, "The Internet, Public Spheres, and Political Communication: Dispersion and Deliberation," *Political Communication* 2005, 22(2): 147–162. See also Peter Dahlgren, *Media and Political Engagement: Citizens, Communication, and Democracy* (Cambridge: Cambridge University Press, 2009); Kazys Varnelis, ed., *Networked Publics* (Cambridge, MA: MIT Press, 2008); danah boyd, "Social Network Sites as Networked Publics," in Zizi Papacharissi, ed., *A Networked Self: Identity, Community, and Culture on Social Network Sites* (New York: Routledge, 2011): 39–58. See also Ganaele Langlois, Elmer Greg, Fenwick McKelvey, and Zachary Devereaux, "Networked Publics: The Double Articulation of Ode and Politics on Facebook," *Canadian Journal of Communication* 2009, 34(3): 415–434; John Postill, "Localizing the Internet Beyond Communities and Networks," *New Media & Society* 2008, 10(3): 413–431. The roots of social network analysis date to Mark Granovetter, "The Strength of Weak Ties," *American Journal of Sociology* 1973, 78(6): 1360–1380. Social field theorists include Rodney Benson, "News Media as a 'Journalistic Field': What Bourdieu Adds to New Institutionalism, and Vice Versa," *Political Communication* 2006, 23(2): 187–202; Nick Couldry, "Bourdieu and the Media: The Promises and Limits of Field Theory," *Theory and Society* 2007, 36: 209.

3　Bennett and Segerberg, *The Logic of Connective Action*, 42.

4　Francois Cooren, *The Organizing Property of Communication* (Amsterdam/ Philadelphia, PA: John Benjamins, 2000); Francois Cooren, Timothy Kuhn, Joep Cornelissen, and T. Clark, "Communication, Organizing and Organization: An Overview and Introduction to the Special Issue," *Organization Studies* 2011, 32(9): 1149–1170.

5　Cooren et al., "Communication, Organizing, and Organization."

6　Cooren et al., "Communication, Organizing, and Organization," 1152.

7　Jose Van Dijck, *The Culture of Connectivity: A Critical History of Social Media* (Oxford: Oxford University Press, 2013).

8　Dan Zahavi, *Husserl's Phenomenology* (Stanford, CA: Stanford University Press, 2003); Martin Heidegger, "Introduction," *The Basic Problems of Phenomenology* (Indianapolis, IN: Indiana University Press, 1975).

9　Christopher Zurn, "Intersubjectivity," *International Encyclopedia of the Social Sciences*, 2008, accessed June 23, 2016, www.encyclopedia.com/doc/ 1G2-3045301173.html.

10　Zurn, "Intersubjectivity."

11　Kate Crawford, "Following You: Disciplines of Listening in Social Media," *Continuum: Journal of Media & Cultural Studies* 2009, 23(4): 525–535. Gershon further argues that the selected medium through which one chooses to communicate becomes part of its relational meaning in Ilana Gershon, *The Breakup 2.0: Disconnecting over New Media* (Ithaca, NY: Cornell University Press, 2010).

12　Martin Friedman, *Martin Buber and the Human Sciences* (New York: SUNY Press, 1996); Kenneth Kramer and Mechthild Gawlick, *Martin Buber's I and Thou: Practicing Living Dialogue* (Mahwah, NJ: Paulist Press, 2003).

13 Chantal Mouffe, *On the Political* (Thinking in Action) (New York: Routledge, 2005).

14 Sherry Turkle, *Alone Together: Why We Expect More from Technology and Less from Each Other* (New York: Basic Books, 2011); Gershon, *The Breakup* 2.0.

15 Nancy Baym, *Personal Connections in the Digital Age*, 2nd ed. (New York: Polity, 2015).

16 John Durham Peters, *Speaking into the Air: A History of the Idea of Communication* (Chicago, IL: University of Chicago Press, 1999).

17 Peters, *Speaking into the Air*, 4.

18 Peters, *Speaking into the Air*, 16.

19 Joseph B. Walther, "Anticipated Ongoing Interaction Versus Channel Effects on Relational Communication in Computer-Mediated Interaction," *Human Communication Research* 1994, 19(1): 3–43; Ronald Rice and Gail Love, "Electronic Emotion: Socioemotional Content in a Computer-Mediated Communication Network," *Communication Research* 1987, 14(1): 85–108; Starr Roxanne Hiltz and Murray Turoff, *The Network Nation: Human Communication Via Computer* (Reading, MA: Addison-Wesley, 1978); Baym, *Personal Connections*, cited each of these research reports in her own work, noting that in Rice and Love's study, only 0.2 percent of online messages were antagonistic.

20 Nina Eliasoph, *Avoiding Politics: How Americans Produce Apathy in Everyday Life* (Cambridge: Cambridge University Press, 1998).

21 Eliasoph, *Avoiding Politics*. Also see Diana C. Mutz, *Hearing the Other Side: Deliberative versus Participatory Democracy* (Cambridge: Cambridge University Press, 2006).

22 Kjerstin Thorson, "Facing an Uncertain Reception: Young Citizens and Political Interaction on Facebook," *Information, Communication & Society* 2014, 17(2): 213. See also Jennifer Stromer-Galley, Lauren Bryant, and Bruce Bimber, "Context and Medium Matter: Expressing Disagreements Online and Face-To-Face in Political Deliberations," *Journal of Public Deliberation* 2015, 11(1), www.publicdeliberation.net/jpd/vol11/iss1/. People do have an imagined audience in mind when they post, although as Litt and Hargittai found, those imagined audiences don't accurately correspond to the actual audience. See Eden Litt and Eszter Hargittai, "The Imagined Audience on Social Network Sites," *Social Media + Society* 2016, 2(1), doi: 10.1177/2056305116633482

23 Carey, *Communication as Culture*, 18.

24 Arendt later shifted her focus from action to the characteristics of the mind that made action possible. This occurred as she wrote about the Eichmann trial, and the way that Eichmann regarded his own role in the extermination of Jews under the Nazi regime. She observed that Eichmann viewed his actions through a lens of efficiency rather than as actions rooted in either hatred or evil. See Hannah Arendt, *Eichmann in Jerusalem: A Report on the Banality of Evil* (London: Faber & Faber, 1963).

25 Arendt shared Levinas's concern that too much of the work of political philosophers at the time of the early twentieth century was focused

on ideas and not enough on action. See Hannah Arendt, *On Revolution* (New York: Penguin, 1961).

26 Arendt, *On Revolution.*

27 Hannah Arendt, *The Origins of Totalitarianism* (New York: Houghton Mifflin Harcourt, 1973).

28 Majid Yar, "Hannah Arendt," *Internet Encyclopedia of Philosophy,* 2008, accessed June 23, 2016, www.iep.utm.edu/arendt/.

29 Walter Lippmann, *Public Opinion* (New York: W. W. Norton, 1922); Roger Silverstone, *Media and Morality: On the Rise of the Mediapolis* (Hoboken, NJ: Wiley, 2006).

30 Silverstone, *Media and Morality.*

31 Anna Topolski, "In Search of a Political Ethics of Intersubjectivity: Between Hannah Arendt, Emmanuel Levinas and the Judaic," *Hannah Arendt Journal for Political Thinking,* 2008, Ausgabe 1, Band 4, accessed June 22, 2016, www.hannaharendt.net/index.php/han/article/view/137/240

32 Annabel Herzog, "Levinas on the Social: Guilt and the City," *Theory, Culture & Society* 2015, 32(4): 27–43. This is Herzog's interpretation of Levinas.

33 Emmanuel Levinas, *Paix et Proximité, Les Cahiers de la Nuit Surveillée* (Lagrasse: Verdier, 1984), translated by Peter Atterton and Simon Critchley, "Peace and Proximity," in Adriaan Peperzak, Simon Critchley, and Robert Bernasconi, eds., *Emmanuel Levinas: Basic Philosophical Writings* (Bloomington, IN: Indiana University Press, 1996), 168; translation modified in Herzog,"Levinas on the Social."

34 Herzog, "Levinas on the Social," 30.

35 Emmanuel Levinas, *Totality and Infinity: an Essay on Exteriority* (Hingham, MA: Nijhoff, 1979).

36 Stanley Deetz, "Resistance: Would Struggle by Any Other Name Be as Sweet?" *Management Communication Quarterly* 2008, 21: 387–392.

37 Kimberlee Crenshaw, "Intersectionality: The Double Bind of Race and Gender," *Perspectives Magazine,* 1989/2004, 2. See also Patricia Hill Collins, *Black Feminist Thought: Knowledge, Consciousness, and the Politics of Empowerment* (London: Psychology Press, 1990/2000).

38 Nick Couldry, *Why Voice Matters: Culture and Politics after Neoliberalism* (London: Sage, 2010).

39 Couldry, *Why Voice Matters.*

40 Axel Bruns, *Blogs, Wikipedia, Second Life, and Beyond: From Production to Produsage.* (New York: Peter Lang, 2008), 74. See also Axel Bruns, *Gatewatching: Collaborative Online News Production* (New York: Peter Lang, 2005).

41 Andrew Chadwick, *The Hybrid Media System: Politics and Power,* Oxford Studies in Digital Politics (New York: Oxford University Press, 2013). See also Geoffrey Baym, "*The Daily Show*: Discursive Integration and the Reinvention of Political Journalism," *Political Communication* 2005, 22: 259–276.

42 Russell, *Journalism as Activism;* see also Adrienne Russell, *Networked: A History of Contemporary News in Transition* (London: Polity, 2011). Charlie Beckett and Robin Mansell, "Crossing Boundaries: New

Media and Networked Journalism," *Communication, Culture and Critique* 2008, 1(1): 92–104; Jo Bardoel and Mark Deuze, "Network Journalism: Converging Competences of Media Professionals and Professionalism, *Australian Journalism Review* 2001, 23(2): 91–103. See also Zizi Papacharissi, "Toward New Journalism(s): Affective News, Hybridity, and Liminal Spaces," *Journalism Studies* 2014, 16(1): 27–40.

43 Jeffrey Alexander, *The Civil Sphere* (New York: Oxford University Press, 2006).

44 The idea that disclosure is related to risk is discussed in theories of communication and self-disclosure. See, e.g., Julia Omarzu, "A Disclosure Decision Model: Determining How and When Individuals Will Self-Disclose," *Personality and Social Psychology Review* 2000, 4(2): 174–185; Natalya Bazarova and Yoon Hyun Choi, "Self-Disclosure in Social Media: Extending the Functional Approach to Disclosure Motivations & Characteristics on Social Network Sites," *Journal of Communication* 2014, 64(4): 635–657; V. J. Derlega and J. Grzelak, "Appropriateness of Self-Disclosure," in G. J. Chelune, ed., *Self-disclosure: Origins, Patterns, and Implications of Openness in Interpersonal Relationships* (San Francisco, CA: Jossey-Bass, 1979), 151–176.

45 For example, studies such as "How Millennials Get News: Inside the Habits of America's First Digital Generation," American Press Institute, March 16, 2015, www.americanpressinstitute.org/publications/reports/survey-research/millennials-news/; "What Young Adults Know about Politics," CIRCLE Staff, The Center for Information and Research on Civic Learning and Engagement, January 2013, http://civicyouth.org/wp-content/uploads/2013/01/What-Young-Adults-Know-Fact-Sheet-20131.pdf; Elizabeth Redman, "Fewer Young People Read News Online than Their Parents," World Association of Newspapers and News Publishers, January 27, 2010, www.editorsweblog.org/2010/01/27/fewer-young-people-read-news-online-than-their-parents; "How Millennials Get Their News: Paying for Content," Media Insight Project, www.mediainsight.org/Pages/default.aspx

46 Mimi Ito, Sonja Baumer, Matteo Bittanti, danah boyd, Becky Herr-Stephenson, Heather A. Horst, et al., *Hanging Out, Messing Around, Geeking Out: Living and Learning with New Media* (Cambridge, MA: MIT Press, 2010).

47 Cathy Cohen, Joseph Kahne, Benjamin Bowyer, Ellen Middaugh, and J. Rogowski, *Participatory Politics: New Media and Youth Political Action*, Executive Summary, 2012, accessed October 1, 2015, http://ypp.dmlcentral.net/sites/default/files/publications/Participatory_Politics_Report.pdf

48 Cohen, *Participatory Politics*.

49 Ito et al., *Hanging Out*.

50 danah boyd, *It's Complicated* (New Haven, CT: Yale University Press, 2014); danah boyd, "Why Youth (Heart) Social Network Sites: The Role of Networked Publics in Teenage Life," *MacArthur Foundation Series on Digital Learning – Youth, Identity, and Digital Media* Volume 2007, 119–142.

51 According to the YPP study (Cohen et al., *Participatory Politics*), 17 percent of youth have shared political news or information on social media sites.

52 Ito et al., *Hanging Out*; Henry Jenkins, *Convergence Culture: Where Old and New Media Collide* (New York: New York University Press, 2006), Jenkins et al. *By Any Media Necessary*; Cohen et al. *Participatory Politics*.

53 John Herrman, "Inside Facebook's (Totally Insane, Unintentionally Gigantic, Hyperpartisan) Political-Media Machine," *New York Times*, August 28, 2016, accessed August 28, 2016, www.nytimes.com/2016/08/28/magazine/inside-facebooks-totally-insane-unintentionally-gigantic-hyperpartisan-political-media-machine.html?emc=edit_th_20160828&nl=todaysheadlines&nlid=51992941&_r=0

54 Herrman, "Inside Facebook."

55 Mike Isaac, "50 Million Reasons Buzzfeed Wants to Take Its Content Far Beyond Lists," *New York Times*, August 10, 2014, accessed August 20, 2016, www.nytimes.com/2014/08/11/technology/a-move-to-go-beyond-lists-for-content-at-buzzfeed.html

56 Terri Senft, "The Skin of the Selfie," in Alain Bieber, ed., *Ego Update: The Future of Digital Identity* (Dusseldorf: NRW Forum Publications, 2015).

57 E. Pierson, "Outnumbered but Well-Spoken: Female Commenters in the *New York Times*," Department of Statistics, Oxford University, UK, published in the Proceedings of the 18th Association for Computing Machinery Conference on Computer Supported Cooperative Work and Social Computing, 2015, pp. 1201–1213, http://cs.stanford.edu/people/emmap1/cscw_paper.pdf doi:10.1145/2675133.2675134

58 Ito et al., *Hanging Out*.

59 John Durham Peters, "Witnessing," *Media, Culture and Society* 2001, 23(6): 707–723; Stuart Allan, *Citizen Witnessing: Revisiting Journalism in Times of Crisis* (New York: Polity Press, 2013). Also see: Shoshana Felman and Dori Laub, *Testimony: Crisis of Witnessing in Literature, Psychoanalysis and History* (New York: Routledge,1992).

60 Jose Van Dijck, "Digital Photography: Communication, Identity, Memory," *Visual Communication* 2008, 7(1): 57–76; Jose Van Dijck, "'You Have One Identity': Performing the Self on Facebook and LinkedIn," *Media, Culture and Society* 2013, 35(2): 199–215.

61 Paul D'Amato, "Non-Profit Worker Who Provoked Fury with Disrespectful Arlington Photo Tells How She Lost Her Job, Can't Date and Now Lives in Fear," *The Daily Mail*, February 22, 2015, accessed August 29, 2016, www.dailymail.co.uk/news/article-2964489/I-really-obsessed-reading-Woman-fired-photo-giving-middle-finger-Arlington-National-Cemetery-says-finally-Google-without-fear.html

62 D'Amato, "Non-Profit Worker."

63 Cohen et al., *Participatory Politics*.

64 Cohen et al., *Participatory Politics*.

65 Cohen et al., *Participatory Politics*.

66 Michelle Jackson, "The Mash-Up: a New Archetype for Communication, *Journal of Computer-Mediated Communication* 2009, 14(3): 730–734.

67 W. Lance Bennett, "Changing Citizenship for the Digital Age, " in W. Lance Bennett, ed., *Civic Life Online: Learning How Digital Media Can Engage*

Youth (Cambridge, MA: MIT Press, 2008), 1-24; Fadi Hirzalla and Lisbet Van Zoonen, "Beyond the Online/Offline Divide: How Youth's Online and Offline Civic Activities Converge," *Social Science Computer Review* 2011, 29(4): 481–498.

68 Elisabeth Soep, *Participatory Politics: Next Generation Tactics to Remake Public Spheres* (Cambridge, MA: MIT Press, 2014); David Buckingham, *The Making of Citizens: Young People, News, and Politics* (London: Routledge, 2000); see also Joellen Fisherkeller, ed., *International Perspectives on Youth Media: Cultures of Production and Education* (New York: Peter Lang, 2011).

69 Soep, *Participatory Politics.*

70 Henry Jenkins et al., *By Any Media Necessary.*

71 *Rising Up: Voices from Colorado's Emerging Student Protest Movement Event.* March 4, 2015, University of Colorado at Denver. The event featured eight student leaders from six high schools and three adults in educational leadership positions.

72 See, e.g., Christina Dunbar-Hester, *Low Power to the People: Pirates, Protest and Politics in FM Radio Activism* (Cambridge, MA: MIT Press, 2014). Dunbar-Hester explored how activists negotiate identities when political realities change, and how activists worked with community members to encourage technical competence and confidence, which, she argued, translated into political awareness and participation in actions for change. See also Ndubuisi Goodluck Nwaerondu and Gordon Thompson, "The Use of Educational Radio in Developing Countries: Lessons from the Past," *International Journal of E-Learning & Distance Education* 1987, 2.2: 43–54; Michele McKinley and Line Jensen, "In Our Own Voices: Reproductive Health Radio Programming in the Peruvian Amazon," *Critical Studies in Media Communication* 2003, 20(2): 180–203; Kevin Howley, *Community Media: People, Places and Community Technologies* (Cambridge: Cambridge University Press, 2005). For the role of art in public sharing and community organizing, see Nancy Love and Mark Mattern, *Doing Democracy: Activist Art and Cultural Politics* (New York: SUNY Press); Mark Mattern, *Acting in Concert: Music, Community and Political Action* (New Brunswick, NJ: Rutgers University Press, 1998); Regina Marchi, *Day of the Dead in the USA: The Migration and Transformation of a Cultural Phenomenon* (New Brunswick, NJ: Rutgers University Press, 2009).

73 Digital media extend activism, particularly when activists take advantage of the low costs and the ability to coordinate action without copresence, as argued in Jennifer Earl and Katrina Kimport, *Digitally Enabled Social Change: Activism in the Internet Age* (Cambridge, MA: MIT Press, 2011). See also Jenkins, *Convergence Culture*; Jenkins et al. *By Any Media Necessary*; Teresa M. Harrison and Brea Barthel, "Wielding New Media in Web 2.0: Exploring the History of Engagement with the Collaborative Construction of Media Products," *New Media & Society* 2009, 11(1–2): 155–178.

3 Hope and Disillusionment with Legacy News

1 Interview on Social Media and News, Studio 12, *KBDI 12* (public television), http://video.cpt12.org/video/2228942292. Yonas provided an enhanced interpretation of this discussion during an extended interview in March 2014.

2 On the use of the phrase "legacy news" in scholarship, see Brian L. Massey, "What Job Advertisements Tell Us about Demand for Multiplatform Reporters at Legacy News Outlets," *Journalism & Mass Communication Educator* 2010, 65(2): 142–155; Kenneth Olmstead, Amy Mitchell, and Tom Rosensteil, *Navigating News Online: Where People Go, How They Get There and What Lures Them Away*, Pew Research Center, 2011.

3 Nick Newman with Richard Fletcher, David A. L. Levy and Rasmus Nielsen, *Reuters Institute Digital News Report 2016*. A report of the Reuters Institute for the Study of Journalism, 2016, accessed May 23, 2017, reutersinstitute. politics.ox.ac.uk/sites/default/files/Digital-News-Report-2016.pdf.

4 Thomas Patterson, *Young People and News*, a report of the Kennedy School of Government's Joan Shorenstein Center on the Press, Politics and Public Policy, 2007, accessed May 23, 2017, shorensteincenter.org/wp-content/uploads/2012/03/young_people_and_news_2007.pdf

5 Andrea Caumont, *Twelve Trends Shaping Digital News*, a report of the Pew Research Center FACTANK, October 16, 2013, accessed May 23, 2017, www .pewresearch.org/fact-tank/2013/10/16/12-trends-shaping-digital-news/; Amy Mitchell, Jeffrey Gottfriend, and Katerina Eva Matsa, *Political Interest and Awareness Lower among Millennials*, a report of the Pew Research Center, 2015, accessed May 23, 2017, www.journalism.org/2015/06/01/political-interest-and-awareness-lower-among-millennials/

6 Lee Rainie, Aaron Smith, Kay Lehman Schlozman, Henry Brady, and Sidney Verba, *Social Media and Political Engagement*, Pew Research Center, 2012, accessed May 23, 2017, www.pewinternet.org/2012/10/19/social-media-and-political-engagement/; Johanna Dunaway, *Mobile vs. Computer: Implications for News Audiences and Outlets*, a report of the Kennedy School of Government's Joan Shorenstein Center on the Press, Politics and Public Policy, August 30, 2016, accessed May 23, 2017, shorensteincenter.org/mobile-vs-computer-news-audiences-and-outlets/#_ftn17; see also Kevin Arceneaux and Martin Johnson, *Changing Minds or Changing Channels? Partisan News in an Age of Choice* (Chicago, IL: University of Chicago Press, 2013).

7 *Understanding the Participatory News Consumer*, a report of the Pew Research Center for the People and the Press, 2010, www.pewinternet.org/2010/03/01/understanding-the-participatory-news-consumer-2/

8 Eliasoph, *Avoiding Politics*.

9 W. Lance Bennett, "The Uncivic Culture: Communication, Culture, and the Rise of Lifestyle Politics," *PS: Political Science & Politics* 1998, 31(4): 741–761. Thorson similarly draws attention to this shift; see Kjerstin Thorson, "Facing an Uncertain Reception: Young Citizens and Political Interaction on Facebook, *Information, Communication & Society* 2014, 17(2): 203–216.

10 Eliasoph, *Avoiding Politics*; Diana Mutz, *Hearing the Other Side: Deliberative versus Participatory Democracy* (Cambridge: Cambridge University Press, 2006).

11 Thorson, "Facing an Uncertain Reception." See also Kjerstin Thorson, "Do-It-Yourself Citizenship: Youth, Communication and Politics in the Digital Age," unpublished manuscript, 2012.

12 Thorson, "Facing an Uncertain Reception," 213.

13 Thomas Jefferson to Edward Carrington, 1787, http://press-pubs.uchicago.edu/founders/documents/amendI_speechs8.html

14 Schudson, *Discovering the News*.

15 Rhys H. Williams, "Visions of the Good Society and the Religious Roots of American Political Culture," *Sociology of Religion* 1999, 60(1): 1–34.

16 Letter sent by the Continental Congress (October 26, 1774) to the Inhabitants of Quebec. Source: *Journal of the Continental Congress* 1904, 1: 108.

17 Siebert, Fred Seaton, Theodore Peterson, and Wilbur Schramm, *Four Theories of the Press: The Authoritarian, Libertarian, Social Responsibility, and Soviet Communist Concepts of What the Press Should Be and Do* (Champaign, IL: University of Illinois Press, 1956).

18 Commission on Freedom of the Press, 1947: 92, cited in Siebert, et al. *Four Theories of the Press*.

19 Daniel Hallin, "Commercialization and Professionalization in the American News Media," in James Curran and Michael Gurevitch, eds., *Mass Media and Society* (London: Arnold, 2005), 218–235; Robert McChesney, *Rich Media, Poor Democracy: Communication Politics in Dubious Times* (New York: Free Press, 2000); Robert McChesney, *The Problem of the Media: US Communication Politics in the 21st Century* (New York: Monthly Review Press, 2004); Mauro Porto, "Frame Diversity and Citizen Competence: Towards a Critical Approach to News Quality," *Critical Studies in Media Communication* 2007, 24(4): 303–231; Daniel Schiller, *Digital Capitalism: Networking the Global Market System* (Cambridge, MA: MIT Press, 2000).

20 Jay Rosen, "A Most Useful Definition of Citizen Journalism," *Pressthink*, July 14, 2008, http://archive.pressthink.org/2008/07/14/a_most_useful_d.htmlhttp://archive.pressthink.org/2008/07/14/a_most_useful_d.html

21 Dan Gillmor, *We the Media: Grassroots Journalism by the People* (New York: O'Reilly Media, 2006); Leonard Downie and Michael Schudson, "The Reconstruction of American Journalism," *Columbia Journalism Review*, 2009, www.cjr.org/reconstruction/the_reconstruction_of_american.php

22 Leonard Downie and Robert Kaiser, *The News about the News: American Journalism in Peril* (New York: Vintage, 2003). See also Pablo Boczkowski, *News at Work: Imitation in an Age of Information Abundance* (Chicago, IL: University of Chicago Press, 2010).

23 Adrienne Russell, *Networked: A History of Contemporary News in Transition* (London: Polity, 2011).

24 Mark Deuze, "The Web and Its Journalisms: Considering the Consequences of Different Types of News Media Online," *New Media & Society* 2003,

5(2): 203–230; Zizi Papacharissi, "Affective News and Networked Publics: The Rhythms of News Storytelling on #Egypt," *Journal of Communication* 2012, 62(2): 266–282; Zizi Papacharissi, "Toward New Journalism(s): Affective News, Hybridity, and Liminal Spaces," *Journalism Studies* 2014, 16(1): 27–40.

25 W. Lance Bennett, Lynne A. Gressett, and William Haltom, "Repairing the News: A Case Study of the News Paradigm," *Journal of Communication* 1985, 35: 50–86, p. 85.

26 Adam Seligman, *Modernity's Wager: Authority, the Self, and Transcendence* (Princeton, NJ: Princeton University Press, 2000).

27 C. W. Anderson, *Rebuilding the News: Metropolitan Journalism in the Digital Age* (Philadelphia, PA: Temple University Press, 2013), 51.

28 C. W. Anderson, "What Hating Social Media Means: Perspectives on Journalistic (Non)-Adoption of New Technology," presentation to the conference, Social Media and the Transformation of Public Spaces, Amsterdam, 2014.

29 Dan Byers, "How Politicians, Pollsters and Media Missed Trump's Groundswell," *CNNMoney*, November 9, 2016, http://money.cnn.com/2016/11/09/media/polling-media-missed-trump/

30 Byers, "How Politicians."

31 Beth Rubin et al., "'It's the Worst Place to Live': Urban Youth and the Challenge of School-Based Civic Learning," *Theory into Practice* 2009, 48(3): 213–221; James Youniss, Jeffrey McLellan, and Miranda Yates, "What We Know about Engendering Civic Identity," *American Behavioral Scientist* 1997, (5): 620–631.

32 Times Mirror Center for the People and the Press, *The Age of Indifference: A Study of Young Americans and How They View the News* (Washington, DC: Times Mirror Center, 1990); Charles Quigley, "Civic Education: Recent History, Current Status, and the Future," *Albany Law Review* 1999, 62(4): 1425–1451; Thomas Patterson, *Young People and News*, a report from the Joan Shorenstein Center on the Press, Politics and Public Policy, John F. Kennedy School of Government, Harvard University, 2007, 1–33; David Mindich, *Tuned Out – Why Americans Under 40 Don't Watch the News* (New York: Oxford University Press, 2005).

33 In May 2014, New Orleans became the largest city to lack a daily newspaper, as the *Times-Picayune*, a 175-year-old Pulitzer Prize winning paper, went to three days per week.

34 Ken Doctor, "The Halving of America's Newsrooms," *NiemanLab*, July 28, 2015, www.niemanlab.org/2015/07/newsonomics-the-halving-of-americas-daily-newsrooms/

35 Pew Research Center on Journalism and Media, "The Search for a New Business Model: The Industry Looking Ahead," March 5, 2012, accessed May 11, 2016, www.journalism.org/2012/03/05/industry-looking-ahead/.

36 Speculation abounds that online papers will eventually make up the advertising revenue lost by print papers, but according to 2011 statistics from the Newspaper Association of America, print losses in advertising revenue exceed digital gains by 10 to 1.

37 Robert McChesney and John Nichols, *The Death and Life of American Journalism* (New York: Nation, 2010).

38 Rachel Smolkin, "Cities without Newspapers," *American Journalism Review*, April/May 2009, http://ajrarchive.org/Article.asp?id=4755

39 A 2010 Pew study of the ecosystem of one city – Baltimore – illustrates how little original news is being produced online. In examining *all* outlets that produced local news in Baltimore, they found that 95 percent of stories containing original news information came from traditional print media, mainly the *Baltimore Sun*.

40 *"How News Happens – Still: A Study of the News Ecosystem in Baltimore*, Pew Project for Excellence in Journalism, January 11, 2010.

41 The ownership of these media companies is constantly undergoing consolidation and change. For the most recent configuration, see www.freepress .net/ownership/chart. Porto makes a compelling argument for intentionally including representatives of disadvantaged groups in news so that members of those groups can figure out their political preferences. See Porto, "Frame Diversity."

42 Diversity in Media Ownership, www.freepress.net/diversity-media-ownership

43 Juan Gonzalez and Joseph Torres, *News for All the People: The Epic Story of Race and the American Media* (New York: Verso, 2012).

44 Gonzalez and Torres, *News for All the People*, 6.

45 Rolf Dobelli, "News Is Bad for You – and Giving Up Reading It Will Make You Happier," *The Guardian*, April 12, 2013, www.theguardian.com/media/ 2013/apr/12/news-is-bad-rolf-dobelli

46 *The Times* bestseller list hardback non-fiction, April 21, 2013; *The Sunday Times* bestseller list July 7, 2013 (rank number 4); Crossword book retailer's bestseller list June 2013; *Irish Bestsellers This Week*, May 11, 2013; *The (Singapore) Straits Times* bestseller list non-fiction, April 28, 2013.

47 In agreement with Dobelli was Daniel Weiss, "Are You a News Junkie?" *Brushfires* blog (Inspire, Transform, Engage), www.brushfiresfoundation. org/are-you-a-news-junkie/; Madeleine Bunting, "Rolf Dobelli's Ideas about Not Needing News Are Dangerous," *The Guardian*, April 18, 2013, www.theguardian.com/commentisfree/2013/apr/18/rolf-dobelli-ideas-news-dangerous; Danny Bunting, "News Is Bad for You? Here Are 9 Reasons Why That Idea Is Flat Wrong," *Huffington Post*, April 16, 2013, www.huffingtonpost.com/danny-rubin/news-is-bad-for-you-rebuttal_b_ 3092183.html

48 Dobelli, "News Is Bad for You."

49 Michael Schudson, "The Politics of Narrative Form (1982)," in Barbie Zelizer, ed, *Taking Journalism Seriously: News and the Academy* (Thousand Oaks, CA: Sage, 2004).

50 Mark Allen Petersen, "Journalism as Trope," *Anthropology News* 2010, 51: 8–9. doi:10.1111/j.1556-3502.2010.51408.x

51 Robert Darnton, "Writing News and Telling Stories," *Daedalus* 1975, 104(2): 175–194. See also S. Elizabeth Bird and Robert W. Dardenne, "Myth, Chronicle, Story," in James Carey, ed., *Media, Myths, and Narratives* (Thousand Oaks, CA: Sage, 1988), 333–350.

52 Richard Tofel, "Non-Profit Journalism: Issues around Impact," White paper from Pro Publica, 2012, accessed June 24, 2014, http://s3.amazonaws.com/ propublica/assets/about/LFA_ProPublica-white-paper_2.1.pdf.

53 See, e.g., http://newsfeed.time.com/2012/03/12/kony-2012-documentary- becomes-most-viral-video-in-history/; Nicke Carbone, "KONY 2012," Arts & Entertainment, *Time.com*, December 4, 2012; Lee Rainie, Paul Hitlin, Mark Jurkowitz, Michael Dimock, and Shawn Neidorf, *The Viral KONY 2012 Video*, Pew Internet and American Life Report, March 15, 2012, www .pewinternet.org/2012/03/15/the-viral-kony-2012-video/

54 Toussaint Nothias, "'It Struck a Chord We Never Managed to Strike: Frames, Perspectives and Remediation Strategies in the International News Coverage of KONY 2012," *African Journalism Studies* 2013, 34(1): 123–129.

55 Quoted in Nothias, "'It Struck a Chord," 127.

56 Peter Dahlgren, "Professional and Citizen Journalism: Tensions and Complements," in Jeffrey Alexander, Elizabeth Breese, and Maria Luengo, eds., *The Crisis of Journalism Reconsidered: Democratic Culture, Professional Codes, Digital Futures* (New York: Cambridge University Press, 2016), 247–263.

57 Cheryl D. Jenkins and Donyale R. Griffin Padgett, "Race and Objectivity: Toward a Critical Approach to News Consumption," in Christopher P. Campbell, Kim M. LeDuff, Cheryl D. Jenkins, and Rockell A. Brown, eds., *Race and News: Critical Perspectives* (New York: Routledge, 2012), 232–251; see also Porto's argument that every news source should provide a plurality of perspectives to increase the possibility that news will be clear and of value to readers from differing communities in Porto, "Frame Diversity."

58 MIT Center for Civic Media *About* page, accessed June 22, 2014, http:// civic.mit.edu/about.

59 Barbie Zelizer, *Covering the Body: The Kennedy Assassination, The Media, and the Shaping of Collective Memory* (Chicago: University of Chicago, 1992); see also Lynn Schofield Clark, "Religion and Authority in a Remix Culture: How a Late Night TV Host Became an Authority on Religion," in Gordon Lynch, Jolyon Mitchell, and Anna Strhan, eds., *Religion, Media, & Culture: A Reader* (London: Routledge, 2011), 111–121.

60 Geoffrey Baym, "Emerging Models of Journalistic Authority in MTV's Coverage of the 2004 US Presidential Election," *Journalism Studies* 2007, 8(3): 382–385.

61 Baym, "Emerging Models."

4 Young People "Produsing" and Consuming News

1 Quote from informant introduced in Jennifer Frank, "Millennial Voters and News Consumption" (Ph.D. diss, Fielding Institute, 2013).

2 Legacy media definition from *NetLingo*, accessed May 6, 2016, www .netlingo.com/word/legacy-media.php.

3 As noted in the Introduction, following Axel Bruns we use the term "pro-dusing." Axel Bruns, *Blogs, Wikipedia, Second Life, and Beyond: From Production to Produsage*, Vol. 45 (London: Peter Lang, 2008).

4 Axel Bruns, *Gatewatching: Collaborative Online News Production* (New York: Peter Lang, 2005).

5 Jeffrey Jones, "Toward a New Vocabulary for Political Communication Research: A Response to Michael Delli Carpini," *International Journal of Communication* 2013, 7: 510–530.

6 Eli Pariser, *The Filter Bubble: What the Internet Is Hiding from You* (New York: Penguin, 2011); Cass Sunstein, *Republic.com* 2.0 (Princeton, NJ: Princeton University Press, 2007).

7 Lance Bennett and Alexandra Segerberg, *The Logic of Connective Action*; "The Logic of Connective Action," *Information, Communication & Society* 2012, 15: 739–768.

8 "How Millennials Get Their News," *American Press Institute*, March 16, 2015, www.americanpressinstitute.org/publications/reports/survey-research/millennials-news/

9 Ito et al., *Hanging Out*, borrow this wide definition of the "media ecology" from Marshall McLuhan and the Toronto School of communication theory, although these more recent authors are less interested in media and cognition than in identifying media as constituting an environment in which young people live. This is discussed in Lynn Schofield Clark, "Media Ecology," in Klaus Bruhn Jensen, Robert T. Craig, Jefferson Pooley, and Eric W. Rothenbuhler eds., *International Encyclopedia of Communication Theory and Philosophy* (New York: Wiley), http://onlinelibrary.wiley.com/book/10.1002/9781118766804/titles?filter=M

10 Nico Carpentier, *Media and Participation: A Site of Ideological and Democratic Struggle* (Chicago, IL: University of Chicago Press, 2011).

11 www.peabodyawards.com

12 Emily Yahr, "Why 'Nick News with Linda Ellerbee' Is Finally Going Off the Air in December," *Washington Post*, December 1, 2015, accessed December 19, 2016, www.washingtonpost.com/news/arts-and-entertainment/wp/2015/12/01/why-nick-news-with-linda-ellerbee-is-finally-going-off-the-air-in-december/?utm_term=.7522f2260caa

13 www.Nick.com

14 David Buckingham, *The Making of Citizens: Young People, News, and Politics* (London: Routledge, 2000); Helle Strandgaard Jensen, "TV as Children's Spokesman: Conflicting Notions of Children and Childhood in Danish Children's Television around 1968," *The Journal of the History of Childhood and Youth* 2013, 6(1): 105-128. Project MUSE, doi:10.1353/hcy.2013.0010; Maire Messenger Davies, Stuart Allan, Kaitlynn Mendes, Roy Milani, and Louise Wass, *What Do Children Want from the BBC? Children's Content and Participatory Environments in an Age of Citizen Media*, Cardiff School of Journalism, Media and Cultural Studies, 2009.

15 Alex Molnar and Faith Boninger, *Sold Out: How Marketing in School Threatens Children's Well-Being and Undermines Their Education* (Lanham, MD: Rowman & Littlefield, 2015).

16 Denise Matthews, *Whittle's Channel One: Powerful Effects for Politically Interested High School Seniors*, paper presented at the annual meeting of the International Communication Association meeting, Washington, DC, 1993; Eric Anderman and Jerome Johnston, *Achievement Goals and Current Events Knowledge*, paper presented at the annual meeting of the American Educational Research Association, New Orleans, LA, 1994.

17 *Captive Audience: Advertising Invades the Classroom* (documentary), Media Education Foundation, 2003; Bradley S. Greenberg and Jeffrey E. Brand, "Television News and Advertising in Schools: The Channel One Controversy," *Journal of Communication* 1993, 43(1): 143–151.

18 Jeremy Gerard, "TV News from the Mouths of Babes," *New York Times*, July 6, 1988, www.nytimes.com/1988/07/06/arts/tv-news-from-the-mouths-of-babes.html

19 Gerard, "TV News."

20 Kent Jenkins, "Quayle 'D and C' Precludes Need for Abortion," *Washington Post*, November 3, 1988, www.washingtonpost.com/archive/politics/1988/11/03/quayle-d-and-c-precludes-need-for-abortion/e6a8c6a7-1f7a-47fd-989d-30735531b6e6/?utm_term=.7c32671fofae

21 Jenkins, "Quayle."

22 *Children's Express How To Do It Guide* (Washington, DC: Children's Express Foundation, 1983).

23 Geoffrey Baym, "*The Daily Show*: Discursive Integration and the Reinvention of Political Journalism," *Political Communication* 2005, 22: 259–276; Geoffrey Baym, *From Cronkite to Colbert: The Evolution of Broadcast News* (Boulder, CO: Paradigm, 2010); Sandra Borden and Chad Tew, "The Role of Journalist and the Performance of Journalism: Ethical Lessons from 'Fake' News (Seriously)," *Journal of Mass Media Ethics* 2007, 22(4):300–314; Stephen Harrington, "The Democracy of Conversation: The Panel and the Public Sphere," *Media International Australia* 2005, 116: 75–87; Stephen Harrington, "Future-Proofing Journalism: Youthful Tastes and the Challenge for the Academy," *Continuum: Journal of Media & Cultural Studies* 2008, 22: 395–407; Stephen Harrington, "Popular News in the 21st Century: Time for a Critical Approach?," *Journalism; Theory, Practice and Criticism* 2008, 9: 266–284; Aaron McKain, "Not Necessarily Not the News: Gatekeeping, Remediation, and *The Daily Show*," *Journal of American Culture* 2005, 28(4): 415–430; Graeme Turner, *Ending the Affair: The Decline of Television Current Affairs in Australia* (Sydney: University of New South Wales Press, 2005).

24 *The Philip DeFranco Show* has aired on YouTube since 2007 when he was twenty-one and a college student (10 mins M-Th; signed with ReVision3; supported by Netflix, Ting & State Farm); *SourceFed* (created by DeFranco). *The Young Turks* offers liberal/progressive political and social commentary and is hosted by Cenk Uygur. Uygur was a commentator on MSNBC in 2010, then on Current TV, and then Current TV's chief news officer, succeeding Keith Olbermann until Current was acquired by Al Jazeera in 2013. (They shut it down to use Current's distribution network for AJ America.) *Vice News* is made available by Rupert Murdoch's group and is a subsidiary

of Vice Media. *Current TV* was produced from 2005 to 2013 and was an interest of Al Gore, Joel Hyatt, and Ronald Burkleheld, who held large stakes in the venture; Comcast and DirecTv had smaller stakes.

25 Jeannine Poggi, "In Surreal Election Year, MTV Again Tries to Make Viewers into Voters. Cue Robo-Roundtable," *Advertising Age*, June 1, 2016, accessed June 8, 2016, http://adage.com/article/media/mtv-surreal-election-campaign-robo-rountable/304223/.

26 Poggi, "Surreal Election."

27 Bruce A. Williams and Michael Delli Carpini, *After Broadcast News: Media Regimes, Democracy, and the New Information Environment* (Cambridge: Cambridge University Press, 2011).

28 National Annenberg Election Survey, "*Daily Show* Viewers Knowledgeable about Presidential Campaign, National Annenberg Election Survey Shows," University of Pennsylvania's Annenberg Public Policy Center, 2004, accessed May 1, 2008, www.annenbergpublicpolicycenter.org/Downloads/Political_Communication/naes2004_03_late-night-knowledge-2_9-21_pr.pdf

29 Baym, "*From Cronkite to Colbert*, "The *Daily Show*: Discursive Integration"; Julia Fox, Glory Koloen, and Volkan Sahin, "No Joke: A Comparison of Substance in *The Daily Show with Jon Stewart* and Broadcast Network Television Coverage of the 2004 Presidential Election Campaign," *Journal of Broadcasting and Electronic Media* 2007, 51(2): 213–227; Harrington, "Future Proofing Journalism," "Popular News"; Lauren Feldman, "The News about Comedy: Young Audiences, *The Daily Show*, and Evolving Notions of Journalism," *Journalism: Theory, Practice, & Criticism* 2007, 8(4): 359–380; Marchi, "With Facebook, Blogs and Fake News, Teens Reject Journalistic 'Objectivity,'" *Journal of Communication Inquiry*.

30 Baym, "*The Daily Show*: Discursive Integration," 264.

31 Baym, "*The Daily Show*: Discursive Integration;" Jones, "Toward a New Vocabulary."

32 Baym, "*The Daily Show*: Discursive Integration;" *From Cronkite to Colbert*; Harrington, "Future Proofing Journalism," "Popular News."

33 Baym, *From Cronkite to Colbert*, 104. For more on how young adults do not hold a single notion of news but draw from a variety of cultural and entertainment resources at their disposal, see Stephanie Edgerly, "Making Sense and Drawing Lines: Young Adults and the Mixing of News and Entertainment," *Journalism Studies* 2015, 1–18.

34 Borden and Tew, "The Role of Journalist."

35 Jamie Warner, "Political Culture Jamming: the Dissident Humor of *The Daily Show with Jon Stewart*," *Popular Communication* 2007, 5(1): 23.

36 Lisbet Van Zoonen, *Entertaining the Citizen: When Politics and Popular Culture Converge* (New York: Rowman & Littlefield, 2004).

37 Also see Michael Schudson, *The Good Citizen: A History of American Public Life* (New York: Simon & Schuster, 1998).

38 Tony Kelso and Brian Cogan, "Introduction: At the Intersection of Politics and Popular Culture: Over Two Hundred Years of Great Entertainment," in Tony Kelso and Brian Cogan, eds., *Mosh the Polls: Youth Voters, Popular Culture, and Democratic Engagement* (New York: Lexington Books, 2008), 1–20.

39 Guy Debord and K. Knabb, *Complete Cinematic Works: Scripts, Stills, Documents* (New York: AK Press, 2003); Guy Debord, *The Society of the Spectacle* (New York: Zone Books, 1994).

40 Horace Newcomb and Paul Hirsch, "Television as a Cultural Forum," *Quarterly Review of Film Studies* 1983, 3: 45–55. As cited in Jones, "Toward a New Vocabulary," 14.

41 Jones, "Toward a New Vocabulary."

42 Richard Rorty, *Contingency, Irony, Solidarity* (Cambridge, MA: Harvard University Press, 1989), xvi.

43 Jones "Toward a New Vocabulary," Zizi Papacharissi, *Affective Publics: Sentiment, Technology, and Politics* (New York: Oxford University Press, 2014).

44 Matt Becker, "'I Hate Hippies:' South Park and the Politics of Generation X," in Jeffrey A. Weinstock, ed., *Taking South Park Seriously* (Albany: SUNY Press, 2008), 145–164. The program has also been critiqued for recentering whiteness; see Phil Chidester, "'Respect my Authori-tah': South Park and the Fragmentation/Reification of Whiteness," *Critical Studies in Media Communication* 2012, 29(5): 403–420.

45 Bill Winter, "Trey Parker – Libertarian. Advocates for Self-Government," Retrieved via Way-back machine: https://web.archive.org/web/20080113153236/http://www.theadvocates.org/celebrities/trey-parker.html

46 Marc Leverette, "'Just Don't Bother to Vote or Die, Bitch!' A Giant Douche, a Turd Sandwich, Hard Core Puppet Sex, and the Reinvention of Political (Un)involvement," in Tony Kelso and Brian Cogan, eds., *Mosh the Polls: Youth Voters, Popular Culture, and Democratic Engagement* (New York: Lexington Books, 2008). See also Brian Cogan, *Deconstructing South Park: Critical Examinations of Animated Transgression* (New York: Lexington Books, 2012), 205–238.

47 C. Dow Tate and Sherrie Taylor, *Scholastic Journalism*, 12th ed. (New York: Wiley, 2012).

48 Lynn's observation based on leading workshops on digital technologies at the Colorado High School Student Press Association annual conferences in the late 1990s and early 2000s.

49 American Library Association, *Notable First Amendment Court Cases*, accessed May 15, 2016, www.ala.org/advocacy/intfreedom/censorshipfirstamendmentissues/courtcases

50 *Notable First Amendment Court Cases.*

51 *Notable First Amendment Court Cases.*

52 www.splc.org/article/2015/10/first-amendment-and-censorship-faqs, May 15, 2016.

53 Frank LoMonte, "Pennsylvania Court Extends School's Disciplinary Reach into Student's Off-Campus Joke," *Student Press Law Center*, May 12, 2016, accessed May 15, 2016, www.splc.org/blog/splc/2016/05/pennsylvania-student-facebook-discipline-upheld; Allison Kowalski, "No Laughing Matter: College Comedy Papers Struggle with 'Political Correctness,'" *Student Press Law Center*, May 13, 2016, accessed May 15, 2016, www.splc.org/article/2016/05/no-laughing-matter; Piotr Bobkowski and Patrick

Miller, "Civic Implications of Secondary School Journalism: Associations with Voting Propensity and Community Volunteering," *Journalism and Mass Communication Quarterly* 2016, 93(3): 530–550.

54 Sarah E. Amster, *Seeds of Cynicism: The Undermining of Journalistic Education* (New York: University Press of America, Inc., 2006); Joe Dennis, "Prior Review in the High School Newspaper: Perceptions, Practices and Effects" (MA Thesis, Athens: University of Georgia, 2007); Freedom Forum, *Death By Cheeseburger: High School Journalism in the 1990s and Beyond* (Arlington, VA: The Freedom Forum, 1994); Renee Hobbs, "Building Citizenship Skills through Media Literacy Education," in M. Salvador and P. Sias, eds., *The Public Voice in a Democracy at Risk* (Westport, CT: Praeger Publishers, 1998), 57–75; David Martinson, "School Censorship: It Comes in a Variety of Forms, Not All of Them Overt," *Clearing\House* 2008 (May/June), 81(5): 211–214.

55 Martinson, "School Censorship," 211.

56 Early examples of such community youth media include Youth Communication in Chicago, which in 1977 produced *New Expression* (National Youth Communications); Youth Communication in Wilmington, Delaware, 1978, produced *The Eye*; the Student Press Service in Washington, DC; Youth News in Oakland, CA (Youth on the Air radio program; and New Youth Connections in New York City, 1980).

57 Kathleen Turner, "Mapping the Field of Youth Media Organizations in the United States," in Joellen Fisherkeller, ed., *International Perspectives on Youth Media* (New York: Peter Lang, 2011), 25–49.

58 Turner, "Mapping the Field."

59 Becky Herr Stephenson, Diana Rhoten, Dan Perkel, and Christo Sims, *Digital Media and Technology in After School Programs, Libraries, and Museums*, MacArthur Foundation Report, 2011.

60 Regina Marchi, "Z-Radio, Boston: Teen Journalism, Political Engagement, and Democratizing the Airwaves," *Journal of Radio and Audio Media* 2009, 16: 127–143.

61 See http://evc.org. Also see Steven Goodman, *Teaching Youth Media: A Critical Guide to Literacy, Video Production, and Social Change* (New York: Teacher's College, 2003).

62 Julia Cagé, *Saving the Media: Capitalism, Crowdfunding and Democracy* (Cambridge, MA: Harvard University Press, 2016).

63 Pat Aufderheide and Charles M. Firestone, *Media Literacy: A Report of National Leadership Conference on Media Literacy* (Cambridge: Polity Press, 1993).

64 Renee Hobbs, "The Seven Great Debates in the Media Literacy Movement," Opinion Papers (Washington, DC: US Department of Education, Educational Resources Information Center (ERIC), 1999), 3.

65 Hobbs, "The Seven Great Debates."

66 Ulla Carlson, Samy Tayie, Genevieve Jacquinot-Delaunay, and Jose Manuel Perez Tornero, eds., *Empowerment Through Media Education: An Intercultural Dialogue* (Goteburg, SE: Nordicom, The International Clearing House on Children, Youth, and Media, 2008); see also Douglas Kellner

and Jeff Share, "Toward Critical Media Literacy: Core Concepts, Debates, Organizations, and Policy," *Discourse: Studies in the Cultural Politics of Education* 2005, 26(3): 369–386.

67 JoEllen Fisherkeller, "Introduction," in JoEllen Fisherkeller, ed., *International Perspectives on Youth Media* (New York: Peter Lang, 2011), 4. See also Renee Hobbs, "Digital and Media Literacy: A Plan of Action," Aspen Institute, 2010, www.knightcomm.org/digital-and-media-literacy/

68 Paul Mihailidis, *Media Literacy and the Emerging Citizen: Youth, Engagement and Participation in Digital Culture* (New York: Peter Lang, 2014).

69 Ben Adler, "A Movement's Moment? Common Core Opens the Door for News Literacy to Expand in the Classroom," *Columbia Journalism Review* 2014, Jan/Feb: 48–49.

70 Mihailidis, *Media Literacy*, and Paul Mihaidilis and Benjamin Thevenin, "Media Literacy as Core Competency for Engaged Citizenship in Participatory Democracy," *American Behavioral Scientist* 2013, 7(11): 1611–1622.

71 Renee Hobbs, Katie Donnelly, Jonathan Friesem, and Mary Moen, "Learning to Engage: How Positive Attitudes about the News, Media Literacy, and Video Production Contribute to Adolescent Civic Engagement," *Educational Media International* 2013, 50 (4): 231–246; see also Bobkowski and Miller, "Civic Implications."

72 Tobias Olsson and Peter Dahlgren, eds., *Young People, ICTs, and Democracy: Theories, Policies, Identities, and Websites* (Nordiskt Information Center, 2010).

73 Amy Stornaiuolo, Glynda Hall, and Urvashi Sahni, "Cosmopolitan Imagingings of Self and Other: Youth and Social Networking in a Global World," in Joellen Fisherkeller, ed., *International Perspectives on Youth Media: Cultures of Production and Education* (New York: Peter Lang), 263–280.

74 Elisabeth Soep, "All the World's an Album: Youth Media as Strategic Embedding," in Joellen Fisherkeller, ed., *International Perspectives on Youth Media: Cultures of Production and Education* (New York: Peter Lang, 2011), 246–261.

75 Zeynep Tufecki, "The Real Bias is Built In at Facebook," *The New York Times*, May 19, 2016, accessed May 24, 2017, www.nytimes.com/2016/05/19/opinion/the-real-bias-built-in-at-facebook.html?smid=tw-share

76 Cohen, *Participatory Politics*.

77 Stanford History Education Group, *Evaluating Information*.

78 Gonzalez and Torres, *News for All the People*.

79 Stanford History Education Group, *Evaluating Information*.

80 Vikki Katz, "How Children of Immigrants Use Media to Connect Their Families to the Community," *Journal of Children and Media* 2010, 4(3): 298–315; Vikki Katz, Alfonso Ang, and Roberto Suro, "An Ecological Perspective on U.S. Latinos' Health Communication Behaviors, Access, and Outcomes," *Hispanic Journal of Behavioral Sciences* 2012, 34(3): 437–456; Liesbeth de Block and David Buckingham, *Global Children, Global Media: Migration, Media, and Childhood* (New York: Palgrave, 2007); Regina Marchi, "News Translators: Latino Immigrant Youth, Social Media, and Citizenship Training," *Journalism and Mass Communication Quarterly* 2016, 94(1): 189–212.

81 Marchi, "News Translators"; Clark, *The Parent App.*
82 Katz, "How Children of Immigrants Use Media"; Katz et al., "An Ecological Perspective"; de Block and Buckingham, *Global Children.*
83 Lynn Schofield Clark, "Digital Media and the Generation Gap: Qualitative Research on U.S. Teens and their Parents," *Information, Communication, and Society* 2009, 12(3), www.tandfonline.com/doi/full/10.1080/13691180 902823845; Marchi, "News Translators."
84 William Perez, Roberta Espinoza, Karina Ramos, Heidi Coronado, and Richard Cortes, "Civic Engagement Patterns of Undocumented Mexican Students," *Journal of Hispanic Higher Education* 2010, 9(3): 245–265.
85 Mark H. Lopez, *Fact Sheet: Electoral Engagement Among Latino Youth* (College Park, MD: The Center for Information and Research on Civic Learning and Engagement, 2003).
86 Carpentier, *Media and Participation.*
87 Janet Wasko and Vincent Mosco, *Democratic Communications in the Information Age* (Toronto: Garamond Press, 1992); Douglas Kellner and Jeff Share, "Toward Critical Media Literacy: Core Concepts, Debates, Organizations, and Policy," *Discourse: Studies in the Cultural Politics of Education* 2005, 26(3): 369–386.
88 Bruce Girard, *A Passion for Radio: Radio Waves and Community* (Black Rose Books, 1992); John Downing with Tamara Villareal Ford, Genevieve Gil, and Laura Stein, *Radical Media: Rebellious Communication and Social Movements* (Thousand Oaks, CA: Sage, 2000); Clemencia Rodriguez, *Citizens' Media against Armed Conflict: Disrupting Violence in Colombia* (Minneapolis: University of Minnesota Press, 2011).
89 Thomas J. Schofield and Jennifer M. Weaver, "Democratic Parenting Beliefs and Observed Parental Sensitivity: Reciprocal Influences between Coparents," *Journal of Family Psychology* 2015, doi: 10.1037/fam0000166; Marta Miklikowska and Helena Hurme, "Democracy Begins at Home: Democratic Parenting and Adolescents' Support for Democratic Values," *European Journal of Developmental Psychology* 2011, 8(5): 541–557; see also M. Bruter, S. Banaji, S. Harrison, B. Cammaerts, N. Anstead, and B. Whitwell, *Youth Participation in Democratic Life: Stories of Hope and Disillusion* (Basingstoke: Palgrave Macmillan, 2014).

5 Connective Journalism and the Formation of Youthful Publics and Counterpublics: Inserting Oneself into the Story through Witnessing and Sharing Outrage

1 Strategies 360, "Summary of Findings from a Survey of Teachers and Staff in the Douglas County School District, Final Report 2015," accessed June 9, 2016, http://douglascountyfederation.com/wp-content/uploads/2013/01/ S360-Final-Survey-Results.pdf
2 Colorado is a one-party consent state, meaning that consent to record is required of only one person involved in a conversation. This means a recording can occur without the other person being aware of it. Federal law deems

it illegal to record unless all parties have consented, but thirty-eight states permit one-party consent and only twelve require all-party consent.

3 John Aguilar, "Student Claims Intimidation by Douglas County School Board Members," *Denver Post*, April 20, 2016, accessed June 8, 2016, www.denverpost.com/2016/04/20/student-claims-intimidation-by-douglas-county-school-board-members/

4 Michael Roberts, "Grace Davis' School Board Bullying Claim Leads to Girl Scouts Resignation," *Westword*, April 27, 2016, accessed June 8, 2016, www.westword.com/news/grace-daviss-school-board-bullying-claim-leads-to-girl-scouts-resignation-7847646.

5 John Aguilar, "Defiance, Disruption Mark Raucous Douglas County School Board Meeting," *Denver Post*, June 22, 2016, accessed June 22, 2016, www.denverpost.com/2016/06/21/defiance-disruption-marks-raucous-douglas-county-school-board-meeting/

6 Nicholas Garcia, "Controversial Douglas County Superintendent to Lead Texas School District," *Chalkbeat Colorado*, May 24, 2016, accessed June 8, 2016, www.chalkbeat.org/posts/co/2016/05/24/controversial-douglas-county-superintendent-to-lead-texas-school-district/#.V1iW_JMrL-Y

7 Michael Roberts, "Grace Davis's School Board Bullying Claim Leads to Girl Scouts Resignation," April 27, 2016, http://www.westword.com/news/grace-daviss-school-board-bullying-claim-leads-to-girl-scouts-resignation-7847646

8 Elisabeth Noelle-Neumann, *The Spiral of Silence: Public Opinion – Our Social Skin* (Chicago, IL: University of Chicago Press, 1974/1984).

9 Jurgen Habermas, *The Structural Transformation of the Public Sphere* (Cambridge, MA: MIT Press, 1991).

10 Dahlgren, "Professional and Citizen Journalism."

11 Craig Calhoun, ed., *Habermas and the Public Sphere* (Cambridge, MA: MIT Press, 1992).

12 C. W. Mills, *The Power Elite* (New York: Oxford University Press, 1956/2000). A recent update focusing on income inequalities is Chrystia Freeland, *Plutocrats: The Rise of the New Global Super-Rich and the Fall of Everyone Else* (New York: Penguin Books, 2013).

13 Gill Valentine, "Children Should Be Seen and Not Heard: The Production and Transgression of Adults' Public Space," *Urban Geography* 1996, 17 (March): 205–220. See also Mats Lieberg, "Teenagers and Public Space," *Communication Research* 1995, 22(6): 720–744.

14 Nancy Fraser, "Rethinking the Public Sphere: A Contribution to the Critique of Actually Existing Democracy," in Craig Calhoun, ed., *Habermas and the Public Sphere* (Cambridge, MA: MIT Press, 1992), 122–133.

15 Mouffe, *On the Political*.

16 Dahlgren, "Professional and Citizen Journalism."

17 Michael Warner, "Publics and Counterpublics," *Public Culture* 2002, 14(1): 49–90.

18 Nick Couldry, *Media, Society, World: Social Theory and Digital Media Practice* (Cambridge: Polity, 2010); John Downing and Natalie Fenton, "New Media, Counterpublicity and the Public Sphere," *New Media & Society* 2003, 5(2): 185–202.

19 Lilie Chouliaraki, "Re-mediation, Inter-mediation, Trans-mediation," *Journalism Studies* 2013, 14(2): 267–283; Gayatri Spivak, "Can the Subaltern Speak?" in Cary Nelson and Lawrence Grossberg, eds., *Marxism and the Interpretation of Culture* (Urbana, IL: University of Illinois Press, 1988), 271–313.

20 Lynn is thankful to Peter Dahlgren for a conversation on this point in June 2014.

21 Stine Eckert and Kalyani Chadha, "Muslim Bloggers in Germany: An Emerging Counterpublic," *Media, Culture & Society* 2013, 35(8): 926–942; Dennis K. Leung and Francis F.L. Lee, "Cultivating an Active Online Counterpublic: Examining the Impact of Internet Alternative Media," *International Journal of Press/Politics* 2014, 19(3): 340–359.

22 Dimitra Milioni, "Probing the Online Counterpublic Sphere: The case of Indymedia Athens," *Media, Culture & Society* 2009, 31(3): 409–431.

23 Peter Dahlgren, "The Internet, Public Spheres, and Political Communication: Dispersion and Deliberation," *Political Communication* 2005, 22(2): 147–162.

24 Lynn Schofield Clark, "Participants on the Margins: #Blacklivesmatter and the Role that Shared Artifacts of Engagement Played Among Minoritized Political Newcomers on Snapchat, Facebook, and Twitter," *International Journal of Communication* 2015, 9: 1–18. Mary Gray, *Out in the Country Youth, Media, and Queer Visibility in Rural America* (New York: New York University Press, 2009).

25 See Lynn Schofield Clark, "Book Review of *Affective Publics: Sentiment, Technology, and Politics* by Zizi Papacharissi," *International Journal of Communication*, 2016, 10, http://ijoc.org/index.php/ijoc/article/view/5375

26 Zizi Papacharissi, *Affective Publics: Sentiment, Technology, and Politics* (New York: Oxford University Press, 2015), 125.

27 Papacharissi, *Affective Publics*.

28 Papacharissi, *Affective Publics*, 25.

29 "Exclusive Analysis: Donald Trump and Young Voters," Center for Information & Research on Civic Learning & Engagement (CIRCLE), accessed June 21, 2016, http://civicyouth.org/exclusive-analysis-donald-trump-and-the-youth-vote/; Ariel Edwards-Levy, "Young Voters Couldn't Hate Donald Trump Much More Than They Already Do," *Huffington Post*, April 7, 2016, accessed June 21, 2016, www.huffingtonpost.com/entry/donald-trump-young-voters_us_5706818de4b0a506064e5e06

30 Gretchen Livingston, "Fewer than Half of U.S. Kids Today Live in 'Traditional' Family," FactTank: Pew Research Center, December 22, 2014, accessed June 21, 2016, www.pewresearch.org/fact-tank/2014/12/22/less-than-half-of-u-s-kids-today-live-in-a-traditional-family/

31 "Young Voters in the 2016 General Election," Center for Information & Research on Civic Learning and Engagement (CIRCLE), November 17, 2016.

32 James M. Jasper and Jane D. Poulsen, "Recruiting Strangers and Friends: Moral Shocks and Social Networks in Animal Rights and Anti-Nuclear Protests," *Social Problems* 1995, 42: 493–512; Zeynep Tufekci and Christopher Wilson, "Social Media and the Decision to Participate in Political

Protest: Observations from Tahrir Square," *Journal of Communication* 2012, 62(2): 363–279; Joris Verhulst and Stefaan Walgrave, "The First Time is the Hardest? A Cross-National and Cross-Issue Comparison of First-Time Protest Participants," *Political Behavior* 2009, 31: 455–484.

33 Russell, *Journalism as Activism.*

34 Alice Marwick, *Status Update: Celebrity, Publicity, and Branding in the Social Media Age* (New Haven, CT: Yale University Press 2013).

35 Cheryll Soriano, "Constructing Collectivity in Diversity: Online Political Mobilization of a National LGBT Political Party," *Media, Culture, Society* 2014, 36(1): 20–36; On how people now may choose from a plethora of media platforms for differing levels of engagement, and how differing contexts shape practices, see Mirca Madianou and Daniel Miller, "Polymedia: Towards a New Theory of Digital Media in Interpersonal Communication," *International Journal of Cultural Studies* 2012, 16(2): 169–187; Daniel Miller, *Why We Post: Social Media through the Eyes of the World* (website), accessed May 24, 2017, www.ucl.ac.uk/why-we-post

36 John Blake, "How Ferguson Could Become a Movement: Lessons from History," CNN, 2014, www.cnn.com/2013/08/17/us/four-ways-to-beat-the-man/; Aamer Madhani and Yamiche Alcinor, "Ferguson has Become a Springboard for Many Movements," *USA Today*, December 8, 2014, www.usatoday.com/story/news/nation/2014/12/05/ferguson-protests-broaden-occupy-wall-street/19917015/; Zachary Roth, "After Ferguson, Some See a Movement Taking Shape," MSNBC, December 6, 2014, www.msnbc.com/msnbc/after-ferguson-some-see-movement-taking-shape.

37 Julie Bosman and Emma Fitzsimmons, "Grief and Protests Follow Shooting of a Teenager," *The New York Times*, August 11, 2014, accessed June 17, 2016, www.nytimes.com/2014/08/11/us/police-say-mike-brown-was-killed-after-struggle-for-gun.html.

38 Clark, "Participants on the Margins."

39 Catherine R. Squires, "Rethinking the Black Public Sphere: An Alternative Vocabulary for Multiple Public Spheres," *Communication Theory* 2002, 12(4): 446–468.

40 Squires, "Rethinking the Black Public Sphere," 454.

41 Aaron Smith, *African Americans and Technology Use*, Pew Research Center Report, 2014, www.pewinternet.org/files/oldmedia/Files/Reports/2014/PIP_African%20Americans%20and%20Technology%20Use_010614.pdf

42 Andre Brock, "From the Blackhand Side: Twitter as a Cultural Conversation," *Journal of Broadcasting & Electronic Media* 2012, 56(4): 529–549.

43 Brock, "Blackhand Side," 545; see also Farhad Manjoo, "How Black People Use Twitter," *Slate*, August 10, 2010, www.slate.com/articles/technology/technology/2010/08/how_black_people_use_twitter.2.html

44 Henry L. Gates, "The Blackness of Blackness: A Critique of the Sign and the Signifying Monkey," *Critical Inquiry* 1983, 9(4): 685–723.

45 Brendan Meeder, "Network Structure and Its Role in Information Diffusion and User Behavior" (Ph.D. diss., Carnegie Mellon University, Pittsburgh, PA, 2012).

46 The town where Michael Brown was killed became internationally synonymous with the incident and short hand for police brutality against unarmed black young men.

47 Peter Van Aelst and Stefaan Walgrave, "Who is that (Wo)man in the Street? From the Normalization of Protest to the Normalization of the Protester," *European Journal of Political Research* 2001, 39(4): 461–486.

48 Ellen Middaugh and Joseph Kahne, "Online Localities: Implications for Democracy and Education," *Yearbook of the National Society for the Study of Education* 2009, 108(1): 192–218.

49 Sandrina de Finney, Mackenzie Dean, Elicia Loiselle, and Johanne Saraceno, "All Children Are Equal, But Some Are More Equal than Others: Minoritization, Structural Inequalities and Social Justice Praxis in Residential Care," *International Journal of Child, Youth and Family Studies* 2011, 3–4: 361–384.

50 Henry Giroux, *Fugitive Cultures: Race, Violence, and Youth* (New York: Routledge, 1996).

51 boyd, *It's Complicated.*

52 Tom McGhee, "Denver Protests Spark Dialogue between Police and Students," *Denver Post*, December 4, 2014, www.denverpost.com/news/ci_27069788/denver-protests-spark-dialogue-between-police-and-students

53 Jaclyn Zubrzycki,"As High School Ferguson Protests Snowball, East Students Search for the Story," *Chalkbeat Colorado*, December 4, 2014, http://co.chalkbeat.org/2014/12/04/as-high-school-ferguson-protests-snowball-east-students-search-for-the-story/#.VKmjJGTF-nA

54 Papacharissi, *Affective Publics*; William Gamson, *Talking Politics* (Cambridge: Cambridge University Press, 1992); Paulo Gerbaudo, *Tweets and the Streets: Social Media and Contemporary Activism* (London: Pluto Press, 2012); Francesca Polletta and James Jasper, "Collective Identity and Social Movements," *Annual Review of Sociology* 2001, 27: 283-305, doi.org/10.1146/annurev.soc.27.1.283.

55 Peter Dahlgren, *Media and Political Engagement: Citizens, Communication and Democracy* (Cambridge: Cambridge University Press, 2009).

56 http://legacy.wbur.org/2013/11/06/east-boston-rejects-suffolk-downs

57 Ellen Wartella and Alexis Lauricella, *Children, Media and Race: Media Use among White, Black, Hispanic and Asian American Children*, Center on Media and Human Development, Northwestern University, 2011, http://web5.soc.northwestern.edu/cmhd/wp-content/uploads/2011/06/SOCconfReportSingleFinal-1.pdf

58 www.bostonglobe.com/metro/2013/11/05/suffolk-downs-defeated-boston-will-explore-revere-only-project/o2VK5haGBzosrwvu7mTLiI/story.html

59 Dan Mercea, "Towards a Conceptualization of Casual Protest Participation: Parsing a Case from the Save Rosia Montana Campaign," *East European Politics and Societies* 2014, 28(2): 386–410.

60 Verhulst and Walgrave, "The First Time"; Jasper and Poulsen, "Recruiting Strangers and Friends."

61 Sidney Verba, Kay Lehman Schlozman, and Henry E. Brady, *Voice and Equality Civic Voluntarism in American Politics* (Cambridge, MA: Harvard

University Press, 1995); Alan Schussman and Sarah Soule, "Process and Protest: Accounting for Individual Protest Participation," *Social Forces* 2005, 84:1083–1108.

62 "Spiral of Silence Theory," *Mass Communication Theory* blog, accessed June 8, 2016, https://masscommtheory.com/2010/07/23/quiet-down-heres-spiral-of-silence/

63 Dietram Scheufele, "Spiral of Silence Theory," *The Sage Handbook of Public Opinion Research* (New York: Sage, 2007), 175. Scheufele and Moy pick up on two ideas of Noelle-Neumann: public opinion as rationality and public opinion as social control. The first comes about through careful deliberation and discussion, and thus, they view it as "a necessary condition for generating social change." (p. 5). The spiral of silence, they argue, operates as a form of social control. See Dietram Scheufele and Patricia Moy, "Twenty-Five Years of the Spiral of Silence: A Conceptual Review and Empirical Outlook," *International Journal of Public Opinion Research* 2000, 12(1): 3–28.

64 Shirley S. Ho, "Social-Psychological Influences on Opinion Expression in Face-to-Face and Computer-Mediated Communication," *Communication Research* 2008, 35(2): 190–207.

65 Gray, *Out in the Country*. See also Shelly A. Neill, "The Alternate Channel: How Social Media is Challenging the Spiral of Silence Theory in GLBT Communities of Color" (MA direct research project, part of requirements for the MA in the School of Communication, American University, 2009), accessed June 9, 2016, www.american.edu/soc/communication/upload/09-Neill.pdf.

66 Keith Hampton, Lee Rainie, Weixu Lu, Maria Dwyer, Inyoung Shin, and Kristen Purcell, "Social Media and the 'Spiral of Silence,'" Report of the Pew Research Center, Internet, Science, and Tech category, 2014, accessed June 9, 2016, www.pewinternet.org/2014/08/26/social-media-and-the-spiral-of-silence/. Research by McDevitt, Kiousis, and Wahl-Jorgensen supports this position as well in their own argument about the fact that with new media contexts, the spiral of silence theory must be updated. See Michael McDevitt, Spiro Kirousis, and Karin Wahl-Jorgensen, "Spiral of Moderation: Opinion Expression in Computer-Mediated Discussion," *International Journal of Public Opinion Research* 15(4):454–470.

67 Verhulst and Walgrave, "The First Time."

68 Tufekci and Wilson, "Social Media and the Decision to Participate."

6 Youth Citizen Journalism: The Connective Journalism Practices of Participation and Making the Story

1 Josh Singer, quoted in Carla Iacovetti, "*Spotlight*: The Burden of Truth," *Creative Screenwriting*, January 25, 2016, accessed June 28, 2016, http://creativescreenwriting.com/spotlight-the-burden-of-truth/

2 Lynn Schofield Clark and Rachel Monserrate, "High School Journalism and the Making of Young Citizens," *Journalism: Theory, Practice, Criticism* 2010, 12(4): 417–432.

3 Aufderheide and Firestone, *Media Literacy.*
4 Ranna Daud and Cynthia Carruthers, "Outcome Study of an After-School Program for Youth in a High-Risk Environment," *Journal of Parks and Recreation Administration* 2008, 26(2): 95-114; Joseph Mahoney, Maria E. Parente, and Edward F. Zigler, "Afterschool Programs in America: Origins, Growth, Popularity, and Politics," *Journal of Youth Development* 2009, 4(3): 26-44; Regina Marchi, "Z-Radio, Boston: Teen Journalism, Political Engagement, and Democratizing the Airwaves," *Journal of Radio & Audio Media* 2009, 16(2):127–143; Mihailidis, *Media Literacy and the Emerging Citizen.*
5 Shayne Bowman and Chris Willis, *We Media: How Audiences Are Shaping the Future of News and Information* (Thinking Paper) (Reston, VA: The Media Center at the American Press Institute, July, 2003).
6 J. Kelly, "Red Kayaks and Hidden Gold: The Rise, Challenges and Value of Citizen Journalism," report of the Reuters Institute for the Study of Journalism, 2009, www.slideshare.net/victori98pt/the-rise-challenges-and-value-of-citizen-journalism. See also Stuart Allen, "Histories of Citizen Journalism," in Stuart Allan and Einar Thorsen, eds., *Citizen Journalism* (New York: Peter Lang, 2009), 17–32.
7 https://globalvoices.org/about/ accessed June 28, 2016.
8 Daniela Gerson, Nien-Tsu Chen, Sandra Ball-Rokeach, and Michael Parks, "Website to Weibo: Activing the Local Communication Network and Civic Engagement in a Diverse City," *The Civic Media Project* (Cambridge: MIT Press, 2015), accessed June 28, 2016, http://civicmediaproject.org/works/civic-media-project/from-website-to-weibo-new-media-as-a-catalyst-for-activating-the-local-communication-network-and-civic-engagement-in-a-diverse-city
9 Gerson et al., "Website to Weibo."
10 http://njspark.rutgers.edu
11 https://mediamobilizing.org
12 See, e.g., "7 Things You Should Know about Citizen Journalism" (Louisville, CO: Educause, 2007), accessed June 28, 2016, https://net.educause.edu/ir/library/pdf/eli7031.pdf; Andrew Keen, *The Cult of the Amateur: How the Democratization of the Digital World Is Assaulting Our Economy, Our Culture, and Our Values* (New York; Currency/Doubleday, 2007).
13 Allen and Thorsen, *Citizen Journalism.*
14 Megan Boler, ed., *Digital Media and Democracy: Tactics in Hard Times* (Cambridge, MA: MIT Press, 2010). However, scholars of journalism have also noted that despite claims of a revolution in the approaches to audiences introduced by the phenomenon of user-generated content, it's still business as usual in most newsrooms, as the availability of such content is not disrupting the traditional relationships between producers and consumers of news. See Andy Williams, Claire Wardle, and Karin Wahl-Jorgensen, "Have They Got News for Us? Audience Revolution or Business as Usual at the BBC," *Journalism Practice* 2010, 5(1): 85–99.
15 Dahlgren, "Professional and Citizen Journalism."
16 Barry Checkoway and Lorraine M. Gutierrez, "Introduction: Youth Participation and Community Change," in Barry Checkoway and Lorraine

Gutierrez, eds., *Youth Participation and Community Change* (Binghamton, NY: Haworth Press 2006), 1.

17 Joseph Kahne, Ellen Middaugh, and Danielle Allen, "Youth, New Media, and the Rise of Participatory Politics," in Danielle Allen and Jennifer Light, eds., *From Voice to Influence: Understanding Citizenship in the Digital Age* (Chicago, IL: University of Chicago Press, 2015), 35–58.

18 Cohen et al., *Participatory Politics*; Kahne et al., "Youth, New Media."

19 Danielle Allen and Jennifer Light, eds., *From Voice to Influence: Understanding Citizenship in the Digital Age* (Chicago, IL: University of Chicago Press, 2015); Benjamin Bowyer, Joseph Kahne, and Ellen Middaugh, "Youth Comprehension of Political Messages in YouTube Videos," *New Media & Society* 2015: 1–20; Soep, *Participatory Politics*.

20 Laura Robinson, "A Taste for the Necessary," *Information, Communication & Society* 2009, 12(4): 488–507, doi: 10.1080.13691180902857678; Jen Schradie, "The Digital Production Gap: The Digital Divide and Web 2.0 Collide," *Poetics* 2011, 39(2): 145–168, doi: 10.1016/j.poetic.2011.02.003; Jen Schradie, "The Trend of Class, Race, and Ethnicity in Social Media Inequality," *Information, Communication & Society* 2012, 15(4): 555–571, doi: 10.1080/1369118x.2012.665939.

21 Lucinda Gray, Nina Thomas, and Laurie Lewis, *Teachers' Use of Educational Technology in US Public Schools: 2009* (NCES No. 2010040). (Washington, DC: National Center for Education Statistics, 2009); Peter Tatian, G. Thomas Kingsley, Joe Parilla, and Rolf Pendall, "Building Successful Neighborhoods," *What Works Collaborative*, 2012, accessed March 16, 2016, www.urban .org/sites/default/files/alfresco/publication-pdfs/412557-Building-Successful-Neighborhoods.PDF

22 Sunaina Maira, *Missing: Youth, Citizenship and Empire after 9/11* (Durham, NC: Duke University Press, 2009); Ben O'Loughlin and Marie Gillespie, "Dissenting Citizenship? Young People and Political Participation in the Media–Security Nexus," *Parliamentary Affairs* 2012, 65(1): 115–137.

23 Sangita Shrestova, "Between Storytelling and Surveillance: American Muslim Youth Negotiate Culture, Politics, and Participation" (Youth and Participatory Politics Research Network), http://ypp.dmlcentral.net

24 Shrestova, "Between Storytelling and Surveillance"; Arely Zimmerman, "Documenting DREAMs: New Media, Undocumented Youth, and the Immigrant Rights Movement" (Los Angeles, CA: Annenberg School for Communication and Journalism, University of Southern California, 2012).

25 Christine Bachen, Chad Raphael, Kathleen-M Lynn, Kristen McKee, and Jessica Philippi, "Civic Engagement, Pedagogy, and Information Technology on Websites for Youth," *Political Communication* 2008, 25: 290–310.

26 Natalia Smirnov, Barbara Ferman, and Nuala Cabral, "Poppyn: Presenting Our Perspective on Philly Youth News," *The Civic Media Project* (Cambridge: MIT Press, 2015), accessed June 28, 2016, http://civicmediaproject.org/works/ civic-media-project/poppyn

27 http://www.engagedyouth.org/blog.html

28 Guy Berger, "Empowering the Youth as Citizen Journalists: A South African Experience," *Journalism* 2011, 12(6): 708–726.

29 Berger, "Empowering the Youth."

30 Peter Levine, "A Public Voice for Youth: The Audience Problem in Digital Media and Civic Education," in W. Lance Bennett, ed., *Civic Life Online: Learning How Digital Media Can Engage Youth*, The John D. and Katherine T. Macarthur Foundation Series on Digital Media and Learning (Cambridge, MA: MIT Press, 2008), 119–138.

31 Levine, "A Public Voice for Youth," 152.

32 Andrea Wenzel, Daniela Gerson, and Evelyn Moreno, *Engaging Communities through Solutions Journalism* (New York: Tow Center for Digital Journalism, April 26, 2016); "What Is Solutions Journalism?" Solutions Journalism Network, www.solutionsjournalism.org/about/solutions-journalism-what-it-is-and-what-it-is-not/. In northern Europe, Catherine Gyldensted uses the term "constructive journalism" in reference to similar practices. See Catherine Gyldensted, "Innovating News Journalism through Positive Psychology," University of Pennsylvania Scholarly Commons, 2011, accessed May 25, 2017, http://repository.upenn.edu/mapp_capstone/20/

33 Hava Gordon, *We Fight to Win: Inequality and the Politics of Youth Activism* (New Brunswick, NJ: Rutgers University Press, 2009), 164.

34 Cara DiEnno, Personal conversation at the University of Denver's Center for Community Engagement and Service Learning, 2015.

35 Lynn Schofield Clark and Margie Thompson, "Media-Rich Participatory Action Research," unpublished paper, 2016.

36 Dahlgren, "Professional and Citizen Journalism."

37 Benjamin Thevenin, "Critical Media Literacy in Action: Uniting Theory, Practice, and Politics in Media Education" (Ph.D. diss., University of Colorado, 2012).

38 The story of this was first published as Lynn Schofield Clark, "Padres Y Jovenes Unidos: Student Empowerment through Critical Media Literacy," *The Civic Media Project* (Cambridge: MIT Press, 2015), accessed June 28, 2016, http://civicmediaproject.org/works/civic-media-project/padres-y-jovenes-unidos

39 Restorative justice, as opposed to traditional punitive justice, is a system of criminal justice that focuses on the rehabilitation of offenders through reconciliation with victims and the community at large.

40 Clark, "#BlackLivesMatter and Participants at the Margins."

41 Lynn Schofield Clark, Margie Thompson, David Brennan, and Students, *Research Brief*, presented to the City of Denver's Office of the Independent Monitor, 2015.

42 Mike Barz, "Two Unlikely Groups Connect, Using Media as a Way to Start the Conversation," *Fox31*, October 11, 2015, http://kdvr.com/2015/10/11/two-unlikely-groups-connect-using-media-as-a-way-to-start-the-conversation/

43 The documentary *Busriders Union* (2000) illustrates a similar story that took place in Los Angeles and how young people took the lead in organizing for transportation justice in that city; see http://zinnedproject.org/materials/bus-riders-union/

44 Joe Vacarelli, "Denver's Montbello School Ready to Graduate," *Denver Post*, May 20, 2014, accessed June 28, 2016, www.denverpost.com/2014/05/20/denvers-montbello-high-school-ready-to-graduate-last-class/

45 But see Ryan Warner, "Politico: Metro Denver Transit 'Miracle' and Missed Opportunity: Is Passenger Rail Across Colorado a Pie in the Sky Vision?" Colorado Public Radio, May 19, 2016, www.cpr.org/news/story/politico-metro-denver-transit-miracle-and-missed-opportunity-passenger-rail-across

46 L. Graca (2016, June). "South Students Now Commuting Longer," *The Washington Park Profile*, May 5, 2016, accessed June 28 2016, http://washparkprofile.com/washington-park-profile-news/south-students-now-commuting-longer/

47 Warner, "Publics and Counterpublics."

48 Banaji and Buckingham, *The Civic Web*; Bennett and Segerberg, *The Logic of Connective Action*; Dahlgen, "Professional and Citizen Journalism"; Flanagan, *Teenage Citizens*; Soep, *Participatory Politics*.

7 Moving Forward: What We Can Do

1 Joseph Kahne, Namjin Lee, and Jessica T. Feezell, "The Civic and Political Significance of Online Participatory Cultures and Youth Transitioning to Adulthood," *Journal of Information Technology and Politics* 2012, 10(1): 1–20.

2 Carpentier, *Media and Participation*.

3 Christopher Daggett, "The Auction that Could Transform Local Media," *New York Times*, November 28, 2016, accessed November 29, 2016, http://www.nytimes.com/2016/11/28/opinion/an-auction-that-could transform-local-media.html; Shan Wang, "The FCC Spectrum Auction Is Sending $10 Billion to Broadcasters. Where Will That Money Go?" NiemanLab, April 14, 2017, accessed May 9, 2017, http://www.niemanlab.org/2017/04/the-fcc-spectrum-auction-is-sending-10-billion-to-broadcasters-where-will-that-money-go/

4 April Simpson, "The FCC Spectrum Auction," *Current: News for People in Public Media*, May 1, 2017, accessed May 9, 2017, https://current.org/series/spectrum-auction/

5 "WGBH Spectrum Auction FAQ," accessed May 9, 2017, http://www.wgbh.org/about/WGBH_Spectrum_Auction_FAQs.cfm

6 NiemanLab, April 14, 2017; "Spectrum Auction and Journalism: A Once-in-a-Lifetime Chance to Strengthen Our Communities," New Voices/Free Press, accessed May 9, 2017, www.newsvoices.org/spectrum-auction-and-journalism

7 For more information on News Voices, see: https://www.newsvoices.org/about-news-voices

8 Amster, *Seeds of Cynicism*; Marchi, "From Disillusion to Disengagement"; Jack Dvorak, *High School Journalism Matters* (Arlington, VA: Newspaper Association of America, 2008), 1–19, accessed December 19, 2016, www.americanpressinstitute.org/wp-content/uploads/2013/09/NIE_High-school-journalism-matters.pdf

9 *Boston Public Schools at a Glance 2014–2015.* Boston Public Schools Communications Office, revised June 10, 2015, www.bostonpublicschools. org/cms/lib07/MA01906464/Centricity/Domain/238/BPS%20at%20a%20 Glance%2015-0610.pdf

10 Amster, *Seeds of Cynicism*; Dennis, *Prior Review*; Mark J. Fiore, "Trampling the 'Marketplace of Ideas': The Case against Extending Hazelwood to College Campuses," *University of Pennsylvania Law Review* June 2002, 150(6): 1915–1968; Carol S. Lomicky, "Analysis of High School Newspaper Editorials before and after *Hazelwood School District v. Kuhlmeier*: A Content Analysis Case Study," *Journal of Law and Education* 2000, 463–476; David L. Martinson, "School Censorship: It Comes in a Variety of Forms, Not All of Them Overt," *Clearing\House* May/June 2008, 81(5): 211–214; Frank D. LoMonte, "Momentum Swings towards Legal Protections for Journalism Students," *Student Press Law Center Report* 2016, 35(2): 2.

11 See Student Press Law Center website for more information: www.splc.org

12 www.dailybulletin.com/social-affairs/20151121/how-students-are-fighting-free-speech-limits-at-schools-colleges; http://newvoicesus.com; www.splc .org

13 Ryan Tarinelli, "Big League, Little Speech," *Student Press Law Center Report* Spring 2016, 35(2): 4–7; Also see www.splc.org

14 Lee Becker, Tudor Vlad, and Holly Anne Simpson, *2013 Annual Survey of Journalism and Mass Communication Graduates* (Athens, GA: University of Georgia, 2014). According to the survey, 80 percent of journalism graduates received news from online platforms and more than 90 percent checked social media the day before the survey, as compared to just 30 percent who read a newspaper the day before. www.grady.uga.edu/annualsurveys/ Graduate_Survey/Graduate_2013/Grad_Report_2013_Combined.pdf

15 T. Grier, Most print and online journalists use social media for story research. Poynter Institute for Media Studies, 2010, www.poynter.org/2010/most-print-and-online-journalists-use-social-media-for-story-research/100373/

16 See Stephanie E. Bor, "Teaching Social Media Journalism: Challenges and Opportunities for Future Curriculum Design," *Journalism & Mass Communication Educator* 2014, 69(3): 243–255; Martin Hirst and Greg Treadwell, "'Blogs Bother Me': Social Media, Journalism Students, and the Curriculum," *Journalism Practice* 2011, 5(4): 446–461; Dianne Lynch, "The State of American Journalism Education," in *Above and Beyond: Looking at the Future of Journalism Education* The Knight Foundation, 2015, www.knightfoundation.org/media/uploads/publication_ pdfs/KF-Above-and-Beyond-Report.pdf; Sarah Bartlett, "New No More," *Above and Beyond*, www.knightfoundation.org/features/je-append-sarah-bartlett-new-no-more/

17 Ingrid Hu Dahl and Christine Newkirk, "Understanding News Literacy: A Youth Perspective," *Youth Media Reporter* 2010, (3): 48–50; Kristy Roschke, "Convergence Journalism in High School: How Educators are Keeping Up with Trends in the Media Industry," *Southwestern Mass Communication Journal* 2009, 24(2): 55–64; Angela Washeck, "The Journey to Teaching High School Journalism in Texas," *MediaShift*, July 17, 2014,

http://mediashift.org/2014/07/the-journey-to-teaching-high-school-journalism-in-texas/; Esther Wojcicki, "Teaching Journalism and News Literacy," *Youth Media Reader*, 2010, 3: 51–52; Elia Powers, "Teaching News Literacy in the Age of New Media: Why Secondary School Students Should Be Taught to Judge the Credibility of the News They Consume," Washington University in St. Louis, 2010, http://openscholarship.wustl.edu/cgi/viewcontent.cgi?article=1454&context=etd

18 Dr. Donald Matheson, July 14, 2016. Comments during the "21st Century Ethical Issues in Journalism" panel at the World Journalism Education Congress, Auckland University of Technology. Similarly, the authors of *Social Media for Journalists: Principles and Practices* (Thousand Oaks, CA: Sage, 2013) note that "journalistic ethics vary considerably" regarding social media use and they urge journalists to create "your own set of ethical and social guidelines by which to operate" (p. 132).

19 Howard Schneider and Jim Klurfeld, "The Demand Dilemma and News Literacy in Schools," Media Giraffe Project at the University of Massachusetts-Amherst and the Donald W. Reynolds Journalism Institute. Video. http://newshare.typepad.com/mgpaudio/2008/01/video-the-deman.html. See also http://drc.centerfornewsliteracy.org/glosary-language-news-literacy

20 Some successful models include the summer program for journalists and journalism educators in Salzburg, Austria, directed by Paul Mihailidis; the award-winning student journalism program at Palo Alto High School, www.paloaltoonline.com/news/2014/10/17/a-new-home-for-journalism; the journalism class at Francis Howell North High School in St. Charles, MO, which has a progressive approach to incorporating social media: www.jeadigitalmedia.org/wp-content/uploads/2012/08/beth_phillips_social_media.pdf; and Stanford's J-program, which teaches data-based journalism to help students write compelling and relevant stories using diverse storytelling genres.

21 Laura Sydell, "We Tracked Down a Fake News Creator in the Suburbs. Here's What We Learned," National Public Radio, November 23, 2016, accessed December 3, 2016, www.npr.org/sections/alltechconsidered/2016/11/23/503146770/npr-finds-the-head-of-a-covert-fake-news-operation-in-the-suburbs

22 Stanford History Education Group, *Evaluating Information.*

23 Stanford History Education Group, *Evaluating Information.*

24 Sabrina Tavernise, "As Fake News Spreads Lies, More Readers Shrug at the Truth," *New York Times*, December 6, 2016.

25 Stanford History Education Group, *Evaluating Information*; Farhad Manjoo, "Social Media's Globe-Shaking Power," *New York Times*, November 16, 2016, accessed December 1, 2016, www.nytimes.com/2016/11/17/technology/social-medias-globe-shaking-power.html; William Powers, "Who's Influencing Election 2016?" MIT Media Lab, *Medium*, February 23, 2016, accessed June 11, 2016, https://medium.com/mit-media-lab/who-s-influencing-election-2016-8bed68ddecc3#.7t9pm8xdl); Natt Garun, "How Social Media Platforms Influenced the 2016 Election," *The Verge* (technology news network), November 14, 2016, accessed on November 18, 2016; Matt Kapko, "How Social Media is Shaping the 2016 Presidential Election," *CIO*

Tech News and Analysis website, September 29, 2016, accessed October 28, 2016, www.cio.com/article/3125120/social-networking/how-social-media-is-shaping-the-2016-presidential-election.html

26 Langdon Winner, *The Whale and the Reactor: A Search for Limits in an Age of Technology* (Chicago, IL: University of Chicago Press, 1989).

27 www.bloomberg.com/news/articles/2012-03-01/the-rise-of-the-brogrammer; www.theatlantic.com/business/archive/2013/09/the-brogrammer-effect-women-are-a-small-and-shrinking-share-of-computer-workers/279611/

28 www.techrepublic.com/article/diversity-stats-10-tech-companies-that-have-come-clean/; http://fortune.com/2014/08/29/how-tech-companies-compare-in-employee-diversity/; http://fortune.com/2014/10/02/women-leave-tech-culture/

29 Danny Yadron, "Facebook Controversy Shows Journalists Are More Complicated than Algorithms," *The Guardian*, May 12, 2016, www.theguardian.com/technology/2016/may/12/facebook-twitter-google-snapchat-news-bias; Hannah Kuchler and Matthew Garrahan, "Does Facebook Bend the Trends that Govern Our News?" *Financial Times*, May 13, 2016, https://next.ft.com/content/5c68e88e-18e6-11e6-bb7d-ee563a5a1cc1

30 This recommendation is taken from Emma Pierson, "How to Get More Women to Join the Debate," *New York Times* Opinion Pages, January 6, 2015, http://kristof.blogs.nytimes.com/2015/01/06/how-to-get-more-women-to-join-the-debate/?_r=0

31 Jurgen Habermas, *Between Facts and Norms: Contributions to a Discourse Theory of Law and Democracy* (Cambridge, MA: Massachusetts Institute of Technology, 1996), 351.

32 See D. DeSilver, "US Income Inequality, on Rise for Decades, Is Now Highest since 1928," Pew Research Center, 2013, www.pewresearch.org/fact-tank/2013/12/05/u-s-income-inequality-on-rise-for-decades-is-now-highest-since-1928/; E. Saez and G. Zucman, "Exploding Wealth Inequality in the United States," Washington Center for Equitable Growth, 2014, http://equitable-growth.org/research/exploding-wealth-inequality-united-states/; Someiller et al., *Income Inequality*.

33 Mossberger et al., *Digital Cities*; Pippa Norris, *Digital Divide: Civic Engagement, Information Poverty, and the Internet Worldwide* (Cambridge: Cambridge University Press, 2001).

34 Rideout and Katz, *Opportunity for All?*

35 David McCabe, "House to Consider Blocking Cellphone Subsidies," *The Hill*, June 20, 2016, http://thehill.com/policy/technology/284110-house-to-consider-cell-phone-subsidies-block

36 Brian Fung, "The FCC Is Stopping 9 Companies from Providing Federally Subsidized Internet to the Poor," *The Washington Post*, February 3, 2017, accessed February 15, 2017, www.washingtonpost.com/news/the-switch/wp/2017/02/03/the-fcc-is-stopping-9-companies-from-providing-subsidized-broadband-to-the-poor/?utm_term=.e42877edc377

37 Tim Wu, "Why Everyone Was Wrong about Net Neutrality," *The New Yorker*, February 26, 2016, www.newyorker.com/business/currency/why-everyone-was-wrong-about-net-neutrality

38 Baym, "*The Daily Show*: Discursive Integration," *From Cronkite to Colbert*; Harrington, *The Democracy of Conversation*, "Future Proofing Journalism," "Popular News."

39 According to the show's official HBO website, accessed on June 25, 2016, www.hbo.com/last-week-tonight-with-john-oliver/about/index.html

40 B. Brody, "How John Oliver Transformed the Net Neutrality Debate Once and For All," *Bloomberg Politics*, 2015, www.bloomberg.com/politics/articles/2015-02-26/how-john-oliver-transformed-the-net-neutrality-debate-once-and-for-all

41 According to YouTube as of December 8, 2016, www.youtube.com/watch?v=fpbOEoRrHyU

42 According to the YouTube site where the video was posted, accessed May 9, 2017, https://www.youtube.com/watch?v=92vuuZt7wak

43 Margaret Harding McGill, "John Oliver Again Fires Up Net Neutrality Debate," *Politico*, May 8, 2017, accessed May 9, 2017, www.politico.com/story/2017/05/08/john-oliver-net-neutrality-238132. Also see FCC website, accessed May 9, 2017, www.fcc.gov/ecfs/search/filings?proceedings_name=17-108&sort=date_disseminated,DESC

44 "The War on Drugs is a Failure," *New York Times* Opinion Page, April 19, 2013, www.nytimes.com/video/multimedia/100000002180127/the-war-on-drugs-is-a-failure.html

45 "Melania Trump's Republican Convention Speech," *New York Times*, July 19, 2016, www.nytimes.com/video/us/politics/100000004538452/comparing-melania-and-michelles-speech.html

46 "*Spotlight* Spoof on *Last Week Tonight with John Oliver*," August 7, 2016, www.youtube.com/watch?v=bq2_wSsDwkQ

47 Rory O'Connor and Aaron Cutler, *Shock Jocks: Hate Speech and Talk Radio: America's Ten Worst Hate Talkers and the Progressive Alternatives* (San Francisco, CA: Alternet Books, 2008).

48 Project for Excellence in Journalism, *State of the News Media 2006: An Annual Report on American Journalism*, www.stateofthemedia.org/2006/; *Trends 2005*, Pew Research Center for the People and the Press, www.pewresearch.org/2005/01/20/trends-2005/; Pew Research Center Politics and Policy, www.people-press.org/2009/10/29/fox-news-viewed-as-most-ideological-network/

49 National Study by Suffolk University and *USA Today*, October 2016, www.suffolk.edu/documents/SUPRC/10_26_2016_tables.pdf

50 www.nytimes.com/2016/07/25/business/sponsored-content-takes-larger-role-in-media-companies.html?_r=0

51 John Stauber and Sheldon Rampton, *Toxic Sludge Is Good for You* (Monroe, ME: Common Courage Press, 1995).

52 Facebook Terms of Service, revised January 2015, https://www.facebook.com/terms

53 Professor Adrienne Russell and students in her Emerging Digital Cultures class offer a detailed list of strategies on "How to Protect your Online Privacy," November 13, 2016, accessed December 13, 2016, https://medium.com/@adierussell/how-to-protect-your-online-privacy-20b505eaf9d1#.iqowhoy3k

54 www.theguardian.com/technology/2016/apr/12/the-dark-side-of-guardian-comments; www.washingtonpost.com/news/the-intersect/wp/2015/01/08/why-women-dont-leave-comments-online/; http://kristof.blogs.nytimes.com/2015/01/06/how-to-get-more-women-to-join-the-debate/?_r=0

55 Emma Pierson, *Outnumbered but Well-Spoken: Female Commenters in the New York Times*, unpublished report, http://cs.stanford.edu/people/emmap1/cscw_paper.pdf

56 Pierson, *Outnumbered but Well-Spoken.*

57 Jorge A. Jimenez and José M. Abreu, "Race and Sex Effects on Attitudinal Perceptions of Acquaintance Rape," *Journal of Counseling Psychology* 2003, 50(2): 252–256, http://dx.doi.org/10.1037/0022-0167.50.2.252

58 Emma Pierson, "How to Get More Women to Join the Debate," *New York Times* Opinion Page, January 6, 2015, http://kristof.blogs.nytimes.com/2015/01/06/how-to-get-more-women-to-join-the-debate/?_r=0

59 Taken from The Society of Professional Journalists' *Code of Ethics*, revised and published online on September 6, 2014, www.spj.org/ethicscode.asp

60 https://hendricksproject.wordpress.com/lessons/overview/

61 http://jea.org/blog/category/resources-for-educators/

62 http://learning.blogs.nytimes.com/category/journalism/

63 James S. Leming, Lucien Ellington, and Kathleen Porter, eds., *Where Did Social Studies Go Wrong?* (Washington, DC: Thomas B. Fordham Foundation, 2003), www.edexcellence.net/publications/wheredidssgowrong.html

64 Henry Giroux, *Zombie Politics and Culture in the Age of Casino Capitalism* (New York: Peter Lang 2010).

65 Michelle Alexander, "Why Hillary Clinton Doesn't Deserve the Black Vote," *The Nation*, February 10 2016, accessed August 30, 2016, www.thenation.com/article/hillary-clinton-does-not-deserve-black-peoples-votes/

66 Alexander, "Why Hillary Clinton."

67 Alexander, "Why Hillary Clinton," who notes that some of this was later restored.

68 Alexander, "Why Hillary Clinton."

69 Peter Kelley, "Nearly Half of African-American Women Know Someone in Prison," *University of Washington Today,* June 15, 2015, accessed August 30, 2016, www.washington.edu/news/2015/06/11/nearly-half-of-african-american-women-know-someone-in-prison/

70 *Children and Families of the Incarcerated Fact Sheet* (Rutgers University: National Resource Center on Children & Families of the Incarcerated, 2014), accessed August 30, 2016, https://nrccfi.camden.rutgers.edu/files/nrccfi-fact-sheet-2014.pdf

71 *Children and Families of the Incarcerated Fact Sheet.*

72 Ana Swanson, "Americans Are Less Trusting than Ever Before. That Could Also Make Us Poor," *Washington Post*, August 26, 2016, accessed August 30, 2016, www.washingtonpost.com/news/wonk/wp/2016/08/26/americans-are-less-trusting-than-ever-before-that-could-also-make-us-poor/?wpisrc=nl_wonk&wpmm=1

73 Alex Tabarrock, quoted in Swanson, "Americans Are Less Trusting."

74 Roger Silverstone, *Media and Morality: On the Rise of the Mediapolis* (Cambridge: Polity Press, 2007).

75 Silverstone, *Media and Morality*; Ulrich Beck and Ciara Cronin, *Cosmopolitan Vision* (New York: Polity Press, 2006); Amy Stornaiuolo, Glynda Hall, and Urvashi Sahni, "Cosmopolitan Imagingings of Self and Other: Youth and Social Networking in a Global World," in Joellen Fisherkeller, ed., *International Perspectives on Youth Media: Cultures of Production and Education* (New York: Peter Lang, 2011), 263–280; See also Mark Coeckelbergh, "Violent Computer Games, Empathy, and Cosmopolitanism," *Ethics and Information Technology* 2007, 9(3): 219–231.

76 Shani Orgad and Irene Bruna Seu, "The Mediation of Humanitarianism: Toward a Research Framework," *Communication, Culture & Critique* 2014, 7(1): 6–36.

77 Susan D. Moeller, S. D. *Compassion Fatigue: How the Media Sell Misery, War, and Death* (New York: Routledge, 1999); see also Irene Bruna Seu, "'Your Stomach Makes You Feel That You Don't Want to Know Anything About It': Desensitization, Defense Mechanisms and Rhetoric in Response to Human Rights Abuses," *Journal of Human Rights* 2003, 2(2):183–196; Irene Bruna Seu, "'Doing Denial': Audience Reaction to Human Rights Appeals," *Discourse & Society* 2010, 21(4): 438–457.

78 Katherine N. Kinnick, Dean M. Krugman, and Glen T. Cameron, "Compassion Fatigue: Communication and Burnout Toward Social Problems," *Journalism and Mass Communications Quarterly* 1996, 73(3): 687–707.

79 Lilie Chouliaraki, *The Ironic Spectator: Solidarity in the Age of Post-Humanitarianism* (London: Polity, 2013).

80 Meanwhile, people in Birgitta Hoijer's study of news audiences did not exhibit "compassion fatigue" or distance from suffering so much as they reiterated a "dominant victim code," sometimes in imperialist tones but not without compassion. In other words, her study found that those representations depicting people as most vulnerable, helpless, and passive – that is, as *deserving* victims – engendered more compassion than representations that depicted sufferers as having agency in their lives. This is a troubling finding, given the fact that it suggests people prefer to think of victims as different from and inferior to themselves. See Birgita Höijer, "The Discourse of Global Compassion: The Audience and Media Reporting of Human Suffering," *Media, Culture & Society* 2004, 26(4): 513–531. More hopeful is Chabot Davis's study of the extent to which black popular culture can, in some cases, engender empathy for African Americans among White Americans. Davis found that while some engagement inevitably reproduces imperialist assumptions in a manner similar to Hoijer's viewers, others experienced transformative identifica-tions when such engagement was paired with formal or informal peda-gogical support. Please see: Kimberly Chabot Davis, *Beyond the White Negro: Empathy and Anti-Racist Reading* (Chicago, IL: University of Illinois Press, 2014).

81 Thorson, "Facing an Uncertain Reception."

82 Smith, as cited in Thorson, "Facing an Uncertain Reception," 13.

83 One study, for instance, found that whereas it may be important to dis-cuss trauma, young people talk about trauma in ways that are patterned

and sometimes unhelpful, in that they often focus on their individual emotive responses to trauma rather than on the social and political contexts that caused others' trauma. See Michalinos Zembylas, "Trauma, Justice and the Politics of Emotion: The Violence of Sentimentality in Education," *Discourse: Studies in the Cultural Politics of Education* 2008, 29(1): 1–17; Michalinos Zembylas, "The Politics of Trauma: Empathy, Reconciliation and Peace Education," *Journal of Peace Education* 2007, 2: 207–224.

84 Toni Erskine, "'Citizen of Nowhere' or 'The Point Where Circles Intersect'? Impartialist and Embedded Cosmopolitanisms," *Review of International Studies* 2002, 28 (3): 457–478.

85 Chantal Mouffe proposes that we think about the agonies that people experience and express as what she terms "the agonistic public sphere." See Mouffe, *On the Political*. Mouffe has argued for what she calls a "radical pluralist democracy" that places conflict rather than consensus at its center. She therefore introduces the concept of the agonistic public space, or the spaces in which conflict and discord, rather than consensus, are what we should expect as a part of public life. As Peter Dahlgren writes, "Mouffe sets a course that admonishes citizens to understand and accept that the political is inseparable from social life – it can arise anywhere – and that there is no harmonious, non-conflictual future waiting for us." Dahlgren, "Professional and Citizen Journalism."

86 We are grateful to Amy Villarejo for first introducing Lynn to the work of Geoff Boucher in a conversation in March 2015.

87 Geoff Boucher, *The Charmed Circle of Ideology: A Critique of Laclau and Mouffe, Butler and Zizek* (New York: Anamnesis, 2008). Boucher suggests a turn to the regulation school that first emerged among French economists who were struggling to understand the economic and social instabilities that had emerged in France in the early 1970s and who wanted to consider these instabilities in light of how capitalism had somehow been "regularized" or stable from the middle of the nineteenth century until the 1930s and again from the postwar years until the 1970s. Robert Boyer argued that stability occurred in the early years of industrialization (1850–1930) because businesses invested their profits back into the business and made high productivity gains, and in the later years (1930s–1970) thanks to a regular growth in output, consumption, and income. See Robert Boyer, *The Regulation School: A Critical Introduction*, Trans. C. Charney (New York: Columbia University Press 1990).

88 See, e.g., Alain Lipietz, *Towards a New Economic Order: Postfordism, Ecology and Democracy*, Trans. M. Slater (London: Oxford University Press, 1992); Alain Lipietz, "Rebel Sons: The Regulation School," Entretien avec Jean Jane Jenson, *French Politics and Society* 1987, 5(4); Harvard University (art 750).

89 Andrew Dobson, "Thick Cosmopolitanism," *Political Studies* 2006, 54(1): 165–184, http://onlinelibrary.wiley.com/doi/10.1111/j.1467-9248.2006.00571.x/full#b15/Andrew Linklater, "Cosmopolitanism," in Andrew Dobson and Robyn Eckersley, eds., *Political Theory and the Ecological Challenge* (Cambridge: Cambridge University Press, 2006), 109–128.

90 Dobson,"Thick Cosmopolitanism."

91 Linklater, "Cosmopolitanism."

92 Kwame Anthony Appiah, *Cosmopolitanism: Ethics in a World of Strangers* (New York: W. W. Norton & Co., 2007).

93 Adam Smith, *A Theory of Moral Sentiments* (Strand and Edinburgh: A. Millar; A. Kincaid & J. Bell, 1759).

94 For example, as Ella Shohat has noted, "genders, sexualities, races, classes, nations and even continents exist not as hermetically sealed entities but rather as part of a permeable interwoven relationality." Ella Shohat, "Foreword," in Ella Shohat, ed., *Talking Visions: Multicultural Feminism in a Transnational Age* (Cambridge, MA: MIT Press, 1998), xii.

95 Pablo Barberá, John T. Jost, Jonathan Nagler, Joshua Tucker, and Richard Bonneau, "Tweeting from Left to Right: Is Online Communication More than an Echo Chamber?" *Psychological Science* 2015, doi: 0956797615594620; Seth Flaxman, Sharad Goel, and Justin Rao, "Filter Bubbles, Echo Chambers and Online News Consumption," *Public Opinion Quarterly* 2016, 80: 298–320, doi: 10.1093/poq/nfw006

Methods Appendix

1 Hava Gordon, *We Fight to Win: Inequality and the Politics of Youth Activism* (New Brunswick, NJ: Rutgers University Press, 2010); Heather Horst and Daniel Miller, *The Cell Phone: An Anthropology of Communication* (London: Berg, 2006); Michelle Fine and Maria Torre, "Theorizing Audience, Products and Provocation, in P. Reason and H. Bradbury, eds., *Handbook of Action Research* (Thousand Oaks, CA: Sage, 2007); Maria Torre and Michelle Fine, "Researching and Resisting: Democratic Policy Research By and For Youth," in Shaun Ginwright, Julio Cammarota and Pedro Noguera, eds., *Beyond Resistance: Youth Activism and Community Change: New Democratic Possibilities for Policy and Practice for America's Youth* (New York: Routledge, 2006), 269–285; Sonia Livingstone, *Young People and New Media: Childhood in a Changing Media Environment* (London: Sage, 2002); Sunaina Maira and Elisabeth Soep, eds., *Youthscapes: The Popular, the National, the Global* (Philadelphia, PA: University of Pennsylvania Press, 2013); Mimi Ito, Heather Horst, with Sonia Baumer, M. Bittanti, danah boyd, R. Cody, Becky Herr-Stephenson, P. Lange, D. Mahendran, K. Martinez, C. J. Pascoe, Dan Perkel, Laura Robinson, Christo Sims, and Lisa Tripp, *Hanging Out, Messing Around, Geeking Out: Living and Learning with New Media* (Cambridge, MA: MIT Press, 2009).

2 Clifford Geertz, "Deep Hanging Out (A Review of Books by Anthropologists Pierre Clastres and Clifford James)," *The New York Review of Books*, October 22, 1998, accessed December 20, 2016, www.nybooks.com/articles/1998/10/22/deep-hanging-out/; see also Ben Walmsley, "Deep Hanging Out in the Arts: An Anthropological Approach to Capturing

Cultural Value," *International Journal of Cultural Policy*, 2016 doi: 10.1080/10286632.2016.1153081.

3 Tim Ingold, "Anthropology is not Ethnography," *Proceedings of the British Academy* 2008, 154: 62–92.

4 Greg Dimitriadis, "Coming Clean at the Hyphen: Ethics and Dialogue at a Local Community Center," *Qualitative Inquiry* 2001, 7(5): 578–597; Vicki Mayer, "Research beyond the Pale: Whiteness in Audience Studies and Media Ethnography," *Communication Theory* 2005, 15(2): 148–167.

5 Regina Marchi, *Day of the Dead in the USA: The Migration and Transformation of a Cultural Phenomenon* (New Brunswick. NJ: Rutgers University Press, 2009).

6 S. Ginwright and J. Cammarota, "Youth Activism in the Urban Community: Learning Critical Civic Praxis within Community Organizations," *International Journal of Qualitative Studies in Education* 2007, 20(6): 693–710.

7 See Lynn Schofield Clark, "The Ethics of Engagement," in Bastiaan Vanacker and Don Heider, eds., *Ethics for a Digital Age* (New York: Peter Lang, 2015).

8 Thomas Lindlof and Bryan Taylor, *Qualitative Communication Research Methods* (Thousand Oaks, CA: Sage, 2002).

9 G. Goldkuhl and S. Cronholm, "Adding Theoretical Grounding to Grounded Theory: Toward Multi-Grounded Theory," *International Journal of Qualitative Methods* 2010, 9(2): 187–205.

10 B. G. Glaser and A. L. Strauss, *The Discovery of Grounded Theory: Strategies for Qualitative Research* (Piscataway, NJ: Transaction Publishers, 2009).

References

Adler, B. (2014, January/February). A movement's moment? Common core opens the door for news literacy to expand in the classroom. *Columbia Journalism Review* 48–49.

Aguilar, J. (2016, April 20). Student Claims Intimidation by Douglas County School Board Members. *Denver Post*. Available at: www.denverpost.com/2016/04/20/student-claims-intimidation-by-douglas-county-school-board-members/ Retrieved June 18, 2016.

Aguilar, J. (2016, June 22). Defiance, Disruption Mark Raucous Douglas County School Board Meeting. *Denver Post*. Available at: www.denverpost.com/2016/06/21/defiance-disruption-marks-raucous-douglas-county-school-board-meeting/ Retrieved June 22, 2016.

Allen, S. (2013). *Citizen Witnessing: Revisioning Journalism in Times of Crisis*. New York: Polity.

Allen, S. and Thorsen, E. (2009). *Citizen Journalism: Global Perspectives*. New York: Peter Lang.

Allen, D. and Light, J. (Eds.). (2015). *From Voice to Influence: Understanding Citizenship in the Digital Age*. Chicago, IL: University of Chicago Press.

Alexander, J. (2006). *The Civil Sphere*. New York: Oxford University Press.

Alexander, J. (2016). Introduction: Journalism, democratic culture, and creative reconstruction. In J. Alexander (Ed.). *The Crisis of Journalism Reconsidered: Dramatic Culture, Professional Codes, Digital Future*. Cambridge: Cambridge University Press.

Alexander, M. (2016, February 10). Why Hillary Clinton Doesn't Deserve the Black Vote. *The Nation*. Available at: www.thenation.com/article/hillary-clinton-does-not-deserve-black-peoples-votes/ Retrieved August 30, 2016.

Almasy, S. and Yan, H. (2014, November 26). Protesters Fill Streets across Country as Ferguson Protests Spread Coast to Coast. *CNN*. Available at: www.cnn.com/2014/11/25/us/national-ferguson-protests/

American Press Institute. (2014). How Americans Get Their News. www
.americanpressinstitute.org/publications/reports/survey-research/
how-americans-get-news/

American Press Institute. (2015). How Millennials Get News: Inside the Habits of America's First Digital Generation. www.americanpressinstitute.org/publications/reports/survey-research/millennials-news/ Retrieved July 2, 2015.

Amster, S. E. (2006). *Seeds of Cynicism: The Undermining of Journalistic Education*. New York: University Press of America.

Anderson, B. (1983). *Imagined Communities: Reflections on the Origins and Spread of Nationalism*. New York: Verso.

Anderson, C. W. (2013). *Rebuilding the News: Metropolitan Journalism in the Digital Age*. Philadelphia, PA: Temple University Press.

Anderson, M. and Caumont, A. (2014). How Social Media Is Reshaping News. Pew Research Center. www.pewresearch.org/fact-tank/2014/09/24/how-social-media-is-reshaping-news/

Appiah, K. (2007). *Cosmopolitanism: Ethics in a World of Strangers*. New York: W. W. Norton & Co.

Ardevol, E., Roig, A., San Cornelio, G., Pages, R., and Alsina, P. (2010). Playful practices: Theorizing "new media" cultural production. In B. Brauchler and J. Postill (Eds.). *Theorizing Media and Practice*, pp. 259–280. New York: Berghahn Books.

Arendt, H. (1961). *On Revolution*. New York: Penguin.

Arendt, H. (1963). *Eichmann in Jerusalem: A Report on the Banality of Evil*. London: Faber & Faber.

Barberá, P., Jost, J., Nagler, J., Tucker, J., and Bonneau, R. (2015). Tweeting from left to right: Is online political communication more than an echo chamber? *Psychological Science* 10: 1531–1542. doi: 10.1177/0956797615594620

Barberá, P., Jost, J., Nagler, J., Tucker, J., and Bonneau, R. (1973). *The Origins of Totalitarianism*. New York: Houghton Mifflin Harcourt.

Associated Press. (2008). A New Model for News: Studying the Deep Structure of Young Adult News Consumption. Available at: www.ap.org/newmodel.pdf.

Aufderheide, P. and Firestone, C. M. (1993). *Media Literacy: A Report of National Leadership Conference on Media Literacy*. Cambridge: Polity Press.

Bachen, C., Raphael, C., Lynn, K., McKee, K., and Philippi, J. (2008). Civic engagement, pedagogy, and information technology on websites for youth. *Political Communication* 25: 290–310.

Bardoel, J. and Deuze, M. (2001). Network journalism: Converging competences of media professionals and professionalism. *Australian Journalism Review* 23(2): 91–103.

Barnhurst, K. and Nerone, J. (2002). *The Form of News: A History*. New York: Guilford Press.

Barron, B., Gomez, K., Pinkard, N., and Martin, C. (2015). *The Digital Youth Network*. Cambridge, MA: MIT Press.

Bauman, Z. (2007). *Liquid Times Living in an Age of Uncertainty*. Cambridge: Polity Press.

Baym, G. (2005). *The Daily Show*: Discursive integration and the reinvention of political journalism. *Political Communication* 22: 259–276.

Baym, G. (2007). Emerging models of journalistic authority in MTV's coverage of the 2004 US Presidential election. *Journalism Studies* 8(3): 382–385.

Baym, G. (2010). *From Cronkite to Colbert: The Evolution of Broadcast News.* Boulder, CO: Paradigm.

Baym, N. (2015). *Personal Connections in the Digital Age,* 2nd ed. New York: Polity.

Bazarova, N. N. and Choi, Y. H. (2014). Self-disclosure in social media: Extending the functional approach to disclosure motivations and characteristics on social network sites. *Journal of Communication* 64(4): 635–657. doi:10.1111/jcom.12106

Beck, U. and Cronin, C. (2006). *Cosmopolitan Vision.* New York: Polity.

Beck, U. (2011). Cosmopolitanism as imagined communities of global risk. *American Behavioral Scientist* 55(10): 1346–1361.

Becker, M. (2008). "I Hate Hippies": South Park and the politics of Generation X. In J. A. Weinstock (Ed.). *Taking South Park Seriously,* pp. 145–164. Albany: SUNY Press.

Becker, L., Vlad, T., and Simpson, H. (2013). Annual Survey of Journalism and Mass Communication Graduates. James Cox Center for International Mass Communication, Grady College of Journalism and Mass Communication. Athens, GA: University of Georgia. www.grady.uga.edu/annualsurveys/ Graduate_Survey/Graduate_2013/Grad_Report_2013_Combined.pdf

Beckett, C. and Mansell, R. (2008) Crossing boundaries: New media and networked journalism. *Communication, Culture and Critique* 1(1): 92–104.

Benhabib, S. (1996). *Democracy and Difference: Contesting the Boundaries of the Political.* Princeton, NJ: Princeton University Press.

Benhabib, S. (2011). *Dignity in Adversity: Human Rights in Troubled Times.* London: Polity.

Bennett, W. L., Gressett, L., and Haltom, W. (1985). Repairing the news: A case study of the news paradigm. *Journal of Communication* 35: 50–86, p. 85.

Bennett, W. L., Gressett, L., and Haltom, W. (1998). The uncivic culture: Communication, culture, and the rise of lifestyle politics. *Political Science & Politics* 31(4): 741–761.

Bennett, W. L., Gressett, L., and Haltom, W. (2008) Changing citizenship in the digital age. *Civic Life Online: Learning How Digital Media Can Engage Youth,* pp. 1–24. Cambridge, MA: MIT Press.

Bennett, W. L., Gressett, L., and Haltom, W. and Segerberg, A. (2012) The logic of connective action. *Information, Communication & Society* 15: 739–768.

Bennett, W. L., Gressett, L., and Haltom, W. and Segerberg, A. (2013). *The Logic of Connective Action: Digital Media and the Personalization of Contentious Politics.* Cambridge: Cambridge University Press.

Benson, R. (2006). News media as a "journalistic field": What Bourdieu adds to New Institutionalism, and vice versa. *Political Communication* 23(2): 187–202.

Berger, G. (2011). Empowering the youth as citizen journalists: A South African experience. *Journalism* 12(6): 708–726.

Bird, S. E. and Dardenne, R. W. (1988). Myth, chronicle, and story – Exploring the narrative qualities of news. In J. W. Carey (Ed.). *Media, Myths, and Narratives – Television and the Press*, pp. 67–86. Newbury Park, CA: Sage.

Black Lives Matter Movement, Explained. *Washington Post*. Available at: www.washingtonpost.com/video/national/black-lives-matter-movement-explained/2016/06/21/8a00e59e-16e8-11e6-971a-dadf9ab18869_video .html Retrieved September 1, 2016.

Blake, J. (2014, August 30). How Ferguson Could Become a Movement: Lessons from History. CNN. Available at: www.cnn.com/2013/08/17/us/four-ways-to-beat-the-man/

Bobkowski, P. and Miller, P. (2016). Civic implications of secondary school journalism: Associations with voting propensity and community volunteering. *Journalism and Mass Communication Quarterly* 93(3): 530–550.

Boczkowski, P. (2010). *News at Work: Imitation in an Age of Information Abundance*. Chicago, IL: University of Chicago Press.

Boczkowski, P. and Mitchelstein, E. (2013). *The News Gap: When the Information Preferences of the Media and the Public Diverge*. Cambridge, MA: MIT Press.

Boczkowski, P., Mitchelstein, E., and Matassi, M. (2017, January 4). *Incidental news: How young people consume news on social media*. Presented at the 50th Hawaii International Conference on System Sciences, University of Hawaii at Manoa, doi: hdl.handle.net/10125/41371.

Boler, M. (Ed.). (2010). *Digital Media and Democracy: Tactics in Hard Times*. Cambridge, MA: MIT Press.

Bor, S. (2014). Teaching social media journalism: Challenges and opportunities for future curriculum design. *Journalism & Mass Communication Educator* 69(3): 243–255.

Borden, S. and Tew, C. (2007). The role of journalist and the performance of journalism: Ethical lessons from "fake" news (seriously). *Journal of Mass Media Ethics* 22(4): 300–314.

Bosman, J. and Fitzsimmons, E. (2014). Grief and Protests Follow Shooting of a Teenager. *The New York Times*. Available at: www.nytimes.com/2014/08/11/us/police-say-mike-brown-was-killed-after-struggle-for-gun.html. Retrieved June 17, 2016.

Boston Public Schools at a Glance 2014–2015. Boston Public Schools Communications Office, revised June 10, 2015. Available at: www .bostonpublicschools.org/cms/lib07/MA01906464/Centricity/Domain/238/ BPS%20at%20a%20Glance%2015-0610.pdf

Boucher, G. (2008). *The Charmed Circle of Ideology: A Critique of Laclau and Mouffe, Butler and Zizek*. New York: Anamnesis.

Bowyer, B., Kahne, J., and Middaugh, E. (2015). Youth comprehension of political messages in YouTube videos. *New Media & Society* 1–20. doi: 10.1177/ 1461444815611593

boyd, danah (2011). Social network sites as networked publics. In Zizi Papacharissi (Ed.), *A Networked Self: Identity, Community, and Culture on Social Network Sites*, pp. 39–58. New York: Routledge.

boyd, danah (2013). *It's Complicated: The Social Lives of Networked Teens*. New Haven, CT: Yale University Press.

Boyer, R. (1990). *The Regulation School: A Critical Introduction*. Trans. C. Charney. New York: Columbia University Press.

Brock, A. (2012). From the blackhand side: Twitter as a cultural conversation. *Journal of Broadcasting & Electronic Media* 56(4): 529–549.

Brody, B. (2015). How John Oliver Transformed the Net Neutrality Debate Once and for All. *Bloomberg Politics*. www.bloomberg.com/politics/articles/2015-02-26/how-john-oliver-transformed-the-net-neutrality-debate-once-and-for-all

Brown, E. (2016, March 29). I Go to a Competitive High School in Suburbia. The Stress Is Killing Me. *Vox*. Available at: www.vox.com/2016/3/29/11301078/high-school-stress-college Retrieved September 1, 2016.

Bruter, M., Banaji, S., Harrison, S., Cammaerts, B., Anstead, N., and Whitwell, B.. (2014). *Youth Participation in Democratic Life: Stories of Hope and Disillusion*. Basingstoke, UK: Palgrave Macmillan.

Bruns, A. (2008). *Blogs, Wikipedia, Second Life, and Beyond: From Production to Produsage*. New York: Peter Lang.

Buckingham, D. (2000). *The Making of Citizens: Young People, News, and Politics*. London: Routledge.

Byers, D. (November 9, 2016). How Politicians, Pollsters and Media Missed Trump's Groundswell. *CNNMoney*. Available at: http://money.cnn.com/2016/11/09/media/polling-media-missed-trump/

Cagé, J. (2016). *Saving the Media: Capitalism, Crowdfunding and Democracy*. Cambridge, MA: Harvard University Press.

Calhoun, C. (1992). *Habermas and the Public Sphere*. Cambridge, MA: MIT Press.

Callahan, C. (1998). Race and participation in high school journalism. *Newspaper Research Journal* 19(1):45–53.

Carey, J. (1989) *Communication as Culture*. New York: Routledge.

Carpentier, N. and Cammaerts, B. (2006). Hegemony, democracy, agonism and journalism: An interview with Chantal Mouffe. *Journalism Studies* 7(6): 964–975.

Carpentier. N. (2011). *Media and Participation: A Site of Ideological-Democratic Struggle*. Chicago, IL: University of Chicago Press.

Carter, C., Messenger Davies, M., Allan, S., Mendes, M., Milani, R., and Wass, L. *What Do Children Want from the BBC?* A report of Children's Content and Participatory Environments in an Age of Citizen Media. Cardiff School of Journalism, Media and Cultural Studies, 2009.

Castells, M. (2012). *Networks of Outrage and Hope: Social Movements in the Internet Age*. Cambridge: Polity.

Caumont, A. (2013, October 16). Twelve Trends Shaping Digital News. Pew Research Center FacTank. Available at: www.pewresearch.org/fact-tank/2013/10/16/12-trends-shaping-digital-news/

Chadwick, A. (2013). *The Hybrid Media System: Politics and Power*. Oxford Studies in Digital Politics. New York: Oxford University Press.

Chea, P. and Robins, B. (Eds.). (1998). *Cosmopolitics: Thinking and Feeling beyond the Nation*. Minneapolis, MO: University of Minnesota Press.

Checkoway, B. and Gutierrez, L. (2006). Introduction: Youth participation and community change. In B. Checkoway and L. Gutierrez (Eds.). *Youth Participation and Community Change*, pp. 1–9. Binghamton, NY: Haworth Press.

Chouliaraki, L. (2013). Re-mediation, inter-mediation, trans-mediation. *Journalism Studies* 14(2): 267–283.

Chouliaraki, L. (2013). *The Ironic Spectator: Solidarity in the Age of Post Humanitarianism.* London: Polity.

The Center for Information and Research on Learning and Engagement. (November 9, 2016). 2016 Election Center. General Election Analysis: Young Voters in the 2016 General Elections. Available at: http://civicyouth.org/ quick-facts/2016-election-center/

Clark, L. S. (2011a). Exploring religion and mediatization through a case study of J + K's big day: A response to Stig Hjarvard. *Culture and Religion: An Interdisciplinary Journal* 12:(2):167–184.doi:10.1080/14755610.2011.579717

Clark, L. S. (2011b). Religion and authority in a remix culture: How a late night TV host became an authority on religion. In G. Lynch, J. Mitchell, and A. Strhan (Eds.). *Religion, Media, and Culture: A Reader*, pp. 111–121. London: Routledge.

Clark, L. S. (2013). *The Parent App: Understanding Families in a Digital Age.* New York: Oxford University Press.

Clark, L. S. (2015). Padres y Jovenes Unidos: Student empowerment through critical media literacy. *The Civic Media Project.* Cambridge, MA: MIT Press. Available at: http://civicmediaproject.org/works/civic-media-project/padres-y-jovenes-unidos. Retrieved June 28, 2016.

Clark, L. S. (2016). Media ecology. In K. B. Jensen, R. T. Craig, J. Pooley, and E. W. Rothenbuhler (Eds.). *International Encyclopedia of Communication Theory and Philosophy.* New York: Wiley.

Clark, L. S. (2016). Participants on the margins: #Blacklivesmatter and the role that shared artifacts of engagement played among minoritized political newcomers on Snapchat, Facebook, and Twitter. *International Journal of Communication* 10: 235–253.

Clark, L. S. and Monserrate, R. (2011). High school journalism and the making of young citizens. *Journalism: Theory, Practice, Criticism* 12(4): 417–432.

Clifford, J. (1997). *Routes: Travel and Translation in the Late Twentieth Century.* Cambridge, MA: Harvard University Press.

Coeckelbergh, M. (2007). Violent computer games, empathy, and cosmopolitanism. *Ethics and Information Technology* 9(3): 219–231.

Cohen, C., Kahne, J., Bowyer, B., Middaugh, E., and Rogowski, J. (2012). *Participatory Politics: New Media and Youth Political Action.* Chicago, IL: MacArthur Foundation.

Collins, P.H. (1990/2000). *Black Feminist Thought: Knowledge, Consciousness, and the Politics of Empowerment.* London: Psychology Press.

Cooren, F. (2000). *The Organizing Property of Communication.* Amsterdam: John Benjamins Publishing Company.

Cooren, F., Kuhn, T., Cornelissen, J., and Clark, T. (2011). Communication, organizing and organization: An overview and introduction to the special issue. *Organization Studies* 32(9): 1149–1170.

Corey, C. (2014, October 24). With Ferguson Protests, 20-Somethings Become First-Time Activists. National Public Radio. Available at: www.npr.org/2014/10/24/ 358054785/with-ferguson-protests-20-somethings-become-first-time-activists

Costanza-Chock, S. (2012). *Youth and Social Movements: Key Lessons for Allies.* Report of the Kinder and Braver World Project: Research Series (danah boyd, John Palfrey, and Dena Sacco, eds.), http://cyber.law.harvard.edu/sites/ cyber.law.harvard.edu/files/KBWYouthandSocialMovements2012_0.pdf

Costanza-Chock, S. (2014). *Out of the Shadows, Into the Streets! Transmedia Organizing and the Immigrant Rights Movement.* Cambridge, MA: MIT Press.

Couldry, N. (2010a). *Why Voice Matters: Culture and Politics after Neoliberalism.* London: Sage.

Couldry, N. (2010b). *Media, Society, World: Social Theory and Digital Media Practice.* New York: Polity.

Couldry, N. (2007). Bourdieu and the media: The promises and limits of field theory. *Theory and Society* 36: 209.

Crawford, K. (2009). Following you: Disciplines of listening in social media. *Continuum: Journal of Media & Cultural Studies* 23(4): 525–535.

Crenshaw, K. (1989). Intersectionality: The Double Bind of Race and Gender. *Perspectives Magazine*, 2004, p. 2. See also Patricia Hill, C. (1990/2000). *Black Feminist Thought: Knowledge, Consciousness, and the Politics of Empowerment.* London: Psychology Press.

Dahl, I. and Newkirk, C. (2010). Understanding news literacy: A youth perspective. *Youth Media Reporter* 3: 48–50.

Dahlgren, P. (2005). The Internet, public spheres, and political communication: Dispersion and deliberation. *Political Communication*, 22(2): 147–162.

Dahlgren, P. (2009). *Media and Political Engagement: Citizens, Communication and Democracy.* Cambridge: Cambridge University Press.

Dahlgren, P. (2014, May 1–3). Professional and citizen journalism: Tensions and complements. In J. Alexander et al. (Eds.). *The Crisis of Journalism Reconsidered: Cultural Power*, Barcelona: Social Trends Institute. Available at: www.socialtrendsinstitute.org/experts/experts-meetings/culture-lifestyles/ the-crisis-of-journalism-reconsidered-cultural-power

Dalton, R. (2009). *The Good Citizen: How a Younger Generation Is Reshaping American Politics.* Washington, DC: CQ Press.

Daud, R. and Carruthers, C. (2008). Outcome study of an after-school program for youth in a high-risk environment. *Journal of Parks and Recreation Administration* 26(2): 95–114.

D'Amato, P. (2015, February 22). Non-Profit Worker Who Provoked Fury with Disrespectful Arlington Photo Tells How She Lost Her Job, Can't Date and Now Lives In Fear. *The Daily Mail.* Available at: www.dailymail.co.uk/ news/article-2964489/I-really-obsessed-reading-Woman-fired-photo-giving-middle-finger-Arlington-National-Cemetery-says-finally-Google-without-fear.html Retrieved August 29, 2016.

Darnton, R. (1975) *Writing News and Telling Stories.* Cambridge, MA: MIT Press.

Davis, C. (2014). *Beyond the White Negro: Empathy and Anti-racist Reading.* Chicago, IL: University of Illinois Press.

de Block, L. and Buckingham, D. (2007). *Global Children, Global Media: Migration, Media, and Childhood.* New York: Palgrave.

Debord, G. and Knabb, K. (2003). *Complete Cinematic Works: Scripts, Stills, Documents.* New York: AK Press.

Deetz, S. (2008). Resistance: Would struggle by any other name be as sweet? *Management Communication Quarterly* 21: 387–392.

de Finney, S., Dean, M., Loiselle, E., and Saraceno, J. (2011). "All children are equal, but some are more equal than others": Minoritization, structural inequalities and social justice praxis in residential care. *International Journal of Child, Youth and Family Studies* 3 and 4: 361–384.

Delli Carpini, M. and Keeter, S. (1996). *What Americans Know about Politics and Why it Matters*. New Haven, CT: Yale University Press.

Dennis, J. (2007). Prior Review in the High School Newspaper: Perceptions, Practices and Effects. Masters Degree Thesis. Athens, GA: University of Georgia.

Derlega, V. J., and Grzelak, J. (1979). Appropriateness of self-disclosure. In G. J. Chelune (Ed.). *Self-Disclosure: Origins, Patterns, and Implications of Openness in Interpersonal Relationships*, pp. 151–176. San Francisco, CA: Jossey-Bass.

DeSilver, D. (2013). US Income Inequality, on Rise for Decades, Is Now Highest since 1928. Pew Research Center. www.pewresearch.org/fact-tank/2013/12/05/u-s-income-inequality-on-rise-for-decades-is-now-highest-since-1928/

Deuze, M. (2003). The web and its journalisms: Considering the consequences of different types of news media online. *New Media & Society* 5(2): 203–230.

Dewey, J. (1927) *The Public and Its Problems*. New York: Holt Publishers.

Dobelli, R. (2013, April, 12). News Is Bad for You – and Giving Up Reading It Will Make You Happier. *The Guardian*. Available at: www.theguardian.com/media/2013/apr/12/news-is-bad-rolf-dobelli

Dobson, A. (2006). Thick Cosmopolitanism. *Political Studies* 54(1): 165–184. Available at: http://onlinelibrary.wiley.com/doi/10.1111/j.1467-9248.2006.00571.x/full#b15/.

Doctor, K. (2015, July 28). The Halving of America's Newsrooms. NiemanLab. Available at: www.niemanlab.org/2015/07/newsonomics-the-halving-of-americas-daily-newsrooms/

Dorfman, L. and Schiraldi, V. (2001). Off Balance: Youth, Race, and Crime in the News, Executive Summary. Available at: http://jjpl.org/Publications_JJ_InTheNews/JuvenileJusticeSpecialReports/BBY/media/media.html

Doss, E. (Ed.). (2001). *Looking at Life Magazine*. Washington, DC: Smithsonian.

Downie, L., and Kaiser, R. G. (2003). *The News about the News: American Journalism in Peril*. New York: Vintage.

Downing, J. and Fenton, N. (2003). New media, counterpublicity and the public sphere. *New Media & Society* 5(2), 185–202.

Dunbar-Hester, C. (2014). *Low Power to the People: Pirates, Protest and Politics in FM Radio Activism*. Cambridge, MA: MIT Press.

Dvorak, J. (1998). *Status of Journalism and News Media in the Nation's Secondary Schools*. High School Journalism Institute, Indiana University. Available at: http://journalism.indiana.edu/programs/hsji/high-school-research/status-of-journalism-and-news-media-in-the-nations-secondary-schools/. Accessed January 8, 2010.

Dvorak, J. 2008. *High School Journalism Matters*, pp. 1–19. Arlington, VA: Newspaper Association of America. Available at: www.naafoundation .org/Research/Foundation/Student-Journalism/High-School-Journalism-Matters.aspx. Retrieved October 5, 2010.

Earl, J. and Kimport, K. (2011). *Digitally Enabled Social Change: Activism in the Internet Age.* Cambridge, MA: MIT Press.

Eckert, S. and Chadha, K. (2013). Muslim bloggers in Germany: An emerging counterpublic. *Media, Culture & Society* 35(8): 926–942.

Edgerly, S. (2015). Making sense and drawing lines: Young adults and the mixing of news and entertainment. *Journalism Studies* 1–18. doi: 10.1080/1461670X.2015.1100522

Erskine, T. (2002) "Citizen of nowhere" or "the point where circles intersect"? Impartialist and embedded cosmopolitanisms. *Review of International Studies* 28(3): 457–478.

Ekstrom, M. and Ostman, J. (2015). Information, interaction, and creative production: The effects of three forms of internet use on youth democratic engagement. *Communication Research* 42(6): 796–818.

Ellison, N., Steinfield, C., and Lampe, C. (2011). Connection strategies: Social capital and implications of Facebook-enabled communication practices. *New Media & Society* 3(6): 873–892.

Entman, R. (1992). Blacks in the news: Television, modern racism, and cultural change. *Journalism Quarterly* 69: 341–361.

Entman, R. and Rojecki, A. (2000). *The Black Image in the White Mind: Media and Race in America.* Chicago, IL: University of Chicago Press.

Faber, D. and Krieg, E. (2005). Unequal Exposure to Ecological Hazards: A Report by the Philanthropy and Environmental Justice Research Project of Northeastern University. Boston, MA. Available at: www.northeastern.edu/nejrc/wp-content/uploads/Final-Unequal-Exposure-Report-2005-10-12-05.pdf. Retrieved August 24, 2016.

Farrell, J. and Rabin, M. (1996). Cheap talk. *Journal of Economic Perspectives* 10(3): 103–118.

Feldman, L. (2007). The news about comedy: Young audiences, *The Daily Show*, and evolving notions of journalism. *Journalism: Theory, Practice, & Criticism* 8(4): 359–380.

Felman, S. and Laub, D. (1992). *Testimony: Crises of Witnessing in Literature, Psychoanalysis, and History.* New York: Taylor & Francis.

Fiegerman, S. (2014, June 27). World Cup Highlights Difference between "Real Time" on Facebook, Twitter. *Mashable.* Available at: http://mashable.com/2014/06/27/facebook-twitter-world-cup/

Fiore, M. (2002). Trampling the "marketplace of ideas": The case against extending Hazelwood to college campuses. *University of Pennsylvania Law Review* 150(6): 1915–1968.

Fischer, C. (1992) *America Calling: A Social History of the Telephone to 1940.* Berkeley, CA: University of California Press.

Fisherkeller, J. (2011). Introduction. In J. Fisherkeller (Ed.). *International Perspectives on Youth Media.* New York: Peter Lang.

Flaxman, J., Goel, S., and Rao, J. (2016). Filter bubbles, echo chambers and online news consumption. *Public Opinion Quarterly* 80: 298–320.

Foreman, M. (2005). Straight outta Mogadishu, in S. Maira and E. Soep (Eds.). *Youthscapes: The Popular, The National The Global*, pp. 3–22. Philadelphia, PA: University of Pennsylvania Press.

Forrest, C. (2014, August 28). Diversity Stats: Ten Tech Companies That Have Come Clean. *Tech Republic*. www.techrepublic.com/article/diversity-stats-10-tech-companies-that-have-come-clean/

Fox, J., Koloen, G., and Sahin, V. (2007). No joke: A comparison of substance in *The Daily Show with Jon Stewart* and broadcast network television coverage of the 2004 presidential election campaign. *Journal of Broadcasting and Electronic Media*. 51(2): 213–227.

Fraser, N. (1992). Rethinking the public sphere: A contribution to the critique of actually existing democracy. In Craig Calhoun (Ed.). *Habermas and the Public Sphere*, pp. 122–133. Cambridge, MA: MIT Press.

Fraser, N. and Gordon, L. (1994). Civil citizenship against social citizenship? On the ideology of contract-versus-charity. In B. Van Steenbergen (Ed.). *The Condition of Citizenship*, pp. 98–101. London: Sage.

Friedman, M. (1996). *Martin Buber and the Human Sciences*. New York: SUNY Press.

Freedom Forum. (1994). *Death by Cheeseburger: High School Journalism in the 1990s and Beyond*. Arlington, VA: The Freedom Forum.

Freeland, C. (2013). *Plutocrats: The Rise of the New Global Super-Rich and the Fall of Everyone Else*. New York: Penguin Books.

Frola, L. (2011). Tracking the Teenage Path to News. Available at: www.poynter.org/uncategorized/78339/tracking-the-teenage-path-to-news/

Funt, D. (2016, August 12). A Compulsive Audience and a Complicit Media. *Columbia Journalism Review*. Available at: www.cjr.org/special_report/news_media_health_screens_brain_cost_business.php Retrieved August 16, 2016.

Gamson, W. (1992). *Talking Politics*. New York: Cambridge University Press.

Garcia, N. (2016, May 24). Controversial Douglas County Superintendent to Lead Texas School District. *Chalkbeat Colorado*. Available at: www.chalkbeat.org/posts/co/2016/05/24/controversial-douglas-county-superintendent-to-lead-texas-school-district/#.V1iW_JMrL-Y. Retrieved June 8, 2016.

Gates, H. L. (1983). The blackness of Blackness: A critique of the sign and the signifying monkey. *Critical Inquiry* 9(4): 685–723.

Gamson, W. (1992). *Talking Politics*. Cambridge: Cambridge University Press.

Gauntlett, D. (2011). *Making Is Connecting: The Social Meaning of Creativity, from DIY and Knitting to YouTube and Web 2.0*. Cambridge: Polity Press.

Gerbaudo, P. (2012). *Tweets and the Streets: Social Media and Contemporary Activism*. London: Pluto Press.

Gershon, I. (2010). *The Breakup 2.0: Disconnecting over New Media*. Ithaca, NY: Cornell University Press.

Gerson, D., Chen, N-T., Ball-Rokeach, S., and Parks, M. (2015). Website to Weibo: Activing the local communication network and civic engagement in a diverse city. *The Civic Media Project*. Cambridge, MA: MIT Press.

Gillmor, D. 2006. *We the Media*: Sebastopol, CA: O'Reilly Media, Inc.

Ginwright, S., Noguera, P., and Cammarota, J. (Eds.). (2006). *Beyond Resistance! Youth Activism and Community Change: New Democratic Possibilities for Practice and Policy for America's Youth*. New York: Routledge.

Giroux, H. (1996). *Fugitive Cultures: Race, Violence, and Youth.* New York: Routledge.

Giroux, H. (2010). *Zombie Politics and Culture in the Age of Casino Capitalism.* New York: Peter Lang.

Gonzalez, J. and Torres, J. (2010). *News for All the People: The Epic Story of Race and the American Media.* New York: Verso.

Goodluck, N. and Thompson, G. (1987). The use of educational radio in developing countries: Lessons from the past. *International Journal of E-Learning & Distance Education* 2(2): 43–54.

Goodman, S. (2003). *Teaching Youth Media: A Critical Guide to Literacy, Video Production, and Social Change.* New York: Teachers College Press.

Gordon, H. (2009). *We Fight to Win: Inequality and the Politics of Youth Activism.* New Brunswick, NJ: Rutgers University Press.

Gordon, H. and Taft, J. (2011). Rethinking youth political socialization: Teenage activists talk back. *Youth & Society* 43(4): 1499–1527.

Gottfried, J. and Shearer, E. (2016, May 26). News Use across Social Media Platforms. Report of the Pew Research Center. Available at: www.journalism.org/2016/05/26/news-use-across-social-media-platforms-2016/. Retrieved June 24, 2016.

Gottfried, J. and Shearer, E. and Barthel, M., and Shearer, E. (2016). Changing a Social Media Profile Picture Is One Way To Express Support or Solidarity. FactTank: News in the Numbers. A Report of the Pew Research Center. Available at: www.pewresearch.org/fact-tank/2016/03/28/changing-a-social-media-profile-picture-is-one-way-to-express-support-or-solidarity/ Retrieved June 24, 2016.

Graca, L. (2016, June). South Students Now Commuting Longer. *The Washington Park Profile.* Available at: http://washparkprofile.com/washington-park-profile-news/south-students-now-commuting-longer/. Retrieved June 28, 2016.

Granovetter. M. (1973) The strength of weak ties. *American Journal of Sociology* 78(6): 1360–1380.

Gray, L., Thomas, N.T., and Lewis, L. (2010). *Teachers' Use of Educational Technology in US Public Schools: 2009 (NCES No. 2010040).* Washington, DC: National Center for Education Statistics.

Gray, M. (2009) *Out in the Country: Youth, Media, and Queer Visibility in Rural America.* New York: New York University Press.

Greco-Larsen, S. (2006). *Media and Minorities: The Politics of Race in News and Entertainment.* New York: Rowman & Littlefield.

Greenberg, Bradley S. J. E. Brand (1993). Television news and advertising in schools: The Channel One controversy. *Journal of Communication* 43(1): 143–151.

Grier, T. (2010). Most Print and Online Journalists Use Social Media for Story Research. Poynter Institute for Media Studies. Available at: www.poynter.org/2010/most-print-and-online-journalists-use-social-media-for-story-research/100373/

Griffin, C. (2005). Challenging assumptions about youth political participation: Critical insights from Great Britain. In J. Forbrig (Ed.). *Revisiting Youth Political Participation: Challenges for Research and Democratic Practice in Europe*, pp. 145–154. Strasborg: Council of Europe.

Grossberg, L. (2005). *Caught in the Crossfire: Kids, Politics and America's Future.* Boulder, CO: Paradigm Publishers.

Gyldensted, C. (2011). Innovating news journalism through positive psychology. University of Pennsylvania Scholarly Commons. Available at: http://repository.upenn.edu/mapp_capstone/20/

Habermas, J. (1981). *The Theory of Communicative Action, Volume 1: Reason and the Rationalization of Society.* Boston, MA: Beacon Press.

Habermas, J. (1989). *The Structural Transformation of the Public Sphere.* Trans. T. Burger and F. Lawrence. Cambridge, MA: MIT Press.

Habermas, J. (1996). *Between Facts and Norms: Contributions to a Discourse Theory of Law and Democracy.* Cambridge, MA: MIT Press.

Hallin, D. (2000). Commercialism and professionalism in the American news media. *Mass Media and Society* 3: 243–262.

Hallin, D. (2005). Commercialization and professionalization in the American news media. In James Curran and Michael Gurevitch, eds., *Mass Media and Society*, pp. 218–235. London: Arnold.

Hampton, K., Rainie, L., Lu, W., Dwyer, M., Shin, I., and Purcell, K. (2014). Social Media and the "Spiral of Silence." Report of the Pew Research Center, Internet, Science, and Tech category. Available at: www.pewinternet.org/2014/08/26/social-media-and-the-spiral-of-silence/. Retrieved June 9, 2016.

Harrington, S. (2005). The democracy of conversation: The panel and the public sphere. *Media International Australia* 116: 75–87.

Harrington, S. (2008a). Future-proofing journalism: Youthful tastes and the challenge for the Academy. *Continuum: Journal of Media & Cultural Studies* 22: 395–407.

Harrington, S. (2008b). Popular news in the 21st century: Time for a critical approach? *Journalism; Theory, Practice and Criticism* 9: 266–284.

Harris, A. (2001). Dodging and waving: Young women countering the stories of youth and citizenship. *International Journal of Critical Psychology* 4(2): 183–199.

Harrison, T. M. and Barthel, B. (2009). Wielding new media in web 2.0: Exploring the history of engagement with the collaborative construction of media products. *New Media & Society* 11: 155–178.

Hava, G., and Taft, J. (2011). Rethinking youth political socialization: Teenage activists talk back. *Youth & Society* 43(4): 1499–1527.

Heidegger, M. (1975). Introduction. *The Basic Problems of Phenomenology.* Bloomington, IN: Indiana University Press.

Hermida, A. (2010). Twittering the news: The emergence of ambient journalism. *Journalism Practice* 4(3): 297–508.

Hermida, A. (2012). Social journalism: Exploring how social media is shaping journalism. In E. Siapera and A. Veglis (Eds.), *The Handbook of Global Online Journalism*, pp. 309–328. Wiley-Blackwell: Oxford.

Herring, S. (2004). Computer-mediated communication and woman's place. In M. Bucholtz, (Ed.). *Language and Women's Place: Text and Commentaries*, pp. 216–222. New York: Oxford University Press.

Herr Stephenson, B., Rhoten, D., Perkel, D., and Sims, C. (2011). *Digital Media and Technology in After School Programs, Libraries, and Museums.* MacArthur

Foundation Report. Available at: https://mitpress.mit.edu/sites/default/files/ titles/free_download/9780262515764_Digital_Media_and_Technology_in_ Afterschool_Programs.pdf

Herrmann, J. (2016, August 28). Inside Facebook's (Totally Insane, Unintentionally Gigantic, Hyperpartisan) Political-Media Machine. *New York Times*. Available at: www.nytimes.com/2016/08/28/magazine/inside-facebooks-totally-insane-unintentionally-gigantic-hyperpartisan-political-media-machine.html?emc=edit_th_20160828&nl=todaysheadlines&nlid= 51992941&_r=0 Retrieved August 28, 2016.

Herzog, A. (2015) Levinas on the social: Guilt and the city. *Theory, Culture & Society* 32(4): 27–43.

Hiltz, S. R. and Turoff, M. (1978) *The Network Nation: Human Communication via Computer*. Reading, MA: Addison-Wesley.

Hirst, M. and Treadwell, G. (2011). Blogs bother me: Social media, journalism students, and the curriculum. *Journalism Practice* 5(4): 446–461.

Hirzalla, F. and Van Zoonen, L. (2011). Beyond the online/offline divide: How youth's online and offline civic activities converge. *Social Science Computer Review* 29(4): 481–498.

Hjarvard, S. (2013). *The Mediatization of Society*. London: Routledge.

Ho, S. (2008). Social-psychological influences on opinion expression in face-to-face and computer-mediated communication. *Communication Research* 35(2): 190–207.

Hobbs, R. (1998). Building citizenship skills through media literacy education. In M. Salvador and P. Sias (Eds). *The Public Voice in a Democracy at Risk*, pp. 57–75. Westport, CT: Praeger Publishers.

Hobbs, R. (1999). The Seven Great Debates in the Media Literacy Movement. Opinion Papers. Published by the US Department of Education, Educational Resources Information Center (ERIC), p. 3.

Hobbs, R. (2010). Digital and Media Literacy: A Plan of Action. Aspen Institute. Available at: www.knightcomm.org/digital-and-media-literacy/

Hobbs, R. and Donnelly, K., Friesem, J., and Moen, M. (2013). Learning to engage: How positive attitudes about the news, media literacy, and video production contribute to adolescent civic engagement. *Educational Media International* 50 (4): 231–246.

Höijer, B. (2004). The discourse of global compassion: The audience and media reporting of human suffering. *Media, Culture & Society* 26(4): 513–531.

Holt, T. (1995). Afterword: Mapping the black public sphere. In Black Public Sphere Collective (Eds.). *The Black Public Sphere*, pp. 325–328. Chicago, IL: University of Chicago Press.

Howard, P. and Hussain, M. (2013). *Democracy's Fourth Wave? Digital Media and the Arab Spring*. Oxford Series in Digital Politics. New York: Oxford University Press.

Howley, K. (2005). *Community Media: People, Places and Communication Technologies*. Cambridge: Cambridge University Press.

Hu, W. (2013, May 27). At School Papers, the Ink is Drying Up. *The New York Times*. www.nytimes.com/2013/05/28/nyregion/at-school-papers-the-ink-is-drying-up.html

Hughes, T. (2014, December 3). Cop Critically Hurt at Ferguson Protest in Denver. *USA Today*. Available at: www.usatoday.com/story/news/nation/2014/12/03/denver-high-school-walkout-protest-dont-shoot/19846479/

Hutchby, I. (2001). Technologies, texts and affordances. *Sociology* 35(2): 441–456.

Iacovetti, C. (2016, January 25). *Spotlight*: The Burden of Truth. Creative Screenwriting. Available at: http://creativescreenwriting.com/spotlight-the-burden-of-truth/. Retrieved June 28, 2016.

Ingram, M. (2016, August 16). Facebook Traffic to U.S. News Sites Has Fallen by Double Digits, Report Says. *Fortune*. Available at: http://fortune.com/2016/08/16/facebook-traffic-media/ Retrieved August 17, 2016.

Isaac, M. (2014, August 10). 50 Million Reasons Buzzfeed Wants to Take Its Content Far beyond Lists. *New York Times*. Available at: www.nytimes.com/2014/08/11/technology/a-move-to-go-beyond-lists-for-content-at-buzzfeed.html Retrieved August 20, 2016.

Ito, M. et al. (2010), *Hanging Out, Messing Around, and Geeking Out: Kids Living and Learning with New Media*. The John D. and Catherine T. MacArthur Foundation Series on Digital Media and Learning. Cambridge, MA: MIT Press.

Jackson, M. H. (2009). The mash-up: a new archetype for communication. *Journal of Computer-Mediated Communication*, 14(3): 730–734.

Jamieson, K. H. (2015). *The Challenges Facing Civic Education*, pp. 1–13. New York: The American Academy of Arts and Science.

Jasper, J. M. and Poulsen, J. (1995). Recruiting strangers and friends: Moral shocks and social networks in animal rights and anti-nuclear protests. *Social Problems* 42: 493–512.

Jenkins, C. D. (2006). *Convergence Culture: Where Old and New Media Collide*. New York: New York University Press.

Jenkins, C. D. and Padgett, D. R. G. (2012). Race and objectivity: Toward a critical approach to news consumption. In P. C. Campbell, K. M. LeDuff, C. D. Jenkins, and R. A. Brown (Eds.). *Race and News: Critical Perspectives*, pp. 232–251. New York: Routledge.

Jenkins, C. D., Padgett, D. R. G., Jenkins, H. Clinton, K., Purushotma, R., Robison, A. J., and Weigel, M. (2006). *Confronting the Challenges of Participatory Culture: Media Education for the 21st Century*. Chicago, IL: The MacArthur Foundation. Available at: www.newmedialiteracies.org/files/working/NMLWhitePaper.pdf. Retrieved July 10, 2007.

Jenkins, C. D., Padgett, D. R. G. Jenkins, H., Clinton, K., Purushotma, R., Robison, A. J., Weigel, M. Shrestova, S., Gamber-Thompson, L., Kligler-Vilenchik, N., and Zimmerman, A. (2016). *By Any Media Necessary: The New Youth Activism*. Connected Youth and Digital Futures. New York: New York University Press.

Jimenez, J. A. and Abreu, J. M. (2003). Race and sex effects on attitudinal perceptions of acquaintance rape. *Counseling Psychology* 50(2): 252–256.

Jones, J. P. (2013). Toward a new vocabulary for political communication research: A response to Michael Delli Carpini. *International Journal of Communication* 7: 510–530.

Juris, J. (2012). Reflections on #Occupy Everywhere: social media, public space and emerging logics of aggregation. *American Ethnologist* 39: 259–279.

Kafai, Y. and Peppler, K. (2011). Youth, technology and DYI: Developing participatory competencies in creative media production. *Review of Research in Education* 35(1): 89–119.

Kahne, J, and Middaugh, E. (2011). Youth online activity and exposure to diverse perspectives. *New Media & Society* 14(3): 492–512. doi: 10.1177/1461444811420271

Kahne, J, Lee, N., and Feezell, J. (2012). The civic and political significance of online participatory cultures and youth transitioning to adulthood. *Journal of Information Technology and Politics* 10(1): 1–20.

Kahne, J., Middaugh, E., and Allen, D. (2014). Youth, new media, and the rise of participatory politics. In D. Allen and J. Light (Eds.), *From Voice to Influence: Understanding Citizenship in the Digital Age*, pp. 35–58. Chicago, IL: University of Chicago Press.

Katz, V. (2010). How children of immigrants use media to connect their families to the community. *Journal of Children and Media.* 4(3): 298–315. doi:10.1080/17482798.2010.486136

Katz, V. and Ang, A., and Suro, R. (2012). An ecological perspective on U.S. Latinos' health communication behaviors, access, and outcomes. *Hispanic Journal of Behavioral Sciences* 34(3): 437–456. doi: 10.1177/0739986312445566

Kelley, P. (2015, June 15). Nearly Half of African-American Women Know Someone in Prison. *University of Washington Today.* Available at: www.washington.edu/news/2015/06/11/nearly-half-of-african-american-women-know-someone-in-prison/ Retrieved August 30, 2016.

Kellner, D. and Share, J. (2005). Toward critical media literacy: Core concepts, debates, organizations, and policy. *Discourse: Studies in the Cultural Politics of Education* 26(3): 369–386.

Kelly, J. (2009). Red Kayaks and Hidden Gold: The Rise, Challenges and Value of Citizen Journalism. Report of the Reuters Institute for the Study of Journalism. Available at: www.slideshare.net/victori98pt/the-rise-challenges-and-value-of-citizen-journalism

Kelso, T. and Cogan, B. Introduction: At the intersection of politics and popular culture: Over two hundred years of great entertainment. In T. Kelso and B. Cogan (Eds.). *Mosh the Polls: Youth Voters, Popular Culture, and Democratic Engagement*, pp. 1–20. New York: Lexington Books.

Khamis, S. and Vaughn, K. (2011). Cyberactivism in the Egyptian revolution: How civic engagement and citizen journalism tilted the balance. *Arab Media & Society* 14. Available at: www.arabmediasociety.com/countries/index.php?c_article=249

Kim, Y-C. and Ball-Rokeach, S. (2006). Civic engagement from a communication infrastructure perspective. *Communication Theory* 16(2): 176–197.

King, L. and Stovall, D. (1992). *Classroom Publishing: A Practical Guide to Enhancing Student Literacy.* Hillsboro: OR: Blue Herron Publishing, Inc.

Kinnick, K. N., Krugman, D. M., and Cameron, G. T. (1996). Compassion fatigue: Communication and burnout toward social problems. *Journalism and Mass Communications Quarterly* 73(3): 687–707.

Kirshner, B. (2015). *Youth Activism in an Era of Education Inequality.* Qualitative Studies in Psychology. New York: New York University Press.

Klandermans, B. and Oegema, D. (1987). Potentials, networks, motivations and barriers: Steps towards participation in social movements. *American Sociological Review* 52: 519–531.

Klein, R. (2014, December 1). High School Students around the Country Are Walking Out of Class for Ferguson. *Huffington Post.* Available at: www .huffingtonpost.com/2014/12/01/high-school-students-protest-ferguson_n_ 6249802.html

Kowalski, Allison. (2016, May 13). No Laughing Matter: College Comedy Papers Struggle with "Political Correctness." Student Press Law Center. Available at: www.splc.org/article/2016/05/no-laughing-matter Retrieved May 15, 2016.

Kram, Z. (2014, December 8). A Mass of Voices: An Oral History of Student Involvement in Protests. *Student Life* (online independent newspaper of Washington University in St. Louis), www.studlife.com/scene/2014/12/08/a-mass-of-voices-an-oral-history-of-student-involvement-in-ferguson-protests/

Kramer, K. and Mechthild, G. (2003). *Martin Buber's I and Thou: Practicing Living Dialogue.* Mahwah, NJ: Paulist Press.

Kuchler, H. and Garrahan, M. (2016). Does Facebook Bend the Trends that Govern Our News? *Financial Times.* May 13, 2016. Available at: https:// next.ft.com/content/5c68e88e-18e6-11e6-bb7d-ee563a5a1cc1

Laclau, E. and Mouffe, C. (1985). *Hegemony and Socialist Strategy: Towards a Radical Democratic Politics.* London: Verso.

Langlois, G., Greg, E., McKelvey, F., and Devereaux, Z. (2009). Networked publics: The double articulation of ode and politics on Facebook. *Canadian Journal of Communication* 34(3): 415–434.

Leming, J., Ellington, L., and Porter, K. (Eds.). (2003). *Where Did Social Studies Go Wrong?* Washington, DC: Thomas B. Fordham Foundation. Available at: www.edexcellence.net/publications/wheredidssgowrong.html.

Leung, D. K. and Lee, F. L. (2014). Cultivating an active online counterpublic: Examining the impact of Internet alternative media. *International Journal of Press/Politics* 19(3): 340–359.

Leverette, M. (2008). Just don't bother to vote or die, bitch!' A giant douche, a turd sandwich, hard core puppet sex, and the reinvention of political (un)involvement. In T. Kelso and B. Cogan (Eds.). *Mosh the Polls: Youth Voters, Popular Culture, and Democratic Engagement,* pp. 205–238. New York: Lexington Books.

Levin, D. (2011). "Because it's not really me": Students' films and their potential as alternative media. In J. Fisherkeller (Ed.). *International Perspectives on Youth Media,* pp. 138–154. New York: Peter Lang.

Levinas, E. 1979. *Totality and Infinity: An Essay on Exteriority.* Trans. Alphonso Lingis. The Hague: Martinus Nijhoff Publishers and Duquesne University Press.

(1984) Paix et proximité. Les cahiers de la nuit surveillée 3 Lagrasse: Verdier. Trans. P. Atterton and S. Critchley. Peace and proximity. In A. T. Peperzak, S. Critchley, and R. Bernasconi (Eds.). *Emmanuel Levinas: Basic Philosophical Writings,* Bloomington, IN: Indiana University Press, 1996, p. 168. Translation modified in A. Herzog (2015).

Levine, P. (2005). Creative use of the new media. In R. Lonnie, R. K. Sherrod, and C. Flanagan (Eds.). *Youth Activism: An International Encyclopedia*. Westport, CT: Greenwood.

Levine, P. (2007). A public voice for youth: The audience problem in digital media and civic education. In L. Benett (Ed.). *Civic Life Online: Learning How Digital Media Can Engage Youth*, pp. 119–138. The John D. and Katherine T. Macarthur Foundation Series on Digital Media and Learning. Cambridge, MA: MIT Press.

Lichterman, J. (2015). More Americans Are Getting News on Facebook and Twitter. NiemanLab. Nieman Foundation at Harvard. Available at: www .niemanlab.org/2015/07/new-pew-data-more-americans-are-getting-news-on-facebook-and-twitter/

Lieberg, M. (1995). Teenagers and public space. *Communication Research* 22(6): 720–744.

Lievrouw, L. (2011). *Alternative and Activist New Media*. London: Polity.

Lim, S., Nekmat E., and Vadrevu, S. (2011). Singapore's experience in fostering youth media production: The implications of state-led school and public education initiatives. In J. Fisherkeller (Ed.). *International Perspectives on Youth Media*, pp. 84–102. New York: Peter Lang.

Lin, W-Y., Song, H., and Ball-Rokeach, S. (2010). Localizing the global: Exploring transnational ties that bind in new immigrant communities. *Journal of Communication* 60(2): 205–229.

Linklater, R. Cosmopolitanism. In A. Dobson and R. Eckersley (Eds.). *Political Theory and the Ecological Challenge*. Cambridge: Cambridge University Press.

Lipietz, A. (1992). *Towards a New Economic Order: Postfordism, Ecology and Democracy*. Trans. M. Slater. London: Oxford University Press.

Lipietz, R. (1987) Rebel sons: The Regulation School. Entretien avec Jean Jane Jenson, *French Politics and Society* 5(4), 17–26. Harvard University (art 750).

Lippmann, W. (1922). *Public Opinion*. New York: Free Press.

Litt, E. and Hargittai, E. (2016). The imagined audience on social network sites. *Social Media + Society* 2(1), doi: 10.1177/2056305116633482

Livingstone, S. (2002). *Young People and New Media*. London: Sage.

Livingstone, S. (2003). The changing nature of audiences: From the mass audience to the interactive media user. In A. Valdivia (Ed.). *A Companion to Media Studies*, pp. 337–359. Oxford: Blackwell.

Livingstone, S. (2013). The participation paradigm in audience research. *Communication Review* 16: 21–30.

Livingstone, S. (2015). Children's digital rights. *InterMEDIA* 42(4/5): 20–24.

Livinston, G. (2014, December 22). Fewer than Half of U.S. Kids Today Live in "Traditional" Family. FactTank: Pew Research Center. Available at: www .pewresearch.org/fact-tank/2014/12/22/less-than-half-of-u-s-kids-today-live-in-a-traditional-family/. Retrieved June 21, 2016.

Loader, Brian. (Ed.). (2007). *Young Citizens in the Digital Age: Political Engagement, Young People and New Media*. New York: Routledge.

Lomicky, C. (2000). Analysis of high school newspaper editorials before and after *Hazelwood School District v. Kuhlmeier*: A content analysis case study. *Journal of Law and Education* 463–476.

LoMonte, F. (2016). Momentum swings towards legal protections for journalism students. *Student Press Law Center Report* 35(2): 2.

Lopez, M. H. (2003). Fact Sheet: Electoral Engagement Among Latino Youth. CIRCLE (The Center for Information and Research on Civic Learning and Engagement). College Park, MD: University of Maryland School of Public Policy.

Love, N. and Mattern, M. (2013). *Doing Democracy: Activist Art and Cultural Politics*. New York: SUNY Press.

Lowery, W. (2016, July 11). Aren't More White People than Black People Killed by Police? Yes, but No. *The Washington Post*. Available at: www.washingtonpost .com/news/post-nation/wp/2016/07/11/arent-more-white-people-than-black-people-killed-by-police-yes-but-no/?utm_term=.53230885ce9c. Retrieved date August 18, 2016.

Lunt, P. and Livingstone, S. (2016). Is "mediatization" the new paradigm for our field? A commentary on Deacon and Stanyer (2014, 2015) and Hepp, Hjarvard, and Lundby (2015). *Media, Culture and Society*. Available via LSE Research Online: http://eprints.lse.ac.uk/view/lseauthor/Livingstone,_Sonia.html

Luttrell, W. et al. (2011). Transnational childhoods and youth media: Seeing with and learning from one immigrant child's visual narrative. In J. Fisherkeller (Ed.). *International Perspectives on Youth Media*, pp. 192–208. New York: Peter Lang.

Lynch, D. (2015). Above and Beyond: Looking at the Future of Journalism Education. Knight Foundation. www.knightfoundation.org/features/journalism-education/

Lynds, J. (2016, January 14). FAA Heeds Youths' Findings to Restore Head-to-Head at Logan Airport. *East Boston Times*. Available at: www .eastietimes.com/2015/01/14/faa-heeds-youths-findings-to-restore-head-to-head-at-logan-airport/ Retrieved August 28, 2016.

(2015, October 22). Greenway Extension Nears Completion. *East Boston Times*. Available at: www.eastietimes.com/2015/10/22/greenway-extension-nears-completion/ Retrieved August 26, 2016.

MacMillan, D. (2012, March 1). The Rise of the Brogrammer. *Bloomberg News*. www.bloomberg.com/news/articles/2012-03-01/the-rise-of-the-brogrammer

Madhani, A. and Alcindor, Y. (2014, December 8). Ferguson Has Become a Springboard for Many Movements. *USA Today*. www.usatoday.com/story/news/nation/2014/12/05/ferguson-protests-broaden-occupy-wall-street/19917015/

Madianou, M. and Miller, D. (2012). Polymedia: Towards a new theory of digital media in interpersonal communication. *International Journal of Cultural Studies* 16(2): 169–187.

Mahoney, J., Parente, M.E., and Zigler, E.F. (2009). Afterschool programs in america: origins, growth, popularity, and politics. *Journal of Youth Development* 4(3): 26–44.

Maira, S. and Soep, E. (2005). Introduction. In S. Maira and E. Soep (Eds.). *Youthscapes: The Popular, the National, the Global*, loc 360 (Kindle). Philadelphia, PA: University of Pennsylvania Press.

Maira, S. (2009) *Missing: Youth, Citizenship and Empire after 9/11*. Durham, NC: Duke University Press.

Mangalindan, J. P. (2014, August 29). How Tech Companies Compare in Employee Diversity. *Fortune*. http://fortune.com/2014/08/29/how-tech-companies-compare-in-employee-diversity/

Manjoo, F. (2010, August 10). How Black People Use Twitter. *Slate*. Available at: www.slate.com/articles/technology/technology/2010/08/how_black_people_use_twitter.2.html

Marchi, R. (2009a). Z-Radio, Boston: Teen journalism, political engagement and democratizing the airwaves. *Journal of Radio & Audio Media* 16(2): 127–143. doi: 10.1080/19376529093276981

Marchi, R. (2009 b) *Day of the Dead in the USA: The Migration and Transformation of a Cultural Phenomenon*. New Brunswick, NJ: Rutgers University Press.

Marchi, R. (2011). From disillusion to engagement: Minority teen journalists and the news media. *Journalism: Theory, Practice and Criticism* 13(8):1–16.

Marchi, R. (2012). With Facebook, blogs, and fake news, teens reject journalistic "objectivity." *Journal of Communication Inquiry* 36(3): 246–262.

Marchi, R. (2016). News translators: Latino immigrant youth, social media, and citizenship training. *Journalism and Mass Communication Quarterly* 94(1): 189–212.

Martinson, D. (2008). School censorship: It comes in a variety of forms, not all of them overt. *Clearing\House* 81(5): 211–214.

Marwick, A. (2013). *Status Update: Celebrity, Publicity, and Branding in the Social Media Age*. New Haven, CT: Yale University Press.

Massey, B.L. (2010). What job advertisements tell us about demand for multiplatform reporters at legacy news outlets. *Journalism & Mass Communication Educator* 65(2): 142–155.

Matei, S., Ball-Rokeach, S., Gibbs, W., and Hoyt, E. G. (2001). Metamorphosis: A field research methodology for studying communication technology and community. *The Electronic Journal of Communication*, 11(2), www.cios.org/EJCPUBLIC/011/2/01125.HTML.

Mattern, M. (1998). *Acting in Concert: Music, Community and Political Action*. New Brunswick, NJ: Rutgers University Press.

Mattoni, A. and Trere, E. (2014). Media practices, mediation processes, and mediatization in the study of social movements. *Communication Theory* 24(1): 252–271.

Mayer, V. (2003). *Producing Dreams, Consuming Youth: Mexican Americans and Mass Media*. New Brunswick, NJ: Rutgers University Press.

McCarthy, J. and Wright, P. (2004). *Technology as Experience*. Cambridge, MA: MIT Press.

McChesney, R. (2000). *Rich Media, Poor Democracy: Communication Politics in Dubious Times*. New York: Free Press.

McChesney, R. (2004). *The Problem of the Media: US Communication Politics in the 21st Century*. New York: Monthly Review Press.

McChesney, R. and Nichols, J. (2010). *The Death and Life of American Journalism: The Media Revolution that Will Begin the World Again*. New York: Nation Books.

McDevitt, M., Kiousis, S., and Wahl-Jorgensen, K. (2003). Spiral of moderation: Opinion expression in computer-mediated discussion. *International Journal of Public Opinion Research* 15(4): 454–470.

McGhee, T. (2014). Denver Protests Spark Dialogue between Police and Students. *Denver Post.* www.denverpost.com/news/ci_27069788/denver-protests-spark-dialogue-between-police-and-students

McKain, A. (2005). Not necessarily not the news: Gatekeeping, remediation, and *The Daily Show. Journal of American Culture* 28(4): 415–430.

McKinley, M. and Jensen, L. (2003) In our own voices: Reproductive health radio programming in the Peruvian Amazon. *Critical Studies in Media Communication* 20(2): 180–203.

Meeder, B. (2012). Network Structure and Its Role in Information Diffusion and User Behavior. Ph.D. dissertation, Carnegie Mellon University.

Mercea, D. (2014). Towards a conceptualization of casual protest participation: Parsing a case from the Save Rosia Montana campaign. *East European Politics and Societies* 28(2): 386–410.

Meyrowitz, J. (1985). *No Sense of Place: The Impact of Electronic Media on Social Behavior.* Oxford: Oxford University Press.

Middaugh, E. and Kahne, J. (2009). Online localities: Implications for democracy and education. *Yearbook of the National Society for the Study of Education* 108(1): 192–218.

Middaugh, E. and Kahne, J. and Clark, L. S. (2016). Digital Media, Participatory Politics and Positive Youth Development. Working paper on Participatory Politics and Civic Development, Children and Screens. Institute of Digital Media and Child Development.

Mihaidilis, P. and Thevenin, B. (2013). Media literacy as core competency for engaged citizenship in participatory democracy. *American Behavioral Scientist* 57(11): 1611–1622.

Miller, P.R., Bobkowski, P.S., Maliniak, D., and Rapoport, R. (2015). Talking politics on Facebook: Network centrality and political discussion practice in social media. *Political Research Quarterly* 68(2): 377–391.

Milioni, D. (2009). Probing the online counterpublic sphere: The case of Indymedia Athens. *Media, Culture & Society* 31(3): 409–431.

Mills, C. W. (1956/2000). *The Power Elite.* New York: Oxford University Press.

Mindich, D. (2005). *Tuned Out – Why Americans Under 40 Don't Watch the News.* New York: Oxford University Press.

Mitchell, A., Gottfriend, J., and Matsa, K. (2015) Political Interest and Awareness Lower Among Millenials. Pew Research Center. Available at: www.journalism.org/2015/06/01/political-interest-and-awareness-lower-among-millennials/. Accessed November 30, 2016.

Moeller, S. D. (1999). *Compassion Fatigue: How the Media Sell Misery, War, and Death.* New York: Routledge.

Molnar, A. and Boninger, F. (2015). *Sold Out: How Marketing in School Threatens Children's Well-being and Undermines Their Education.* New York: Rowman & Littlefield.

Morales, L. (2012). US Distrust in Media Hits New High. Gallop Poll. www.gallup.com/poll/157589/distrust-media-hits-new-high.aspx

Morozov, E. (2009, May 19). The Brave New World of Slacktivism. *Foreign Policy.* Available at: http://foreignpolicy.com/?s=Slacktivism

Mossberger, K., Tolbert, C., and Franko, W. (2012). *Digital Cities: The Internet and the Geography of Opportunity.* Oxford Studies in Digital Politics. New York: Oxford University Press.

Mouffe, C. (2005) *On the Political (Thinking in Action).* New York: Routledge.

Mouffe, C. (2013). *Agonistics: Thinking the World Politically.* New York: Verso.

Mutz, D. (2006). *Hearing the Other Side: Deliberative versus Participatory Democracy.* Cambridge: Cambridge University Press.

National Annenberg Election Survey (2004). *Daily Show* Viewers Knowledgeable about Presidential Campaign, National Annenberg Election Survey Shows. University of Pennsylvania's Annenberg Public Policy Center. Available at: www.annenbergpublicpolicycenter.org/Downloads/Political_Communication/naes/2004_03_late-night-knowledge-2_9-21_pr.pdf

National Resource Center on Children and Families of the Incarcerated. (2014). Children and Families of the Incarcerated Fact Sheet. Rutgers University. Available at: https://nrccfi.camden.rutgers.edu/files/nrccfi-fact-sheet-2014.pdf Retrieved August 30, 2016.

Neill, S. (2009). The Alternate Channel: How Social Media is Challenging the Spiral of Silence Theory in GLBT Communities of Color. MA direct research project, part of requirements for the M.A. in the School of Communication, American University. Available at: www.american.edu/soc/communication/upload/09-Neill.pdf. Retrieved June 9, 2016.

Newcomb, H. and Hirsh, P. (1983). Television as a cultural forum: Implications for research. *Quarterly Review of Film Studies.* 8(3): 45–55.

Newman, N., Fletcher, R., Levy, D., and Nielsen, R. K. (2016). Reuters Institute Digital News Report 2016. Reuters Institute for the Study of Journalism. Available at: http://reutersinstitute.politics.ox.ac.uk/sites/default/files/Digital-News-Report-2016.pdf

Newspaper Association of America. (2010). Common Threads: Linking NAA Foundation Research to Today's Young Media Consumers. NAA Media Management Center, Northwestern University. Newspaper Association of America Foundation.

Noelle-Neumann, E. (1974/1984). *The Spiral of Silence: Public Opinion – Our Social Skin.* Chicago, IL: University of Chicago Press.

Nolan, S. and Mezzacappa, D. (2014, November 25). Constitution High students march to Liberty Bell to protest Ferguson. The Notebook (Independent voice of Philadelphia Public Schools). Available at: http://thenotebook.org/blog/147955/constitution-high-school-students-march-liberty-bell-protest-ferguson

O'Connor, R. and Cutler, A. (2008). *Shock Jocks: Hate Speech and Talk Radio: America's Ten Worst Hate Talkers and the Progressive Alternatives.* San Francisco, CA: Alternet Books.

O'Loughlin, B. and Gillespie, M. (2012). Dissenting citizenship? Young people and political participation in the media–security nexus. *Parliamentary Affairs* 65(1): 115–137. doi: 10.1093/pa/gsr055

Olmstead, K., Mitchell, A., and Rosenstiel, T. (2011). Navigating News Online: Where People Go, How They Get There and What Lures Them

Away. Pew Research Center. Available at: www.journalism.org/2011/05/09/ navigating-news-online/

Olsson, T. and Dahlgren, P. (2010). *Young People, ICTs, and Democracy: Theories, Policies, Identities, and Websites*. Gothenburg: Nordicom.

Omarzu, J. (2000). A disclosure decision model: Determining how and when individuals will self-disclose. *Personality and Social Psychology Review* 4(2): 174–185.

Orgad, S. and Irene Bruna S. (2014). The mediation of humanitarianism: Toward a research framework. *Communication, Culture & Critique* 7(1): 6–36.

Ortiz-Healy, V. (2015, April 13). Lack of Money, Interest Forcing Many High School Newspapers to Fold. *Chicago Tribune*. www.chicagotribune.com/ news/ct-high-school-newspapers-dying-met-20150409-story.html

Orttung, N. (2016, June 8). Will Snapchat's Redesign Make the App a Go-To News Source? *The Christian Science Monitor*. Available at: www.csmonitor. com/Technology/2016/0608/Will-Snapchat-s-redesign-make-the-app-a-go-to-news-source?cmpid=gigya-fb Retrieved September 1, 2016.

Owen, T. (2015). *Disruptive Power: The Crisis of the State in a Digital Age*. Oxford Studies in Digital Politics. New York: Oxford University Press.

Polletta, F. and Jasper, J. (2001). Collective identity and social movements. *Annual Review of Sociology* 27: 283–305, doi.org/10.1146/annurev.soc.27.1.283

Palczewski, C. H. (2011). Cyber-movements, new social movements, and counterpublics. In R. Asen and D. Brouwer (Eds.). *Counterpublics and the State*, pp. 161–186. Albany, NY: SUNY Press.

Papacharissi, Z. (2012). Without you, I'm nothing: Performances of the self on Twitter. *International Journal of Communication* 6. Available at: http://ijoc .org/index.php/ijoc/article/view/1484

Papacharissi, Z. and de Fatima Oliviera, M. (2012). Affective news and networked publics: The rhythms of news storytelling on #Egypt. *Journal of Communication* 62(2): 266–282.

Papacharissi, Z. (2014a). *Affective Publics: Sentiment, Technology, and Politics*. New York: Oxford University Press.

Papacharissi, Z. (2014b). Toward new journalism(s): Affective news, hybridity, and liminal spaces. *Journalism Studies* 16(1):27–40.

Pardun, C. and Scott, G. (2004). Reading newspapers ranked lowest versus other media for early teens. *Newspaper Research Journal* 25(3): 77–82.

Pariser, E. (2011). *The Filter Bubble: What the Internet Is Hiding from You*. New York: Penguin.

Patterson, T. (2007). Young People and News. A Report from the Joan Shorenstein Center on the Press, Politics and Public Policy. John F. Kennedy School of Government, Harvard University, pp. 1–33.

Perez, W., Espinoza, R., Ramos, K., Coronado, H., and Cortes, R. (2010). Civic engagement patterns of undocumented Mexican students. *Journal of Hispanic Higher Education* 9(3): 245–265. doi:10.1177/1538192710371007

Peters, J. D. (1999). *Speaking into the Air: A History of the Idea of Communication*. Chicago, IL: University of Chicago Press.

(2001). Witnessing. *Media, Culture and Society* 23(6): 707–723.

Petersen, M. (2010). Journalism as Trope. *Anthropology News* 51: 8–9. doi:10.1111/j.1556-3502.2010.51408.x

Pew Project for Excellence in Journalism. (2010, January 11). How News Happens – Still: A Study of the News Ecosystem in Baltimore. Available at: www.journalism.org/2010/01/11/how-news-happens/

Pew Research Center on Journalism and Media. (2012, March 5). The Search for a New Business Model: The Industry Looking Ahead. www.journalism.org/2012/03/05/industry-looking-ahead/. Retrieved May 11, 2016.

Pew Project for Excellence in Journalism (2012, March 19). State of the New Media in 2012: New Devices, Platforms Spur News Consumption. Available at: www.pewresearch.org/2012/03/19/state-of-the-news-media-2012/

Pew Research Center. (2015, July 14). The Evolving Role of News on Twitter and Facebook. www.journalism.org/2015/07/14/the-evolving-role-of-news-on-twitter-and-facebook/

Picone, I., Courtois, C., and Paulsen, S. (2014). When news is everywhere: Understanding participation, cross-mediality and mobility in journalism from a radical user perspective. *Journalism Practice* 9(1): 35–49.

Pierson, E. (2015) Outnumbered But Well-spoken: Female Commenters in the New York Times. Department of Statistics, Oxford University, UK. Published in the Proceedings of the 18th Association for Computing Machinery Conference on Computer Supported Cooperative Work and Social Computing, pp. 1201–1213. http://cs.stanford.edu/people/emmap1/cscw_paper.pdf doi:10.1145/2675133.2675134

Pierson, E. (2016, January 6). How to Get More Women to Join the Debate. *The New York Times*. http://kristof.blogs.nytimes.com/2015/01/06/how-to-get-more-women-to-join-the-debate/?_r=0

Poell, T. and van Dijck, J. (2015). Social media and activist communication. *The Routledge Companion to Alternative and Community Media*. London: Routledge.

Poggi, J. (2016, June 1). In Surreal Election Year, MTV Again Tries to Make Viewers into Voters. Cue Robo-Roundtable. *Advertising Age*. Available at: http://adage.com/article/media/mtv-surreal-election-campaign-robo-rountable/304223/. Retrieved June 8, 2016.

Porto, M. (2007). Frame diversity and citizen competence: Towards a critical approach to news quality. *Critical Studies in Media Communication* 24(4): 303–231.

Postill, J. (2008). Localizing the Internet beyond communities and networks. *New Media & Society* 10(3): 413–431.

Postill, J. (2013). Democracy in an age of viral reality: A media epidemiography of Spain's indignados movement. *Ethnography* 15(1): 51–69.

Powers, E. (2010). Teaching News Literacy in the Age of New Media: Why Secondary School Students Should Be Taught to Judge the Credibility of the News They Consume. Washington University in St. Louis: All Theses and Dissertations (ETDs). http://openscholarship.wustl.edu/cgi/viewcontent.cgi?article=1454&context=etd

Putnam, R. (2000). *Bowling Alone: the Collapse and Revival of American Community.* New York: Simon & Shuster.

Quigley, C. (1999). Civic education: recent history, current status, and the future. *Albany Law Review* 62(4): 1425–1451.

Rainie, L., Smith, L., Lehman Schlozman, K., Brady, H., and Verba, S. (2012, October 19). Social Media and Political Engagement. Pew Research Center. Available at: www.pewinternet.org/2012/10/19/social-media-and-political-engagement/

Reuters Institute for the Study of Journalism. (2015). Digital News Report: Social Networks and Their Role in News. www.digitalnewsreport.org/survey/2015/social-networks-and-their-role-in-news-2015/

Rice, R. and Love, G. (1987). Electronic emotion: Socioemotional content in a computer-mediated communication network. *Communication Research* 14(1): 85–108.

Richardson, V. (2014, December 9). Denver Mayor Tells Protesting Students to Return to Class After Walk-Outs. *Washington Times*. Available at: www.washingtontimes.com/news/2014/dec/9/denver-mayor-tells-protesting-students-return-clas/

Rideout, V. and Katz, V. (2016). Opportunity for All? Technology and Learning in Low Income Families. The Joan Ganz Cooney at Sesame Workshop. Available at: www.joanganzcooneycenter.org/publication/opportunity-for-all-technology-and-learning-in-lower-income-families/

Roberts, M. (2016, April 27). Grace Davis' School Board Bullying Claim Leads to Girl Scouts Resignation. *Westword*. Available at: www.westword.com/news/grace-daviss-school-board-bullying-claim-leads-to-girl-scouts-resignation-7847646. Retrieved June 8, 2016.

Robinson, L. (2009). A taste for the necessary. *Information, Communication & Society* 12(4): 488–507. doi: 10.1080.13691180902857678.

Rodriguez, C. (2011). *Citizens' Media against Armed Conflict: Disrupting Violence in Colombia.* Minneapolis: University of Minnesota Press.

Romesburg, D. (2008). The tightrope of normalcy: Homosexuality, developmental citizenship and American adolescence, 1890–1940. *Journal of Historical Sociology* 21(4): 417–442.

Rorty, R. (1989). *Contingency, Irony, Solidarity.* Cambridge, MA: Harvard University Press.

Rosaldo, R. (2003). *Cultural Citizenship in Island Southeast Asia: Nation and Belonging in the Hinterlands.* Los Angeles, CA: University of California Press.

Roschke, K. (2009). Convergence journalism in high school: How educators are keeping up with trends in the media industry. *Southwestern Mass Communication Journal* 24(2): 55–64.

Rosen, J. (2008, July 14). A Most Useful Definition of Citizen Journalism. *Pressthink.* Available at: http://archive.pressthink.org/2008/07/14/a_most_useful_d.html

Roth, Z. (2014). After Ferguson, Some See a Movement Taking Shape. MSNBC. www.msnbc.com/msnbc/after-ferguson-some-see-movement-taking-shape

Rubin, B.C. (2007). "There's still no justice": Youth civic identity development amid distinct school and community contexts. *Teachers College Record* 109: 449–481.

Rubin, B. C., Hayes B., and Benson, K. (2009). "It's the worst place to live": Urban youth and the challenge of school-based civic learning. *Theory Into Practice* 48(3): 213–221.

Russell, A. (2011). *Networked: A History of Contemporary News in Transition.* London: Polity.

Russell, A. (2013). Innovation in hybrid spaces: 2011 UN Climate Summit and the expanding journalism landscape. *Journalism* 14(7): 904–920.

Russell, A. (2016). *Journalism as Activism: Recoding Media Power.* New York: Polity Press.

Saez, E. and Zucman, G. (2014). Exploding Wealth Inequality in the United States. Washington Center for Equitable Growth. http://equitablegrowth.org/research/exploding-wealth-inequality-united-states/

Scheufele, D. (2007). Spiral of silence theory. *The Sage Handbook of Public Opinion Research*, pp. 175–183. New York: Sage.

Schiller, D. (2000). *Digital Capitalism: Networking the Global Market System.* Cambridge, MA: MIT Press.

Schneider, H. and Klurfeld, J. (2008). The Demand Dilemma and News Literacy in Schools. Media Giraffe Project at the University of Massachusetts-Amherst and the Donald W. Reynolds Journalism Institute. Video. http://newshare.typepad.com/mgpaudio/2008/01/video-the-deman.html. See also: http://drc.centerfornewsliteracy.org/glossary-language-news-literacy

Scholastic Journalism Institute. (2010). White Paper on Threats to Scholastic Journalism Programs. Reno, NV: University of Nevada. http://thinksji.org/threats-initiative/ti-white-paper/

Schradie, J. (2011). The digital production gap: The digital divide and web 2.0 collide. *Poetics* 39(2): 145–168, doi: 10.1016/j.poetic.2011.02.003.

Schradie, J. (2012). The trend of class, race, and ethnicity in social media inequality. *Information, Communication & Society* 15:(4): 555–571, doi: 10.1080/1369118x.2012.665939.

Schudson, M. (1978). *Discovering the News: A Social History of American Newspapers.* New York: Basic Books.

Schudson, M. (1998). *The Good Citizen: A History of American Public Life.* New York: Simon & Schuster.

Schussman, A. and Soule, S. A. (2005). Process and protest: Accounting for individual protest participation. *Social Forces* 84: 1083–1108.

Schwartz, J. (2016, August 14). U.S. media publishers and publications – ranked for July 2016. DigitalVision (SimilarWeb). Available at: www.similarweb.com/blog/us-media-publishers-july-2016. Retrieved August 17, 2016.

Schworm, P. (2014, December 16). Boston Students Leave Class Early to Rally for Equality. *Boston Globe.* Available online: www.bostonglobe.com/metro/2014/12/16/students-walk-out-boston-schools-protest/amorEGYE2EmXO-qCyqcPH8L/story.html

Seligman, A. (2000). *Modernity's Wager: Authority, the Self, and Transcendence.* Princeton, NJ: Princeton University Press.

Senft, T. (2015). *The Skin of the Selfie.* In A. Bieber (Ed.). *Ego Update: The Future of Digital Identity.* Dusseldorf: NRW Forum Publications.

Seu, I. B. (2003) "Your stomach makes you feel that you don't want to know anything about it": Desensitization, defense mechanisms and rhetoric in response to human rights abuses. *Journal of Human Rights* 2(2): 183–196. doi: 10.1080/1475483032000078170

Seu, I. B. (2010). "Doing denial": Audience reaction to human rights appeals. *Discourse & Society* 21(4): 438–457.

Sherrod, L., Flanagan, C., and Youniss, J. (2002). Dimensions of citizenship and opportunities for youth development: The who, what, why, where and who of citizenship development. *Applied Developmental Science* 6(4): 264–272.

Shirky, C. (2008). *Here Comes Everybody: The Power of Organizing without Organization.* New York: Penguin Books.

Shohat, E. (1998). Foreword. In E. Shohat (Ed.). *Talking Visions: Multicultural Feminism in a Transnational Age.* Cambridge, MA: MIT Press.

Shresthova, S. (2013). Between Storytelling and Surveillance: American Muslim Youth Negotiate Culture, Politics and Participation. A Case Study Report. Working Paper of the Media, Activism, and Participatory Politics Project. Available at: http://ypp.dmlcentral.net/publications/161

Siebert, F., Peterson, T., and Schramm, W. (1963). *Four Theories of the Press.* Chicago, IL: University of Illinois Press.

Silverstone, R. (2007). *Media and Morality: On the Rise of the Mediapolis.* Cambridge: Polity Press.

Smirnov, N., Ferman, B., and Cabral, N. (2015). *Poppyn: Presenting Our Perspective on Philly Youth News. The Civic Media Project.* Cambridge, MA: MIT Press. Available at: http://civicmediaproject.org/works/civic-media-project/poppyn. Retrieved June 28, 2016.

Smith, A. (1759). *A Theory of Moral Sentiments.* Strand and Edinburgh: A. Millar; A. Kincaid and J. Bell.

Smith, A. (2014). African Americans and Technology Use. Pew Research Center Report. Available at: www.pewinternet.org/files/old-media/Files/Reports/2014/PIP_African%20Americans%20and%20Technology%20Use_010614.pdf

Smith, C. (2011). *Lost in Transition: The Dark Side of Emerging Adulthood.* New York: Oxford University Press.

Snow, McAdam, D. (1988). Micromobilization contexts and the recruitment to activism. In B. Klandermans, H. Kriesi, and S. Tarrow (Eds.). *From Structure to Action*, pp. 125–154. Greenwich: JAI Press.

Snyder, K. (2014, October 2). Why Women Leave Tech: It's the Culture, Not Because "Math Is Hard." *Fortune.*, http://fortune.com/2014/10/02/women-leave-tech-culture/

Soep, E. (2011). All the world's an album: Youth media as strategic embedding. In J. Fisherkeller (Ed.). *International Perspectives on Youth Media: Cultures of Production and Education*, pp. 246–261. New York: Peter Lang.

Soep, E. (2014). *Participatory Politics: Next Generation Tactics to Remake Public Spheres.* Cambridge, MA: MIT Press.

Soler, M. and Garry, L. (2009). Disproportionate Minority Contact, pp. 1–12. US Department of Justice. www.ncjrs.gov/pdffiles1/ojjdp/218861.pdf.

Sommeiller, E., Price, M., and Wazeter, E. (2016). Income Inequality in the U.S. by State, Metropolitan Area, and County. Report of the Economic Policy Institute. Available at: www.epi.org/files/pdf/107100.pdf Retrieved August 18, 2016.

Soriano, C. R. (2014). Constructing collectivity in diversity: Online political mobilization of a national LGBT political party. *Media, Culture, Society* 36(1): 20–36.

Spigel, L. (1992). *Make Room for TV: Television and the Family Ideal in Postwar America*. Chicago, IL: University of Chicago Press.

Spivak, G. (1988). Can the subaltern speak? In C. Nelson and L. Grossberg, (Eds.). *Marxism and the Interpretation of Culture*, pp. 271–313. Urbana, IL: University of Illinois Press.

Squires, C. R. (2002). Rethinking the black public sphere: An alternative vocabulary for multiple public spheres. *Communication Theory* 12(4): 446–468.

Stanford History Education Group. (November 2016). Evaluating Information: The Cornerstone of Civic Online Reasoning, pp. 1–29. Stanford, CA: Stanford University. Available at: https://sheg.stanford.edu/upload/V3LessonPlans/Executive%20Summary%2011.21.16.pdf

Stornaiuolo, A., Hall, G., and Sahni, U. (2011). Cosmopolitan imagingings of self and other: Youth and social networking in a global world. In J. Fisherkeller (Eds.). *International Perspectives on Youth Media: Cultures of Production and Education*, pp. 263–280. New York: Peter Lang.

Stromer-Galley, J., Bryant, L., and Bimber, B. (2015). Context and medium matter: Expressing disagreements online and face-to-face in political deliberations. *Journal of Public Deliberation* 11 (1), www.publicdeliberation.net/jpd/vol11/iss1/art1.

Sunstein, C. (2007). *Republic.com 2.0*. Princeton, NJ: Princeton University Press.

Stauber J. and Rampton, S. (1995). *Toxic Sludge is Good For You: Lies, Damn Lies and the Public Relations Industry*. Monroe, ME: Common Courage Press.

Swaine, J. (2014, October 8). Ferguson Protest Leaders: "We'll Take Our Anger Out on People Who Failed Us." *The Guardian*. Available at: www.theguardian.com/us-news/2014/oct/08/ferguson-protest-leaders-rally-new-york-michael-brown-shooting

Swanson, A. (2016, August 26). Americans Are Less Trusting than Ever Before. That Could Also Make Us Poor. *The Washington Post*. Available at: www.washingtonpost.com/news/wonk/wp/2016/08/26/americans-are-less-trusting-than-ever-before-that-could-also-make-us-poor/?wpisrc=nl_wonk&wpmm=1 Retrieved August 30, 2016.

Tate, C. D. and Taylor, S. (2012). *Scholastic Journalism*, 12th ed. New York: Wiley.

Tatian, P., Kingsley, G. T., Parilla, J., and Pendall, R. (2012). Building Successful Neighborhoods. What Works Collaborative. Available at: www.urban.org/sites/default/files/alfresco/publication-pdfs/412557-Building-Successful-Neighborhoods.PDF. Retrieved March 16, 2016.

Tewksbury, D. and Rittenberg, J. (2012). *News on the Internet: Information and Citizenship in the 21st Century*. New York: Oxford University Press.

Thiruvengadam, M. (2013). Instagram for Newsrooms: A Community Tool, a Reporting Tool, and a Source of Web Content. Poynter Institute. www.poynter.org/2013/instagram-for-newsrooms-a-community-tool-a-reporting-tool-a-source-of-web-content/214435/

Thorson, K. (2012). Do-It-Yourself Citizenship: Youth, Communication and Politics in the Digital Age. Unpublished manuscript.

Thorson, K. (2014). Facing an uncertain reception: Young citizens and political interaction on Facebook. *Information, Communication & Society* 17(2): 203–216.

Times Mirror Center for the People and the Press. (1990). *The Age of Indifference: A Study of Young Americans and How They View the News.* Washington, DC: Times Mirror Center.

Tiranelli, R. (2016). Big league, little speech. *Student Press Law Center Report* 35(2): 4–7.

Tofel, R. (2012). Non-Profit Journalism: Issues around Impact. White paper from Pro Publica. Available at: http://s3.amazonaws.com/propublica/assets/about/LFA_ProPublica-white-paper_2.1.pdf. Retrieved June 24, 2014.

Topolski, A. (2008). In search of a political ethics of intersubjectivity: Between Hannah Arendt, Emmanuel Levinas and the Judaic. *Hannah Arendt Journal for Political Thinking.* Ausgabe 1, Band 4. Available at: www.hannaharendt .net/index.php/han/article/view/137/240 Retrieved June 22, 2016.

Toussaint N. (2013). It struck a chord we never managed to strike: Frames, perspectives and remediation strategies in the international news coverage of KONY 2012. *African Journalism Studies* 34(1): 123–129.

Tufekci, Z. and Wilson, C. (2012). Social media and the decision to participate in political protest: Observations from Tahrir Square. *Journal of Communication* 62(2): 363–279.

Tufte, T. and Enghel, F. (2009). Youth engaging with media and communication: Different, unequal and disconnected? *Youth Engaging with the World: Media, Communication and Social Change,* pp. 11–18. Yearbook. Goteberg, Sweden: Nordicom.

Turkle, S. (2011). *Alone Together: Why We Expect More from Technology and Less from Each Other.* New York: Basic Books.

Turner, G. (2005). *Ending the Affair: The Decline of Television Current Affairs in Australia.* Sydney: University of New South Wales Press.

Turner, K. (2011). Mapping the field of youth media organizations in the United States. In J. Fisherkeller (Ed.). *International Perspectives on Youth Media,* pp. 25–49. New York: Peter Lang.

Ulla, C., Tayie, S., Jacquinot-Delaunay, G., and Perez Tornero, J. (2008). Empowerment through Media Education: An Intercultural Dialogue. UNESCO Communication and Information Resources. www.unesco .org/new/en/communication-and-information/resources/publications-and-communication-materials/publications/full-list/empowerment-through-media-education-an-intercultural-dialogue/

Vacarelli, J. (2014, May 20). Denver's Montbello School Ready to Graduate. *Denver Post.* Available at: www.denverpost.com/2014/05/20/denvers-montbello-high-school-ready-to-graduate-last-class/. Retrieved June 28, 2016.

Valentine, G. (1996). Children should be seen and not heard: The production and transgression of adults' public space. *Urban Geography* 17: 205–220.

Van Aelst, P. and Walgrave, V. (2001). Who is that (wo)man in the street? From the normalization of protest to the normalization of the protester. *European Journal of Political Research* 39(4): 461–486.

Van Dijck, J. (2008). Digital photography: Communication, identity, memory. *Visual Communication* 7(1): 57–76.

Van Dijck, J. (2013). *The Culture of Connectivity: A Critical History of Social Media*. New York: Oxford University Press.

Van Zoonen, L. (2004). *Entertaining the Citizen: When Politics and Popular Culture Converge*. New York: Rowman & Littlefield.

Varnelis, K. (Ed.). (2008). *Networked Publics*. Cambridge, MA: MIT Press.

Verba, S., Schlozman, K. L., and Brady, H. E. (1995). *Voice and Equality Civic Voluntarism in American Politics*. Cambridge, MA: Harvard University Press.

Verhulst, J. and Walgrave, S. (2009). The first time is the hardest? A cross-national and cross- issue comparison of first-time protest participants. *Political Behavior* 31: 455–484.

Vogt, N. and Mitchell, A. (2016). Crowdfunded Journalism: A Small but Growing Addition to Publicly Driven Journalism. A Report of the Pew Research Center. Available at: www.journalism.org/2016/01/20/crowdfunded-journalism/. Retrieved June 24, 2016.

Vygotsky, L. (1978). *Mind in Society: The Development of Higher Psychological Processes*. Cambridge, MA: Harvard University Press.

Walgrave, S. and Verhulst, J. (2006). Towards "new emotional movements"? A comparative exploration into a specific movement type. *Social Movement Studies* 5: 275–304.

Walther, J. B. (1994). Anticipated ongoing interaction versus channel effects on relational communication in computer-mediated interaction. *Human Communication Research* 19(1): 3–43.

Warner, J. (2007).Political culture jamming: The dissident humor of *The Daily Show with Jon Stewart*. *Popular Communications* 5(1): 17–36.

Warner, M. (2002). Publics and counterpublics. *Public Culture* 14(1): 49–90.

Wartella, E. and Lauricella, A. (2011). Children, Media and Race: Media Use among White, Black, Hispanic and Asian American Children. Northwestern University. http://web5.soc.northwestern.edu/cmhd/wp-content/uploads/2011/06/SOCconfReportSingleFinal-1.pdf

Washeck, A. (2014, July 17). The Journey to Teaching High School Journalism in Texas. *MediaShift*. http://mediashift.org/2014/07/the-journey-to-teaching-high-school-journalism-in-texas/

Weissmann, J. (2013, September 12). The Brogrammer Effect: Women Are a Small (and Shrinking) Share of Computer Workers. *The Atlantic*. www.theatlantic.com/business/archive/2013/09/the-brogrammer-effect-women-are-a-small-and-shrinking-share-of-computer-workers/279611/

Williams, A., Wardle, C., and Wahl-Jorgensen, K. (2010). "Have they got news for us?" Audience revolution or business as usual at the BBC. *Journalism Practice* 5(1): 85–99.

Williams, B. A. and Delli Carpini, M. (2011).*After Broadcast News: Media Regimes, Democracy, and the New Information Environment*. Cambridge: Cambridge University Press.

Williams, R. (1983). Community. *Keywords: A Vocabulary of Culture and Society*. Revised Edition. New York: Oxford University Press.

Williams, R. 1999. Visions of the good society and the religious roots of American political culture. *Sociology of Religion* 60(1): 1–34.

Wilson, C. and Gutiérrez, F., and Chao, L. (2003). *Racism and Sexism in the Media: The Rise of Class Communication in Multicultural America.* Thousand Oaks, CA: Sage Publications.

Winner, L. (1989). *The Whale and the Reactor: A Search for Limits in an Age of Technology.* Chicago, IL: University of Chicago Press.

Wojcicki, E. (2011). The Slow Death of High School Journalism. *The Huffington Post.* Available at: www.huffingtonpost.com/esther-wojcicki/the-slow-death-of-high-sc_b_45158.html

Wojcicki, E. (2010). Teaching journalism and news literacy. *Youth Media Reader* 3: 51–52.

Wu, T. (2003). Network neutrality, broadband discrimination. *Journal on Telecom and High Technology Law* 2: 141–180.

Yadron, D. (2016, May 12). Facebook Controversy Shows Journalists Are More Complicated than Algorithms. *The Guardian.* Available at: www.theguardian.com/technology/2016/may/12/facebook-twitter-google-snapchat-news-bias

Yar, M. (2008). Hannah Arendt. *Internet Encyclopedia of Philosophy.* Available: www.iep.utm.edu/arendt/. Retrieved June 23, 2016.

Youniss, J., McLellan, J., and Yates, M. (1997). What we know about engendering civic identity. *American Behavioral Scientist* 5: 620–631.

Zahavi, D. (2003). *Husserl's Phenomenology.* Redwood City, CA: Stanford University Press.

Zelizer, B. (1992). *Covering the Body: The Kennedy Assassination, The Media, and the Shaping of Collective Memory.* Chicago, IL: University of Chicago.

Zelizer, B. (2004). *Taking Journalism Seriously: News and the Academy.* Thousand Oaks, CA: Sage.

Zembylas, M. (2007). The politics of trauma: Empathy, reconciliation and peace education. *Journal of Peace Education* 4(2): 207–224.

Zembylas, M. (2008).Trauma, justice and the politics of emotion: The violence of sentimentality in education. *Discourse: Studies in the Cultural Politics of Education* 29(1): 1–17.

Zimmerman, A. M. (2012). *Documenting DREAMs: New Media, Undocumented Youth, and the Immigrant Rights Movement.* Los Angeles, CA: Annenberg School for Communication and Journalism, University of Southern California.

Zubrzycki, J. (2014, December 4). As High School Ferguson Protests Snowball, East Students Search for the Story. *Chalkbeat Colorado.* http://co.chalkbeat.org/2014/12/04/as-high-school-ferguson-protests-snowball-east-students-search-for-the-story/#.VKmjJGTF-nA

Zukin, C., Keeter, S., Andolina, M. W., Jenkins, K., and Delli Carpini, M. X. (2006). *A New Engagement: Political Participation, Civic Life, and the Changing American Citizen.* New York: Oxford University Press.

Zurn, C. (2008). Intersubjectivity. *International Encyclopedia of the Social Sciences.* www.encyclopedia.com/doc/1G2-3045301173.html. Retrieved June 23, 2016.

Index

Montreal School, 22–23, 36
organization and, 22–23, 36
political communication theory, 13
"public sphere" and, 21–22
relational approach to (*see* Relational
approach to communication)
ritual approach to, 220n. 4
Toronto School, 237n. 9
"Communication failure," 43
Community
communication and, 21–23
democracy and, 21–23
Community citizen journalism, 141, 145–
146, 190–191
Community youth media, 99–100
"Compassion fatigue," 194, 258n. 79
Compensatory justice, 196–197
Concentration of ownership in legacy
journalism, 68–69
Concerns of young people, 4
Conflict-driven news, 69–70
Connective action
affective publics and, 117
connective journalism and, 35–36, 44
Connective journalism
overview, 15, 20, 35–36, 53–54,
164–165
action in, 75–76
advocacy in, 75–76
connective action and, 35–36, 44
counterpublics and, 113–114
critical citizenship and, 42–46
defined, 13
discord and, 196–197
emerging model of, 16–17
as emotion-based approach to
news, 14–15
expanded news in, 42–46
"gatewatching" in, 43–44, 45
"inserting self into the story" in, 46,
49–50 (*see also* Counterpublics)
"making the story" in, 46, 51–53,
137–138 (*see also* Youth citizen
journalism)
networks and, 35
political nature of, 44–45
as proto-political, 43–44
recommendations regarding (*see*
Recommendations regarding
connective journalism)
"sharing the story" in, 46–49

story versus identity in, 14
voice and, 44
youth-oriented journalism and, 81–82
Connectivity
intersubjectivity and, 36–40
in social media, 36–40
Consumerism, youth and, 24–25
Cosmopolitanism, 195, 196–197
Costanza-Chock, Sasha, 223n. 44
Costera Meijer, Irene, 6
Couldry, Nick, 7, 44
Counterpublics
overview, 16, 112–114, 115–117, 137,
166–167
affective publics and, 117–119
agonistic democracy and, 115
artifacts of political engagement and,
113–114
Black Lives Matter and, 118
"Black public," 121–122
"Black Twitter," 122–123
case studies, 120–123
connective journalism and, 113–114
embodied participation and, 115–116
Ferguson protests (*see* Ferguson
protests)
"No Eastie Casino" movement,
129–133, 166–167
social media and, 116–117, 135
"spiral of silence" and, 133–135
Cox Center (University of Georgia),
175–176
Crawford, Kate, 37–38
Critical approaches to youth
citizenship, 26–27
Critical citizenship, 42–46
Critical media literacy
analytical skills and, 100–103
immigrants and, 104–106
production skills and, 100–103
providing training on social media in
context of, 175–178
texting and, 103
Critiques of current news, 190
Cross-curriculum partnerships, 175
Crowd funding, legacy journalism
and, 30–31
Cullors, Patrisse, 26–27
Current TV, 87, 238n. 24
Cutler, Aaron, 185
Cynicism, 25–26

Other Books in the Series (*continued from page iii*)